T0219330

Machine Learning for
Healthcare Applications

Scrivener Publishing
100 Cummings Center, Suite 541J
Beverly, MA 01915-6106

Publishers at Scrivener
Martin Scrivener (martin@scrivenerpublishing.com)
Phillip Carmical (pcarmical@scrivenerpublishing.com)

Machine Learning for Healthcare Applications

Edited by

Sachi Nandan Mohanty
G. Nalinipriya
Om Prakash Jena
and
Achyuth Sarkar

Scrivener
Publishing

WILEY

Wiley Global Headquarters
111 River Street, Hoboken, NJ 07030, USA

For details of our global editorial offices, customer services, and more information about Wiley prod-ucts visit us at www.wiley.com.

Library of Congress Cataloging-in-Publication Data

ISBN 9781119791812

Cover image: Pixabay.Com
Cover design by Russell Richardson

Set in size of 11pt and Minion Pro by Manila Typesetting Company, Makati, Philippines

Contents

11 Comparison of MobileNet and ResNet CNN Architectures in the CNN-Based Skin Cancer Classifier Model   169

Subasish Mohapatra, N.V.S. Abhishek, Dibyajit Bardhan, Anisha Ankita Ghosh and Shubhadarshinin Mohanty

Part 5: Case Studies of Application Areas of Machine Learning in Healthcare System

21 Future of Telemedicine with ML: Building a Telemedicine Framework for Lung Sound Detection

Sudhansu Shekhar Patra, Nitin S. Goje, Kamakhya Narain Singh,
Kaish Q. Khan, Deepak Kumar, Madhavi and Kumar Ashutosh Sharma

22 A Lightweight Convolutional Neural Network Model for Tuberculosis Bacilli Detection From Microscopic Sputum Smear Images

Rani Oomman Panicker, S.J. Pawan, Jeny Rajan and M.K. Sabu

Preface

Machine learning is one of the principal components of computational methodology. In today's highly integrated world, when solutions to problems are cross-disciplinary in nature, machine learning promises to become a powerful means for obtaining solutions to problems very quickly, yet accurately and acceptably.

When considering the idea of using machine learning in healthcare, it is a Herculean task to present before the reader the entire gamut of information in the field of intelligent systems. It was therefore our objective to keep the presentation narrow and intensive. The approach of this book is distinct from others in that it presents detailed computer simulations for all models presented with explanations of the program code. It includes unique and distinctive chapters on disease diagnosis, telemedicine, medical imaging, smart health monitoring, social media healthcare, and machine learning for COVID-19. These chapters help develop a clear understanding of the working of an algorithm while strengthening logical thinking. In this environment, answering a single question may require accessing several data sources and calling on sophisticated analysis tools. While data integration is a dynamic research area in the database community, the specific needs of research have led to the development of numerous middleware systems that provide seamless data access in a result-driven environment.

Since this book is intended to be useful to a wide audience, students, researchers and scientists from both academia and industry may all benefit from this material. It contains a comprehensive description of issues for healthcare data management and an overview of existing systems, making it appropriate for introductory and instructional purposes. Prerequisites are minimal; the readers are expected to have basic knowledge of machine learning.

This book is divided into 22 real-time innovative chapters which provide a variety of application examples in different domains. These chapters illustrate why traditional approaches often fail to meet customers' needs. The presented approaches provide a comprehensive overview of current technology. Each of these chapters, which are written by the main inventors of the presented systems, specifies requirements and provides a description of both the chosen approach and its implementation. Because of the self-contained nature of these chapters, they may be read in any order. Each of the chapters use various technical terms which involve expertise in machine learning and computer science.

The chapters of the book are organized as follows:

- Chapter 1 introduces the fundamental concepts of machine learning and its applications, and describes the setup used throughout the book. It is now realized that complex real-world problems require intelligent systems that combine knowledge, techniques and methodologies from various sources.

- Chapter 2 describes the actual machine learning algorithms that are most widely used in practice, and discusses their advantages and shortcomings. It is therefore necessary to work through conventional machine learning algorithms while relating the underlying theme to cutting-edge neuroscience research findings.
- Chapter 3 explains the study of neuromarketing with EEG signals and machine learning techniques. This is followed by a detailed review of the global function of classifiers and the inner workings. Such a premise provides the fabric for presentation of ideas throughout this text.
- Chapter 4 elaborates on an expert system-based clinical decision support system for hepatitis B prediction and diagnosis. It develops a working model of the decision support system and its application domain. The clinical decision helps to improve the diagnostic performance.
- Chapter 5 works on disease prediction to develop an intuitive understanding of fundamental design principles. These concepts are carried to their fullest complexity with neural networks and their learning. The working of artificial neurons and the architecture stands in stark contrast with their biological counterparts.
- Chapter 6 introduces machine learning as a public safety tool. A solid discussion on the relationship between public safety and video surveillance systems is provided. The topic of offline crime prevention leads to the extremely important topic of public safety, which is discussed in the context of machine learning theory.
- Chapter 7 introduces semantic web ontology, multi-agent system in a semantic framework, decision-making ontology and query optimizer agent. These unified methods open up a new avenue of research.
- Chapter 8 focuses on the detection, prediction and intervention strategies of attention deficiency in the brain. These important topics are missing from many current texts on machine learning.
- Chapter 9 summarizes the issues concerning the progression of osteoporosis using machine learning and the treatment models, and culminates in the presentation of K-nearest neighbor and decision tree algorithms.
- Chapter 10 covers the issues in biomedical text processing and the food industry. It addresses the latest topics of face recognition systems for domestic cattle, assortment of vegetables and fruits, plant leaf disease detection and approaches for sentiment analysis on drug reviews.
- Chapter 11 discusses hyperparameter tuning of the MobileNet-based CNN model and also explains ResNet5.0. It presents a variety of important machine learning concepts found in the literature, including confusion matrix and classification results.
- Chapter 12 presents a detailed introduction to the theory and terminology of deep learning, image classifier, and data preprocessing with augmentation. It talks about malaria cell detection and finally the results are tabulated in a meaningful manner for further fruitful research.
- Chapter 13 considers various approaches for the design of transfer learning, including CNN architecture with ROC curve as a core neural network

model, which can incorporate human expertise as well as adapt themselves through repeated learning.

- Chapter 14 provides a model for early stage detection. It gives a variety of application examples in different domains such as multivariate regression, model building, and different learning algorithms.
- Chapter 15 presents the concept of using the internet of things (IoT) in healthcare applications. It focuses on networking system using the IoT, smart hospital environments, emerging vulnerabilities and threat analysis.
- Chapter 16 explains real-time health monitoring. It proposes a framework for model construction, supervised learning, neural networks for classification and decision-making. An application is presented that supports health monitoring by implementing IoT concepts. A multiple linear regression algorithm and random forest algorithm are used to map the requirement of distance health monitoring.
- Chapter 17 introduces ontology in healthcare. It also explains NLP-based retrieval for COVID-19 dataset. Query formulation and retrieval from a knowledgebase are handled in an effective manner. Included are several examples in the literature to travel further in this research direction.
- Chapter 18 summarizes the topics necessary for COVID-19 research. It details the public discourse and sentiment during the coronavirus pandemic. Moreover, how to understand text semantics and semantic analysis using social media are explained.
- Chapter 19 is devoted to basic COVID-19 research and its relationship to various data mining techniques. Prediction and analysis of COVID-19 dataset, dataset collection, backpropagation neural network, and several algorithms are discussed in detail.
- Chapter 20 details automated diagnosis of COVID-19. Topics treated include the feature extraction, genetic algorithm and image segmentation technique. The presented approach provides a description of both the chosen approach and its implementation.
- Chapter 21 provides users and developers with a methodology to evaluate the present system. It focuses on the future of telemedicine with machine learning. The state-of-the-art, existing solutions and new challenges to be addressed are emphasized. Fast electronics health record retrieval, intelligent assistance for patient diagnosis and remote monitoring of patients are discussed very clearly.
- Chapter 22 discusses the challenges faced by chronic disease patients and the lightweight convolutional neural network used to address these challenges. Experimental results are tabulated, leading to active research in the healthcare field
- Chapter 23 discusses disease diagnosis. Active solutions using machine learning techniques are given along with the generalize tools used to implement the concepts. A wide range of research areas are also given for future work.
- Chapter 24 explains the detection of disease and its related solution in machine learning. The chapter continues with the treatment of machine leaning algorithms that are dynamic in nature. It presents a number of powerful

machine learning models with the associated learnings. A discussion section is provided that briefly explains what can be computed with the models.

Finally, we would like to sincerely thank all those involved in the successful completion of the book. First, our sincere gratitude goes to the chapters' authors who contributed their time and expertise to this book. Second, the editors wish to acknowledge the valuable contributions of the reviewers regarding the improvement of quality, coherence, and content presented in the chapters.

The Editors
February 2021

Part 1

INTRODUCTION TO INTELLIGENT HEALTHCARE SYSTEMS

Innovation on Machine Learning in Healthcare Services—An Introduction

Parthasarathi Pattnayak[1]* and Om Prakash Jena[2]

[1]*School of Computer Applications, KIIT Deemed to be University, Bhubaneswar, Odisha, India*
[2]*Department of Computer Science, Ravenshaw University, Cuttack, Odisha, India*

Abstract

The healthcare offerings in evolved and developing international locations are seriously important. The use of machine gaining knowledge of strategies in healthcare enterprise has a crucial significance and increases swiftly. In the beyond few years, there has been widespread traits in how system gaining knowledge of can be utilized in diverse industries and research. The organizations in healthcare quarter need to take benefit of the system studying techniques to gain valuable statistics that could later be used to diagnose illnesses at a great deal in advance ranges. There are multiple and endless Machine learning application in healthcare industry. Some of the most common applications are cited in this section. Machine learning helps streamlining the administrative processes in the hospitals. It also helps mapping and treating the infectious diseases for the personalised medical treatment. Machine learning will affect physician and hospitals by playing a very dominant role in the clinical decision support. For example, it will help earlier identification of the diseases and customise treatment plan that will ensure an optimal outcome. Machine learning can be used to educate patients on several potential disease and their outcomes with different treatment option. As a result it can improve the efficiency hospital and health systems by reducing the cost of the healthcare. Machine learning in healthcare can be used to enhance health information management and the exchange of the health information with the aim of improving and thus, modernising the workflows, facilitating access to clinical data and improving the accuracy of the health information. Above all it brings efficiency and transparency to information process.

Keywords: Machine learning, healthcare, EHR, RCT, big data

1.1 Introduction

The human services is one of the significant possessions inside the general public. In any case, because of expedient development social orders' desires for human services surpass the substances of ease and reachable consideration. As need for medicinal services develops, granting enough human services to the general public is the essential need of the principles in social insurance zone. The state of the well-being zone fluctuates relying upon the

---

Corresponding author: parthafca@kiit.ac.in

Sachi Nandan Mohanty, G. Nalinipriya, Om Prakash Jena and Achyuth Sarkar (eds.) Machine Learning for Healthcare Applications, (3–16) © 2021 Scrivener Publishing LLC

nation's populace, social turn of events, regular sources, political and money-related gadgets. Increment of importance given to medicinal services and the excellent level of social insurance, expands resistance among well-being gatherings and offers a critical commitment to the improvement of the world. Medical problems influence human lives. During clinical thought, prosperity associations secure clinical real factors around each particular affected individual, and impact data from the overall people, to conclude how to manage that understanding. Information along these lines plays out a basic situation in tending to medical problems, and advanced insights is basic to upgrading influenced individual consideration. Without question, one of the most imperative components that influences human services area is time. In spite of speedy increment in social orders and in social orders' requirement for medicinal services, todays' propelling period can be one of the most essential components that can react to the need of human services contributions in social orders. Fortunately, nowadays we've a convoluted age in human services structures which could help settling on choices dependent on gathered information. This ability of the age in medicinal services structures is as of now becoming accustomed to aggregate information roughly any manifestation that an influenced individual has, to analyze special afflictions before they happen at the influenced individual, and to forestall any of these sicknesses with the guide of playing it safe. With the assistance of that innovation, numerous victims have just been protected from various dreadful ailments. Utilizing realities, machine considering has driven advances in numerous areas comprehensive of PC creative and judicious, NLP, and robotized discourse fame to gracefully puissant structures (For instance, engines with driver less, non-open associates enacted voice, mechanized interpretation).

Thinking about calm masses to perceive causes, chance factors, ground-breaking meds, and sub sorts of sickness has for a long while been the space of the study of disease transmission. Epidemiological systems, for instance, case-control and unpredictable controlled starters ponders are the establishments of verification upheld prescription. In any case, such techniques are dreary and expensive, freed from the inclinations they are planned to fight, and their results may not be material to authentic patient peoples [1]. All inclusive, the gathering of electronic prosperity records (EHRs) is growing a direct result of frameworks and associations that help their usage. Techniques that impact EHRs to react to questions took care of by disease transmission specialists [2] and to manufacture precision in human administrations transport are as of now ordinary [3].

Data assessment approaches widely fall into the going with classes: expressive, explorative, deductive, insightful, and causative [4]. An elucidating examination reports outlines of information without understanding and an explorative investigation distinguishes relationship between factors in an informational index. At last, a causal examination decides how changes in a single variable influence another. It is vital to characterize the sort of inquiry being posed in an offered examination to decide the kind of information investigation that is fitting to use in addressing the inquiry. Prescient examinations used to anticipate results for people by building a measurable model from watched information and utilizing this model to create an expectation for an individual dependent on their interesting highlights. Prescient displaying is a sort of algorithmic demonstrating, by which information are created to be obscure. Such displaying approaches measure execution by measurements, for example, accuracy, review, and adjustment, which evaluate various ideas of the recurrence.

AI is the way toward acquisition of a sufficient factual model utilizing watched information to foresee results or classify perceptions in future information. In particular, administered AI techniques string a model utilizing perceptions on tests where the classes or anticipated estimation of the result of intrigue are now known (a best quality level). The subsequent framework—which is frequently a punished relapse of some structure—is normally applied to new examples to sort or foresee estimations of the result for before-hand inconspicuous perceptions, and its presentation assessed by contrasting anticipated qualities with real qualities for a lot of test tests. In this manner, AI "lives" in the realm of algorithmic demonstrating and ought to be assessed in that capacity. Relapse frameworks created utilizing AI techniques can't and ought not to be assessed utilizing measures from the universe of information demonstrating. To do so would create wrong evaluations of a model's presentation for its proposed task, conceivably deceptive clients into off base under-standing of the model's yield.

EHRs give access to an enormous number and assortment of factors that empower top notch grouping and prediction, while AI offers the strategies to deal with the huge bulk of high-dimensional information that are common in a medicinal services setting. Subsequently, the utilization of AI to EHR information investigation is at the bleeding edge of current clinical informatics [5], filling propels in practice of medication and science. We portray the operational and methodological difficulties of utilizing AI in practice and research. Finally, our viewpoint opens doors for AI in medication and applications that have the most noteworthy potential for affecting well-being and social insurance conveyance.

This area spreads the extraordinary specific challenges that should be considered in AI systems for restorative administrations endeavors, especially as execution between arranged structures and human pros limits [6]. Failure to intentionally consider these troubles can demolish the authenticity and utility of AI for human administrations. We present levels of leadership of clinical possibilities, sifted through into the going with general groupings: automating clinical endeavors, offering clinical assistance, and developing clinical cut-off points. We close by depicting the open entryways for investigate in AI that have explicit significance in therapeutic administrations: satisfying developments in data sources and instruments, ensuring systems are interpretable, and recognizing incredible depictions

1.2   Need for Change in Healthcare

Much has been created concerning the way medicinal services is changing, with a partic-ular highlight on how incredibly immense measures of data are by and by being routinely accumulated during the ordinary thought of patients. The usage of AI procedures to change these ever-forming measures of data into interventions that can improve steady outcomes seems like it should be an unquestionable method to take. In any case, the field of AI in social insurance is still in its beginning phases. This book, mercifully maintained by the Institution of Engineering and Technology, intends to give a "delineation" of the state of back and forth movement investigate at the interface among AI and restorative administra-tions. Basically, this is a fragmentary and uneven testing of the state of force analyses, yet then we have expected to give a wide-going preamble to the significance and size of work that is being endeavoured far and wide. In picking material for this modified volume, we have set exceptional complement on AI broadens that are (or are close) achieving improve-ment in determined outcomes. For certain, reasons, uncovered contrastingly in a bit of the parts that follow, it is an adage that "therapeutic administrations is hard"; there are stand-out restrictions that exist, and consideration that must be taken, when working with human services data. Regardless, for all of its difficulties, working with restorative administrations data is particularly satisfying, both to the extent the computational troubles that exist and to the extent the yields of exploration having the choice to impact the way social protection is passed on. There are barely any application regions of AI that have such assurance to benefit society as does that of human administrations.

1.3   Opportunities of Machine Learning in Healthcare

Tending to the pecking order of chances in medicinal services makes various open doors for advancement. Importantly, clinical staff and AI scientists frequently have integral aptitudes, and some high-sway issues must be handled by community oriented endeavors. We note a few promising bearings of research, explicitly featuring such issues of information non-stationary, model interpretability, and finding proper portrayals. Regardless of the methodological difficulties of working with EHR information and analysts have however to exploit the universe of EHR-determined factors accessible for prescient displaying, there are many energizing open doors for AI to improve well-being and human services conveyance. frameworks that separate patients into various hazard classifications to advise practice the executives have tremendous potential effect on human services esteem and strategies that can anticipate results for singular patients bring clinical practice one bit nearer to exactness medication [7]. Distinguishing significant expense and high-hazard patients [8] so as to endeavor focused on intercession will turn out to be progressively essential as medicinal services suppliers assume the budgetary danger of handling their patients. AI address has just been utilized to portray and foresee an assortment of well-being dangers. Late work in our gathering utilizing punished strategic relapse to distinguish patients with undiscovered fringe corridor malady and foresee their mortality chance found that such a methodology beats an easier stepwise calculated relapse as far as precision, alignment, and net renaming. Such prescient frameworks have been executed in clinical work on, bringing about progressively proficient and better quality consideration. AI has additionally been applied to medical clinic and practice the board, to smooth out tasks and improve quiet results. For instance, frameworks have been created to anticipate interest for crisis division beds [9] and elective medical procedure case volume [10], to advise emergency clinic staffing choices. As expenses for medicinal services deteriorate at verifiably high costs and the requirement for clinical oversight expands, machine learning for huge scope unstructured information may end up being the answer for this ever-developing issue. A few organizations what's more, people have set up themselves in the market today with their AI innovation applied to current medication with both unstructured information and organized information. In medicinal services, 50% of the absolute costs originate from 5% of absolute patients; furthermore, the quantity of constant conditions requiring steady, consistent consideration has progressively expanded the nation over. At long last, AI isn't a panacea, and not everything that can be anticipated will be significant. For instance, we might have the option to precisely anticipate movement from stage 3 to arrange 4 constant renal disappointments. Without viable treatment alternatives—other than kidney transplant and dialysis—the expectation doesn't do a lot till improve the administration of the sick person. AI can demonstrate to distinguish patients who might be increasingly inclined to repeating diseases what's more, help analyse patients. Also, near 90% of crisis room visits are preventable. AI can be utilized to help analyze and direct patients to legitimate treatment all while minimizing expenses by keeping patients out of costly, time escalated crisis care focuses.

1.4   Healthcare Fraud

Social insurance extortion is a serious issue. It is a crime committed by people who make false claims to gain financial gain. In order to identify misrepresentation inside human services framework, the procedure of evaluating is followed by examination. On the off chance that records are cautiously inspected, it is conceivable to recognize suspicious strategy holders and suppliers. In a perfect world, all cases ought to be examined cautiously what's more, exclusively. In any case, it is difficult to review all cases by any down to earth implies as these structure immense heaps of information including arranging tasks and complex calculation [11]. Besides, it is hard to review specialist co-ops without pieces of information concerning what examiners ought to be searching for. A reasonable methodology is to make short records for investigation and review patients and suppliers dependent on these rundowns. An assortment of expository methods can be utilized to accumulate review short records. Deceitful cases every now and again incorporate with designs that can be seen utilizing prescient models.

1.4.1   Sorts of Fraud in Healthcare

Human services misrepresentation is isolated into four sorts: (Section 1.4.2) clinical specialist co-ops, (Section 1.4.3) clinical asset suppliers, (Section 1.4.4) protection strategy holders, and (Section 1.4.5) insurance strategy suppliers. Figure 1.1 shows the review of fake exercises found in social insurance.

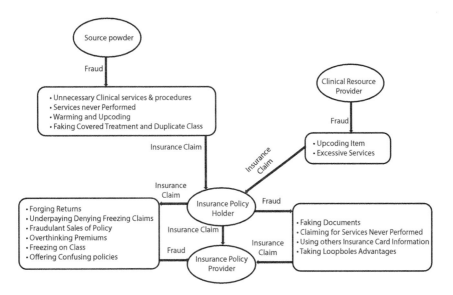

Figure 1.1 Categorization of healthcare fraud.

1.4.2   Clinical Service Providers

Clinical specialist co-ops can be medical clinics, specialists, attendants, radiologists and other research centre specialist organizations, and emergency vehicle organizations. Exercises including Clinical Services are comprised of the following:

- ✓ Justify certain patient related medical service or procedure or diagnosis which is not relevant medically [12],
- ✓ Claiming certain services which never took place or claiming extra money by altering the original claims [12],
- ✓ Charging insurance companies an excess amount i.e., the part of an insurance claim to be paid by the insured [12],
- ✓ Charging insurance companies something which is not necessary for the patient, for example, by increasing the frequency of the check-ups [12, 13],
- ✓ charging amount for certain expensive procedures or services which were never performed for the patient [12, 13]
- ✓ By using illegitimate schemes for which the providers of the healthcare exchange money which alternatively could have been provided by Medicare [13]

1.4.3   Clinical Resource Providers

Clinical asset suppliers include pharmaceutical organizations, clinical gear organizations that gracefully items like wheelchairs, walkers, specific emergency clinic beds what's more, clinical units. Exercises including Clinical resources provide may include:

- ✓ Charge insurance companies amount for the equipment which was never procured by modifying or changing the original bill [14].
- ✓ Resource providers in connivance with the corrupt doctor satisfy their selfish motive [15].
- ✓ Falsely charging insurance companies for an up-coding item [15].
- ✓ Making patient available unnecessary or undesirable services which are not required by them.

1.4.4   Protection Policy Holders

Protection strategy holders comprise of people and gatherings who convey protection arrangements, including the two patients and managers of patients. Exercises including Protection Policy Holders may include:

- ✓ Providing counterfeit eligibility record to take advantage of the benefits [16]
- ✓ Submitting false claims for the services which were not performed ever before [16]
- ✓ Availing insurance benefits by using illegitimate or fake card information, and
- ✓ Exploiting the flaws in the insurance policy to self-benefit.

In 2007, a misrepresentation case was submitted by erroneously documenting a disaster protection guarantee. The fake proprietor faked his own demise in a kayaking mishap and carried on a mystery life in his home for a long time [17].

1.4.5   Protection Policy Providers

Protection strategy suppliers are the elements that pay clinical costs to an approach holder as a by-product of their month to month premiums. Protection strategy suppliers can be private insurance agencies or government administrated medicinal services offices counting operators and intermediaries. Almost no examination has been led with respect to misrepresentation submitted by protection strategy suppliers as most protection extortion information are conveying the suppliers. It is assessed that around $85 billion are lost yearly due misrepresentation submitted by insurance agencies [15]. Exercises including Insurance Strategy Providers may include:

✓ Filing illegal return on the service statement by paying too little,
✓ Insurance companies resort to unfair means and do not accept the legally endorsed documents and thus discourse the policy holders to the extent that the patients ultimately give up [15],
✓ Deny the claims without examining them appropriately [15],
✓ Forcing the client to pay an exorbitant premium by providing them with wrongly interpreted information [15],
✓ Extract exorbitant premium by selling counterfeit policies.

Among these four kinds of misrepresentation talked about over, the specialist organizations alone submit most of the misrepresentation. Albeit most specialist organizations are dependable, those couple of unscrupulous specialist organizations submit misrepresentation and account the failure of thousands and thousands of dollars to the human services framework. At times, more than one of the above mentioned types is engaged with submitting human services misrepresentation. Identifying misrepresentation in such a half and half cases can be unpredictable and testing [16]. Henceforth, it is pressing that analysts find compelling approaches to find examples and connections in information that might be utilized to make a substantial forecast about false cases. Because of this squeezing demand, high end information mining and AI procedures holds a guarantee to give refined devices to distinguish potential indicators that portray the false practices dependent on the chronicled information [16].

1.5   Fraud Detection and Data Mining in Healthcare

Data mining method is used to distinguish misrepresentation and maltreatment in human services framework. The immense amounts of information created by human services insurance agencies are hard to process and assess utilizing traditional strategies. Data mining gives the strategies and mastery to change over these stores of information into the valuable assortment of realities for dynamic [18]. This sort of investigation has become important, as money-related weight has expanded the prerequisite for social insurance enterprises to develop decisions dependent on the investigation of financial and clinical information. Data and investigations acquired through information mining can improve working effectiveness, decline expenses, and increment benefits while safeguarding a high level of care.

The information mining applications for the most part build up standards for identifying extortion and misuse. At that point, these applications recognize irregular patters of cases by facilities, research centres, and doctors. Alongside different subtleties, these information mining applications can give data about strange referrals, remedies, clinical claims and fake protection claims. Data mining procedures can be arranged into administered strategies and unaided techniques.

1.5.1   Data Mining Supervised Methods

Supervised method uses labeled data. In this case the models are trained to use these data. The sole objective of the supervised ML method is to train the model in a manner such that it can predict the outcome when it is provided with some new set of data. This method can be used in particular case where both inputs and the corresponding outputs are known. The important feature of this method is that it provides the most accurate results. We can categorize supervised ML into regression problem and classification problem. This method is not considered to be close to true Artificial intelligence because the model is first trained for each available data, and then it predicts the correct outcome. Supervised ML includes various algorithms i.e., Linear Regression, Support Vector Machine, Multi-class Classification, Decision tree, Bayesian Logic, etc.

1.5.2   Data Mining Unsupervised Methods

In unsupervised Data mining systems, independent procedures don't get any objective yield or focal points from their natural variables. In spite of the fact that it is hard to envision how a machine can be prepared with no reaction from its surroundings, these techniques function admirably. It is probably going to assemble a legitimate model for individual learning techniques bolstered on the possibility that the component's point is to utilize input portrayal to predict imminent information, adequately communicating the contribution to another system, dynamic, etc. It very well may be said that solo learning can discover designs in an information which can likewise be unstructured clamor. Bunching and dimensionality decrease are the exemplary instances of unaided learning [20]. The benefit of using supervised techniques over unsupervised is that once the classifier has been trained, it can be easily utilized on any same kind of datasets [21] which settles on it a most ideal decision for a misrepresentation identification program which includes screening and observing. In this part, we just consider directed machine learning methods and give a top to bottom review of their application in identifying extortion in the social insurance framework.

1.6   Common Machine Learning Applications in Healthcare

Here are multiple and endless Machine learning applications in healthcare industry. Some of the most common applications are cited in this section. Machine learning helps streamlining the administrative processes in the hospitals. It also helps mapping and treating the infectious diseases for the personalized medical treatment. Machine learning will affect physician and hospitals by playing a very dominant role in the clinical decision support. For example, it will help earlier identification of the diseases and customize treatment plan that will ensure an optimal outcome. Machine learning can be used to educate patients on several potential disease and their outcomes with different treatment option. As a result it can improve the efficiency hospital and health systems by reducing the cost of the healthcare. Machine learning in healthcare can be used to enhance health information.

1.6.1   Multimodal Machine Learning for Data Fusion in Medical Imaging

Clinical picture combination method is a valuable and huge strategy to examine infections by getting the reciprocal data from various multimodality clinical pictures. These methodologies have been reliably and continuously applied in clinical practice. Multimodal picture examination and group learning methodologies are growing quickly and conveying noteworthy motivating force to clinical applications. Driven by the on-going accomplishment of applying these learning methodologies to clinical picture taking care of, specialists have proposed algorithmic structure to regulate multimodal picture examination with cross-system blend at the part learning level, classifier level, and at the dynamic level too. By then structure an image division system subject to significant convolutional neural frameworks is executed to shape the wounds of fragile tissue sarcomas using multimodal pictures, including those from appealing resonation imaging, enlisted tomography, and positron release tomography. The framework arranged with multimodal pictures shows better execution stood out to frameworks arranged from single-particular pictures.

1.6.2   Machine Learning in Patient Risk Stratification

In social insurance, hazard delineation is comprehended as the way toward ordering patients into sorts of dangers. This status relies upon information acquired from different sources, for example, clinical history, well-being pointers, and the way of life of a populace. The objective of delineating hazard incorporate tending to populace the board difficulties, individualizing treatment intends to bring down dangers, coordinating danger with levels of care, and adjusting the training to esteem based consideration draws near. Customary models for anticipating hazard generally relies on the ability and experience of the expert. ML doesn't request human contributions—to investigate clinical and money related information for quiet hazard definition, by utilizing the accessibility of volumes of information, for example, clinical reports, patients' records, and protection records, and apply ML to give the best results.

1.6.3   Machine Learning in Telemedicine

Tele-well-being in human services is a significant industry. It makes the patient consideration process simpler for the two suppliers and patients. This industry is developing at a quicker pace around the world. The progression of new innovation, for example, ML in the human services has furnished clinical experts with really veritable instruments and assets to deal with the day by day convergence of patients. AI can assist these experts with another approach to break down and decipher volumes of crude patient information and offer intriguing experiences and headings towards accomplishing better well-being results.

1.6.4   AI (ML) Application in Sedate Revelation

Machine learning (ML) approaches, have assumed a key job during the time spent medication disclosure in the ongoing occasions. It has limited the high disappointment rate in medicate advancement by utilizing the accessibility of enormous great information. There are numerous difficulties in ML for medicate advancement. One of the significant difficulties is to guarantee sedate security. One of the difficult and complex undertakings during the time spent medication revelation is to examine and decipher the accessible data of the known impacts of the medications and expectation of their symptoms. Specialists from different rumoured colleges/organizations and obviously, numerous pharmaceutical organizations have been constantly utilizing ML to acquire pertinent data from clinical information utilized in clinical preliminaries. Breaking down and deciphering these information utilizing ML in the context of drug security is a functioning region of research as of late. Most importantly, the computational arrangement in drug disclosure has helped fundamentally lessen the cost of introducing drugs to the market.

1.6.5   Neuroscience and Image Computing

Neuroscience Image Computing (NIC) gives specific consideration for the improvement of advanced imaging approaches, and its understanding into clinical studies. NIC contemplates endeavor to find the ethology of mind issues, including mental issues, neuro degenerative issues and horrendous cerebrum wounds by utilizing trend setting innovations.

1.6.6   Cloud Figuring Systems in Building AI-Based Healthcare

AI when all is said in done and ML specifically have seen enormous development in the ongoing occasions as a result of its capacity to utilize gigantic volumes of information and produce precise and profound comprehension about the current issues. Distributed computing has made it conceivable that are more practical and its capacity to deal with expanding market request. Models utilizing ML are believed to be progressively powerful that are utilizing distributed computing assets. The distributed computing assets can follow information from gadget wearable gadgets and well-being trackers. At that point they can stream and total it cost adequately in cloud-based capacity. The enormous volume of information can be broke down productively utilizing cloud-based process foundation. This permits the ML models to be progressively precise and strong.

1.6.7   Applying Internet of Things and Machine Learning for Personalized Healthcare

Web of Things (IoT) in social insurance has made it progressively conceivable to associate an enormous number of individuals, things with shrewd sensors, for example, wearable and clinical gadgets and situations. Understanding vitals and different kinds of constant information are caught by sensors and shrewd resources in IoT gadgets. Information investigation advances, for example, ML, can be utilized to convey esteem based consideration to the individuals. For example, operational upgrades improve efficiencies that give quality consideration at diminished expenses. Likewise, clinical enhancements guarantee speedier and generally exact conclusions. It likewise guarantees progressively tolerant driven, logical assurance of the best restorative way to deal with help better well-being results. ML utilizes gathered dataset to improve disease development strategy and disorder estimate. Informative models by utilizing ML are fused into different human administrations applications. These models commonly separate the gathered data from sensor contraptions and various sources to perceive individual lead norms and clinical conditions of the patient.

1.6.8 Machine Learning in Outbreak Prediction

Multiple episode expectation models are broadly utilized by specialists in the ongoing occasions to settle on most fitting choices and execute significant measures to control the flare-up. For instance, specialists are utilizing a portion of the standard models, for example, epidemiological and factual models for forecast of COVID-19. Expectation rising up out of these models end up being less strong and less exact as it includes immense vulnerability and lack of applicable information. As of late, numerous specialists are utilizing ML models to make long haul expectation of this episode. Scientists have demonstrated that AI based models end up being progressively powerful contrasted with the elective models for this flare-up.

1.7 Conclusion

Human administrations are one of the speediest creating divisions in the current economy; more people require care, and it is ending up being progressively exorbitant. Government spending on social protection has shown up at a record-breaking high while the inherent prerequisite for redesigned open minded specialist affiliation ends up being expeditiously clear. Advancements like tremendous data and AI can bolster the two licenses and providers to the extent better thought and lower costs. Computer-based intelligence strategies applied to EHR data can make important bits of information, from upgrading understanding peril score structures, to foreseeing the start of ailment, to streamlining clinical facility exercises. Quantifiable structures that impact the variety and luxury of EHR-decided data (as opposed to using a little plan of ace picked and also by and large used features) are still modestly phenomenal and offer an invigorating street for extra investigation. New kinds of data, for instance, from wearable's, bring their own odds and troubles. Challenges in effectively using AI strategies consolidate the availability of staff with the aptitudes to build, evaluate, and apply learned systems, similarly as the looking over this current reality cash sparing bit of leeway trade off of embedding's a model in a social protection work process. To build up a well-working human services framework, it is essential to have a decent misrepresentation recognition framework that can battle extortion that as of now exists and extortion that may develop in future. In this section, an endeavor has been made to characterize misrepresentation in the social insurance framework, distinguish information sources, describe information, and clarify the administered AI extortion identification models. Despite the fact that an enormous sum of exploration has been done around there, more provokes should be worked out. Misrepresentation identification isn't restricted to finding false examples, however to likewise giving quicker methodologies with less computational cost when applied to tremendous measured datasets.

References

1. Mason, E., Jain, S., Kendall, M., Mostashari, F., Blumenthal, D., The regional extension center program: Helping physicians meaningfully use health information technology. *Ann. Intern. Med.*, 153, 666–670, 2010.
2. Mossialos, E., Wenzl, M., Osborn, R., Sarnak, D., *International Profiles of Healthcare Systems*, The Commonwealth Fund, New York, NY, 2016.
3. Parikh, R.B., Kakad, M., Bates, D.W., Integrating predictive analytics into high-value care: the dawn of precision delivery. *JAMA*, 315, 651–652, 2016.
4. Goldstein, B.A., Navar, A.M., Pencina, M.J., Ioannidis, J.P., Opportunities and challenges in developing risk prediction models with electronic health records data: A systematic review. *J. Am. Med. Inform. Assoc.*, 27, 1, 198–208, 2016.
5. Jung, K., Covington, S., Sen, C.K., Januszyk, M., Kirsner, R.S., Gurtner, G.C. *et al.*, Rapid identification of slow healing wounds. *Wound Repair Regen.*, 24, 181–188, 2016.
6. Pencina, M.J. and Peterson, E.D., Moving from clinical trials to precision medicine: The role for predictive modeling. *JAMA*, 315, 1713–1714, 2016.
7. Chen, R. and Michael, S., Promise of personalized comics to precision medicine. *Wiley Interdiscip. Rev. Syst. Biol. Med.*, 5.1, 77–82, 2013.
8. Nickel, M. and Kiela, D., Poincare Embeddings for Learning Hierarchical Representations arXiv:170508039, abs/1705.08039, 1–10, 2017.
9. Lin, C., Jain, S., Kim, H., Bar-Joseph, Z., Using neural networks for reducing the dimensions of single-cell RNA-Seq data. *Nucleic Acids Res.*, 45, 17, e156–e156, 2017.
10. Choi, E., Bahadori, M.T., Song, L., Stewart, W.F., Sun, J., GRAM: Graph-based attention model for healthcare representation learning. *International Conference on Knowledge Discovery and Data Mining (KDD)*, ACM, pp. 787–795, 2017.
11. Silver, M., Sakata, T., Su, H.C., Herman, C., Dolins, S.B., O'Shea, M.J., Case study: How to apply data mining techniques in a healthcare dataware house. *Healthcare Inf. Manage.*, 15, 2, 155–164, 2001.
12. NHCAA, https://www.nhcaa.org, 2020.
13. FBI Reports and publications: Financial, https://www.fbi.gov/starts-services/publications, 2009.
14. FBI Scams and Safety: Common fraud schemes, https://www.fbi.gov/, Scams-and-safety, 2011.
15. Spencer, K. and Herbert, D., Mass Marketing of Property and Liability Insurance, Department of Transportation, United States of America, 1970.
16. Li, J., Huang, K., Jin, J., Shi, J., A survey on statistical methods for healthcare fraud detection. *Healthcare Manage. Sci.*, 11, 275–287, 2008.
17. London: The Guardian. The mystery of John Darwin, https://www.theguardian.com, 2007.
18. Relles, D., Ridgeway, G., Cater, G., Data mining and the implementation of a prospective payment system for inpatient rehabilitation. *Health Serv. Outcomes Res. Method*, 3, 3–4, 247–266, 2002.
19. Koh, H. and Tan, G., Data mining applications in healthcare. *J. Healthc Inf. Mgmt.*, 19, 2, 64–72, 2005.

20. Hall, C., Intelligent data mining at IBM: New products and applications. *Intel Software Strategy*, 7, 5, 1–11, 1996.
21. Jeffries, D., Zaidi, I., Jong, B., Holland, M., Miles, D., Analysis of flow cytometry data using an automatic processing tool. *Cytometry Part A,* 73A, 9, 857–867, 2008.

Part 2

MACHINE LEARNING/DEEP LEARNING-BASED MODEL DEVELOPMENT

A Framework for Health Status Estimation Based on Daily Life Activities Data Using Machine Learning Techniques

Tene Ramakrishnudu*, T. Sai Prasen and V. Tharun Chakravarthy

National Institute of Technology-Warangal, India

Abstract

In the current generation, it is very important to monitor our health. With the busy lives of people nowadays, many are experiencing health-related issues at an early age. Many of these issues arise because of our daily life activities. People are interested in many activities, but they hardly know the consequences of those activities. Hence it is very important to detect daily life activities that affect the health of a person and predict the diseases that may come in the future. However, there are existing methods for predicting a particular kind of disease like diabetes, tuberculosis, etc., based on electronic health records. The proposed system predicts the overall health status of a person using machine learning techniques. The overall health status includes how well a person is sleeping, eating, doing physical activity, etc. Also, the proposed system monitors the health of persons and alerts when they are deviating from a normal state. In this chapter, we will discuss the data collection approach, architecture of the system, overall health estimation models, implementation details, and the analysis of the result.

Keywords: Healthcare data analysis, machine learning in healthcare, data analytics, health status estimation

2.1 Introduction

2.1.1 Health Status of an Individual

The overall health status of a person is assessed by comparing the level of wellness with the level of illness. The health status can be estimated through many parameters. Some of the parameters are (i) Sleep status: the health level of a person is depending on his/her sleep timings, (ii) Screen status: the health level of a person is depending on the amount of time spent on screen, (iii) Drink status: the health level of a person is depending on his/her drinking habits, (iv) Smoke status: the health level of a person is depending on his/her smoking activities (v) Calories status: the health level of a person is depending on the calories consumed and physical activities.

**Corresponding author*: trk@nitw.ac.in

Sachi Nandan Mohanty, G. Nalinipriya, Om Prakash Jena and Achyuth Sarkar (eds.) Machine Learning for Healthcare Applications, (19–32) © 2021 Scrivener Publishing LLC

2.1.2   Activities and Measures of an Individual

The things that an individual does daily can be referred to as activities. Some of the activities include sleeping, watching television, consuming alcohol, smoking cigarette, listening to the radio, reading books, etc. Measures of an Individual include physical measures like height, weight, and some other measures like age, gender, etc. Basically, many of the measures are permanent they will not change frequently, whereas the activities might change frequently.

2.1.3   Traditional Approach to Predict Health Status

In general, health status can be predicted by consultancy experts. If an individual wants to know about their sleep status (i.e. whether their sleep pattern is good? And whether they are taking the adequate amount of sleep?), they can consult an expert at sleep centers. If an individual wants to know about their calorie status (i.e. How much calories they need to consume to maintain/increase/decrease weight? How much exercise they need to do to maintain the calories in balance?), they can consult physicians.

But what the experts do, they give some suggestions by considering the measures and activities mentioned previously. For this, the experts use some rules and conditions on the measures and activities. For example, 'A boy of age 21, height 176 cm, weight 63 kg with a less physical activity needs to consume 1,950 calories per day to maintain weight'. But the limitation of this approach is not considered some of the important parameters like (i) Different Health Parameters (Sleep Status, Calorie Status, etc.) have different consultants. (ii) They may not be very accurate in predicting them manually without any calculations. (iii) Consulting experts might be costly for a low-middle and middle-class family.

Thus, it demands the need for designing a model that can predict their health status from daily life activities.

2.2   Background

It is important for everyone to understand their health status, it helps to avoid future diseases. As mentioned previously some of the parameters of the health status are sleep status, smoke status, drink status, disease status, etc. Directly or indirectly they depend on the individual's daily life activities and physical measures. In healthcare data management, a huge amount of structured or unstructured data related to the patient is generated from the diagnostic reports, doctor's prescription, and the wearable devices. In recent years the healthcare data analysis and estimating the future health status are the major focused domains in healthcare. Disease Prediction has a major impact on healthcare analytics as it predicts outbreaks of epidemics to avoidable diseases and improves the quality of life. Some of the recent works proposed a verity of models to predict health status a person with the help of various factors. Researchers Sahoo, Mohapatra, and Wu [10], proposed a cloud-based probabilistic data acquisition method and also, designed an approach to predict the impending health state of a person based on the current health status. A work by Hirshkowitz *et al.* [5], proposed a method to evaluate and recommended sleep duration for individuals based on their age categories. Researchers [9], proposed a new approach for the disease risk prediction, in that they also proposed the Convolutional Neural Network (CNN) based on unimodal disease risk prediction and CNN-based Multimodal Disease Risk Prediction. Reseachers Weng, Huang, and Han [2], discussed different types of artificial neural network (ANN) techniques for disease prediction and evaluated all the methods based on statistical tests. Researchers [7], proposed a system to collect health data through some questionnaires and analyzed using deep learning architectures.

A work by Tayeb *et al.* [12], proposed a method based on the popular machine learning algorithm KNN to predict heart disease and chronic kidney failure. Researchers [6] proposed an automated system for the prediction of stroke based on Electronic Medical Claims (EMCs), and they compared the Deep Neural Network (DNN) with the gradient boosting decision tree (GBDT), logistic regression (LR) and support vector machine (SVM) approach. Researchers [8] proposed the cloud-based smart clothing system for sustainable monitoring of human health. They also discussed the technologies and the implementation of methodologies. Reseachers Schmidt, Tittlbach, Bös & Woll [11], analyzed varieties of physical activity, fitness and health, they considered 18 years duration for study and identified interesting insights. In a recent work on Analyzing University Fitness Center data [14], the user's fitness activity data is collected to predict the crowd at the fitness center. But the fitness activity data can be used to predict more than that.

A lot of research was done on measuring health parameters numerically. Also, there are many works on calculating some health parameters from other parameters. A work by Harris-Benedict [4] calculates Basal Metabolic Rate from an individual's physical measures. It is used to estimate the number of calories needed for an individual to maintain good health. Our work incorporated the effect of daily life activities on health status. But that data can be used to personalize health predictions and suggestions. This motivated to design a model that predicts health status from the daily life activities of individuals.

2.3   Problem Statement

Let A_t be the set of daily life activities done by an individual t day's back. Thus, A_0 is the set of activities done by an individual today, A_1 be the set of activities done by an individual yesterday, and so on. A is the collection of the activities of an individual for many days. M be the set of physical measures of an individual. H be the health status matrix.

Definition 1: Health Status Matrix: A health status matrix M describes the outcome of various parameters of health status. Each row of the matrix is considered as a vector of possible outcomes of the respective parameter of the health status. Examples of health status parameters are sleep status, smoke status, drink status, etc.

Given a set of daily life activities and physical measures of users over a few days and their health status. The health status of a set of users already defined, known as labeled users U_L. Whereas the health status of other sets of users is not defined, known as unlabeled users U_V. The aim of the proposed model is to learn a function that uses the information of the labeled users' U_L and find the health status of the unlabeled users U_V.

Given a series of activities from last t days, the objective is to learn a function F,

$$H = F(M, A_0, A_1, A_2, \dots A_t),$$

where *M* is the set of physical measures of a user A_t is the set of activities of the user *t* days back. *H* is a health status matrix

2.4   Proposed Architecture

Figure 2.1 describes the architecture of the proposed model. The set of daily life activities and physical measures of an individual is taken from the users and fed into a pre-processor phase, which processes the input by reducing the number of features and does the required data pre-processing operations.

2.4.1   Pre-Processing

The daily life activities of an individual that are mainly considered are screen time, sleep time, physical activity, number of cigarettes smoked, units of alcohol consumed. The measures that are mainly considered are age, gender, height, weight, calorie intake. Thus, there are ten features that are collected from an individual. Then, in the pre-processing step, the number of features is reduced by removing the activities and measures that do not have any direct effect on health status. This is achieved by using the Harris-Benedict Equation [4].

The Harris–Benedict Equation [4] is a method used to estimate an individual's basal metabolic rate (BMR). It says

For Men	BMR = (10 × Weight in kg) + (6.25 × Height in cm) − (5 × Age in years) + 5
For Women	BMR = (10 × Weight in kg) + (6.25 × Height in cm) − (5 × Age in years) − 161

As per the Harris–Benedict Equation [4], the calories to be consumed is depending on the BMR value and the physical activity.

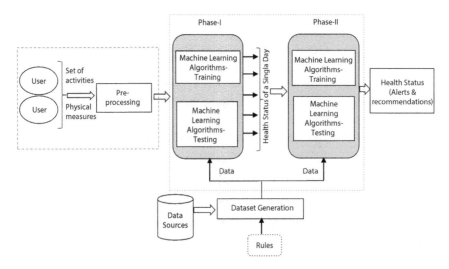

Figure 2.1 Architecture of the model.

Calories to be consumed = BMR * Physical Activity
Calories Difference = (Calories Consumed) − (Calories to be consumed).

In the proposed method the number of features is reduced to seven. They are age, gender, sleep time, screen time, number of cigarettes, units of alcohol consumed, and calorie intake.

2.4.2   Phase-I

The Phase-I of the model, process the data received from both the data sources and the user. In this phase, a decision tree classifier is used to estimate the health parameter of the user. Initially, the model is trained with the dataset received from the data sources. The Phase-I of the model estimates the health status of an individual for a particular day. But an individual's health status can't be accurate just by considering one day's output. In Phase-I the decision tree classifier is used, it takes the activities of an individual as input and produces the status of the health parameters for one day. Thus, the output of Phase-I is collected over a week and feeds it to Phase-II.

2.4.3   Phase-II

The Phase-II of the model, process the data received from the data sources and the output of the Phase-I. In this phase, the decision tree classifier is used to estimate the health parameter of the user. Initially, the model is trained with the dataset received from the data sources. The Phase-II of the model estimates the health status of an individual for a week. The output of Phase-II estimates the health status and generates the alerts and suggestions that are to be notified to the individual. In Phase-II the decision tree classifier is used, it takes the daily status of the health parameters over a week as input (i.e. the output of Phase-I) and outputs alerts & predictions of that health parameter.

2.4.4   Dataset Generation

Sub-section below provides the details of the rules collection and the dataset generation. The generated dataset is used for training the model proposed in the previous section.

2.4.4.1   Rules Collection

For preparing the datasets a proper set of rules is required on how the daily life activities of an individual affect his health status. The rules are collected from different trusted sources [5] and [1]. Based on the activities and measures of an individual, these rules give the overall health status of an individual. For example, the recommended sleep time for the person aged between 6 and 13 years is 9 to 11 h. If the sleep time is between 7 and 8, it is a little less than normal. if the sleep time is between 11 and 12, it is a little more than normal. if the sleep time is more than 12 or less than 8, then it affects health.

2.4.4.2   Feature Selection

Selecting the features from the rules that are collected and these rules depend on some activities and measures of an individual. For example, alcohol consumption rules for females are different from males. Similarly, the calorie value recommended for a person of 100 kg is different than that of a person of 50 kg [1]. In these examples, gender and weight are the features that are selected. In a similar fashion all the features like age, gender, height, weight, calorie intake, units smoked, units drunk, physical activity, screen time and sleep time were collected.

2.4.4.3   Feature Reduction

Although the features were collected, some of them might not affect the health status of a person directly. Thus, the collected features need to be transformed into the actual features which affect the health status. Here, the Harris–Benedict equation is used to reduce the features. The Harris–Benedict equation [4] is a method used to estimate an individual's basal metabolic rate (BMR). It says that the calories to be consumed depends on the BMR value and physical activity.

For example, If the physical activity is sedentary or a little active, then the calories to be consumed is 1.2 * BMR. If the physical activity is lightly active, then the calories to be consumed is 1.375 * BMR. If physical activity is moderate, then the calories to be consumed is 1.55 * BMR. If physical activity is an intense exercise, then the calories to be consumed is 1.725 * BMR. If physical activity is an extra hard exercise, then the calories to be consumed is 1.9 * BMR.

$$\text{Calories Difference} = (\text{Calories Consumed}) - (\text{Calories to be consumed}) \quad (2.1)$$

Thus, the total number of inputs is reduced to seven. They are Age, Gender, Number of units smoked, Units of Alcohol Consumed, Screen Time, Sleep Time, Calories Difference.

2.4.4.4   Dataset Generation From Rules

Based on the rules discussed in Section 2.4.4.1, all the required features are extracted. The features include daily life activities and physical measures of an individual. From the features extracted, the number of features is reduced using some standard techniques as discussed [4].

There are two phases in the proposed system. Thus, the Phase-I needs one dataset and the Phase-II needs a different dataset with class labels. The example dataset is described in Table 2.1.

2.4.4.5   Example

Let the individual's activities and measures for a day are:

Input = (Age = 21) ∩ (Gender = Male) ∩ (No. of cigars smoked = 0) ∩ (Units of Alcohol Consumed = 2) ∩ (Screen Time = 6) ∩ (Sleep Time = 8) ∩ (Height = 176) ∩ (Weight = 63) ∩ (Calorie Intake = 1,800) ∩ (Physical Activity = Lightly Active).

Table 2.1 Sample Dataset for Phase-I.

Class	Condition	Class label	Description
Sleep			
0	for age less than 2 sleep value between 11 and 14 For age between 3 and 5 sleep value between 10 and 13 For age between 6 and 13 sleep value between 9 and 11 For age between 14 and 17 sleep value between 8 and 10 For age between 18 and 25 sleep value between 7 and 9 For age between 26 and 64 sleep value between 7 and 9 For age greater than 65 sleep value between 7 and 8	normal	It tells the optimal sleep value for different age groups
1	for age less than 2 sleep value between 9 and 10 For age between 3 and 5 sleep value between 8 and 9 For age between 6 and 13 sleep value between 7 and 8 For age between 14 and 17 sleep value between 7 and 8 For age between 18 and 25 sleep value between 6 and 7 For age between 26 and 64 sleep value between 6 and 7 For age greater than 65 sleep value between 5 and 6	less sleep	It tells the sleep value is less than the optimal value for different age groups
2	for age less than 2 sleep value between 15 and 16 For age between 3 and 5 sleep value between 13 and 14 For age between 6 and 13 sleep value between 11 and 12 For age between 14 and 17 sleep value between 10 and 11 For age between 18 and 25 sleep value between 9 and 10 For age between 26 and 64 sleep value between 9 and 10 For age greater than 65 sleep value between 8 and 9	more sleep	It tells the sleep value is more than the optimal value for different age groups

(Continued)

Table 2.1 Sample Dataset for Phase-I. (*Continued*)

Class	Condition	Class label	Description
	Smoke		
0	if the number of cigars smoked is 0	good smoke status	
1	if the number of cigars smoked is between 1 and 4	smoking status is reasonable	
2	if the number of cigars smoked is between 5 and 15	bad smoking status	
3	if the number of cigars smoked is more than 15	dangerous smoking status	
	Drink		
0	if the number of units consumed is 0	drinking status is good	
1	if gender is male and the number of units consumed is less than 2 If gender is female and the number of units consumed is less than 1	drinking status is reasonable	
2	if gender is male and the number of units consumed is between 3 and 4 If gender is female and the number of units consumed is less than 2 and 3	drinking status is bad	

2.4.5 Pre-Processing

$$BMR = (10 \times \text{Weight in kg}) + (6.25 \times \text{Height in cm}) - (5 \times \text{Age in years}) + 5 \text{---------}[4]$$
$$BMR = 10 \times 63 + 6.25 \times 176 - 5 \times 21 + 5 = 1630$$
Calories needs to be consumed = BMR × Physical Activity = 1630 × 1.375 = 2241.25
Calorie Difference = Calories consumed − Calories needs to be consumed = 1,800 − 2241.25 = −441.25.

Thus, inputs after pre-processing are:

Input1 = (Age = 21) ∩ (Gender = Male) ∩ (No. of cigars smoked = 0) ∩ (Units of Alcohol Consumed = 2) ∩ (Screen Time = 6) ∩ (Sleep Time = 8) ∩ (Calorie Difference = −441.25).

2.5   Experimental Results

We have developed two models in this chapter based on the two popular machine learning algorithms which are Decision tree and Random forest and tested both the models based on the synthetic dataset. We have developed a web-based application to demonstrate the models proposed in this chapter. A few screenshots of the application shown in Figure 2.2.

2.5.1   Performance Metrics

To analyze the effectiveness and the performance of the model proposed in this chapter, we used the standard performance metrics [13] and [3] accuracy, precision, recall, and F1-score.

2.5.1.1   Accuracy

The accuracy of the model is calculated using the equation given below.

$$Accuracy = \frac{(TP+TN)}{(TP+FP+TN+FN)}$$

Table 2.2 shows the accuracy of the model for the decision tree proposed in this chapter.

Figure 2.3 shows the accuracy comparison between the two models which are proposed in this chapter and it is observed the model-II gives more accuracy than the model-I.

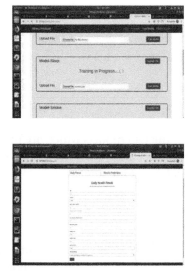

Figure 2.2 Screenshots of the web application.

Table 2.2 Accuracy of the model.

Health status	Model 1		Model 2	
	Accuracy: Phase-I	Accuracy: Phase-II	Accuracy: Phase-I	Accuracy: Phase-II
Sleep	90.54	93.64	91.54	94.64
Smoke	92.21	94.01	94.21	96.01
Drink	94.63	95.99	96.63	97.99
Screen	93.11	94.76	94.11	95.76
Calories	94.00	97.83	95.00	98.83

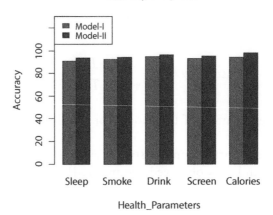

Figure 2.3 Accuracy: Model-I vs Model-II.

2.5.1.2   Precision

The precision of the model is calculated using the equation given below.

$$Precision = \frac{TP}{(TP+FP)}$$

Figure 2.4 shows the precision comparison between the two models which are proposed in this chapter and it is observed the model-II gives more accuracy than the model-I. Table 2.3 shows the Precision comparison between the model-1 and model-2.

2.5.1.3   Recall

The recall of the model is calculated using the equation given below.

$$Recall = \frac{TP}{(TP+FN)}$$

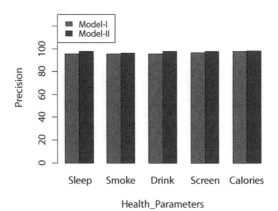

Figure 2.4 Precision: Model-I vs Model-II.

Table 2.3 Precision of the model.

Health status	Model 1		Model 2	
	Precision: Phase-I	Precision: Phase-II	Precision: Phase-I	Precision: Phase-II
Sleep	95.5555556	97.826087	95.6043956	97.8723404
Smoke	95.6989247	95.8333333	95.8333333	97.8947368
Drink	95.5555556	97.8723404	97.8947368	98.9473684
Screen	96.7032967	97.8494624	97.826087	96.8421053
Calories	97.3494624	97.9381443	97.8494624	98.9690722

Table 2.4 Recall of the model.

Health status	Model 1		Model 2	
	Recall: Phase-I	Recall: Phase-II	Recall: Phase-I	Recall: Phase-II
Sleep	93.4782609	94.7368421	94.5652174	95.8333333
Smoke	95.6989247	97.8723404	97.8723404	97.8947368
Drink	93.4782609	96.8421053	97.8947368	98.9473684
Screen	95.6521739	95.7894737	95.7446809	97.8723404
Calories	95.78941737	98.9583333	96.8085106	98.9690722

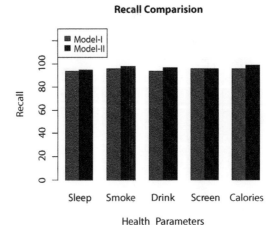

Figure 2.5 Recall: Model-I vs Model-II.

Table 2.4 shows the Recall comparison between the model-1 and model-2.

Figure 2.5 shows the Recall comparison between the two models which are proposed in this chapter and it is observed the model-II gives more accuracy than the model-I.

2.5.1.4   F1-Score

The F1-score is the harmonic mean of precision and recall. Below equation used to calculate the F1-score.

$$F1 - Score = \frac{2 * Precision * Recall}{Precision * Recall}$$

Figure 2.6 shows the F1-score comparison between the two models which are proposed in this chapter and it is observed the model-II gives more accuracy than the model-I. Table 2.5 shows the F1-Score comparison between the model-1 and model-2.

Table 2.5 F1-score of the model.

Health status	Model 1		Model 2	
	F1-score: Phase-I	F1-score: Phase-II	F1-score: Phase-I	F1-score: Phase-II
Sleep	94.50549	96.25668	95.08197	96.84211
Smoke	95.69892	96.84211	96.84211	97.89474
Drink	94.50549	97.3545	97.89474	98.94737
Screen	96.17486	96.80851	96.77419	97.3545
Calories	96.80851	98.4456	97.3262	98.96907

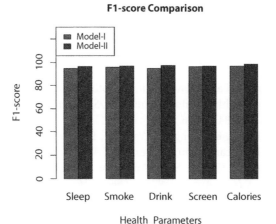

Figure 2.6 Recall: Model-I vs Model-II.

2.6   Conclusion

In this chapter, we have proposed an architecture based on machine learning algorithms. Basically, we focus on a challenging problem of predicting the overall health status of an individual based on their daily life activities and measures. The proposed system predicts the overall health status of a person and future diseases using machine learning techniques. To demonstrate the proposed model, we have created a web-based application. The proposed model helps the user to understand their health status by submitting their details. For training and testing we used the synthetic data, in the future we need to test the proposed model using the real data by collecting from the users. In this work, we attempted a general healthcare problem and a lot more has to be done in the future. The future work is to predict the diseases based on the overall health status estimation using the models proposed in this chapter.

References

1. Bjartveit, K. and Tverdal, A., Health consequences of smoking 1–4 cigarettes per day. *Tobacco Control*, 14, 5, 315–320, 2005.
2. Weng, C.-H., Huang, T.C.-K., Han, R.-P., Disease prediction with different types of neural network classifiers. *Telematics Inf.*, 33, 2, 277–292, 2016.
3. Alpaydın, E., *Introduction to Machine Learning*, 2nd edition, the MIT press, Cambridge, Massachusetts, 2010.
4. Harris, J.A. and Benedict, F.G., A Biometric Study of Human Basal Metabolism. *Proc. Natl. Acad. Sci. U.S.A.*, 4, 12, 370–373, 1918.
5. Hirshkowitz, M., Whiton, K., Albert, S.M., Alessi, C., Bruni, O., DonCarlos, L., Hillard, P.J.A., National Sleep Foundation's sleep time duration recommendations: Methodology and results summary. *Sleep Health*, 1, 1, 40–43, 2015.
6. Hung, C.-Y., Chen, W.-C., Lai, P.-T., Lin, C.-H., Lee, C.-C., Comparing deep neural network and other machine learning algorithms for stroke prediction in a large-scale population-based

electronic medical claims database. *39th Annual International Conference of the IEEE Engineering in Medicine and Biology Society*, pp. 3110–3113, 2017.

7. Nie, L., Wang, M., Zhang, L., Yan, S., Zhang, B., Chua, T.S., Disease inference from health-related questions via sparse deep learning. *IEEE Trans. Knowl. Data Eng.*, 27, 8, 2107–2119, 2015.

8. Chen, M., Ma, Y., Song, J., Lai, C., Hu, B., Smart clothing: Connecting human with clouds and big data for sustainable health monitoring, in: *ACM/Springer Mobile Networks and Applications Mobile*, vol. 21, 5, pp. 825–845, 2016.

9. Chen, M., Hao, Y., Hwang, K., Wang, L., Wang, L., Disease Prediction by Machine Learning over Big Data from Healthcare Communities. *IEEE Access*, 5, 8869–8879, 2017.

10. Sahoo, P.K., Mohapatra, S.K., Wu, S.-L., Analyzing healthcare big data with prediction for future health condition. *IEEE Access*, 4, 9786–9799, 2016.

11. Schmidt, S.C.E., Tittlbach, S., Bös, K., Woll, A., Different Types of Physical Activity and Fitness and Health in Adults: An 18-Year Longitudinal Study. *BioMed Res. Int.*, 2017, 2017.

12. Tayeb, S., Pirouz, M., Sun, J., Hall, K., Chang, A., Li, J., Latifi, S., Toward Predicting Medical Conditions Using kNearest Neighbors. *IEEE International Conference on Big Data*, pp. 3897–3903, 2017.

13. Mitchell, T.M., *Machine Learning*, McGraw Hill International Edition, New Yak City, 1997.

14. Du, Y., Gebremedhin, A.H., Taylor, M.E., Analysis of university fitness center data uncovers interesting patterns, enables prediction. *IEEE Trans. Knowl. Data Eng.*, 31, 8, 1478–1490, 2019.

Study of Neuromarketing With EEG Signals and Machine Learning Techniques

S. Pal[1], P. Das[1], R. Sahu[2] and S.R. Dash[3]*

[1]Infogain India Pvt. Ltd., Bengaluru, India
[2]School of Computer Science & Engineering, KIIT University, Bhubaneswar, Odisha, India
[3]School of Computer Applications, KIIT University, Bhubaneswar, Odisha, India

Abstract

Neuromarketing is the most rising yet undelved technique even though it has shown immense potential. It has many uses and benefits in the commercial sector as supposedly it can tell which product has potential while analyzing your competition and also stop from manufacturing products which might fail in upcoming market trends. It is supposed to fill the gap between survey results and the actual behavior of the customer at the shop.

It has not been researched well in the past due to limitations of cost-effectiveness of an EEG device. But with the promise of cheap, portable and reliable devices like Emotiv Epoc sensors and Neurosky Mindwaves, we are now able to conduct trials and evaluation in a cost-effective, portable and fast manner in comparison to conventional EEG setups. The chapter has analyzed and studied consumers' choice with regards to various products and found out the pattern of EEG signals using machine learning techniques according to like and dislike.

In this chapter, we have observed and conducted trials on 25 subjects. We recorded all EEG signals using Emotiv Epoc+ Sensor device with 14 channels recording EEG data from 25 volunteers while observing common products on a display. All volunteers are between 18 and 38 years of age. A set of 13 various products were displayed wherein products had 3 different brands which invariably created 42 unique product images. In total 1,050 EEG signals were captured for all the 25 volunteers. Like and dislike are labeled by each participant for the unique image during the experiment to capture the labeled emotions with their corresponding EEG data. Every product was displayed for 4 s. In the data collection, it is instructed to the volunteers to label their honest opinion towards the products. The proposed approaches have shown the feasibility towards the marketing and provide an additional method to the traditional method for forecasting a product's performance. These machine learning methods with EEG signals may develop strategies, introduce new products, and find out inflation in the business world. We have noticed that Kernel SVM has performed better than other classifiers.

Keywords: Neuromarketing, bagging decision tree, gaussian bayes, kernel SVM, random forest, EEG signals

---

Corresponding author: satyaranjan.dash@gmail.com

Sachi Nandan Mohanty, G. Nalinipriya, Om Prakash Jena and Achyuth Sarkar (eds.) Machine Learning for Healthcare Applications, (33–56) © 2021 Scrivener Publishing LLC

3.1   Introduction

Brain is perhaps the most significant organ of our body which consists of billions of neurons which in turn use electric pulses for communicating among themselves. There is immense amount of electrical activity in our brain because of transmission of neuro signals in the form of electric pulses. These neuro signals are what is collectively known as brainwaves. They consist of synchronized and sequential electric pulses from neurons to various parts of our body via nerves. These brainwaves can be analyzed and detected by an equipment called Electroencephalograph. Traditionally the machines used to detect EEG signals where very large and costly but nowadays they have been miniaturized into EEG biosensors. EEG is a significant part of signal analysis because its amplitude graphs depict the various stimulations as well as brain states.

3.1.1   Why BCI

The objective of our study is empowering the users to explore the different avenues that come under the field of Brain Computer Interfaces (BCI), implementing user-friendly and economical equipment which have been recently been made viable for common public use. The domain of BCI is the influential force behind the goal of full utilization of Electroencephalography (EEG). We use electrodes on the scalp of users to record the brain activity. In the past, we have focused highly on creating solutions from a medical context, helping extreme cases of paralysis or disablement in regard to motor functions by mapping EEG signals to the respective cognitive actions.

But now BCI solutions are no longer limited to just patients for treatment, with the change in focus of general public towards living a healthier lifestyle with the aid of modern technology, young people are a prime target group who are willing to adapt to EEG devices as a dimension giving them timely updates about their mental ability and wellness. It starts with treatment and can go till far as entertainment as more and more companies start working on Mind-Controlled gaming technology. This exciting phase makes EEG to be more available, cost effective and firms become more willing to invest into this technology for general purpose uses.

One of the prime manufacturers of cost-effective EEG headsets is Emotiv with a slogan "Neurotech for the Global Community". They have an EEG device named Emotiv EPOC+ sensor device which is a low-cost and portable headset aimed for the consumer market. Historically EEG machines were reserved for rich people but now it can be used by anyone in the shape of a user, developer or analyst. This helps us to accelerate the growth and research done in the field of BCI. The strategy of our study is to utilize this piece of technology and create viable results in Neuromarketing.

3.1.2   Human–Computer Interfaces

Since past few years, major advances have been done in the approach for interaction of users with machines. Standard physical interactive devices for computers were keyboard and mouse, but now more user-centric devices are being developed to deeply incorporate them into the lifestyle of users.

Most of the previous devices required an action to be performed for interacting with the machine. EEG counters this point by controlling the actions via brains stimuli functions. This in turn becomes life-saving for people with limited motor skills due to diseases and disabilities like paralyzed patients. This solution is also known as Mind–Machine Interface or "Brain Machine Interface" which is a direct path from brain to an external device.

3.1.3   What is EEG

An Electroencephalogram is basically a reading of brain's electric voltage fluctuations as read on scalp electrodes. It is the approximate cumulative electrical activity of neurons. This process is one of the best non-penetrative interfaces because of its temporal resolution. But it has hindrances like susceptibility to noise which is a very prominent barrier to implementing EEG devices as BCI solutions. It requires extensive training for users and models to provide substantial results in a consistent manner.

As for example, Niels Birbaumer from University of Tubingen had brought paralyzed patients in mid-1990s for training them to control the slow cortical potentials to be utilized in order for them to control a computer's cursor by binary signaling. They were slow, as in they required 1 h to write 100 characters and training them took several months but it appeared as a breakthrough possibility.

3.1.4   History of EEG

Hans Berger was the man who discovered that there is significant electrical activity in the brain and developed the initial process known as Electroencephalography today. In the year 1924 he captured the first brain signal and by analyzing them he found oscillatory activity in the form of alpha wave (8–12 Hz) called Berger's wave. During early days he inserted silver wires in the scalp of patients then after graduating to using silver foils which in turn were connected to a "Lippmann Capillary Electrometer". Later on he experimented with galvanometers and after significant analysis he started creating brain maps of electrical pulses for specific brain diseases. This all led to the discovery of EEG and created new possibilities in human advancement.

3.1.5   About Neuromarketing

Generally marketing procedures or tools include surveying, interviews, target groups, etc. where participants willingly give feedback for their thoughts and opinions on a product. These procedures have a drawback of not considering the unconscious decision-making characteristics. EEG has the potential to identify these emotions and influence the decision-making process. It is found that 90% of the decision making consists of factors from the subconscious mind. In this domain, the analysis of the subconscious mind presents the true choices of users more accurately than other methods. It has the potential to factor in characteristics about decision making in users which cannot be accurately pin-pointed in other methods. Neuromarketing fills the gap between the results of traditional marketing methods and real decisions of consumers.

In order to analyze the consumer's behavior we factor in his sensorimotor and mental feedback with the combination of eye-tracking, skin conductance, galvanic skin response and facial electromyography which all in turn contribute to create a sequential flow chart of a consumer's response and various stimuli which resulted in the failure or successful of purchase of the product.

This technology came around prominence in 2002 with the initiatives of Brighthouse and SalesBrain who developed marketing solutions based on Neuromarketing and also offered studies on the client's product base from a consumer's EEG data. Thus, major powerhouses in FMCG markets have started to adopt Neuromarketing techniques to exploit the consumer's behaviour from a marketing and psychological angle.

3.1.6   About Machine Learning

"Machine Learning" is the process of enabling computing devices to try, learn, do and verify assigned tasks to be performed on their own without being hard-coded to do so. The learning process in the code needs to evolve on its own with the changing parameters and perform accordingly. Earlier on human used to analyze all the scenarios in a task and we would dictate the steps required to the computer but during wider and more complex situations we realized it's better for the computers to develop its own algorithm.

This domain of Machine Learning implements various tracks to help computers automatedly accomplish tasks where no correct sequence of steps is known. It involves training the computer through a vast number of situations and label them as successful or not and accordingly perform the correct sequence of action for the respective situation. This is called training data which is used to improve the effectiveness and efficiency of an algorithm. We have extensively used this procedure to achieve significant results in regard to our efficiency in predicting the choice of a consumer and also establishing a brain map for like/dislike.

3.2   Literature Survey

In this section, we shall briefly mention most of the studies and research done currently in the field of EEG and Neuromarketing relevant to our study.

Primarily we got a solid foundation [1] to work on from Dr. Partha Pratim Roy's and his associates' paper on Analysis of EEG signals and application of Neuromarketing, in his paper he has used the deep learning method of Hidden Markov Model and recorded the dataset using user-independent test approach. He also proposed a predictive modelling framework to acquire the consumer's knowledge about what all he like/dislikes amongst the sample products using an Emotiv EPOC+ sensor. We have borrowed his dataset for initial study as an ice-breaker and it has helped us in leaps.

After reading his paper, we inherently searched for the spectrum of mind which consciously makes the decision of a person liking/disliking a product in a natural environment. We had encountered lot of reasons such as presentation, composition of materials, past experiences, cost and brand value which a person uses to determine its likeability. But perhaps this wasn't enough. So, we decided to delve a little into emotion recognition for identifying which all areas in brain elicit an emotion. Following will be our concise notes on emotion recognition and after which we shall provide the methodological research of models.

This paper [2] is about automatic emotional classification by EEG data using DEAP dataset led by Samarth Tripathi and his associates, applying Convolutional and Deep Neural Networks on DEAP datasets. Earlier emotion recognition involved text, speech, facial, etc. as analyzing parameter s. An emotion is a psychophysiological operation started by a voluntary or involuntary reception of a situation.

In this paper, peripheral physiological signals of 32 subjects were recorded while they watched videos and were evaluated on levels of arousals & valence. They used a 32 EEG-channel 512 Hz Biosemi Active2 device that utilizes active AgCl electrodes to compile the data.

Neural networks implement functions based on large datasets of unknown inputs by training & statistic models. Here, 2 neural models are used 1. Deep Neural Network (DNN) and 2. Convolutional Neural Network (CNN). The dataset is of 8064 signal data from 40 channels for each subject. A total of 322,560 readings were recorded for the models to process. The first model, i.e., DNN used 4 neural levels whose output became input for the subsequent levels. As the dataset was limited, they implemented dropout technique with superior Epoch which could keep the count of all training vectors for updating weights. The datasets were divided into groups for easier use and they all go through learning algorithms before Epoch update occurs. The data was trained in 310 groups with Epoch of 250. For the second model, i.e., CNN, the DEAP data is converted to 2D images for the 101 readings each totaling to a size of 4,040 units. CNN's first layer used 'Tan Hyperbolic' as activation function in valence classification model & 'Relu' as activation for arousal model. The subsequent levels used 100 filters and $3 * 3$ sized kernel with the very same 'Tan Hyperbolic' function as activation function for both classifier models. The last dense layer used 'Softplus' as its activation function using CCE as loss function and SGD as an optimizer.

The learning rates were found to be 0.00001 for valence, 0.001 for arousal & a gradient momentum of 0.9. These models resulted in 4.51 & 4.96% improvement in classifying valence and arousal respectively among 2 classes (High/Low) in valence & 3 classes (High/Normal/Low) in arousal. The learning rate is marginally more useful, but dropout probability secures the best classification across levels. They also noted that wrong choice of activation functions especially 1st CNN layer will cause severe defects to models. The models were highly accurate with respect to previous researchers and prove the fact that neural networks are the key for EEG classification of emotions in a step to unlocking the brain.

Hence Deep Neural Networks are used to analyze human emotions and classify them by PSD and frontal asymmetry features. Training model for emotional dataset are created to identify its instances. Emotions are of 2 types—Discrete, classified as a synchronized response in neural anatomy, physiology & morphological expressions and Dimensional, i.e., they can be represented by a collection of small number of underlying effective dimensions, in other words, vectors in a multidimensional space.

The aim of this paper is to identify excitement, meditation, boredom and frustration from the DEAP emotion dataset by a classification algorithm. The Python language is used including libraries like SciKit Learn Toolbox, SciPy and Keras Library. The DEAP dataset contains physiological readings of 32 participants recorded at a sampling rate of 512 Hz with a "bandpass frequency filter" with a range of 4.0 to 45.0 Hz and eliminated EOG artifacts. Power Spectral Density (PSD), based on Fast Fourier Transform, decomposes the data into 4 distinct frequency ranges, i.e., theta (4–8 Hz), alpha (8–13 Hz), beta (13–30 Hz) and gamma (30–40 Hz) using the avgpower function available in Python's Signal Processing toolbox. The left hemisphere of brain has more frequently activation with positive valence and the right hemisphere has negative valence.

$$Valence = \left(\frac{Left_\beta}{left_\alpha} \right) - \left(\frac{right_\beta}{right_\alpha} \right)$$

$$Arousal = np.\log_2 (front\_\beta/front\_\alpha)$$

Emotion estimation on EEG frontal asymmetry:

$$Valence = ln\ (frontal\ \alpha^{(left)} - ln\ (frontal\ \alpha^{\ (right)})$$

$$Arousal = np.\log_2\ (front\_\beta/front\_\alpha)$$

"Ramirez *et al.* classified emotional states by computing levels of arousal as prefrontal cortex and valence levels as below":

$$Valence = \alpha(f4)\beta(F4) - \alpha(F3)\beta(F3)$$

$$Arousal = \alpha(AF3 + AF4 + F3 + F4)\beta(AF3 + AF4 + F3 + F4)$$

"Whenever the arousal was computed as beta to alpha activity ratio in frontal cortex, valence was computed as relative frontal alpha activity in right lobe compared to left lobe as below":

$$Valence = \alpha(F4) - \beta(F3)$$

$$Arousal = \beta(AF3 + AF4 + F3 + F4)\alpha(AF3 + AF4 + F3 + F4)$$

"A time-frequency transform was used to extract spectral features alpha (8–11 Hz) and beta (12–29 Hz). Lastly Mean absolute error (MAE), Mean squared error (MSE) and Pearson Correlation (Corr) is used."

$$MAE = Mean\ (1n_i = 1n)\ of\ absolute\ errors\ |e_i| = |f_i = y_i|$$

$$where\ f_i = prediction/y_i = true\ value.$$

$$MSE\ is\ mean\ (1ni = 1n\ |e_i|)\ of\ square\ of\ errors\ ((y_i - y_i)^2)$$

By scaling (1–9) into valence & arousal (High & Low) we see that feeling of frustration and excitement triggers as high arousal in a low valence area and high valence area respectively whereas meditation and boredom triggers as low arousal in high valence area and in low valence area respectively.

The DNN classifier has 2,184 units with each hidden layer having 60% of its predecessor's units. Training was done using roughly 10% of the dataset divided into a train set, validation set and a test set. After setting a dropout of 0.2 for input layer & 0.5 for hidden layers, the model recognized arousal & valence with rates of 73.06% (73.14%), 60.7% (62.33%), and 46.69% (45.32%) for 2, 3, and 5 classes, respectively. The kernel-based classifier was observed to have better accuracy compared to other methods like Naïve Bayes and SVM. The result was a set of 2,184 unique features describing EEG activity during each trial. These extracted features were used to train a DNN classifier & random forest classifier. This was exclusively successful for BCI where datasets are huge.

Emotion monitoring using LVQ and EEG is used to identify emotions for the purpose of medical therapy and rehabilitation purposes. [3] proposes a monitoring system for humane emotions in real time through wavelet and "Learning Vector Quantization". Training data from 10 trials with 10 subjects, "3 classes and 16 segments (equal to 480 sets of data)" is processed within 10 seconds and classified into 4 frequency bands. These bands then become input for LVQ and sort into excited, relaxed or sad emotions. The alpha waves appear frequently when people are relaxed, beta wave occurs when people think, theta wave occurs when people are under stress, tired or sleepy and delta wave occurs when people are in deep sleep. EEG data is captured using an Emotive Insight wireless EEG on 10 participants. They used wireless EEG electrodes on "AF3", "T7", "T8" and "AF4" with a 128 Hz sampling frequency to record at morning, noon and night. 1,280 points are recorded in a set, which occurs every 3 min segmented every 10 s. Each participant is analyzed with excited, relaxed or sad states. Using the "LVQ wavelet transform", EEG was extracted into the required frequencies. "Discrete wavelet transforms (DWT)" again X(n) signal is described as follows:

$$C\,(j, k) = 12j\ nx(n) \star (2 - j \star n - k)$$

Known as wavelet base function. Approximation signal below is a resulted signal generated from convoluted processes of original signal mapping with high pass filter.

$$Approximation\ Signal = yhigh[k]$$

$$= \sum_{n} x[n] * g[n-k]$$

$$= ylow[k]$$

$$= \sum_{n} x[n] * h[n-k]$$

Where, $x(n)$ = original signal
$g(n)$ = low pass filter coeff
$h(n)$ = high pass filter coeff
K, n = index 1 = till length of signal

Scale function coefficient (Low pass filter)
  g0 = 1 − 342, g1 = 3 − 342, g2 = 3 + 3, 342, g3 = 1+342
Wavelet function coefficient (High pass filter)
  h0 = 1 − 342, h1 = − 3 − 342, h2 = 3 + 3, 342, h3 = − 1 + 342

When each input data with class label is known, a supervised version of vector quantization called "Learning Vector quantization" can be used to obtain the class that depends on the Euclidean distance between reference vectors and weights. Each training data's class was compared based on:

$$D_i = \sum_{j=i}^{n} \left\| x_{ij} - y_{ij} \right\|^2$$

Following is the series of input identification systems:

$x(n)$

$$= \begin{cases} t_{1-8}, s=1, AF3, a_{1-12}, s=1, AF3, b_{1-36}, s=1, AF3, \ldots, \\ t_{1-8}, s=10, AF3, a_{1-12}, s=10, AF3, b_{1-36}, s=10, AF3, \ldots, \\ t_{1-8}, s=1, T8, a_{1-12}, s=1, T8, b_{1-36}, s=1, T8, \ldots, \\ t_{1-8}, s=10, T8, a_{1-12}, s=10, T8, b_{1-36}, s=10, T8, \ldots, \\ et_{1-8}, s=1, AF3-AF4, ea_{1-12}, s=1, AF3-AF4, eb_{1-36}, s=1, AF3-AF4, \ldots, \\ et_{1-8}, s=10, AF3-AF4, ea_{1-12}, s=10, AF3-AF4, eb_{1-36}, s=10, AF3-AF4, \ldots, \\ et_{1-8}, s=1, T7-T8, ea_{1-12}, s=1, T7-T8, eb_{1-36}, s=1, T7-T8, \ldots, \\ et_{1-8}, s=10, T7-T8, ea_{1-12}, s=10, T7-T8, eb_{1-36}, s=10, T7-T8, \ldots, \end{cases}$$

"As stated, The LVS algorithm attempted to correct winning weight Wi with minimum D by shifting the input by the following values:

1. If the input xi and wining w_i have the same class label, then move them closer together by $\Delta W_i(j) = B(j)(X_{ij} − W_{ij})$.
2. If the input xi and wining w_i have a different class label, then move them apart together by $\Delta W_i(j) = −B(j)(X_{ij} − W_{ij})$.
3. Voronoi vectors/weights w_j corresponding to other input regions are left unchanged with $\Delta w_i(t) = 0$."

"The parameters used to train the LVQ model has a learning rate of 0.01 to 0.05 with 0.001 of learning rate reduction and the maximum epoch of 10,000." The learning rate of 0.05 resulted in the highest accuracy. An accuracy of 72% was achieved without extraction, 87% with extraction using a subset of pair symmetric channel called asymmetric wave and 84% accuracy without asymmetric wave. Using LVQ resulted in computation time being under a minute without any loss of accuracy. Generalization of data in LVQ training was relatively faster and more stable than Multilayer Perceptron. 10 seconds of signal data was identified in 0.44 s in each test.

Here 6 different emotional states such as sorrow, fear, happiness, frustration, satisfaction and enjoyment can be classified using different methods by extracting features from EEG signals. Decent accuracy was achieved by extracting appropriate features for emotional states such as discrete wavelet transforms and ANN recognizer system. In Ref. [4] this model, valence emotions range from negative to positive whereas arousal emotions go from calm to excitement. Discrete Wavelength transforms were applied on brain signal to classify different feature sets. The models used here is the 2-dimensional Arousal-Valence model. We invoked stimulus in the participant's neural signals using IAPS datasets. The IAPS Dataset contains 956 images with each of them projecting all emotional states. The participants of IAPS rated every picture for valence and arousal. 18 electrodes of a 21-electrode headset are used with 10–20 standard system and a sampling rate of 128 Hz. Since every subject's emotion are different, a self-assessment manikin (SAM) using the 2-dimensional space (arousal/valence) model where each of them having 5 levels of intensity was taken by the subjects needed to rate his or her emotion. The test was attended by 5 participants between the ages of 25 and 32. Each participant was given a stimulus of 5 s since the duration of each emotion is about 0.5 to 4 s.

To do this the data is derived from 4 frequency bands—alpha, beta, theta, delta. ECG (heart) artefacts which are about 1.2 Hz, "EOG" artefacts (Blinking) is below 4 Hz and EMG (Muscle) artefacts about 30 Hz and Non-Physiological artefacts power lines which is above 50 Hz which removed in preprocessing. In DWT all frequency bands are used and for each trial, the feature vector is $18 * 3 * 9 * 4 = 1,944$ (18 electrodes, 3 statistical features, 9 temporal windows & 4 frequency bands). In our instance, an "artificial neural network" has been used as a form of classifier of "backpropagation" algorithm for learning models implemented on the network. The architecture consists of 6 outputs and 10 hidden layers for all the different states of emotion. The accuracies "10-fold cross-validation technique" was used to avoid overfitting while estimating accuracies for the classifiers. As user's emotion can be affected by many factors such as their emotional state during the experiment, the best achieved accuracy for the network was 55.58%.

They applied Support Vector Machine to explore the bond between neural signals elated in prefrontal cortex based on taste in music. They [5] explored the effects of music on mental illnesses like dementia. It was observed that music enabled listeners to regulate negative behaviors and thoughts occurring in the mind. A BCI-based music system is able to analyze the real time activities of neurons and possible to provide physiological information to the therapist for understanding their emotions. The methods used to evaluate the data depended on the subjects.

The BCI music system consisted of EEG capturing system, a Bluetooth module for transmitting data from the EEG signals to analyze real time issue and also accordingly control the music. 3 major categories of music were considered to trigger positive emotions in the brain, namely the subject's favorite songs, K448 and high focus audio. The high focus audio comprised of non-vocal instrumentals produced by "The Brain Sync Company". It consisted of classic white noise elements such as those found in nature like falling rain or a cricket's cry, etc. The company claimed that these audio clippings helps a person reach their peak performance brain state with relative ease and without getting distracted. 28 participants attended the experiment having a mean age of 21.75 years.

> 'Fast fourier transform with 0.5 overlap to average power with a frequency band.'
> Each power was normalized by the valve of the baseline in same frequency band across the scalp. ($N = 3$)
> $NEEGS, F = EEGS, F1/N * S = 1NBEEGS, F$
> To investigate the asymmetric response of alpha power of PFC, a relation ratio (RR) = $RP - LPRP + LP * 100$, RP = alpha power from right hemisphere of PFC (FP2) & LP is from (FP1).

SVM was used utilizing a "non-linear kernel function" to recognize the responses of EEG signals. In one-sample test setting the median to 128 with a range between 0 and 255, it was seen that values went from highest to lowest in favorite songs, "K448" and High Focus, in that order. This proved that SVM recognized emotions with high accuracy. This approach did vary vastly from other approaches such as using musical properties such as tempo and melody as a metric to judge emotional response.

It is used to pretreat EEG signals for recognizing emotions. Emotions and their states are divided broadly as being either optimistic or pessimistic. This study [6] is able to scientifically explain emotion driven events such as rash driving and creativity. "DEAP" datasets were used to divide the EEG signals into sub-band analysis using "Fisher's Linear Discriminant" and then used "Naive Bayes Classifier" to classify emotions as being optimistic or pessimistic. 40 different locations of the brain were tracked for recording the EEG signals.

> The result of X, are the size of filters. Defining hk as the kth convolution of any depth, then sampled feature is: $hk = f(Wk * X + bk)$, where,
> W = weight of filter, b = bias of filter, $*$ = convolution,
> $f(.)$ = non linear activation function.
> When CNN is trained, cross–entropy function is usually used as the cost function.
> $Cost = 1n \; x[y \; Ln \; y + (1 - y)Ln \; (1 - y)]$, where, n = no. of training samples, x = input samples, y = actual output, y = target output. It defines the smaller the cost function, the closer the classification results is to target output. The convolution layer input samples are $\{X, Y\} = \{\{X1, Y1\}, \{X2, Y2\}, ..., \{X_i, Y_i\}\}$, $i = \{1, 2, ..., n\}$.
> X = feature of ith sample, Y = label of ith sample. $X = \{A * B * C\}$, a = channel of EEG signals. b = Down sampled EEG signals, f = sampling frequency. C = duration of EEG signals, t = time of video. C is the depth of 2 dimensional feature vector.
> Labels are:
> $Y_i = \{0, 0 < labels \; i < 4.5, 1, 4.5 < labels \; i < 9\}$
> $Y_i = \{0, 0 < labels \; i < 3, 1, 3 < labels \; i < 6, 2, 6 < labels \; i < 9\}$
> In 2 category recognition algorithm, 0 = optimism & 1 = pessimism. In 3 category recognition algorithm 0 = optimism, 1 = calm & 2 = pessimistic.
> $tan(hk) = ehk - e - hkehk + e - hk$
> The full connection layers use following as an activation function:
> $Softplus(y) = Log \; (1 + e^y)$

When trained, a stochastic gradient descent is used as an optimization algorithm to update the weights:

$$\hat{y} = \sum_{j=1}^{m} \theta_j x_j$$

$$J(\theta) = \frac{1}{m} \sum_{i=1}^{n} \frac{1}{2} (y_i - \widehat{y_\theta}(x_i))^2$$

$$= \frac{1}{m} \sum_{i=1}^{n} cost(\theta, (x_i, y_i))$$

$$\theta_{j+1} = Mt \times \theta_j - \lambda \frac{\partial J(\theta_j)}{\partial \theta_j}$$

y() = output of CNN, J() is loss value which is mean of multiple cost function values. The program is written in python and implemented using keras library toolkit and theano.

Regarding Neuromarketing techniques, we read up n the recent research that linked EEG signals with predicting consumer behavior and emotions on self-reported ratings.

The correlation between neurons' activities and the decision-making process is studied [7] during shopping have extensively been exploited to ascertain the bond between brain mapping and decision-making while visualizing a supermarket. The participants were asked to select one of every 3 brands after an interval of 90 stops. They discovered improvement in choice-predictions brand-wise. They also established significant correlations between right-parietal cortex activation with the participant's previous experience with the brand.

The researchers [8] explored the Neuro-signals of 18 participants while evaluating products for like/dislike. It also incorporated eye-tracking methodology for recording participant's choice from set of 3 images and capturing Neuro-signals at the same time. They implemented PCA and FFT for preprocessing the EEG data. After processing mutual data amongst preference and various EEG bands, they noticed major activity in "theta bands" in the frontal, occipital and parietal lobes.

The authors [9] tried to analyze and predict the 10 participant's preference regarding consumer products in a visualization scenario. In the next procedure, the products were grouped into pair and presented to participants which recorded increase frequencies on mid frontal lobe and also studied the theta band EEG signals correlating to the products.

It has implemented an application-oriented solution [10] for footwear retailing industry which put forward the pre-market prediction system using EEG data to forecast demand. They recorded 40 consumers in store while viewing the products, evaluating them and asked to label it as bought/not with an additional rating-based questionnaire. They concluded that 80–60% of accuracy was achieved while classifying products into the 2 categories.

A suggestive system [11] was created based on EEG signal analysis platform which coupled pre and post buying ratings in a virtual 3D product display. Here, they factored the emotions of the subjects by analyzing beta and alpha EEG signals.

The authors created a preference prediction system [12] for automobile brands in a portable form while conducting trial on 12 participants as they watched the promotional ad. The Laplacian filter and Butterworth band pass was implemented for preprocessing and 3 tactical features—"Power-Spectral Density", "Spectral Energy" and "Spectral Centroid" was procured from alpha band. The prediction was done by "K-Nearest Neighbor" and "Probabilistic Neural Network" classification with 96% accuracy.

They used the scenario of predicting the consumer's choice based on EEG signal analysis [13] while viewing the trailers which resulted in finding significant gamma and beta high frequencies with high correlation to participants and average preferences.

Participants were assessed on self-arousal and valence features while watching particular scenes in a movie [14]. They analyzed the data while factoring in 5 peripheral physiological signals relating them to movie's content-based features which inferred that they can be used to categorize and rank the videos.

Here 19 participants were shown 2 colors for an interval of 1 s and during the time EEG oscillations were analyzed [15] on Neural mechanisms for correlations of color preferences.

They had 18 participants who were subjected to a set of choices and analyzed their Neuro-activity and Eye-tracking activity to brain-map regions associated with decision making and inter-dependence of regions for the said task [16]. They concluded with high synchronization amongst frontal lobe and occipital lobe giving major frequencies in theta, alpha and beta waves.

They are trying to establish a bond between Neuro-signals and the learning capacity of a model software [17] while assuming that the model has the capability to train itself for dominant alpha wave participants.

"Independent Component Analysis (ICA)" to separate multivariate signals coming from 120 channels of electro-cortical activity [18]. This was done to convert those signals into additive subcomponents. Patterns of sensory impulses were recorded which matched movement of the body.

They have used filter is as a stabilizing and filtering element in the ECG data of 26 volunteers and then applied Approximate Entropy on it for inter-subject evaluation of data as the part of a retrospective approach [19] while adding truthfulness to Entropy windows for its stable distribution. This filter is very extensively being used in Signal processing which led us to adopt it.

The study [20] is an experiment on ECG signals of 26 participants where approximate entropy method is implemented for examining the concentration. Approximation entropy window was taken less for intra-patient comparing to inter-patient and for filtering the noisy signals S-Golay method was implemented.

They have innovatively preprocessed the ECG signal using S–Golay filter technique [21]. With both quadratic degrees of smoothing and differentiation filter methods combinedly has processed ECG signals having sampling rate 500 Hz with seventeen points length.

A very unique "double-class motor imaginary Brain Computer Interface" was implemented with Recurrent Quantum Neural Network model for filtering EEG signals [22].

In the paper [23] using the S-Golay filter, the artifacts due to blinking of eyes are found out and it is eliminated adapting a noise removal method.

3.3   Methodology

3.3.1   Bagging Decision Tree Classifier

Among the many Machine Learning algorithms, this method forms a group of algorithms where several instances are created of black-box estimators on variable subsets from the base training set after which we aggregate their solo predictions to form a resultant prediction. This process is used as a path to minimize the variance of the foundation estimator i.e. a decision tree by including randomization within its creation process and building an ensemble from it. In multiple scenarios, this method consists a simple path to improve with regard to a single model, avoids making it a necessity to acclimatize to a foundation algorithm. It works best with fully developed decision trees as it reduces overfitting in comparison to boosting methods which generally work best in shallow decision trees. This classifier comes in many flavors but majorly differ from each other by the path that they draw variable subsets of the training set. In our case samples were extracted with replacement called as Bagging.

3.3.2   Gaussian Naïve Bayes Classifier

This classifier is based on probability which is combined within a Machine Learning model. Hence, it is based on "Bayes Theorem" which states that, we can derive the probability of an event1 given that a retrospective event2 has happened. Here, event2 is the witness and event1 is the hypothesis. The assumption here is that the features are non-dependent which means that the existence of one feature does not affect the other which is why it's called Naïve. When predictions allocate a continuous value without being discrete, we can ascertain that those values are derived from gaussian distribution. Following is the general formula for Bayes theorem (3.1).

$$P(A \mid B) = \frac{P(B \mid A)P(A)}{P(B)} \tag{3.1}$$

Since our case has a different set or input, our formula for this implementation changes to Equation (3.2).

$$P(x_i \mid y) = \frac{1}{\sqrt{2\pi\sigma_y^2}} \exp\left(-\frac{(x_i - \mu_y)^2}{2\sigma_y^2}\right) \tag{3.2}$$

3.3.3   Kernel Support Vector Machine (Sigmoid)

The separable data with non-linear attributes cannot be tackled by a simple Support Vector Machine algorithm due to which we use a modified version of it called Kernel Support Vector Machine. Essentially in K-SVM it presents the data from a non-linear lower dimension to a linear higher dimension form as such that the attributes belonging to variable classes are assigned to different dimensions. We use a simple Python-SciKit Learn Library to implement and use K-SVM.

For training purposes, we use the SVC class of the library. The difference is in the values for the Kernel parameters of SVC class. In simple SVM's we use "Linear" for Kernel parameters but in K-SVM we use Gaussian, Sigmoid, Polynomial, etc. wherein we have used Sigmoid.

The only limitation observed in our case is that though this method achieves the highest accuracy but not up to the mark. Hence more advanced models like Deep Learning may be applied in near future for more concrete results.

3.3.4   Random Decision Forest Classifier

It is a variant of supervised machine learning algorithm founded on the schematic of ensembled learning. Ensemble learning is an algorithm where you join multiple or single algorithm into multiple types of algorithms of multiple or same variant to create a complex and advanced prediction model. It also combines many algorithms of same variant as decision trees, forest trees, etc. so the name "Random Forest". It is used for regression and classification tasks.

The way it works is it picks a part of the dataset and builds a decision tree on these records, and after selection of number of trees you want this process is repeated. Each tree represents the prediction in that category for which the new record belongs. The only limitation here is that there forte lies in their complexity and for that we need substantial computing resources when huge number of decision trees can be brought together which in turn will better train themselves.

3.4   System Setup & Design

We have used an Emotiv EPOC+ biosensor device for capturing Neuro-Signals in the following manner. Figure 3.1 represents the channels on the brain from signals collected and the equipment used for collection. The signals are collected from 14 electrodes positioned at "AF3, AF4, F3, F4, F7, F8, FC5, FC6, O1, O2, P7, P8 T7 and T8" according to International 10–20 system viewed in the figure below. There are reference electrodes positioned above ears at CMS and DRL. By default, the device has a sampling frequency of 2,048 Hz which we have down-sampled to 128 Hz per channel. The data acquired is transmitted using Bluetooth connectivity to a system. Before every sample collection sensor felt pads are rubbed with saline, connected via the Bluetooth USB and charged after with a USB cable as shown in the figure below.

The device is placed on the participants and then showed a particular set of common usage items for the purpose of our experiment, during which all the EEG activity is recorded and later on they are asked to label their choice of purchase amongst each set of products i.e. 1 among 3 items of from each set of products. The process diagram can be seen below in Figure 3.2.

After the data collection, the signals are preprocessed, and some features are extracted using wavelet transformation method and then the classification models were run on the

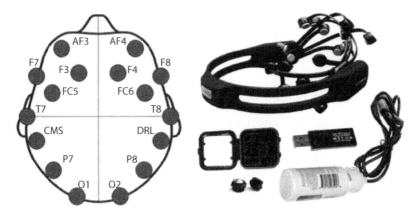

Figure 3.1 Brain map structure and Equipment used.

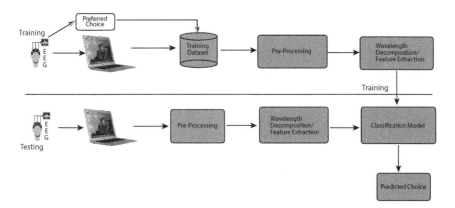

Figure 3.2 Workflow diagram.

resultant as mentioned before. A part of the data was is preprocessed and decomposed to test the training model. The labeling was done majorly into Like/Dislike.

3.4.1 Pre-Processing & Feature Extraction

We shall discuss how we used S-Golay filter to even out the signals and then DWT based wave-let analysis to extract features from Neuro-signals.

3.4.1.1 Savitzky–Golay Filter

In layman words [24] if we try to understand this filter, it is a polynomial based filter in which least square polynomial method find out the filtered signals with combinedly evaluating the neighbor signals. It can be computed for a signal such as $S_j = f(t_j)$, $(j = 1, 2, ..., n)$ by following Equation (3.3).

$$Q_j = \sum_{i=-\frac{m-1}{2}}^{\frac{m-1}{2}} c_i S_{j+i}, \quad \frac{m+1}{2} \leq j \leq n - \frac{m-1}{2} \tag{3.3}$$

Here, 'm' is frame span, c_i is no. of convolution coeffs. and Q is the resultant signal. 'm' is used to calculate instances of c_i with a polynomial. In our case, this was used to smoothen Neuro-signals by a frame size of 5 with a polynomial of degree 4.

3.4.1.2   Discrete Wavelet Transform

In layman words, it is used to convert incoming signal into sequences of smaller waves using multi-stage decomposition. This enables us to analyze multiple oscillatory signals in an approximation and detail coefficient form. Figure 3.3 has shown the decomposing structural of brain neuron signals when it is preprocessed using low & high filtering methods. Low filter pass method (L) removes high voltage fluctuations and saves slow trends. These in turn provide approximation (A) of the signal. High pass filter method (H) eliminates the slow trends and saves the high voltage fluctuations. The resultant of (H) provides us with detail coefficient (D) which is also known as Wavelet coefficient. The Wavelet function is shown in Equations (3.4) and (3.5).

$$\int_{-\infty}^{+\infty} \psi(t)\,dt = 0 \tag{3.4}$$

$$\psi_{m,n}(t) = a_0^{\frac{-m}{2}}\, \psi(a_0^{-m}t - nb_0) \tag{3.5}$$

Here 'a' and 'b' are scaling parameter and translation parameter containing discrete values. 'm' is frequency and 'n' is time belonging to Z. The computation of (A) and (D) is shown in scaling function (3.6) and wavelet function (3.7).

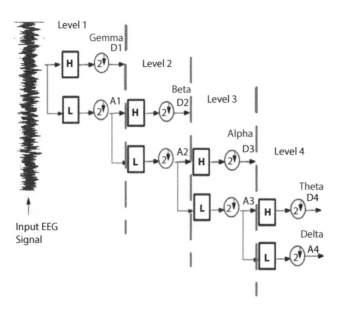

Figure 3.3 DWT schematic.

$$\phi_{j,k}(n) = 2^{j/2}h(2^j n - k) \tag{3.6}$$

$$\omega_{j,k}(n) = 2^{j/2}g(2^j n - k) \tag{3.7}$$

Here, $\varphi_{j,k}(n)$ is the scaling function belonging to (L) and $\omega_{j,k}(n)$ is the wavelet function belonging to (H), M is length of signal, n is the discrete variable lies between 0 and M − 1, $J = \log_2(M)$, with k and j taking values from $\{0 - J - 1\}$. The values of A_i and D_i are computed below by Equations (3.8) and (3.9).

$$A_i = \frac{1}{\sqrt{M}} \sum_n x(n) \times \phi_{j,k}(n) \tag{3.8}$$

$$D_i = \frac{1}{\sqrt{M}} \sum_n x(n) \times \omega_{j,k}(n) \tag{3.9}$$

In previous works we have seen that theta (4–8 Hz) is preferably explored for finding judgement tasks, studying the cortical activity in left side of brain. We used 4-levels of signal decomposition by Daubechies 4 wavelet technique which results into a group of 5 wavelets coeffs where one group represent one oscillatory signal and presents Neuro-signal pattern through D1–D4 and A4. They have "5 frequency bands—(1–4 Hz), (4–8 Hz), (8–13 Hz), (13–22 Hz) and (32–100 Hz)".

3.4.2   Dataset Description

We recorded Neuro-signals from 25 participants through 14 channels who all were aged between 18 and 38 years of age belonging to IIT Roorkee. They were shown 39 (13 product types × 3 samples of each product) images. A total of 325 (13 × 25) Neuro-signals were recorded wherein each image was displayed for 4 s. After the collection we asked users to label their choice for each item in terms of Like/Dislike. All participants were instructed to truly evaluate and label correct choices. The following Figures 3.4 and 3.5 shall provide an overview of the image and dataset.

3.5   Result

3.5.1   Individual Result Analysis

Here, we display the output of the 5 classification algorithms we used on the given dataset for deliberating on Neuromarketing using Machine Learning Algorithms. The output was user-independent as we assume that for predicting the choice of a user his/her training data is not required. In Figure 3.6 we depict the overall accuracy received while running it on the mentioned columns, i.e., Decision Tree, Bagging Decision Tree, Gaussian Naïve Bayes Classifier, Kernel SVM and Random Forest Classifier.

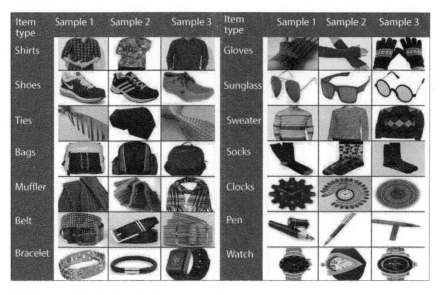

Figure 3.4 Images used for visual evaluation.

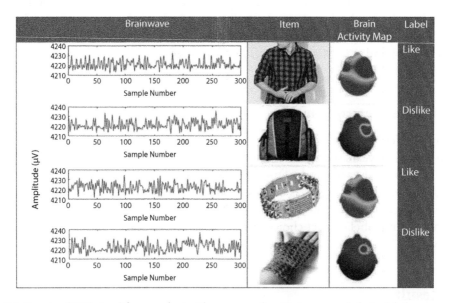

Figure 3.5 Sample of EEG signal for a product with corresponding Brain map and choice label.

We compiled all participant's EEG data into a single file called as "Master file" with appropriate like=1/dislike=0 labelling for all rows. We observe here that Kernel SVM has the highest achieved accuracy followed by Decision Tree whereas all other 3 produce near about close results.

In Figure 3.7, we shall be showing the individual ROC AUC curve results in the graphical form for all the algorithms used on Master file showing true positive and false positive rates by its axes depicting the performance of a classification model at all classification thresholds.

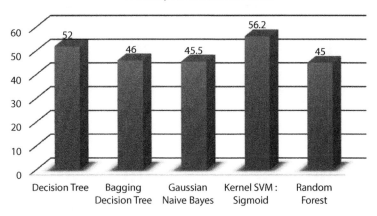

Figure 3.6 Accuracy for all users (compiled).

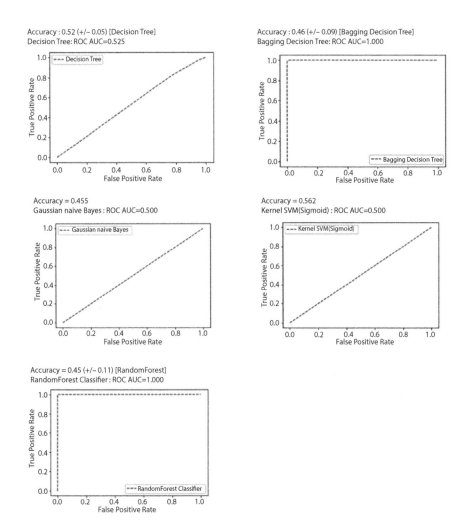

Figure 3.7 Individual result of each algorithm.

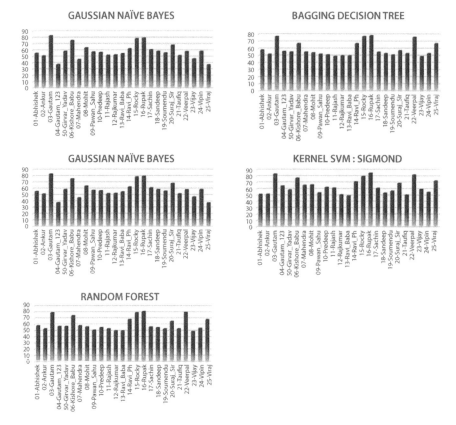

Figure 3.8 Result of 25-users with different algorithms.

In Figure 3.8 we shall be showing the individual 25 participant's resultant accuracy with respect to Decision Tree, Bagging Decision Tree, Gaussian naïve Bayes Classifier, Kernel SVM and Random Forest Classifier in the respective order.

3.5.2   Comparative Results Analysis

In Figure 3.9, we shall be doing a comparative analysis of each user's data's performance regarding each individual algorithm in a chart form.

In this study, we applied our knowledge of EEG data and Machine Learning to cohabit in a system for correctly analyze and predict the consumer's choice when surveying different brands of same type of products. We had 25 males perform this initial study and it resulted in a viable feasibility for developing solutions using EEG data to enhance productivity, cut down on losses and shifting the paradigm of marketing to new heights. We have noticed that on a user-level Kernel SVM has performed better than others in majority of the cases for identifying like/dislike. It has also recorded the highest accuracy in Master file run of 56.2% among others. We have observed that Kernel SVM: Sigmoid is significant to our study and we shall try different kernels in this form to test better results.

In the following Figures 3.10 and 3.11 we shall be showing you the Approximate Brain's EEG activity map we have derived for like/dislike states of mind in our Neuromarketing study.

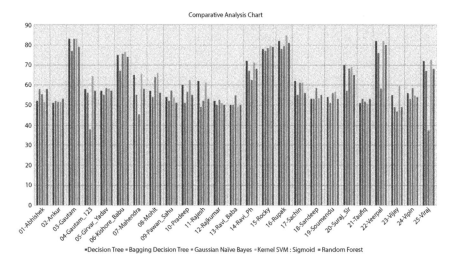

Figure 3.9 Result of 25-users compared with different algorithms.

3.6 Conclusion

In our study we did not achieve high yield of results for now in predicting like/dislike of users as this is a feasibility study based on trials. Thus, we have inferred that we need to use higher complexity models of Deep Learning for achieving better accuracy in near future. We also need to work on a method to tackle fake-responses. We have future plans to provide the

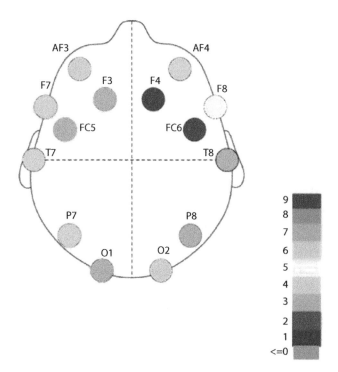

Figure 3.10 Approximate brain EEG map for dislike state.

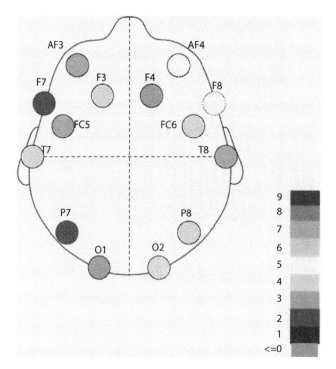

Figure 3.11 Approximate brain EEG map for like state.

participants with a wide variety of choice and more neutral choices to objectively analyze the decision-making process while tracking their eye-movement as an additional parameter while delving deeper into complex classifiers for achieving higher predictions accuracy. We also think that additional methods can be added on to this process like eye-tracking coupled with higher complexity models of classifiers to take our prediction accuracy to a higher level.

References

1. Yadava, M., Kumar, P., Saini, R., Roy, P.P., Dogra, D.P., Analysis of EEG signals and its application to neuromarketing. *Multimedia Tools Appl.*, 76, 18, 19087–19111, 2017.
2. Tripathi, S., Acharya, S., Sharma, R.D., Mittal, S., Bhattacharya, S., Using Deep and Convolutional Neural Networks for Accurate Emotion Classification on DEAP Dataset. *Twenty-ninth IAAI conference*, pp. 4746–4752, 2017.
3. Djamal, E.C. and Lodaya, P., EEG based emotion monitoring using wavelet and learning vector quantization. *2017 4th international conference on Electrical Engineering, Computer Science and Informatics (EECSI)*, pp. 1–6, IEEE, 2017.
4. Al-Nafjan, A., Hosny, M., Al-Wabil, A., Al-Ohali, Y., Classification of human emotions from electroencephalogram (EEG) signal using deep neural networ. *Int. J. Adv. Comput. Sci. Appl*, 8, 9, 419–425, 2017.

5. Tseng, K.C., Lin, B.S., Han, C.M., Wang, P.S., Emotion recognition of EEG underlying favourite music by support vector machine. *2013 1st International Conference on Orange Technologies (ICOT)*, pp. 155–158, IEEE, 2013.

6. Cheng, C., Wei, X., Jian, Z., Emotion recognition algorithm based on convolution neural network. *2017 12th International Conference on Intelligent Systems and Knowledge Engineering (ISKE)*, IEEE, pp. 1–5, 2017.

7. Ambler, T., Braeutigam, S., Stins, J., Rose, S., Swithenby, S., Salience and choice: Neural correlates of shopping decisions. *Psychol. Marketing*, 21, 4, 247–261, 2004.

8. Khushaba, R.N., Greenacre, L., Kodagoda, S., Louviere, J., Burke, S., Dissanayake, G., Choice modeling and the brain: A study on the Electroencephalogram (EEG) of preferences. *Expert Syst. Appl.*, 39, 16, 12378–12388, 2012.

9. Vecchiato, G., Kong, W., Giulio Maglione, A., Wei, D., Understanding the impact of TV commercials. *IEEE Pulse*, 3, 3, 3–65, 2012.

10. Baldo, D., Parikh, H., Piu, Y., Müller, K.M., Brain waves predict success of new fashion products: A practical application for the footwear retailing industry. *J Creating Value*, 1, 1, 61–71, 2015.

11. Guo, G. and Elgendi, M., A new recommender system for 3D e-commerce: An EEG based approach. *J. Adv. Manage. Sci.*, 1, 1, 61–65, 2013.

12. Murugappan, M., Murugappan, S., Gerard, C., Wireless EEG signals based neuromarketing system using Fast Fourier Transform (FFT). *2014 IEEE 10th International Colloquium on Signal Processing and its Applications*, IEEE, pp. 25–30, 2014.

13. Boksem, M.A. and Smidts, A., Brain responses to movie trailers predict individual preferences for movies and their population-wide commercial success. *J. Marketing Res.*, 52, 4, 482–492, 2015.

14. Soleymani, M., Chanel, G., Kierkels, J.J., Pun, T., Affective ranking of movie scenes using physiological signals and content analysis. *Proceedings of the 2nd ACM workshop on Multimedia semantics*, pp. 32–39, 2008.

15. Kawasaki, M. and Yamaguchi, Y., Effects of subjective preference of colors on attention-related occipital theta oscillations. *NeuroImage*, 59, 1, 808–814, 2012.

16. Khushaba, R.N., Wise, C., Kodagoda, S., Louviere, J., Kahn, B.E., Townsend, C., Consumer neuroscience: Assessing the brain response to marketing stimuli using electroencephalogram (EEG) and eye tracking. *Expert Syst. Appl.*, 40, 9, 3803–3812, 2013.

17. Stickel, C., Fink, J., Holzinger, A., Enhancing universal access–EEG based learnability assessment. *International Conference on Universal Access in Human–Computer Interaction*, Springer, Berlin, Heidelberg, pp. 813–822, 2007.

18. Holzinger, A., Scherer, R., Seeber, M., Wagner, J., Müller-Putz, G., Computational sensemaking on examples of knowledge discovery from neuroscience data: Towards enhancing stroke rehabilitation. *International Conference on Information Technology in Bio- and Medical Informatics*, Springer, Berlin, Heidelberg, pp. 166–168, 2012.

19. Holzinger, A., Stocker, C., Bruschi, M., Auinger, A., Silva, H., Gamboa, H., Fred, A., On applying approximate entropy to ECG signals for knowledge discovery on the example of big sensor data. *International Conference on Active Media Technology*, Springer, Berlin, Heidelberg, pp. 646–657, 2012.

20. Hargittai, S., Savitzky–Golay least-squares polynomial filters in ECG signal processing. *Comput. Cardiol.*, 2005, 763–766, IEEE, 2005.

21. Gandhi, V., Prasad, G., Coyle, D., Behera, L., McGinnity, T.M., Quantum neural network-based EEG filtering for a brain–computer interface. *IEEE Trans. Neural Networks Learn. Syst.*, 25, 2, 278–288, 2013.

22. Abd Rahman, F. and Othman, M.F., Real time eye blink artifacts removal in electroencephalogram using Savitzky–Golay referenced adaptive filtering. *International Conference for Innovation in Biomedical Engineering and Life Sciences*, Springer, Singapore, pp. 68–71, 2015.
23. Awal, M.A., Mostafa, S.S., Ahmad, M., Performance analysis of Savitzky–Golay smoothing filter using ECG signal. *Int. J. Comput. Inf. Technol.*, 1, 02, 24–29, 2011.
24. Kaur, B., Singh, D., Roy, P.P., A novel framework of EEG-based user identification by analyzing music-listening behavior. *Multimedia Tools Appl.*, 76, 24, 25581–25602, 2017.

An Expert System-Based Clinical Decision Support System for Hepatitis-B Prediction & Diagnosis

Niranjan Panigrahi[1]*, Ishan Ayus[1] and Om Prakash Jena[2]

[1]Department of CSE, Parala Maharaja Engineering College, Berhampur, India
[2]Ravenshaw University, Cuttack, India

Abstract

Viral hepatitis is a commonly occurring liver infection which appears in almost all part of the world. According to World Health Organization report of 2017, among all Hepatitis viruses, Hepatitis-B is highly endemic and has highest mortality rate. In India, it is also a significant health problem but the awareness is very low among the general public and mostly in rural area. In this context, expert system-based Clinical Decision Support System (CDSS) which is a dual of Machine Learning (ML) will be a better solution. In the absence of experienced physician at rural and remote area, expert system can assist health workers to diagnose the disease. Hence, this chapter presents fundamentals of CDSS and applications of expert system based CDSS for prediction and diagnosis of Hepatitis-B. A knowledge base consisting of 59 rules is designed for the expert system. The planned system is implemented in ES-builder, a web-based Expert System Shell (ESS). To check the efficiency of the system, an extensive testing has been carried out by querying the proposed system.

Keywords: Decision support system, artificial intelligence, expert system, hepatitis-B

4.1 Introduction

Hepatitis remains one of the most infectious global health problems, due to which the mortality and morbidity rate is increasing [1]. The symptoms for Hepatitis-B virus (HBV) are: fever, weakness, muscle pain, appetite loss and jaundice infection [3]. Generally, most of the transmission cases, i.e., more than 90% in infants are transmitted through perinatal transmission. In contrast to this, more than 95% adults get infected with HBV by the transfer of body fluid [2]. Acute hepatitis generally lasts less than six months whereas chronic hepatitis lasts more than six months.

Human HBV is a type of Hepadnaviridae family, which are structurally small, enveloped, with hepatotropic DNA viruses. These viruses have a special affinity for the liver and they are inoculated into hepatocytes, replicates and assemble exclusively in hepatocytes, and this result in a change in antigen structure. Thus, the body recognizes them as a foreign body

---

Corresponding author: niranjan.cse@pmec.ac.in

Sachi Nandan Mohanty, G. Nalinipriya, Om Prakash Jena and Achyuth Sarkar (eds.) *Machine Learning for Healthcare Applications*, (57–76) © 2021 Scrivener Publishing LLC

and our immune system triggered to perform self-mediated immune damage of the liver. Thus resulting in gradual damage of liver leading to liver failure due to different viral factors. The diagnosis test for chronic HBV infection involves: (i) HBV marker assessments, and (ii) liver disease assessments. Under HBV marker assessments: HBsAg, HBeAg, and HBV DNA (Hepatitis-B virus DNA) are some of the test conducted to detect HBV. Under Liver disease assessments: (a) biochemical parameter: ALT (Alanine Transaminase), and (b) fibrosis marker are used to determine the condition of the liver. Treatment for HBV may include entecavir, tenofovir, disoproxil, or tenofoviralafenamide. Pegylated interferon-alfa treatment considered for average chronic Hepatitis-B patients [1]. India is a highly populated country. Even if a person suspects that he has the disease getting a diagnosis from a certified medical institution may not be financially feasible. In remote rural areas and places with difficultly accessible terrain like Ladakh and North-East India, finding an expert medical professional, who could detect, diagnose and guide patients regarding proper treatment process is not easy.

Hence, the emerging health crisis of the year 2020 requires a reliable, feasible, systematic, and automated decision support system for such deadly diseases that can work at the user-level that can assist people in early prediction of the disease and suggestion for possible treatment under the guidance of healthcare personnel. Artificial Intelligence (AI) technology has the potential in developing such systems to assist the general healthcare personnel for effective detection and diagnosis of the disease, who may not have expert knowledge about the particular disease, thus, creating a new hope for the people in rural area.

Artificial intelligence (AI) with its related technologies are having greater impact on the growth of business and society and thus equipping healthcare with new technological weapons to fight battle against diseases. The potential of this technology is increasing with the technological development with many aspects of patient care. Development of technology is eventually increasing in the domain of expert systems, which is a sub-domain of artificial intelligence [5]. It is a decision support system that consists of a KB, IE, and UI. The KB consists of evidence in the form of rules for a specific domain and IE is used to infer the best possible solution for the given query asked by the end-user. Many expert systems have evolved in the late '80s for disease detection and diagnosis. Some of the popular expert systems in the field of medicine are MYCIN, DXplain, Germwatcher, HELP, PEIRS, CADeT, Puff, SETH [6]. Therefore, the expert system can be a considered as a better solution for the early prediction of Hepatitis-B and reliable diagnosis.

The significant contributions of this chapter are given below:

1. A brief overview of the decision support system and its classification is presented.
2. A comprehensive survey about AI-based approaches for Hepatitis-B disease is highlighted.
3. An expert system based CDSS is proposed for Hepatitis-B by defining 59 rules from different reliable sources.
4. A thorough implementation and validation of the system is done using ES-builder, a web-based ESS.

The organization of rest of the chapter is as follows. Section 4.2 gives a brief outline of the decision support system and its classification. Section 4.3 presents a comprehensive summary of different AI-based approaches for Hepatitis-B prediction and diagnosis. In Section 4.4, the proposed expert system is described along with its rules set, inference mechanism, and its implementation in ES-builder. The testing of the system is highlighted in Section 4.5, followed by conclusion in Section 4.6.

4.2   Outline of Clinical DSS

This section briefly highlights the fundamentals of clinical DSS, its types, and its architecture.

4.2.1   Preliminaries

Decision support systems are generally information-based computer system equipped with decision-making capability in a specific domain. According to the context of healthcare domain, it is helpful for patients as it assists common healthcare professionals for diagnosis and treatment of diseases in particular domain [7]. It minimizes the possibility of any analytical errors by alerting healthcare personnel of significant harmful drug interactions, and their treatment procedures to help in proper diagnosis. The main advantages of medical decision support system are:

- Assisting patients in consultation process without intervention of medical expert.
- Recommending optimal treatment methods for case-specific patients.
- Helping common healthcare personnel to gain expert's suggestions for better diagnosis and treatment.

In Ref. [8], a review was carried out on 100 patients where it was observed that decision support system has enhanced performance of practitioner in 64% of the studies out of total 97 studies. A similar conclusion was derived in the same year by Duke University which carried out a review on 70 different types of cases. So, decision support system has shown successful implementation in medical field since its inception. The following is a brief historical perspective on the progress of medical decision support system [9].

- MYCIN: It was developed by Edward Shortliffe at Stanford University in 1972 which is well known as the first ever interactive clinical decision support system. The earliest backward chaining expert system, which is designed to diagnose and suggest treatment for bacteria causing bacteraemia or meningitis. The knowledge in MYCIN is stored as production rules to diagnoses the bacterial infection.
- Internist-1: It was developed at Pittsburgh University in the year 1974. It has a list of diagnosis based on disease profiles and knowledge present in memory. The "Greek Oracle" model for medical expert system, which was experimentally use as a consultant program, educational quizmaster and it could be helpful to people in rural areas, outer space and foreign military base [10].
- QMR: It uses the INTERNIST knowledge base and it helps the physicians for the diagnosis of over 4,000 diseases.

- DXplain: It is a diagnosis decision support system, which is specially designed for the healthcare professionals who are unable to work with the computer system. It accepts a list of clinical manifestations and based on which it proposes diagnostic hypothesis. It was developed with the support of American Medical Association (AMA) and distributed to medical community through AMA/NET.
- Puff: It was a decision support system developed in the laboratory of Pacific Presbyterian Medical Centre in San Francisco in 1977, which diagnose the presence and treatment of lung diseases. The focus of this system is to diagnose the results of pulmonary function tests [5].

4.2.2   Types of Clinical DSS

Traditionally, DSS is classified into different types in different domain [12]. Clinical DSSs are broadly classified into 2 categories: Non-knowledge base and Knowledge base decision support system [28]. But some recent works combine both of them to create hybrid decision support system [13, 17]. The following sections briefly describe the different categories as shown in Figure 4.1.

4.2.3   Non-Knowledge-Based Decision Support System (NK-DSS)

In NK-DSS, user-defined knowledge-base is not present as reference to make decision. The machine is completely dependent on raw clinical data which are needed to be processed before using it for decision making with AI technique called machine learning. In machine learning, the system "learns" from both past experience and raw data through series of iterative computation. Some well-known machine learning methods used in such type of decision support systems are: Artificial Neural Net (ANN), Probabilistic Regression, SVM, and Decision tree [23, 25]. Recently, Deep Learning (DL), which is a sub-domain of machine learning, is getting popularity as a backbone for decision support systems [4].

- ANN in NK-DSS
  ANN mimics the architecture of human brain, which performs better than conventional algorithm. The simulation of associative memory is performed due to data structure and functionality of neural nets. The essential component for neural network is nodes similar to the neurons of biological neural network connected with weighted edges or links, which corresponds to axon-synapse-dendrite connection. Generally, ANN has 3 layers of nodes.

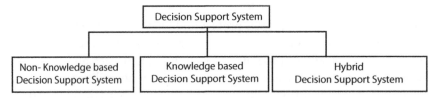

Figure 4.1 Classification of clinical DSS.

The input layer receives the data, which is processed through a series of weighted computation, and finally the output layer gives the final result. Training phase and amount of data are generally considered as essential factor to determine the accuracy of the system. In this stage, a clinical dataset is used as input, which is analyzed further to hypothesize the correct output. This trained output are further compared with the actual result, weight are updated to minimize the error. This process of comparison and updating of weight performed iteratively until the correct prediction is made with some acceptable error. In the field of healthcare, an ANN based DSS, which takes patient's clinical test data as input, and assesses ANN in disease diagnosis for heart and nephritis disease [23].

The ANN facilitates as it minimizes the need to consult a medical specialist, it simply collects disease related diagnostic information and generates the knowledge-base which could be used for diagnosis. The limitation of ANN-based DSS include: The iterative error correction and training phase are generally time-consuming. It is incapable of reasoning some of the steps used for inference. Thus, reliability is a major issue in such ANN-based systems.

- Logistic Regression in NK-DSS
  Logistic regression is a statistical model generally used for modeling data, which is classified as binomial, multinomial, and ordinal. In binomial the target variable can take either value 1or 0 with certain probabilities of success 'p' and probabilities of failure '1 − p' respectively. In multinomial the target variable have three or more possible type without order. In ordinal the target variable have ordered categories based on which classification is performed. Further, it finds an approximate model relating the target variable with the independent input variables. Logistic regression computes the probability of whether the given value can be drawn from the target variable instead of predicting the value for target variable. In healthcare field, it predicts the probability of a patient suffering from a specific disease. The probabilistic function used in logistic regression is mostly a non-linear sigmoid function, which is represented as:

$$p(n) = 1/\{1 + e^{-(a + bm)}\}$$

Where $p(n)$ represents the probability that the target variable n occurs based on input variab le m, a = constant, and b = coefficient of the independent input variable.

- Decision Tree in NK-DSS
  Decision tree is the most commonly used method for decision support system. It is mainly a top-down method used for searching a particular solution. It is a tree-like model used to analyse the chance of an event where each node represents a test for a given input attribute's values. The testing at node separates the data into more homogeneous sub-groups, based on target variable.

The testing process are generally carried out for different attributes at each level of the hierarchy until no further division of data is possible into subgroups. The leaf nodes of a decision tree act as the different groups or classes. In Ref. [22], the authors proposed a system using this method to assist clinical personnel to diagnose tuberculosis patients with positive tuberculin skin tests.

- SVM in NK-DSS
  Support vector machine (SVM) is an example of supervised ML methods, used for solving problems dealing with classification analysis, regression analysis and other task like outliers detection. A statistical learning framework, based on VC theory proposed by Vapnik and Chervonekis in 1963. They can be used to find solution for both linear and non-linear classification problem. Basically, the examples can be represented as a nonprobabilistic linear classifier using Kernel trick in which the data points are represented in space, mapped in such a way that they represent separate classes divided by a clear gap, known as hyper plane. In SVM, the data is viewed as n-dimensional vector (a list of n numbers) and it is required to find a (p-1)-dimensional hyper-plane, which can split data points into different classes. It is used in many disease predictions like cancer, heart disease, etc. [24, 25].

- DL in NK-DSS
  Deep learning is a particular kind of unsupervised ML, which is a subdomain of artificial intelligence (AI) that has capability of learning different forms of data, which is unstructured or unlabelled. The depth allows the computer to learn a multi-step program assisted with parallel execution and transformation of input data into abstract representation. Deep convolution neural network can be used for the skin cancer classification [4].

- Genetic Algorithm in NK-DSS
  Genetic algorithm generally follows Darwin's evolution theory which describes the entire process to be carried out. This algorithm begins with the collection of randomly generated solution for the given problem. Further evaluating the fitness or quality of each solution using a fitness function. Then ranking of fitness provide us with the fit solution for "breeding" performed by mutual exclusion to produce the most appropriate solution. This process is repeated iteratively to produce the best optimal solution [27].

4.2.4   Knowledge-Based Decision Support System (K-DSS)

The K-DSS mainly consists of 3 parts, KB, IE and UI. In K-DSS, there exists a predefined reference table which is known as KB. The IE uses KB to deduce conclusions and UI is the user interface. Knowledge in K-DSS can be classified into two types:

1. Declarative knowledge: It consists of propositions and sentences. The statements are that are either 'T' or 'F' are known as proposition which are joined by operators like 'V', '∧', to form sentences. It is an argument, which reaches from general fact to specific fact.

2. Procedural knowledge: It is also known as imperative knowledge which provides more explicit information based on facts and data. The information is related to what step can be carried out or what result can be inferred from declarative knowledge. It is an argument, which reaches from specific fact to general fact [11].

KDSS can also be categorized based on the knowledge representation schemes are generally of following categories:

- Logic in K-DSS.
  Logic seems to be a language with some user-defined concrete rules. It is considered as the well-known representation format in the field of AI that is commonly used by researcher. Logical representation generally draws a conclusion depending on various conditions. It precisely consists of semantics and syntax support of the inference system. Syntax generally focuses on the legal rules used for the construction of the legal sentence. In contrary, semantic are rules helps in the process of interpretation of the sentences in the logic. Logical representation enables researcher to perform logical reasoning.

- Weak slot and filler structure in K-DSS
  Generally, weak slot and filler structure do not have hard and fast rules based on which we can perform the representation.

  i) Semantic network is one of the common graphical network representations of knowledge. Here nodes or vertices represent the object whereas arcs or links can represent relation between those objects. There are two types of commonly used link they are IS-A (an instance or individual to a generic class) and A-KIND-OF (AKO i.e. super-class).

  ii) A frame represents a record type of data structure, which is divided into substructure or sub frames for stereotype situation. Each information is held as slot, which may contain fact, or data, procedure, default values and sub frames. Some researcher work describes a frame based RDBS, which is embedded in the expert system [15].

- Strong slot and filler structure in K-DSS
  These are the some of the powerful theories, which provide detailed and specific ideas of what kind of object and relation are allowed.

  i) Conceptual Dependency: It is a theory to conceptualize the type of knowledge about events that normally appears in natural language sentence. The aim is represented in such a manner that it can draw inference from the sentence of the independent of language. This concept is accompanied by some predefined rules based on which knowledge representation is performed.

ii) Script: It represents flow of events in the context of a specific domain. It has a set of slots which is filled with some information related to type of values it may include along with a default value. They are useful as they deal with real time problems.

- Production Rule in K-DSS
  A production rules based system consist of (condition, action) tuple, i.e., "IF < Condition > THEN <action>". The production rules set and description are stored in working memory when there is a match then production rule fire out. The associated problem solving steps performed on the action. A system is developed to diagnose some of the common diseases using rule based knowledge for the diagnosis of malaria, breast cancer typhoid fever, tuberculosis, and cholera [16].

4.2.5   Hybrid Decision Support System (H-DSS)

In the recent years due to the increasing demand for intelligent systems the intelligent clinical decision support system are developed by using H-DSS. H-DSS is the combination of both NK-DSS and K-DSS used for different application of DSS. Generally, data mining of knowledge bases (KB) with different knowledge representation of KDSS is combined with different techniques of NK-DSS like artificial neural network (ANN) to develop intelligent and hybrid clinical decision support system. A work is done to create a DSS for prediction to a patient regarding the risk of Type-1 Diabetes which has used feed-forward neural net (FNN), regression method and rule induction [17].

4.2.6   DSS Architecture

According to Marakas [29], a generic decision support system has three fundamental layers as shown in Figure 4.2: (i) user interface layer, (ii) data management layer, and (iii) application processing layer. Here the user is essential component of DSS as they are the one

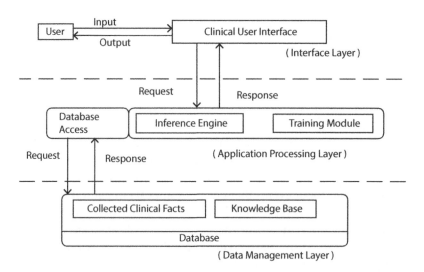

Figure 4.2 Architecture of CDSS [29].

who feed input to the system i.e. symptoms of disease in this case. Data management layer generally handles internal and external database. The knowledge engine consists of knowledge base and inference engines. Knowledge bases store knowledge according to different knowledge representation scheme whereas inference engine infer possible solution for the given problem using inference rule. User interface provide an interface to the end user for interaction with the system.

4.3   Background

Computer scientists these days are getting involved in many humanitarian services aiming to provide a better life for the common people through technology. Diagnosis and detection of diseases is also an area of research in which many researchers have presented their work. In this section, we will discuss about some earlier works related to Hepatitis-B. The first paper addresses a user-friendly application software program, which has capability to monitor, diagnose the disease. J2SE or any other IDE have been utilized to create the interface using java programming language. MySQL is used as back-end relational database and knowledge representation is based on production rule [3]. The second thesis uses VP expert system programming, which is a special programming file, which runs under the disk operating system (DOS), and the analysis is based on 20 patients from Turkey and North Cyrus who had chronic Hepatitis-B. This program is abbreviated as CHBDX, short for chronic Hepatitis-B diagnosing expert system [18]. The third paper focused on ANN-based approach with regression theory for Hepatitis-B diagnosis. It can determine whether a patient is infected by Hepatitis-B or not and if yes, then what is its severity. The system consists of two major parts: an inference mechanism and a neural net which can work on multi-functional database [19, 20]. The fourth paper has described the adaptive learning expert system, in which the rules are inferred by using both forward and backward chaining to provide feasible advices. The system is capable of adapting dynamic knowledge through generalization of rules and learning new rules given by domain specialist without intervention of knowledge engineer. This system uses SWI-PROLOG editor for development of expert system [21].

4.4   Proposed Expert System-Based CDSS

This section presents the proposed expert system based CDSS for Hepatitis-B prediction and diagnosis.

4.4.1   Problem Description

The problem of designing a CDSS using KB-based expert system for Hepatitis-B prediction and diagnosis can be logically represented as follows.

Given, the input set, $I = \{I_1, I_2,...,I_n\}$, it is required to design an expert system which can predict and suggest, the output set, $O = \{O_1, O_2, ..., O_n\}$.

If I = set of symptoms and clinical test results, then O = set of predictions and diagnostic suggestions.

The design phase involves creating a knowledgebase (KB) and an inference engine (IE) to deduce the output set O. The KB is created by consulting medical experts and other reliable sources. The knowledge thus acquired is represented using some standard knowledge representation techniques in the KB.

4.4.2   Rules Set & Knowledge Base

The generation rules of the proposed expert system-based DSS are formulated which include five important attribute which serves as the input of this system.

1. WHAT IS YOUR HBsAg?
2. WHAT IS YOUR HBeAg?
3. WHAT IS YOUR HBV_DNA?
4. WHAT IS YOUR ALT?
5. WHAT IS YOUR Liver_disease (Fibrosis test)?

The design of expert system is accomplished in ES-builder, an ESS (Expert System Shell) which provides an online template where attribute determines the different questions, asked when the system enters into the situation of uncertainty for determining the presence of disease, clarifying the mystery. The attributes, values and conclusion are three components used to build the decision tree. The knowledge base used in this context are generally referred from EASL clinical practice guideline [1], WHO prescribed guidelines for chronic Hepatitis [26] and many other reliable resources were analysed to develop the rule set. The rule set consists of 59 rules which are incorporated in the knowledge base. A sample consisting of 20 rules is shown in Table 4.1.

4.4.3   Inference Engine

The proposed inference engine (IE) uses decision tree approach which matches the users' input with rules present in the KB to reach appropriate answers as shown in Figure 4.3. This is done by using forward chaining on the decision tree. The proposed system has used IF–THEN rule based knowledge representation technique. When users access the expert system, it will ask certain queries regarding those persons 'clinical test results and symptoms which that person might have been tested. According to that persons' observations of his/her symptoms, the system will infer the information by the user in a forward-chaining approach with the expert's data present in the knowledge base and finally conclude the result about the disease.

4.5   Implementation & Testing

The proposed system is designed on ES-builder [30], a web-based ESS. Figures 4.4(a)–(g) show the snapshots user interfaces (UI) and testing of the system in ES-builder. The proposed system can tested in real-time by visiting the following link: https://www.mcgoo. com.au/esbuilder/viewer/viewES.php? es=485b5cff9962a96ab1073ae66022ca48.

Table 4.1 Sample rule set for the proposed expert system.

SL. no.	Rule
1	**IF** what is your HBsAg? Negative **THEN** the conclusion is **Not_Hepatitis B**.
2	**IF** what is your HBsAg? Positive **AND** what is your HBeAg? Positive **AND** what is your HBV_DNA? more_than_10^7 **AND** what is your ALT? between_0_55**AND** what is your Liver_disease? Zero **THEN** the conclusion is **Chronic_Hepatitis_follow_with_doctor**.
3	**IF** what is your HBsAg? Positive **AND** what is your HBeAg? Positive **AND** what is your HBV_DNA? more_than_10^7 **AND** what is your ALT? between_0_55**AND** what is your Liver_disease? One **THEN** the conclusion is **Chronic_Hepatitis_follow_with_doctor**.
4	**IF** what is your HBsAg? Positive **AND** what is your HBeAg? Positive **AND** what is your HBV_DNA? more_than_10^7 **AND** what is your ALT? between_0_55**AND** what is your Liver_disease? two_or_three**THEN** the conclusion is **Please_check_your_test_result**.
5	**IF** what is your HBsAg? Positive **AND** what is your HBeAg? Positive **AND** what is your HBV_DNA? more_than_10^7 **AND** what is your ALT? between_0_55**AND** what is your Liver_disease? Four **THEN** the conclusion is **Please_check_your_test_result**.
6	**IF** what is your HBsAg? Positive **AND** what is your HBeAg? Positive **AND** what is your HBV_DNA? more_than_10^7 **AND** what is your ALT? more_than_55**AND** what is your Liver_disease? Zero **THEN** the conclusion is **Please_check_your_test_result**.
7	**IF** what is your HBsAg? Positive **AND** what is your HBeAg? Positive **AND** what is your HBV_DNA? more_than_10^7 **AND** what is your ALT? more_than_55**AND** what is your Liver_disease? One **THEN** the conclusion is **Please_check_your_test_result**.
8	**IF** what is your HBsAg? Positive **AND** what is your HBeAg? Positive **AND** what is your HBV_DNA? more_than_10^7 **AND** what is your ALT? more_than_55**AND** what is your Liver_disease? two_or_three**THEN** the conclusion is **Chronic_Hepatitis_need_for_treatment**.
9	**IF** what is your HBsAg? Positive **AND** what is your HBeAg? Positive **AND** what is your HBV_DNA? more_than_10^7 **AND** what is your ALT? more_than_55**AND** what is your Liver_disease? four **THEN** the conclusion is **Chronic_Hepatitis_need_for_treatment**.
10	**IF** what is your HBsAg? Positive **AND** what is your HBeAg? Positive **AND** what is your HBV_DNA? between_10^4_10^7 **AND** what is your ALT? between_0_55**AND** what is your Liver disease? Zero **THEN** the conclusion is **Please_check_your_test_result**.

(Continued)

Table 4.1 Sample rule set for the proposed expert system. (*Continued*)

SL. no.	Rule
11	**IF** what is your HBsAg? Positive **AND** what is your HBeAg? Positive **AND** what is your HBV_DNA? between_10^4_10^7 **AND** what is your ALT? between_0_55**AND** what is your Liver disease? One **THEN** the conclusion is **Please_check_your_test_result.**
12	**IF** what is your HBsAg? Positive **AND** what is your HBeAg? Positive **AND** what is your HBV_DNA? between_10^4_10^7 **AND** what is your ALT? between_0_55**AND** what is your Liver disease? two_or_three **THEN** the conclusion is **Please_check_your_test_result.**
13	**IF** what is your HBsAg? Positive **AND** what is your HBeAg? Positive **AND** what is your HBV_DNA? between_10^4_10^7 **AND** what is your ALT? between_0_55**AND** what is your Liver disease? Four **THEN** the conclusion is **Please_check_your_test_result.**
14	**IF** what is your HBsAg? Positive **AND** what is your HBeAg? Positive **AND** what is your HBV_DNA? between_10^4_10^7 **AND** what is your ALT? more_than_55**AND** what is your Liver_disease? Zero **THEN** the conclusion is **Please_check_your_test_result.**
15	**IF** what is your HBsAg? Positive **AND** what is your HBeAg? Positive **AND** what is your HBV_DNA? between_10^4_10^7 **AND** what is your ALT? more_than_55**AND** what is your Liver_disease? One **THEN** the conclusion is **Please_check_your_test_result.**
16	**IF** what is your HBsAg? Positive **AND** what is your HBeAg? Positive **AND** what is your HBV_DNA? between_10^4_10^7 **AND** what is your ALT? more_than_55**AND** what is your Liver_disease? two_or_three **THEN** the conclusion is **Chronic_Hepatitis_need_for_treatment.**
17	**IF** what is your HBsAg? Positive **AND** what is your HBeAg? Positive **AND** what is your HBV_DNA? less_than_2000**AND** what is your ALT? between_0_55**AND** what is your Liver_disease? zero **THEN** the conclusion is **Please_check_your_test_result.**
18	**IF** what is your HBsAg? Positive **AND** what is your HBeAg? Positive **AND** what is your HBV_DNA? less_than_2000**AND** what is your ALT? between_0_55**AND** what is your Liver_disease? One **THEN** the conclusion is **Please_check_your_test_result.**
19	**IF** what is your HBsAg? Positive **AND** what is your HBeAg? Positive **AND** what is your HBV_DNA? less_than_2000**AND** what is your ALT? between_0_55**AND** what is your Liver_disease? two_or_three **THEN** the conclusion is **Please_check_your_test_result.**
20	**IF** what is your HBsAg? Positive **AND** what is your HBeAg? Positive **AND** what is your HBV_DNA? less_than_2000**AND** what is your ALT? between_0_55**AND** what is your Liver_disease? four **THEN** the conclusion is **Please_check_your_test_result.**

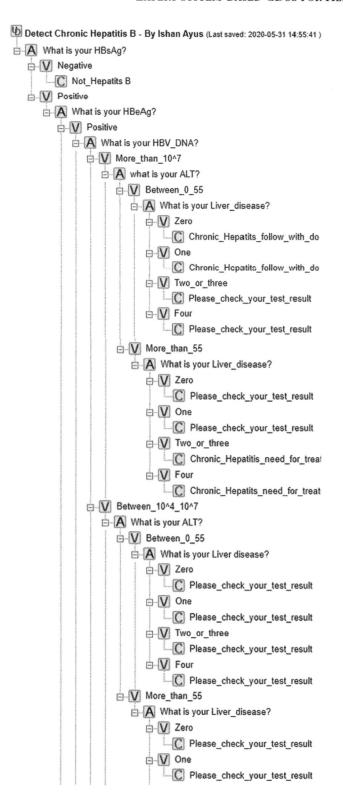

Figure 4.3 Inference using decision tree for the proposed system.

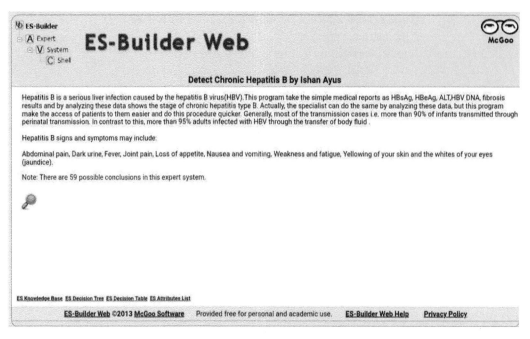

Figure 4.4 (a) First level UI of the system in ES-Builder.

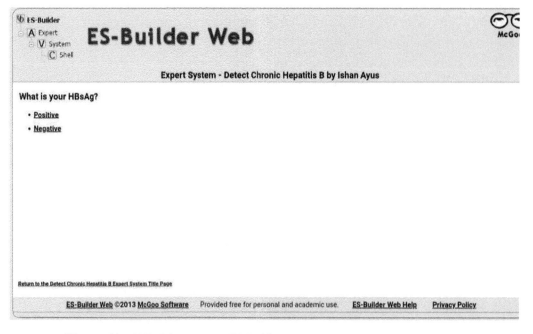

Figure 4.4 (b) Second level UI of the system in ES-Builder.

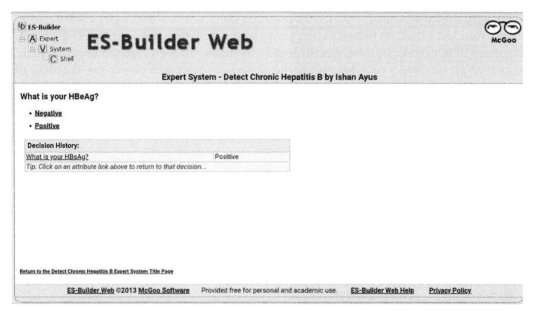

Figure 4.4 (c) Third level UI of the system in ES-Builder.

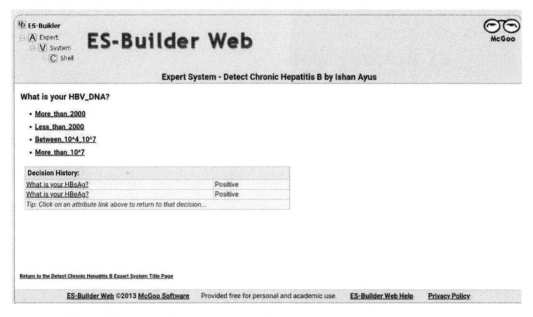

Figure 4.4 (d) Fourth level UI of the system in ES-Builder.

The system provides three results: if the person is affected with chronic Hepatitis-B, please checks your test result, no hepatitis. Thus, if person is suffering from chronic Hepatitis-B, they need to undertake treatment according to the advice of the proposed expert system. In case of 'please checks your test result', the person needs to take care as per the stage of Hepatitis-B. In case of 'no hepatitis', the person is normal.

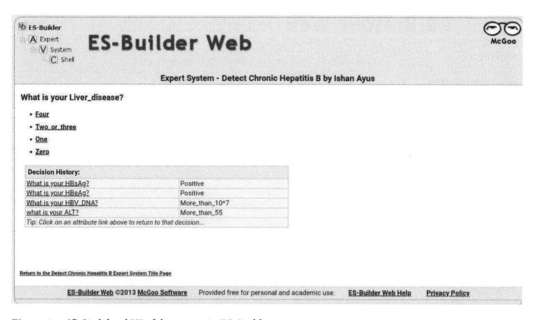

Figure 4.4 (e) Fifth level UI of the system in ES-Builder.

Figure 4.4 (f) Sixth level UI of the system in ES-Builder.

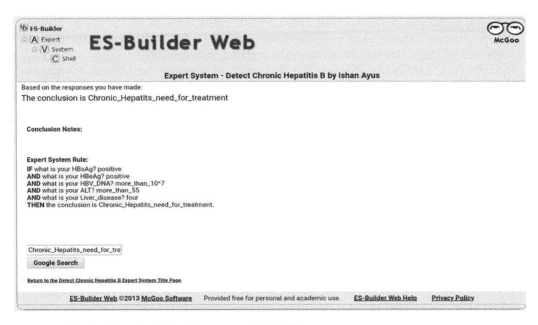

Figure 4.4 (g) Conclusion level UI of the system in ES-Builder.

4.6   Conclusion

This chapter presents a brief overview of CDSS, its classification and architecture. A comprehensive survey is highlighted on AI-based approaches for Hepatitis-B prediction and diagnosis. Further, an expert system based decision support system for Hepatitis-B prediction and diagnosis is proposed, implemented and tested using ES-builder, a web-based expert system shell. The recognition of such a deadly disease with its apparent sign and symptoms must be done by using an intelligent system in a stipulated period. Moreover, the common people can be directly benefited. This system could even avoid unnecessary test performed by doctors under the pressure of private hospitals, facilitating transparency. This technology helps the people at rural areas as it could assist the local healthcare workers. Thus, this decision support system is open source, reliable, feasible, and easily accessible and beneficial for the society.

References

1. Lampertico, P., Agarwal, K., Berg, T., Buti, M., Janssen, H.L.A., Papatheodoridis, G., Zoulim, F., Tacke, F., EASL 2017 Clinical Practice Guidelines on the management of hepatitis B virus infection. *J. Hepatol.*, 67, 2, 370–398, 2017. https://doi.org/10.1016/j.jhep.2017.03.021.
2. Morikawa, K., Shimazaki, T., Takeda, R., Izumi, T., Umumura, M., Sakamoto, N., Hepatitis B: Progress in understanding chronicity, the innate immune response, and cccDNA protection. *Ann. Transl. Med.*, 4, 18, 337–337, 2016. https://doi.org/10.21037/atm.2016.08.54.
3. Mailafiya, I. and Isiaka, F., Expert System for Diagnosis of Hepatitis B. *West Afr. J. Ind. Acad. Res.*, 4, 1, 1–10, 2012. Retrieved from https://www.ajol.info/index.php/wajiar/article/view/86892.

4. Esteva, A., Kuprel, B., Novoa, R.A., Ko, J., Swetter, S.M., Blau, H.M., Thrun, S., Erratum: Corrigendum: Dermatologist-level classification of skin cancer with deep neural networks. *Nature*, 546, 7660, 686–686, 2017. https://doi.org/10.1038/nature22985.

5. Smith, D.H., Artificial Intelligence: The Technology of Expert Systems, in: *ACS Symposium Series*, pp. 1–16, American Chemical Society, Washington, DC, 1986, https://doi.org/10.1021/bk-1986-0306.ch001.

6. Wai, K.S., Rahman, Abd. L.B.A., Zaiyad, M.F., Aziz, A.A., Expert System in Real World Applications, pp. 1–14, generation 5, 2005, November. Retrieved from http://www.generation5.org/.

7. Kanakaraj, G. and Thenmalar, Dr. S., Review of Clinical Decision Support Systems Implementations. *Eurasian J. Anal. Chem.*, 13, 339–344, 2019. Retrieved from https://pdfs.semanticscholar.org/5737/c6591427f0e62a6e85181a1c6dc16bd3ef73.pdf.

8. Garg, A.X., Adhikari, N.K.J., McDonald, H., Rosas-Arellano, M.P., Devereaux, P.J., Beyene, J., Sam, J., Haynes, R.B., Effects of Computerized Clinical Decision Support Systems on Practitioner Performance and Patient Outcomes. *JAMA*, 293, 10, 1223, 2005. https://doi.org/10.1001/jama.293.10.1223.

9. Moore, M. and Loper, K., An Introduction to Clinical Decision Support Systems. *J. Electron. Resour. Med. Libraries*, 8, 348–366, 2011. https://doi.org/10.1080/15424065.2011.626345.

10. Nath, P., AI & Expert System in Medical Field: A study by survey method. *AITHUN*, Volume-I, 100, 2015.

11. Kong, G., Xu, D.-L., Yang, J.-B., Clinical Decision Support Systems: A Review of Knowledge Representation and Inference under Uncertainties. *Int. J. Comput. Intell. Syst.*, 1, 2, 159, 2008. https://doi.org/10.2991/ijcis.2008.1.2.6.

12. Marin, G., Decision support systems. *J. Inf. Syst. Oper. Manage.*, 2, 2, 513–520, 1–4, 2008. Retrieved from http://www.rebe.rau.ro/RePEc/rau/jisomg/FA08/JISOM-FA08-A19.pdf.

13. Basu, R., Thomas, U.F., Sartipi, K., Incorporating Hybrid COSS in Primary Care Practice Management, in: *McMaster EBusiness Research Centre (MeRC) Working Paper #40*, Retrieved from https://www.semanticscholar.org/paper/Incorporating-hybrid-CDSS-in-primary-care-practice-Basu-Fevrier-Thomas/10c2dfde9eb0650f639f7c21aaa3abfe5e9c5ec3.

14. Kim, J.T., Application of Machine and Deep Learning Algorithms in Intelligent Clinical Decision Support Systems in Healthcare. *J. Health Med. Informat.*, 9, 321, 1–6, 2018. https://doi.org/10.4172/2157-7420.1000321.

15. Rattanaprateep, C. and Chittayasothorn, S., A Frame-based Object-Relational Database Expert System Architecture and Implementation. *Conference Proceedings: 5th WSEAS Int. Conf. on Artificial Intelligence, Knowledge Engineering and Data Bases*, pp. 327–332, 2006, Retrieved from http://citeseerx.ist.psu.edu/viewdoc/download?doi=10.1.1.492.1229&rep=rep1&type=pdf.

16. Adewole, K.S., Hambali, M.A., Jimoh, M.K., Rule Based Expert System for Diseases Diagnosis. Longe, O.B., Jimoh, R.G. and Ebem, D.U. (Eds), *Book of Proceedings, International Science, Technology, Engineering, Arts, Management and Social Sciences (iSTREAMS) Multidisciplinary Conference*, University of Ilorin, Nigeria, 7, pp. 183–190, 2015. Retrieved from https://www.researchgate.net/publication/279487549_RULE-BASED_EXPERT_ SYSTEM_FOR_DISEASE_DIAGNOSIS/link/5593a85208aed7453d467c34/download.

17. Skevofilakas, M., Zarkogianni, K., Karamanos, B., Nikita, K., A hybrid Decision Support System for the Risk Assessment of retinopathy development as a long term complication of Type 1 Diabetes Mellitus. *Conference Proceedings: Annual International Conference of the IEEE Engineering in Medicine and Biology Society*, IEEE Engineering in Medicine and Biology Society. Conference, pp. 6713–6, 2010.

18. Mirzaei, O., Diagnosis Chronic Hepatitis B Using Expert System, Near East University, Nicosia, 2019.

19. Panchal, D. and Shah, S., Artificial Intelligence Based Expert System For Hepatitis B Diagnosis. *Int. J. Model. Optim.*, 1, 4, 362–366, 2011. https://doi.org/10.7763/ijmo.2011.v1.61.

20. Ogah, U.S., Zirra, P.B., Sarjiyus, O., Knowledge Based System Design For Diagnosis of Hepatitis B Virus (HBV) Using Generalized Regression Neural Network (GRNN). *Am. J. Comput. Eng.*, 1, *1*, 1–19, 2017. Retrieved from https://ajpojournals.org/journals/index.php/AJCE/article/view/270.

21. Yared Agizew, H., Adaptive Learning Expert System for Diagnosis and Management of Viral Hepatitis. *Int. J. Artif. Intell. Appl.*, 10, 02, 33–46, 2019. https://doi.org/10.5121/ijaia.2019.10204.

22. Gerald, L.B., Tang, S., Bruce, F., Redden, D., Kimerling, M.E., Brook, N., Dunlap, N., Bailey, W.C., A Decision Tree for Tuberculosis Contact Investigation. *Am. J. Respir. Crit. Care Med.*, 166, 8, 1122–1127, 2002. https://doi.org/10.1164/rccm.200202-124oc.

23. Qeethara, A.-S., Artificial Neural Networks in Medical Diagnosis. *Int. J. Comput. Sci. Issues*, 8, 150–154, *IJCSI (Int. J. Comput. Sci. Issues)*, 8, 2, 2011. Retrieved from www.IJCSI.org.

24. Sweilam, N.H., Tharwat, A.A., Abdel Moniem, N.K., Support vector machine for diagnosis cancer disease: A comparative study. *Egypt. Inf. J.*, 11, 2, 81–92, 2010. https://doi.org/10.1016/j.eij.2010.10.005.

25. Shylaja, S. and Muralidharan, Dr. R., A Novel Method to Predict Heart Disease Using SVM Algorithm. *AJMR*, 7, 6, 141–150, 2018.

26. WHO, *Guidelines for the prevention, care and treatment of persons with chronic hepatitis B infection*, World Health Organization, Geneva, Switzerland, 2015.

27. Goldberg, D.E., *Genetic Algorithms in search, optimization and machine learning*, Pearson Education, India, 1989.

28. Farooq, K., Khan, B.S., Niazi, M.A., Leslie, S.J., Hussain, A., Clinical decision support systems: A visual survey. *Informatica (Slovenia)*, 42, 4, 485–505, 2018. https://doi.org/https://doi.org/10.31449/inf.v42i4.1571.

29. Marakas, G., *Decision Support Systems in the 21st Century*, Prentice Hall, Inc. Upper Saddle River, NJ, 1999.

30. Retrieved from https://www.mcgoo.com.au/esbuilder/index.php [ES-Builder website used for implementation].

Deep Learning on Symptoms in Disease Prediction

Sheikh Rafiul Islam[1], Rohit Sinha[2], Santi P. Maity[1*] and Ajoy Kumar Ray[3]

[1]*Dept. of Information Technology, Indian Institute of Engineering Science and Technology, West Bengal, India*
[2]*The Neotia University, Jhinger Pole, Diamond Harbour Rd, Sarisha, West Bengal, India*
[3]*JIS Institute of Advanced Studies and Research, Sector V, Bidhannagar, Kolkata, Arch Waterfront, GP Block, India*

Abstract

Increasing healthcare crises due to overpopulation and lack of supportive infrastructures together make it difficult and challenging to avail the healthcare support by the patients in need. Furthermore, the usages of various modern clinical modalities to diagnose the diseases by the medical practitioners are the demands of the days. Machine Learning (ML) techniques thus show huge promises and potentials for the accurate symptom analysis followed by disease prediction. This chapter makes studies on Deep learning (DL) for autonomous disease diagnosis from symptoms. As an outline to the solution, a Graph Convolution Network (GCN) is suggested as the disease–symptom network to link the disease and symptoms. A Deep Neural Network (DNN) follows the GCN determines the most probable diseases associated with the given symptoms with ~98% accuracy.

Keywords: Disease prediction, symptom–disease graph, graph convolutional network, disease classifier, symptom–disease sorting

5.1 Introduction

Accurate prognosis, diagnosis, detection and assessment of various health conditions for the human being using Machine Learning (ML) techniques show a huge promise and potential in the healthcare sector. As the ratio of physicians to patients in most developing countries is very low, it is almost impossible for a medical professional to pay attention and medical services to people in need in time. In a recently published report, the World Health Organization (WHO) has estimated that 57 countries suffer from the lack of physicians, nurses and midwives, thereby probing a shortage of healthcare professionals for essential functioning like diagnosis, drug prescription, hygiene attendance, etc. An Artificial Intelligence (AI)-led solution can be used for assisted diagnosis and prognosis with little to almost no intervention from the trained clinicians, thereby increasing the chances to a lot of people for receiving the required healthcare support in time. The corner stone problems

---

Corresponding author: santipmaity@it.iiests.ac.in

Sachi Nandan Mohanty, G. Nalinipriya, Om Prakash Jena and Achyuth Sarkar (eds.) *Machine Learning for Healthcare Applications*, (77–88) © 2021 Scrivener Publishing LLC

that can be addressed by AI would be improving the diagnosis time of any serious condition, extensive care and reducing healthcare costs. It also opens up the possibility of using the potential benefit of Computer Aided Diagnosis (CAD) system in pandemic situations like COVID-19.

Many industries have seen a widespread implementation of AI-led solutions, while the healthcare sector is lagging behind. There are many contributing factors to constrain the AI solutions in healthcare. Most of the healthcare data are under Health Insurance Portability and Accountability Act (HIPAA) compliance, so they are not made public even for research purposes, as a result of which developing new AI-driven systems for healthcare becomes difficult. The small volume of data that are made available, often too small in size for the use in an AI-based system development that the conventional ML methods need. Furthermore, most of the data collected are skewed and biased, as the number of patients and the healthy individuals participating in a medical study are highly imbalanced. The sample size of the group for which data is collected is not typically very large thus the imbalance in data becomes difficult to rectify. In addition, the lack of transparency in the process of data collection, is another critical concern for developing AI-based healthcare systems.

Despite the above mentioned challenges, the benefits of an AI-led healthcare system outweighs. Thus development of a robust and accurate predictive system that can facilitate the need of the minimum healthcare support by providing an initial diagnosis to an individual becomes of utmost importance. The combination of the concept of classical ML and Deep Learning (DL) [1] can be used in developing the AI-based system to address the challenges. The DL enables learning and extraction of the latent and the hidden patterns from the data. This can then be used to find the underlying connections among the symptoms and the disease. The chapter aims to explore deep learning on the symptoms for the disease prediction.

The remainder of the chapter is structured as follows: A brief review on the related state-of-the-art approaches and scope of DL in disease prediction is materialized in Section 5.2. Section 5.3 describes the related mathematical models used in this work. Section 5.4 presents an outline of DL-based approach to predict diseases. Section 5.5 then accesses the proposed solution while Section 5.6 concludes the article.

5.2   Literature Review

Traditionally, Deep Neural Network (DNN) has shown promising results in modeling assisted diagnosis and disease prediction based on the symptoms given. In Ref. [2], chi-squared statistical method is used to remove the irrelevant features and the configuration of the NN is optimized by an exhaustive search over the hyper parameter space for predicting heart disease. Lei *et al.* [3] proposed a data-driven framework that employs ML methods along with hierarchical knowledge graphs of symptoms to study the effects of various factors on disease classification in data constructed from the medical records. Hao *et al.* [4] proposed a multimodal covolutional recurrent network to predict the degree of risk of a disease. The methods efficiently extracts the non-linear relationship between the disease and the symptoms by extracting the features from the data. The approach also uses Deep Belief Network (DBN) to combine the features extracted from the structured and the unstructured data. In Ref. [5], temporal information-directed disease network is developed and is combined with a recommendation system to provide the risk prediction of the multiple diseases. However, the risk prediction of a disease requires prior data available from the previous hospitalization of the patient.

In Ref. [6], a multi-view deep convolution network is proposed for large scale mammography based breast cancer screening. The performance of the method has been recognized by a committee of radiologists. In Ref. [7], a unified approach is provided using the Residual neural Network (ResNet) architecture for identifying abnormalities present in a radiology image. This is then explored in disease identification and treatment planning using the same underlying model for all type of images. In Ref. [8], a CNN is proposed to segment the non-contrast Computed Tomography (CT) for coronary calcium deposits, which is an important bio-marker of cardiovascular disease to predict Agatstone score, that shows the extent of coronary artery calcification. De *et al.* [9] proposed a novel architecture applied on heterogeneous set of a 3D optical coherence tomography of patients for diagnosis of retinal disease. The work done by Ref. [10] seems to be the first one in the field to implement AI-based approach in In Vitro Fertilization (IVF) for automated embryo assessment. This method proposed a DNN framework based on Google's Inception model. The goal was to predict blastocytes quality to select the highest quality embryo using embryo time lapse images. However, these methods are very specific to detect or predict a limited number of diseases based on the given imaging modalities.

A system or a framework focusing on human body, in general, followed by some predictive, diagnostic and prognostic task is of utmost importance. Development of such a system will greatly benefit people having a nominal healthcare support and from the areas with lack in the clinicians to the patients ratio. This study explores the scope and challenges for the development of a generalized AI-led disease prediction system. The contributions may be highlighted as follows:

- A graph-like relationship between the diseases and the symptoms is developed using Disease Symptom Network (DSN) [11].
- A geometric DL method i.e. Graph Convolution Network (GCN) is used to learn the representation of the disease symptom graph.
- A DNN is used as a universal approximator to predict the diseases based on the learned representation by the GCN.

5.3   Mathematical Models

This section makes an introduction to various mathematical models of graphs and related DL techniques that help in ease of understanding the article.

In simplistic terms, an Artificial Neural Network (ANN) can be seen as a function approximator. The purpose of the ANN is to estimate a $\hat{f}(\cdot)$ such that $\hat{f}(x) \approx y$, where x is an input and $y = f(x)$ is the respective output. For an ANN to learn, huge amount of the historical (previous) data is required, where data is normally in the form of pairs of (x, y).

A system that predicts disease based on symptoms needs to capture the intrinsic causal relation between the disease and its symptoms. The modeling of such systems can be done using the graphs structures, where the diseases and the symptoms are the nodes and their relations are represented by the edges/links of the graph.

5.3.1   Graphs and Related Terms

Graphs are mathematical structures that are used to model the linked relationships among objects.

Definition 5.3.1.1 *(Graph)*: A graph G is defined as a pair $G = (N, E)$, where $N = \{n_1, n_2,..., n_k\}$ is a set of vertices connected by edges $E = \{e_1, e_2,...,e_l\}$. An edge e_k connects a pair of vertices (n_i, n_j) where $n_i, n_j \in N$. For a graph if there exists a function $f{:}e_k \rightarrow w_k$ that assigns a weight w_k to an edge e_k connecting vertices (n_i, n_j) then it is called a weighted graph, else it's an unweighted graph. A graph is said to be undirected if existence of $e_l \in E$ connecting the vertices $(n_i, n_j) \in E$ implies the existence of $e_k \in E$ connecting the vertices $(n_i, n_j) \in E$.

Definition 5.3.1.2 *(Degree Matrix)*: The degree $deg(n_i)$ of n_i a vertex the number of edges connected to the vertex in an unweighted graph, while the degree of a vertex n_i of a weighted graph is the sum of the edges connected to it. A degree matrix D of a graph $G = (N, E)$ is a $|N| \times |N|$ diagonal matrix, where $D_{jj} = deg(n_j)$.

Definition 5.3.1.3 *(Adjacency Matrix)*: An adjacency matrix A for a graph $G = (N, E)$ is a $|N| \times |N|$ matrix, where the rows and the columns are indexed by nodes N. In adjacency matrix, the element $A_{i,j}$ denotes, whether the node i and the node j have an edge between them or not (i.e adjacent or not). For an unweighted graph, adjacency matrix has binary values $A \in \{0,1\}^{|N|\times|N|}$, and for a weighted graph, the adjacency matrix has real values $W \in R^{|N|\times|N|}$.

Definition 5.3.1.4 *(Laplacian Matrix)*: Laplacian matrix L is a form of adjacency matrix $|N| \times |N|$ that combines information about the degree of vertices. For an undirected graph, L, D and A relate as, $L = D - A$.

5.3.2   Deep Learning in Graph

Many advancement has been made in learning representation of the complex structured data. Extracting information and learning representation from these complex relational structured data is very essential for implementing an AI model trained on these data. Defining the graphs with concrete structures is a challenging task, as structures in graph is arbitrary and can vary significantly. Thus CNN cannot be directly applied for the graphs, as convolution operation cannot be used on irregular structured data. Furthermore, the convolution operation relies on the geometric priors (like shift invariance), therefore, can be applied to Euclidean data as shown in Figure 5.1(a).

It is reported in Ref. [11], that the relation between the disease and the symptoms can be better modeled by non-Euclidean data like graph as shown in Figure 5.1(b). The challenges on the learning representations from the graphs can be addressed using Geometric Deep Learning (GDL) [12]. The GDL tries to learn a graph representation in low dimension, known as embedding and is discussed below about this.

5.3.3   Network Embedding

Network embedding is learning of a function that maps the discrete graph into a continuous space. For a graph $G = (N, E)$ with its adjacency matrix, weighted $W \in R^{|N|\times|N|}$ or unweighted $A \in \{0,1\}^{|N|\times|N|}$, the aim is to learn a representation in lower dimension

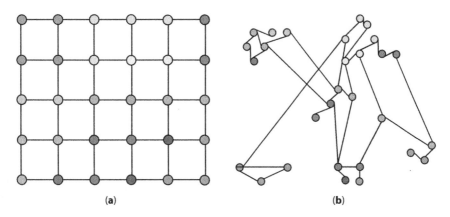

Figure 5.1 Graphs: (a) Euclidean graph, (b) Non-euclidean graph.

Z_i for $i \in N$ in such a way that the global and the local properties of the graph are preserved. For instance if in the original graph, the two nodes are close together, then their embedding in Z should also be close together. Let $Z \in R^{|N| \times k}$ is the embedding matrix, where $k \ll |N|$. A graph can have node attributes and edge attributes that provide useful information about the graph. A node feature can be represented as $X \in R^{|N| \times n_0}$, where n_0 is the dimension of input feature space. In network embedding, if the node features are used then the structural and the semantic information of the graph can be captured, but if the node features are not taken into consideration, then only the structural information is captured.

5.3.4 Graph Neural Network

The graph structured relationship between the disease and its causal symptoms could be efficiently handled by the DL methods introduced in Ref. [13]. These methods perform the graph embedding through information diffusion mechanism. Here the information continues to propagate from a node to its neighbors, until a stable equilibrium is achieved.

In GNN, the updation of the node embedding can be expressed using the following global output function F. This is formed by stacking $|N|$ instances of f, where $s_n = f\left(l_{c_0[n]}, l_{n_e[n]}, s_{n_e[n]}, l_n\right)$:

$$X^{t+1} = F(X^t, l, \theta) \tag{5.1}$$

Here X is an initialized node embedding, l represents the labels that are formed by stacking l_n and l_{ei}. Here l_n is label associated with the node n, and l_{ei} is the label associated with the edge $e_i \in E$. The θ is the network parameter. The set $n_e[n]$ represents the neighbors of the node n. The $c_0[n]$ is the set of the edges connected to the node n.

The final network embedding can be obtained using the following global output function G. This is formed by stacking the $|N|$ instances of g, where $o_n = g(s_n, l_n)$:

$$O = G(X, l_N, \varnothing) \tag{5.2}$$

Here l_N is stacked up node labels. With each node n, a state $s_n \in R^x$ is associated based on the information of its neighbors.

According to Scarselli *et al.* [13], the function mapping $f(.)$ is multi-layered perceptron (MLP) constrained to be contraction mapping. The parameters θ and ϕ are learned through back propagation by Almeda–Pineda algorithm as described in Ref. [13]. Based on the assumption that the iteration mapping is a contraction mapping, Banach's fixed point theorem guarantees the convergence of the Equation (5.1) to a unique solution.

5.3.5   Graph Convolution Network

The classical convolution operation cannot be applied directly to the graph due to its unstructured nature. The approach taken is to apply convolution operation to the Laplacian matrix of the graph in spectral domain, by approximating spectral filters as described in GCN [14].

For a graph $G = (N, E)$ and the input feature matrix $X \in R^{|N| \times d_0}$ the GCN produces a node level-output $X \in R^{|N| \times f_0}$. The d_0 and f_0 is the dimension of the input and the output feature vector, respectively. The output of the lth layer of the GCN can be expressed as

$$K^{l+1} = f(K^l, A); \quad 0 \le l \le L \tag{5.3}$$

where $K^0 = X$, and $K^L = Z$.

The propagation rule used in GCN can be written as follows:

$$f_\theta(K^l, A) = \sigma(A k^l \theta^l) \tag{5.4}$$

where θ^l is the learnable parameter of the lth layer, and σ is the non-linear activation function.

Equation (5.4) does not consider the feature vector of the node itself as $A_{i,i} = 0$. Thus the adjacency matrix is adjusted as $\hat{A} = A + I$. The GCN normalizes A to avoid the exploding gradients or numerical instability. The normalization is done by using $A \rightarrow D^{-\frac{1}{2}} A D^{-\frac{1}{2}}$.

Now the graph convolution layer becomes as follows:

$$f_\theta(K^l, A) = \sigma\left(D^{-\frac{1}{2}} \hat{A} D^{-\frac{1}{2}} K^l \theta^l \right) \tag{5.5}$$

5.4   Learning Representation From DSN

With the brief introduction to the related mathematical models, this section explores their uses in the present problem of disease prediction. This study implements the GCN [14] that encapsulates the graph embedding methods including GNN as based on the message passing [13] and the graph convolution [14]. This work uses the relationship between the diseases and the symptoms which is represented by a network as shown in Figure 5.2, as described in Ref. [11].

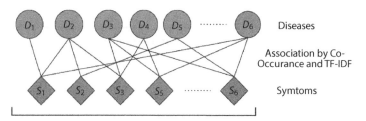

Figure 5.2 Representation of DSN.

5.4.1   Description of the Proposed Model

This subsection describes the proposed network architecture, the input given to the network along with the target output and the objective function used during training. The proposed model considers an undirected weighted graph $G = (N, E)$ as input, with adjacency matrix $W \in R^{|N| \times |N|}$, node feature $X \in \{0,1\}^{|N| \times d_i}$ and edge feature $K \in R^{|E| \times d_e}$ where d_e is the edge feature dimension. The supervision target given to our model is $S = \{N\}$, where N represents the node. This work uses a graph embedding network that creates the embedding of the graph followed by the classification network to provide the prediction of the disease class.

Graph Embedding Model: The graph embedding model uses GCN to embed the input graph, as shown in Figure 5.3. The f_{gcn} of Figure 5.3 is a multi-layer GCN, that can be described by Equation (5.6).

$$f_{gcn}(H^l, W; \theta) = \sigma \left(D^{-\frac{1}{2}} \widehat{W} D^{-\frac{1}{2}} H^l \theta^l \right)$$ (5.6)

The model provides the embedded graph that is represented as an embedding matrix $Z \in R^{|N| \times d_0}$. The operation performed by the GCN model can be described by the following Equation:

$$Z = f_{gcn}(W, X; \theta)$$ (5.7)

After performing the graph convolution operation by GCN, the input is mapped to an embedding space, which can be described by Equation (5.8).

$$f_{gcn}(\theta) : R^{|N| \times |N|} \times R^{|N| \times d_i} \rightarrow R^{|N_d| \times d_0}$$ (5.8)

The embedding space is $R^{|N_d| \times d_0}$, where $|N_d|$ is the number of diseases.

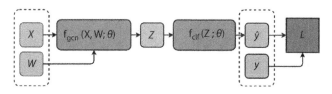

Figure 5.3 Training steps of the model.

Table 5.1 Description of network architecture.

Layer name	Activation function (σ)	Output dimension
Input	–	4,219
GCNConv	ReLu	1,024
GCNConv	ReLu	512
GCNConv	ReLu	256
Ln	ReLu	128
Ln	ReLu	512
Ln	ReLu	1,024
Ln	LogSoftmax	4,219

Classification Network: A classification network, as shown in Figure 5.3, is required to provide the desired predicted diseases using the graph embeddings Z, provided by GCN f_{gcn}. This work uses a Fully Connected (FC) DNN as the classification network as described in Equation (5.9).

$$\hat{y} = f_{clf}(Z;\varnothing) \tag{5.9}$$

The network outputs a probability distribution over the output label $\hat{y} \in \gamma^{|N_d|}$, where $\gamma^{|N_d|}$ represents the disease (node) label space.

The network, with their different components used in this model, is reported in Table 5.1. The table describes the layer information of the network, activation function used and the dimension of the output of the each layer.

5.4.2   Objective Function

This work uses the loss function, as shown in Equation (5.10), to optimize the learnable parameters of the proposed model during training.

$$\mathcal{L}(y,\hat{y}) = \sum_{i|v_i \in N_d} -\hat{y}_y + \log\left(\sum_j \exp(\hat{y}_j)\right) \tag{5.10}$$

The loss function compares the predicted value $\hat{y}$ with the ground truth label y. Here $\hat{y}$ is the probability distribution of the model while y is the class of the ground truth.

5.5   Results and Discussion

The development and the training of the model is done in Google's Colaboratory (Colab). The 'runtime' type was chosen as 'Python3' and the 'hardware accelerator' was chosen as 'GPU' in Colab. The PyTorch and PyTorch-Geometric libraries are used in the development environment. This section shows an outline of the performance of the stated model in terms of its evaluation capability on disease prediction.

5.5.1   Description of the Dataset

This study uses the dataset available from the work done by Ref. [11]. The dataset contains 322 unique symptoms and 4,219 unique diseases. The dataset also contains co-occurrence and Term Frequency-Inverse Document Frequency (TF-IDF) score of each disease-symptom pair in PubMed and other related bibliographic medical records [11]. The dataset contains 147,978 data points in the form of disease–symptom pair. This work uses 75%, 15% and 10% randomly chosen data as training, validation and testing dataset, respectively.

5.5.2   Training Progress

This subsection presents the performance of the proposed approach showing its variations on the loss and the accuracy with the epochs. Figures 5.4(a) and (b) show performance of the proposed approach in terms of the loss evaluated using Equation (5.10) and accuracy, for the training and validation data. Both the training and the validation losses go on reducing with the progress on the learning process as expected and is shown in Figure 5.4(a). The accuracy increases with the development of the learning process for both the training and the validation dataset as expected and shown in Figure 5.4(b). In Figure 5.4, a bump is seen in the loss graph (dip in the accuracy graph). This phenomena could be interpreted as the learning rate for that epoch is a bit high so the update based on the gradient overshoots the minima. However, eventually the loss converges to the minima (accuracy converges to a maxima). The values of the hyper parameters used during the training of the network are mentioned in Table 5.2.

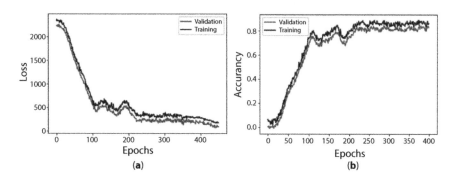

Figure 5.4 Training Performance: (a) Loss, (b) Accuracy.

Table 5.2 Description of the hyper parameters.

Hyper parameter	Value
Learning rate	0.006
Momentum	0.99
Learning Algorithm	SGD

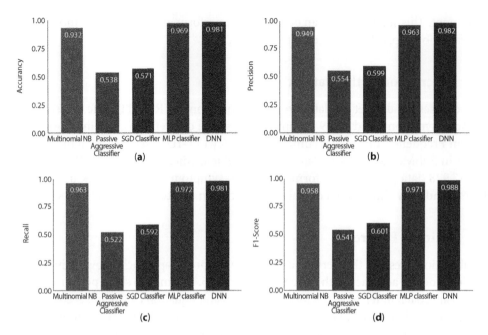

Figure 5.5 Performance comparison: (a) Accuracy, (b) Precision, (c) Recall, (d) F1-score.

5.5.3   Performance Comparisons

Performance of the model is evaluated in terms of Precision, Recall, Accuracy and F1-measure.

This work implements a multi-layer perception (MLP) and a DNN as classification networks to p redict the diseases. A comparative study is done between this work and the other classical classification methods like multinomial naive Bayes, Stochastic Gradient Descent (SGD) Classifier and Passive Aggressive Classifier (PAC) available in scikit-learn package [15].

Figures 5.5(a–d) show the comparative study in terms of the accuracy, precision, recall and F1-score, respectively between the classical and the proposed method. Performance improvement in terms of accuracy, precision, recall and f1-score is at least 3.7%, 1.4%, 0.9% and 1.3%, respectively when MLP is used. The DNN improves accuracy, precision, recall and f1-score by 1.2%, 1.9%, 0.9% and 1.7%, respectively when compared to MLP. As can be seen from the improved values of the evaluation metrics, the proposed approach is found to be efficient to learn from DSN for the disease prediction.

5.6   Conclusions and Future Scope

The chapter highlights the relevance and the role of AI-led automatic disease diagnosis. A geometric DL approach learns efficiently the inherent graph relationship between the disease and the symptoms leading to an accuracy of ~98% in disease diagnosis when a DNN is used as a classifier. Some future issues may be as follows:

- Determining the probable interaction of protein with the given symptoms and diseases.
- Some imaging modality works on subsample measurements or huge data of symptoms need sparse representation, thus suggesting the development of a sparse-symptom diagnosis using DL.

References

1. LeCun, Y., Bengio, Y., Hinton, G., Deep learning. *Nature*, 521, 7553, 436–444, 2015.
2. Ali, L., Rahman, A., Khan, A., Zhou, M., Javeed, A., Khan, J.A., An automated diagnostic system for heart disease prediction based on χ^2 statistical model and optimally configured deep neural network. *IEEE Access*, 7, 34938–34945, 2019.
3. Lei, Z., Sun, Y., Nanehkaran, Y.A., Yang, S., Islam, M.S., Lei, H., Zhang, D., A novel data-driven robust framework based on machine learning and knowledge graph for disease classification. *Future Gener. Comput. Syst.*, 102, 534–548, 2020.
4. Hao, Y., Usama, M., Yang, J., Hossain, M.S., Ghoneim, A., Recurrent convolutional neural network based multimodal disease risk prediction. *Future Gener. Comput. Syst.*, 92, 76–83, 2019.
5. Wang, T., Qiu, R.G., Yu, M., Zhang, R., Directed disease networks to facilitate multiple-disease risk assessment modeling. *Decis. Support Syst.*, 129, 113171, 2020.
6. Geras, K.J., Wolfson, S., Shen, Y., Wu, N., Kim, S., Kim, E., Cho, K., High-resolution breast cancer screening with multi-view deep convolutional neural networks, arXiv preprint arXiv:1703.07047, 2017.
7. Li, Z., Wang, C., Han, M., Xue, Y., Wei, W., Li, L., Fei-Fei, L., Thoracic disease identification and localization with limited supervision, in: *Proceeding of the Conference on Computer Vision and Pattern Recognition*, pp. 8290–8299, 2018.
8. Shadmi, R., Mazo, V., Bregman-Amitai, O., Elnekave, E., Fully convolutional deep-learning based system for coronary calcium score prediction from non-contrast chest CT, in: *Proceedings of the 15th International Symposium on Biomedical Imaging (ISBI)*, pp. 24–28, 2018.
9. De Fauw, J., Ledsam, J.R., Romera-Paredes, B., Nikolov, S., Tomasev, N., Blackwell, S. *et al.*, Clinically applicable deep learning for diagnosis and referral in retinal disease. *Nat. Med.*, 24, 9, 1342–1350, 2018.
10. Khosravi, P., Kazemi, E., Zhan, Q., Malmsten, J.E., Toschi, M., Zisimopoulos, P. *et al.*, Deep learning enables robust assessment and selection of human blastocysts after *in vitro* fertilization. *NPJ Digital Med.*, 2, 1, 1–9, 2019.
11. Zhou, X., Menche, J., Barabási, A.-L., Sharma, A., Human Symptoms–disease network. *Nat. Commun.*, 5, 1, 1–10, 2014.
12. Bronstein, M.M., Bruna, J., LeCun, Y., Szlam, A., Vandergheynst, P., Geometric deep learning: Going beyond euclidean data. *IEEE Signal Process. Mag.*, 34, 4, 18–42, 2017.
13. Scarselli, F., Gori, M., Tsoi, A.C., Hagenbuchner, M., Monfardini, G., The graph neural network model. *IEEE Trans. Neural Networks*, 20, 1, 61–80, 2008.
14. Kipf, T.N. and Welling, M., Semi-supervised classification with graph convolutional networks, arXiv preprint arXiv:1609.02907, 2016.
15. Pedregosa, F., Varoquaux, G., Gramfort, A., Michel, V., Thirion, B., Grisel, O., Duchesnay, E., Scikit-learn: Machine Learning in Python. *J. Mach. Learn. Res.*, 12, 2825–2830, 2011.

Intelligent Vision-Based Systems for Public Safety and Protection via Machine Learning Techniques

Rajitha B.

Department of Computer Science & Engineering, Motilal Nehru National Institute of Technology Allahabad, Prayagraj, India

Abstract

Video surveillance has increased a lot in the past few years, securing lives in both private and public places. These footages are processed or analyzed only when a abnormal behavior is reported which makes it passive. But, an active/automated systems are required for immediate, fast and accurate responses/actions from the authorities when ever an abnormality happens. This could save the lives of many by proving the services like hospitality, police and etc. This leads to develop an intelligent video surveillance systems which can detect the abnormality/incident dynamically and accordingly raise an alarm to the nearest police stations, hospitals as per requirement. Thus this chapter presents a detailed review on such cases, challenges and work done in the respective area to date. It also details how AI-based computer vision analysis tools and secured network platform generation helps in incident authentication and transmission of data over the web.

Keywords: Video surveillance systems, machine learning, theft detection, video segmentation, feature extraction, vehicle accident detection, Alextnet

6.1 Introduction

Abnormal behavior detection from on-line/offline videos is an emerging field in the area of computer vision. This plays a vital role in video surveillance-based applications to provide safety for humans at public places such as traffic signals, shopping malls, railway stations, etc. Surveillance cameras are meant to act as digital eyes i.e. watching over activities at public places and provide security. Nowadays there are number of cameras deployed at various public places to provide video surveillance. But in reality they are used or analyzed only after some incident happens. Moreover a human watch is needed in-order to detect the person/cause of the incident. This makes the surveillance cameras passive. For example if a theft/murder occurred at some CCTV monitored area, and then the footage is manually checked for crime identification and localization after complaint has been raised. Thus there is huge demand to develop an intelligent video surveillance system which can

Email: rajitha@mnnit.ac.in

Sachi Nandan Mohanty, G. Nalinipriya, Om Prakash Jena and Achyuth Sarkar (eds.) Machine Learning for Healthcare Applications, (89–102) © 2021 Scrivener Publishing LLC

detect the abnormality/incident dynamically and accordingly raise an alarm to the nearest police stations, hospitals as per requirement. Current developments in computer vision via Artificial Intelligence (AI) have grown vastly by providing high computational video analysis power. Through this high dimension computation power CCTV data analysis tools can be provided intelligence i.e. brains to automatically detect any theft, murder, vehicle accidents, etc. If AI-supported CCTV systems are deployed at commercial and traffic areas then we can easily detect the incidents/crimes and they can be traced fastly.

AI-based video analytics machines include: detecting the humans via face recognition software's, vehicles detection via number-plate/vehicle model (through image processing techniques) and pedestrians detection, etc. They can also be used to detect that a human is waiting at a bus-stop, running from locations A to B, driving a vehicle in some area, etc. But they fail to detect that a human has murdered a person at location A and running to location B, a man waiting at some bus-stop is a criminal, a person has just robbed a vehicle, a person had hit a car during his journey, etc. These problems occur daily in almost all the cities of our country. But, our efficient policemen are unaware of the incident until any complaint/report (either written or phone-called) has been made manually to them. Thus these problems led us to think and develop systems which can generate an auto-alarm to Police stations, Ambulance services, Fire stations, etc. via a secured channel whenever a crime or accident occurs at commercial and traffic areas, and from any CCTV covered locations. Thus this chapter is mainly aimed to focus on these issues and discusses some solutions using AI-based computer vision analysis tools and secured network platform generation for incident authentication and transmission of data over web.

6.1.1   Problems Intended in Video Surveillance Systems

In recent years most of the public places and organizations (such as banks, business work stations, universities, hospitals, shopping malls, etc.) are deploying the cameras i.e. CCTVs (Closed-Circuit Television) for various purposes such as to monitor the public, pedestrian detection, density based traffic signal allocation, crime identification at mass locations, women safety, robbery prevention/identification, murderer identification, etc. [1–3]. Some of these videos are accessible without any password credentials and some require authorized access. These camera footages could be utilized to develop the intelligent surveillance systems to increase public safety both at personal and public places [4]. It can also help the police in guiding and identifying the other safer routes for common public daily journey without any mishap (after/during any incident). Even the governments of U.S., U.K., India, etc. are deploying surveillance video systems at various cities respectively. They are trying to steam the real-time public networks cameras data for public safety such as abnormal action detection or prevention via central server. These cameras data can be used to identify perpetrator after the crime. Law enforcement agencies in India, United States, Washington and New York [5–7] are embracing the community policies philosophy from past few years in-order to enforce public safety. This might lead to develop and incorporate more efficient and effective strategies to enforce the law. In order to achieve higher accuracy in these applications a vast number of network cameras must be installed to cover all angles of crime/anomaly detection. A number of new and cost-effective software tools and machines must be deployed. In order to create such efficient systems some challenges might be encountered such as follows:

Challenges in current video surveillance systems

- Where exactly to Locate Cameras
- Choosing Best Cameras for public places
- Latest Technology Integration i.e. deep learning with available Software Tools such as Vision Processing Units, OpenCV, Python libraries, etc.
- How to Incorporate the Privacy Policies
- How to Incorporate the Active and Dynamic CCTV Monitoring
- How to analyze the Video footage for anomaly detection and prevention
- Dynamic Tracking of perpetrator/vehicle.
- Multi-casting the perpetrator info to nearest police stations in secured channel.

6.1.2   Current Developments in This Area

Police monitored cameras are placed in United States from past few years. They are mostly used after the crime has occurred and to identify the suspects. In the U.S. and U.K. the CCTVs are placed in most of the organizations, schools, commercial areas, railways stations, apartments, etc. for monitoring the people, prevent/detect the theft suspects, and to identify any misconduct. However, they all are passive (not an auto detecting systems). To develop such high dimensional capable software tools, higher broadband services are required for efficient and faster data transfer over web. Currently U.K. stands among the top 20 in providing the broadband services. In Indian communities there is lack of high-speed broadband services in the earlier years. But, this has changed drastically from last three to four years. Now India also provides high-speed Internet services at most of the metropolitan cities. Thus implementing intelligent and smart CCTVs in India for law enforcement can improve the technical growth of the country and reduce the crime.

6.1.3   Role of AI in Video Surveillance Systems

Governments of various countries are now interested in funding the agencies to setup a wireless networks with 4G technology in order to increase the communication among the police stations to respond immediately after an serious incident. Though they are costly the governments of U.S., U.K., Canada, etc are willing to install high-definition CCTVs in order to reduce the crime rate. Grant Fredericks, a constable and forensic video analysis expert from Columbia, Canada had monitored and evaluated number of the CCTVs located at public transports, city centers, transport locations, apartments, vehicle parking, etc. (these analytics was carried-out manually). Simon Goudie, Brandon Welsh and David Farrington, Anne Mellbye, Tanya Kristiansen from Campbell Collaboration and RBUP, Norway have published an article review named as *"17 Effects of Closed Circuit Television Surveillance on Crime"* [8]. Their study was conducted in hospitals, residential areas; public transports, etc. in U.K., USA, Canada, Norway and Sweden and found that *"CCTVs are not effective until some intelligence is provided, otherwise they are just passive"*.

6.2   Public Safety and Video Surveillance Systems

The CCTV-based network controlled systems are still in development stage in most of the states of India and other countries. Delhi police has installed CCTV networks at various traffic signals to monitor the traffic and crime. The CCTV are also been used by criminals at their respective houses/offices. Gurgaon police commissionerate also installed central surveillance systems in urban areas by municipal corporation costing 3.37 crores. Around 61 CCTV cameras are installed and monitored at police headquarters. These areas covered most of the public transport routes. M.N. Anucheth, deputy commissioner of police (administration), said "CCTV can be used as electronic evidence while investigating criminals. The Journalist Gauri Lankesh murder case has benefitted through this CCTV footage for indentifying the suspects during the absence of an eyewitness."

6.2.1   Offline Crime Prevention

In offline crime identification, crime related information is gathered once some manual alert (either by phone call/personal complaint) is received to the police. This process is very time consuming and sometimes it might lead to some major loss like deaths, murders, thefts, misleading the case, suspect, etc.

6.2.2   Crime Prevention and Identification via Apps

Increasing number of crimes in public places and private places had lead to fear in minds of public. This increasing crime rate had resulted to impose strict rules and regulations on daily routine of common public. People have to fallow these rules wither willingly or unwillingly. So, government is trying to gradually reduce this burden on common public and introduce/develop some new technology based applications which automatically recognizes the crime or incidents and populates the information among the police to enforce the law. There are numerous numbers of software apps developed for public safety, which need to be deployed in people's personal mobile phones. Women's safety is one of the major concerns in current public safety aims. In this regard, Eyewatch SOS app was designed to record audio and video of surroundings of the women and automatically transfers them to registered contacts indicating an alert message. iGoSafely app, sends position of the GPS to emergency contact upon activation. Criminal Identification and Localizations is another concerned area of public safety. Police of various states in India, developed separate apps for criminal identification though mobile phones instantly. These apps are trained to search the criminal through face as well as textual information. Tables 6.1 and 6.2 summarize and compare some of the existing mobile apps developed for public safety and security.

6.2.3   Crime Prevention and Identification via CCTV

Software's apps on smart phones are mainly user initiated processes. So the alternative is to measure and provide public safety via Artificial Intelligence-enabled surveillance cameras. Currently, in almost all the major cities huge numbers of CCTV cameras are installed

Table 6.1 Comparison of existing software apps.

Software/App name	Users	Purpose
PoliceOne	Police officers	It's an iPhone application for sharing the official news, photos, tactical tips, etc. among the police officials.
CrimeSceneTracker	Any Individual	This app facilitates the individual who is at the crime scene to take photos, document the scene information in standard format and share with the nearest police station.
Police Field Interview FI Card	Security Officers	Suspects Face can be detected from the records of crime data
US Cop	Street Officers	Helpful for patrolling police.
Police Spanish Guide	Police working and cannot speak Spanish	App converts your speech to Spanish while enquiring with Spanish people
My Police Department	For police officials	Can track the nearest police station and inform the suspects information immediately from the scene.
Karnataka State Police App	Police officials	Users can trace the nearest police stations and lodge complaint directly via app including the Images of suspects
COP Connect by Telangana	Police Officials	It's an group chart app through which the police officials can make groups at different levels like district, zone, sub-division, circle levels, etc. and share the suspects information like images, audios, videos and documents.
Delhi Police app	Police Officials	Police can notify the people about the helpline numbers in case of emergency, shortcuts to all police official cites, etc.
RAIDS Online	Police officers and public	People can inform about the public safety routes, informs/alerts about the high-crime areas. They can also view details about a crime including crime type, date, time, address, and distance from current location.

at public and private places. These camera recoding are used for crime identification and tracking the suspect. They are used after the incident has occurred and it might take at least 1 to 24 h to trace the suspect after the incident. Hence a highly efficient software system is required to detect the incident immediately from the CCTV footage and track perpetrator in very minimal time, which is lacking in the current available systems.

Table 6.2 Comparison of previous approaches.

Approach	Limitations	Software designed	Evaluation-Parameter
Accelerometer and GPS tracking [8]	SPOF	Yes	Accuracy
Smart Phone [32]	SPOF	Yes	Accuracy
Atmel Micro-controller [33]	SPOF	Yes	Time
Sensors [34]	Informs one mobile number.	Yes	Accuracy
Based on Speed [35]	SPOF	GSM and GPS Modem	Time
Smart Phone [36]	SPOF	Yes	Accuracy
Vehicle Features [37]	Delay in the message sending	Prototype	Accuracy
Vector Machine [38]	Not a rescue system	Rea-time Traffic	Accuracy
Smart Phone [39]	SPOF	Yes	Accuracy
Camera on Vehicle [40]	SPOF	Yes	Accuracy

6.3   Machine Learning for Public Safety

The abnormal behavior doesn't happen on daily basis at traffic signals or roots, they occur very often (rare cases). So, detecting such incidents need slots of learning. Thus developing software's must be processed on many video footages in order to classify the normal and abnormal behavior. These models can be broadly categorized as Semi-Supervised, Supervised and Unsupervised approaches [9–11]. If the training dataset is mixture of labeled and unlabelled data then semi-supervised approaches can be used to classify. If the training dataset is labeled then it is split in the ratio of n:m for training and testing respectively.

Another special case of learning method is Active Learning [12], here the system interacts with the user during the process of predicting the class i.e. takes a user input for better class predictions rates. This type of prediction methods are used when there is huge number of unlabeled datasets and cannot be labeled manually with minimal time. All the learning methods first train the system or model by splitting the available dataset into m:n ratio (where m + n is the total number of samples in the dataset). For example, if 1000 sample images exist in dataset and 80:20 is chosen for splitting the dataset then 800 will be in training and 200 will be in testing respectively. But, in real time the dataset increases or grows dynamically. Thus, researches have proposed another learning mechanism named as Re-enforcement learning [13]. Based on these basic learning methods the machine is trained and tested on test data. The normal learning becomes the deep learning when deep feature are extracted from the training data as well as from test data.

But, to classify the a human face from another human face manual features may not give better results, thus require deep features. Thus, machine learning techniques are playing vital role in developing smart and efficient approaches for various vision based applications.

6.3.1 Abnormality Behavior Detection via Deep Learning

Abnormality behavior detection can be broadly categorized in to the following:

- Model-Based approaches: These approaches train the model using a group of parameters. These parameters are learnt via statistical methods. Some of them are regression based methods and Gaussian mixture models [14–15]. If the structure data feature is created dynamically then it is non-parametric method. Some of them are Bayesian network models [16], Dirichlet process mixture models [17] and histogram based models [18].
- Classification-Based approaches: For a given feature dataset space if one can distinguish a line or model (either liner or non-linear separator) then it is said to be a classification. In general the classification approaches are categorized into two: binary class classification and multiclass classification. Rule based classifier [19] is one such approach where a set of rules are created or formalized on the train data and their attribute relationships and finally classifies the test data on these rules. Decision tress, Bayesian classifiers are also of the similar category. Support vector machine [20] is an advanced and latest approach which classifies both in binary and multiclass data.
- Prediction-Based approaches: Here anomaly detection is achieved by estimating the differences between predicted and actual class characteristics. LSTM (Long Short Term Memory) [21] and HMM (Hidden Markov Model) [22] are some of the examples of these categories.
- Reconstruction-Based approaches: This method assumes that the normal image data can be re-represented through a different or lower dimensional representation for differentiating the normal and abnormal behavior image data. For example an image can be re-represented just as a scaled down feature map such as point distribution model, Principal Component Analysis [23], Auto-Encoder, etc.
- Other variant approaches: Clustering [24], here the generated features are grouped into two or multiple sub groups/clusters. The grouping is done on the concept of the data elements within a group has similar properties and data from two different groups has different properties.

Deep Learning Approaches and its Variants
Here a computer machine is aimed to take automated decisions. They should also include intelligence while processing. If a machine takes an automated decision with intelligence then it is said to be machine learning based approach. From late 1990s new approaches came into existence based on this methodology both in computer vision and big-data analytics. The advancements in neural networks and artificial intelligence has given rise to new approaches called Convolutional Neural Networks (CNN) [25]. Hubel and Wiesel have

inspired the formation this architecture. First CNN model was designed by LeCun in the year 1989 for topological data processing (represented in grid-from). Its action is similar to human brain processing unit such as Neocortex. It processes the information through multiple layers in brain and extracts the meaningful information or knowledge automatically. Thus it resembles the human brain visual cortex. CNN also tries to learn and minimize the cost function using backpropogation. It can extract high, low and middle level features by varying the filter size and filter type. Thus with all these key features it can learn efficiently from any raw input image (pixels data in 2D matrix form).

CNN is a subclass of neural networks. It has a powerful ability while extracting the features from an image. It includes many hidden layers which automatically learns the inner features of the image. CNN has gained much importance due to vast growing rate of vision data and new developments in processing devices. CNN architecture contains: various activation functions, loss functions, regularization, optimization parameters and processing units etc. This CNN is further enhanced to make it Deep CNN (DCNN). DCNN is constructed by modulating the basic CNN architecture in more depth. CNN uses block based processing units instead of structural layers. Hence gained substantial importance and attention. CNN network architecture has multiple learning layers or stages which combine: Convolutional Layers, Processing units with non-linearity and sampling layer. Every layer transforms the given image data to the next layer using a bank of convolutional filters (kernals). Here the input image is divided into smaller blocks or slices. Local features are extracted on these blocks via a set of filters. The resultant images are forwarded to non-liner processing units. This will help in understanding the semantics of the image. Next, the results are forwarded to subsampling layer, which combines the results of multiples filters and makes them geometric distortion invariant.

Deep CNN architecture is advantages over shallow architecture or manual approaches for feature extractions and classification. The complex tasks require a rigorous learning of features. The complex learning ability is gained due to multiple non-linear and linear processing units stacking unlike normal CNN. That is DCNN is combination of collection of normal CNN's one after another or in parallel. The hardware advancements like GPU's with high computing capable systems are also the cause of attractions and attention towards its development. Thus it shows high performance over conventional approaches. It also has the ability to learn from unlabelled data, extracting the invariant representation, handle hundreds of categories and etc. DCNN has many variants and a short description is given in following:

LeNet-5 (1995): It is designed by LeCun and *et al.* in the year 1995 [26]. This is pioneering convolutional neural network with 7 level layers. This is trained to classify the numerals or digits. Several researchers have used this network for recognizing the hand-written numbers, numbers on checks, etc. The input image is resized to 32×32 image size in grayscale format. The high resolution image datasets of numbers require high computational layers in designed CNN model where in this model lacks the performance.

AlexNet (2012): This architecture [27] is also similar to LeNet but, it is much deeper and has more number of layers with huge number of convolutional layers stacked. It has won the first rice by resolving almost all the challenges of co competitors and outperformed the results with top-5 error rates to 15.3% on an average. It base model contained 11×11 convolutional layers at first stage, 5×5 and 3×3 convolutional layers in the remaining layers. Each stage has max pooling layers, dropout layers, ReLU activations, data augmentations and SGD momentum. ReLU layer is at every individual convolutional layer and at fully connected layer. It was trained on Nvidia Geforce GPUs for almost six days simultaneous. As it is taking too much time they split the network into two pipelines. Alex Krizhevsky, Ilya Sutskever and Geoffrey Hinton together designed this architecture in SuperVision group.

ZFNet (2013): In the year 2013 another modified variant of CNN was proposed by [28] named ZFNet. It is the winner of ILSVRC in that year. This network has error rate as 14.8% which is lower than the existing approaches till that date.

GoogLeNet/Inception (2014): GoogleNet [29] also known as Inception V1 was the winner of ILSVRC in the year 2014 conference competition. The error is further reduced here to just 6.67% in comparison to existing approaches. This was very similar to human brain level thinking. It was hard to beat this error rate challenge during that year. But, after some days a human expert tried hard and achieved 5.1% error rate (Andrej Karpathy) for single model and for ensemble he achieved 3.6% error rate. It was inspired by LeNet but had a novel architecture. This architecture had batch normalization, RMS prop and image distortions. Several small level convolutional filters are designed in order to reduce the parameters. They constructed a 22-layer stacked deep convolutional neural network and reduced the parameters from 60 million to just 4 million as compared to AlextNet.

VGGNet (2014): Simonyan and Zisserman developed a variant of CNN model called VGGNet [30]. It was the runner up of ILSVRC conference competition in the year 2014. It is very interesting and appealing with uniform architecture and includes 16 convolution layers. Its architecture is similar to AlextNet but has 3×3 convolution layers along with more number of filters. They trained the machine for 2 to 3 weeks on four GPU machines. Due to its simple and most profound architecture it gained much importance in DCNN's domain and is the top most preferred model over researchers. It has been widely adopted by many people over web and its architecture and weight configuration is publicly available. One issue with VGGNet is that it has around 138 million number of parameters.

ResNet (2015): Kaiming He *et al.* [31] have designed an architecture having skip connections and heavy batch normalization for features. These skip connections are known as gated recurrent units or gated units which has similarity to RNN's. They trained this neural network with 152 numbers of layers which is much lesser than the VGGNet. This architecture has even beaten the human expert error rate with 3.57% of GoogleNet. This model has won the completion of ILSVRC in the year 2015 and named the network as ReNet (Residual Neural Network). It has residual connections unlike the two networks for AlexNet and inception for GoogleNet.

6.3.2 Video Analytics Methods for Accident Classification/Detection

Yun *et al.* pointed that the vehicle accident detection techniques are broadly classified into the following: *Traffic Flow Modeling Patterns*: Here only law-full patterns are considered such as U-Turn, go-straight, right-turn, etc. Thus, it is suitable for normal traffic and cannot detect collisions. *Vehicle Activities Analysis*: Here moving vehicles are detected and then their features like: acceleration, distance between vehicles, direction etc are extracted. This method works fine only in low crowded traffic. *Modeling of vehicle interactions:* This method is inspired by sociological concepts. The model is trained using large number of images.

Some of the video-based anomaly detection challenges are Illumination of video footages, Pose and Perspective of cameras, Heterogeneous object handling, Sparse vs. Dense traffic, Curtailed tracks, Lack of real-life datasets, etc. Thus machine learning based approaches can be helpful to handle all such challenges and develop more efficient automated traffic analysis systems.

6.3.3   Feature Selection and Fusion Methods

It is also important to detect good features from these videos so that the incident can be identified automatically and accurately. The uncommon behavior of a suspect can be identified only when the features are extracted correctly and according to the type of incident. The special and frequency transform filter will help in identifying the boundaries via wavelet transforms. The Histogram of Gradients will detect the human very efficiently and vehicles in the desired areas. The list of low level and high level feature models used for video surveillance system incident detection are: Gaussian process regression, Gaussian Mixture Model (GMM), Dynamic Patch Grouping, Fuzzy clustering Techniques, Unsupervised Kernel learning, SVM classifier, HOG & SVM, Hidden Markov Model, KNN and Convolution Neural Networks. Table 6.3 shows the summary of existing approaches for accident detection. The current available trained networks in video surveillance systems are not capable to handle multiple incidents (though they use deep convolution networks). The available models of deep learning in this field are still passive. The incidents can be any one from the following but not limited to: (a) Vehicle Accidents at public places, (b) Murder in public places through gunshot and knife, (c) Bomb blasts detection, (d) Gang fights/wars in public places. These features are stored in the form of vectors and used for classification. Once the incident is classified, the information must be forwarded to next nearest police stations and sub monitoring systems for tracking the perpetrator immediately after the incident.

Table 6.3 Comparison of various DCNNs.

CNN model	Year of publication	Developed by	Competition position	Error-rate of Top-5	Total no. of parameters
LeNet 5	1998	LeCun *et al.*			60 Thousand
AlexNet	2012	Krizhevsky *et al.*	1st Position	15.3%	60 Million
ZFNet	2013	Zeiler *et al.*	1st Position	14.8%	–
GoogleNet	2014	Szegedy *et al.*	1st Position	6.67%	4 Million
VGGNet	2014	Simonyan *et al.*	2nd Position	7.3%	138 Million
ResNet	2015	He, Kaiming *et al.*	1st Position	3.6%	–

6.4   Securing the CCTV Data

6.4.1   Image/Video Security Challenges

Distribution of digital data/information/image over the network is an essential task these days and it is cost-effective. These applications need secured information transmit, copyright protection systems, etc. But, storing and sharing this data over communication channels is a challenging task till date. In literature its was found that encryption methods and watermarking techniques provide better confidentiality, availability, integrity, authenticity, efficient indexing, tampering detection, reduced memory, ownership identification, etc. It is also found that transform based watermarking techniques are better than the spatial based watermarking techniques.

6.4.2   Blockchain for Image/Video Security

This section discusses a decentralized autonomous application for video content storage and transmission using blockchain technology (Secure and scalable data sharing is essential). In recent years blockchain technology has gained much popularity due to its unique features in providing security. They are highly resistant to data modifications i.e. the data cannot be modified once it is created/secured using blockchain mechanism. Bitcoin is among the most successful blockchain mechanism in digital cryptocurrency applications. That is why it is becoming more and more popular in current research trends. These days all innovative applications where insecurity is a major issue this blockchain is being used widely. Violating the cybersecurity rules might also cause some serious problems in the daily routine of human life (misguiding the public) and in some cases, it might lead to deaths. Thus, there is an urgent need to secure video data over surveillance systems. Inspired by the massive success of blockchain in this aspect, there a need to focuses on understanding the basics of advanced concepts and critical challenges in blockchain.

6.5   Conclusion

This chapter discussed the various methods for abnormal behavior detection from on-line/off-line videos. It is an emerging filed in the area of computer vision. This plays a vital role in video surveillance based applications to provide safety for humans at public places such as traffic signals, shopping malls, railway stations, etc. Surveillance cameras are meant to act as digital eyes i.e. watching over activities at public places and provide security. They are used or analyzed only after some incident has happened. Hence this chapter has detailed some of the learning approaches for supervised, semi supervised and unsupervised-based models in depth. Machine Learning is also the important concept which is widely used in computer vision for various applications like: Pattern recognition, classification, optimization, etc. Chapter has detailed some of them such as convolutional neural network model in depth followed by its variants: LeNet, AlexNet, GoogleNet, ZFNet, ResNet, VGGNet, etc. All these are modified versions of normal CNN model. They all are based on AI-Enabled algorithms so that better and fast detection rate can be achieved. Finally it is concluded that there is a huge demand to develop an intelligent video surveillance system which can detect the abnormality or incident dynamically and accordingly raise an alarm to the nearest police stations, hospitals as per requirement. If AI-supported CCTV systems are deployed at commercial and traffic areas then we can easily detect the incidents/crimes and they can be traced in minimal time.

References

1. National Institute of Justice (NIJ), US Department of Justice, Office of Justice Programs, United States of America, *CCTV: Constant cameras track violators*, vol. 249, pp. 16–23, NIJ Journal, Cornell University, 2003.
2. Armitage, R. To CCTV or not to CCTV. A review of current research into the effectiveness of CCTV systems in reducing crime. 2002.
3. Nieto, M., *Public video surveillance: Is it an effective crime prevention tool?*, California Research Bureau, California State Library, Sacramento, CA, 1997.
4. Skogan, W.G., Community Policing: Common Impediments to Success: The Past, Present and Future, in: *Community Policing: The Past, Present and Future*, The Annie E. Casey Foundation, Northwestern University, Washington, D.C., 2004.
5. Fridell, L.A. and Wycoff, M.A. (Eds.), *Community policing: The past, present, and future*, Annie E. Casey Foundation and Police Executive Research Forum, Washington, DC, United States of America, 2004.
6. Braga, A.A. and Weisburd, D.L., Police innovation and crime prevention: Lessons learned from police research over the past 20 years, David L. Weisburd and Anthony A. Braga (Eds.), Jul 20, 2006.
7. La Vigne, N.G., Lowry, S.S., Markman, J.A., Dwyer, A.M., *Evaluating the use of public surveillance cameras for crime control and prevention*, US Department of Justice, Office of Community Oriented Policing Services, Urban Institute, Justice Policy Center, Washington, DC, 2011.
8. Zhao, Y., Mobile phone location determination and its impact on intelligent transportation systems. *IEEE Trans. Intell. Transp. Syst.*, 1, 1, 55–64, 2000.
9. Zhu, X. and Goldberg, A.B., Introduction to semi-supervised learning. *Synth. Lect. Artif. Intell. Mach. Learn.*, 3, 1, 1–130, 2009.
10. Niculescu-Mizil, A. and Caruana, R., Predicting good probabilities with supervised learning, in: *Proceedings of the 22nd International Conference on Machine Learning*, ACM, pp. 625–632, 2005.
11. Coates, A., Ng, A., Lee, H., An analysis of single-layer networks in unsupervised feature learning, in: *Proceedings of the Fourteenth International Conference on Artificial Intelligence and Statistics*, pp. 215–223, 2011.
12. Beygelzimer, A., Dasgupta, S., Langford, J., Importance weighted active learning, *In Proceedings of the 26th annual international conference on machine learning*, Jun 14, pp. 49–56, 2009.
13. Zoph, B. and Le, Q.V., Neural architecture search with reinforcement learning, arXiv preprint arXiv:1611.01578, 2016.
14. Cleveland, W.S., Grosse, E., Shyu, W.M., Chapter 8, Local regression models (1992), in: *Statistical Models in S*, pp. 309–376, Routledge, 2017.
15. Reynolds, D., Gaussian mixture models, in: *Encyclopedia of Biometrics*, pp. 827–832, 2015.
16. Maldonado, A.D., Uusitalo, L., Tucker, A., Blenckner, T., Aguilera, P.A., Salmerón, A., Prediction of a complex system with few data: Evaluation of the effect of model structure and amount of data with dynamic bayesian network models. *Environ. Model. Softw.*, 118, 281–297, 2019.

17. Liu, C., Li, H.-C., Liao, W., Philips, W., Emery, W.J., Variational Textured Dirichlet Process Mixture Model with Pairwise Constraint for Unsupervised Classification of Polarimetric SAR Images. *IEEE Trans. Image Process.*, 28, 8, 4145–4160, 2019.

18. Srivastava, D., Rajitha, B., Agarwal, S., An efficient image classification using bag-of-words based on SURF and texture features, in: *2017 14th IEEE India Council International Conference (INDICON)*, IEEE, pp. 1–6, 2017.

19. Gu, X., Angelov, P.P., Zhang, C., Atkinson, P.M., A massively parallel deep rule-based ensemble classifier for remote sensing scenes. *IEEE Geosci. Remote Sens. Lett.*, 15, 3, 345–349, 2018.

20. Liu, P., Choo, K.-K.R., Wang, L., Huang, F., SVM or deep learning? A comparative study on remote sensing image classification. *Soft Comput.*, 21, 23, 7053–7065, 2017.

21. Cui, Y., Yang, G., Veit, A., Huang, X., Belongie, S., Learning to evaluate image captioning, in: *Proceedings of the IEEE Conference on Computer Vision and Pattern Recognition*, pp. 5804–5812, 2018.

22. Guo, Q., Wang, F., Lei, J., Tu, D., Li, G., Convolutional feature learning and Hybrid CNN-HMM for scene number recognition. *Neurocomputing*, 184, 78–90, 2016.

23. Kang, X., Xiang, X., Li, S., Benediktsson, J.A., PCA-based edge-preserving features for hyperspectral image classification. *IEEE Trans. Geosci. Remote Sens.*, 55, 12, 7140–7151, 2017.

24. Dey, N. and Ashour, A. (Eds.), *Classification and clustering in biomedical signal processing*, IGI Global, Hershey, 2016.

25. LeCun, Y., Kavukcuoglu, K., Farabet, C., Convolutional networks and applications in vision, in: *Proceedings of 2010 IEEE International Symposium on Circuits and Systems*, IEEE, pp. 253–256, 2010.

26. LeCun, Y., Jackel, L.D., Bottou, L., Brunot, A., Cortes, C., Denker, J.S., Drucker, H. *et al.*, Comparison of learning algorithms for handwritten digit recognition, in: *International Conference on Artificial Neural Networks*, vol. 60, pp. 53–60, 1995.

27. Krizhevsky, A., Sutskever, I., Hinton, G.E., Imagenet classification with deep convolutional neural networks, in: *Advances in Neural Information Processing Systems*, pp. 1097–1105, 2012.

28. Zeiler, M.D. and Fergus, R., Visualizing and understanding convolutional networks, in: *European Conference on Computer Vision*, pp. 818–833, Springer, Cham, 2014.

29. Szegedy, C., Liu, W., Jia, Y., Sermanet, P., Reed, S., Anguelov, D., Erhan, D., Vanhoucke, V., Rabinovich, A., Going deeper with convolutions, in: *Proceedings of the IEEE Conference on Computer Vision and Pattern Recognition*, pp. 1–9, 2015.

30. Simonyan, K. and Zisserman, A., Very deep convolutional networks for large-scale image recognition. arXiv preprint arXiv:1409.1556, Cornell University, under Computer Science: Computer Vision and Pattern Recognition, 2014.

31. He, K., Zhang, X., Ren, S., Sun, J., Deep residual learning for image recognition, in: *Proceedings of the IEEE Conference on Computer Vision and Pattern Recognition*, pp. 770–778, 2016.

32. Ali, H.M. and Alwan, Z.S., *Car accident detection and notification system using smartphone*, LAP LAMBERT Academic Publishing, Saarbrucken, 2017.

33. Tushara, D.B. and Harsha Vardhini, P.A., Wireless vehicle alert and collision prevention system design using atmel microcontroller, in: *2016 International 22 Conference on Electrical, Electronics, and Optimization Techniques (ICEEOT)*, IEEE, pp. 2784–2787, 2016.

34. Yee, T.H. and Lau, P.Y., Mobile vehicle crash detection system, in: *2018 International Workshop on Advanced Image Technology (IWAIT)*, IEEE, pp. 1–4, 2018.

35. Dogru, N. and Subasi, A., Traffic accident detection using random forest classifier, in: *Proceedings of the 2018 15th Learning and Technology Conference (LT)*, Jeddah, Saudi Arabia, 2526 February, p. 4045, 2018.

36. Faiz, A.B., Imteaj, A., Chowdhury, M., Smart vehicle accident detection and alarming system using a smartphone, in: *2015 International Conference on Computer and Information Engineering (ICCIE)*, IEEE, pp. 66–69, 2015.

37. Fogue, M., Garrido, P., Martinez, F.J., Cano, J.-C., Calafate, C.T., Manzoni, P., A system for automatic notification and severity estimation of automotive accidents. *IEEE Trans. Mob. Comput.*, 13, 5, 948–963, 2013.

38. Liang, G., Automatic Traffic Accident Detection Based on the Internet of Things and Support Vector Machine. *Int. J. Smart Home*, 9, 4, 97–106, 2015.

39. Bhatti, F., Shah, M.A., Maple, C., Islam, S.U., A novel internet of things-enabled accident detection and reporting system for smart city environments. *Sensors*, 19, 9, 2071, 2019.

40. G. Spampinato, S. Curti, N.I. Guarneri, A.R. Bruna, Method for advanced and low cost cross traffic alert, related processing system, cross traffic alert system and vehicle, U.S. Patent Application 10/242,272, filed March 26, 2019.

7

Semantic Framework in Healthcare

Sankar Pariserum Perumal[1*], Ganapathy Sannasi[2], Selvi M.[3] and Kannan Arputharaj[3]

[1]*Department of Information Science and Technology, College of Engineering Guindy, Anna University, Chennai, India*
[2]*School of Computer Science and Engineering, Vellore Institute of Technology, Chennai Campus, India*
[3]*School of Computer Science and Engineering, Vellore Institute of Technology, Vellore, India*

Abstract

Healthcare applications are diverse in nature and they are in critical need of compatible and understandable systems through which they can communicate effectively. A semantic framework for such disparate applications is very necessary so that the resultant seamless communication between them would boost up the patient information access and healthcare improvement processes. Semantic interoperability among various healthcare data sources is a challenging task for efficient healthcare delivery within and across communities. Semantic Web is introduced for extracting meaningful contents from different kinds of healthcare data. It is followed by multiple agent systems that help in regularizing the discovery of information from such curated data. A primitive multiple agent system that enhances the semantic data retrieval and translation process is explained in this chapter. By leveraging Resource Description Framework (RDF) as the information representation medium between the different data models to achieve semantic interoperability, structured mapping definitions and ontologies for Semantic Web Services and decision making, a translation system for healthcare instance data is proposed. Different agents employed in this framework assist the users in invoking the required services and monitor the system performance. This system finds out the linkages between data model elements aimed at improved accuracy in healthcare instance matching.

Keywrods: EHR, semantic framework, semantic web ontology, RDF, multi-agent system, SPARQL, STTL, healthcare instance data

7.1 Introduction

Healthcare domain is in need of a well-defined semantic framework among individuals as well as groups so that various healthcare data providers could collaborate with each other aiming at enhanced healthcare data management [1]. It is very challenging to attain at a healthcare semantic framework in today's healthcare IT cloudstream given the complexity of different data sources. These data are presented in various forms—from unstructured, semi-structured to structured formats and they are also sourced from different data

Corresponding author: tell.sankar@gmail.com, ORCID 0000-0002-6004-3534

Sachi Nandan Mohanty, G. Nalinipriya, Om Prakash Jena and Achyuth Sarkar (eds.) Machine Learning for Healthcare Applications, (103–120) © 2021 Scrivener Publishing LLC

centers—clinical laboratory databases, Electronic Health Record (EHR) systems, diverse and voluminous data delivered by various medical devices, each of which will be subjected to different algorithmic computational tasks. This leads to expensive and long standing data communication process in between them.

To curb out the issue of various healthcare data forms and formats, the single adaptable representation that is being widely used is RDF (Resource Description Framework) recommended by W3C [2]. RDF is globally recognized across various healthcare data providers and is not bound to a particular schema. It represents information in the form of triples, the combination of Subject, Predicate and Object. SQL queries can also be represented in RDF format [3] to denote the abstract syntax of other language identifiers. Fresnel [4] created a RDF vocabulary that details the specific data to be displayed in RDF graph with browser independent presentation. Healthcare clinical and patient information present in different data sources are connected through respective RDF triples' predicates, thereby representing such data in the form of a substantial linked graph. By making use of RDF as the generic information rendering medium, a semantic framework is proposed to attain the data concordance among various healthcare data clusters.

7.2   Semantic Web Ontology

Ontologies play an important role in semantic Web [5]. They provide a regulated and crisp approach for defining the meanings of Web resources. It comes up with the suitable domain fields, their attributes, value ranges and their connections. The key note is the design of related fields, their properties and the meaning based connections between them which makes any ontology, an efficient domain processor based on semantic context and not on the syntactical analytic ability or associations established among the physical attributes. Ontology need not be a completely different entity, even a meta data repository that indicates the physical as well as conceptual properties of the fields that are associated to a certain user group is deemed to be an ontology. So, a Semantic Web Ontology with respect to a knowledge base refers to the process of listing out the attributes within the knowledge base, well understood by a group of resources as well as systems that read such associations and share the semantic relationships among them.

RDFS (Resource Description Framework Schema) prescribes language for showcasing the RDF vocabularies on the Web, based on which other technologies like OWL (Ontology Web Language) or SKOS (Simple Knowledge Organization System) are built. It is represented by a set of classes, sub-classes of individual nodes and their attributes. RDF and RDFS are proposed by W3C community and they stand as the medium of representing various Web resources or the components for an ontology design tool or base for developing a simple metadata repository. URIs (Uniform Resource Identifier) are used to refer the properties from one ontology or a metadata repository to another. Figure 7.1 shows the association of URI with RDF Vs HTML. Though RDFS does not derive any meanings from a specific domain, it restates the attributes from other ontologies through URIs.

Though the same URI is catered, the RDF and HTML descriptions vary. Both are two different documents where the Web server responds with a location HTTP along with the URL of the corresponding document. Based on the content negotiation chosen by the Web server, URL of the HTML representation or RDF is sent. Further, HTTP requests are

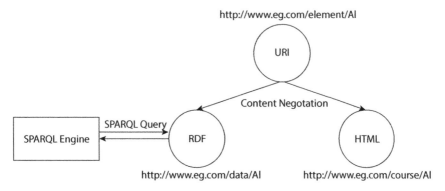

Figure 7.1 Sample association between URI, RDF and SPARQL.

pointed to HTML URLs whereas the RDF data requests are pointed to corresponding RDF documents [6]. These RDF documents would in turn store information about the RDF triples using the appropriate URI.

Similar to an XML schema that restricts the structure of its document, a RDFS schema interprets its classes, sub classes and concepts with the corresponding vocabulary to be well understood by the downstream systems. Such parent–child level relationships boost up the hierarchical structure of sub-classes deriving their descriptions, attributes and constraints from their super classes. Unlike other traditional hierarchies, an RDFS ontology's first two levels—resource (level 1) and class & attribute (level 2) are defined at RDFS schema level whereas the fields in all the bottom levels represent one or more parent class or attribute. Table 7.1 lists examples for some of the well-known ontologies.

It is not necessary for all attributes in a RDFS ontology to have possible attribute values, though its structure provides all required vocabulary contents. Establishment of semantic linkages between all classes and/or attributes is treated to be an external process outside RDFS ontology. Also, rule-based definitions by the agents are allowed in RDFS schema to spot the knowledge associations among its members or a new member. A Semantic Web ontology is said to contain a complete vocabulary only when its value matched. In other words, the inventory of meta classes, sub classes and concepts of the ontology should be matched against their appropriate concept values. There is a difference between a regular dictionary and a Semantic Web ontology. A regular dictionary has all of its words and their

Table 7.1 Examples of some types of ontologies.

Ontology type	Examples
Linguistic Ontology	WordNet, BabelNet, OpenCyc
Research Ontology	KA2 (Knowledge Annotation Initiative of Knowledge Acquisition community)
Domain Ontology	SWEET (Semantic Web for Earth and Environmental Terminology), MeSH (Medical Subject Headings)
General Ontology	eCl@ss, PSCS (Products and Services Categorization Standards)

meanings arranged in an alphabetical order. In the same way, if the elements in a Semantic Web ontology are arranged in an alphabetical order, their semantic linkage will be lost. So, none of the sequential ordering methods is employed in it.

In any natural language processing context, a meaningful and conceptual account base could be developed that is open for analysis and maintenance in a machine-readable language within a team working on a common domain and shared purpose so that the benefitting agents could interpret and understand the inherent meanings in these accounts and even derive novel and insightful information out of it. A Semantic Web ontology is a mixture of well-defined vocabularies and multi-level hierarchies which are collaborated into a distinct scheme of data interpretation [7]. Its semantic logic enables the data to be exchanged among different ontologies that might belong to different domains. It proves to be a common medium of knowledge sharing among various user groups. This throws an option to revisit all the traditionally built knowledge bases and modify them based on the ever evolving semantic relationships and knowledge representations over a period of time so that the resulting Semantic Web ontology is precise and upto date.

7.3 Multi-Agent System in a Semantic Framework

An agent showcases the involvement exhibited by a specific information system and presents a liaison feature between the host and other information agents. In any dataflow environment, an agent might have to alter the existing service or restrict the service to lower levels. In such cases, an agent's interaction with other fellow agents in the system plays an important role. A multi agent system is in need of an ardent system to analyze and react to the data flow changes in the existing framework, which calls for a shared knowledge pool among such agents. One of the main goals of agents involved in Semantic Web is autonomous transaction, i.e., ability to respond to the system changes automatically with very less human intervention. Agents have the potential to instantly identify, implore and comprehend the reactions with respect to the actions performed by already interacted as well as new agents entered into the system. The pace of such reactions is significantly impacted by the agent's consistency level and how it articulates the incoming signals.

Services and clients in a Semantic Web service framework have several agent goals, but not limited to [8–10]:

- Agents should be able to understand and respond to all ontologies available over the internet and enable seamless interaction among such ontologies.
- Agents acting as service providers should be able to sell their semantic interpretation potentials over the Web, so that agents acting as service consumers should be able to choose certain services and send messages to other agents using them.
- Agents should be able to cross check the semantic explanations given by the service provider agents and use them to keep modifying the sub goals set for the neighboring agents until it eases out the interaction process from the first agent to the last agent and vice versa.

- Application of multi agents should be restricted to particular facets of information flow, but spread across all areas including data maintenance, decision making, data reproduction or data wrangling.
- Agents should be able to dynamically handle the constantly changing system requirements and execute suitable adaptations in the Semantic Web context.

There are so many applications of multi agent systems for healthcare domain out of which literature study of few of them are discussed. An applications named 'AgentHospital' [11] is developed and cross validated for multi agent environment in hospital logistics environment at modeling and implementation stages. A semantic framework with many individual sub-models are created at the modelling level. All other infrastructure and granular services are validated at the implementation level. Koutkias *et al.* [12] come up with a multi agent system to support continuous monitoring of adults in a generic medical contact center (MCC) for prolonged illnesses. Another approach [13] is designed for the surveillance and maintenance of critical care patients with multi agents aimed at the betterment of their health through rule based agent sharing knowledge system. Another rule-based agent system named 'Geriatric Ambient Intelligence' (GerAmI) provided physical assistance as well as reasoning guide [14]. The target audience were the patients infected by Alzheimer's disease. Multi agent system named 'SHAREIT' (Supported Human Autonomy for Recovery and Enhancement of Cognitive and motor disabilities using Agent Technologies) produced sensor based user collaborative tool for motor disabilities. The 'Context aware Hospital Information System' (CHIS) [15] is another multi-agent system that provides secure collaboration among colleagues in the hospital set ups. The autonomous feature of the agents help the intended technicians to promote privacy-aware emergency responding systems with high availability [16]. Unbounded semantic descriptions could be taken out from such multi agent based Semantic Web services. Some of the existing healthcare semantic frameworks are discussed in detail.

7.3.1   Existing Healthcare Semantic Frameworks

7.3.1.1   AOIS

Agents and Ontology based Information Sharing (AOIS) is a hierarchical multi-agent system that promotes a user group over internet to share knowledge [17]. It is redefined on the earlier version called Remote Assistant for Information Sharing (RAIS) based on Google Desktop search. AOIS works on semantic topic ontology principle where the top topic terms having similar semantic distance are populated and the topology gets updated in every iteration. Topic ontologies created and maintained by other users are also utilized in AOIS. A sold file-sharing system, BitTorrent is employed in AOIS where the idea is to communicate files in a distributed system and not via any main hub.

There are many components in AOIS system—(i) JADE (Java Agent DEvelopment) framework for developing multi-agent applications and FIPA (Foundation for Intelligent Physical Agents) built on top of JADE [18, 19], (ii) BitTorrent DHT [20] that constitutes a server to load and track the torrent files and DHT (Distributed Hash Table) indexing in a peer-to-peer network, (iii) JAWS (Job Access with Speech) [21], an API that provides Java applications to read and retrieve data from other systems, (iv) Nutch [22], an open source software for online search within a local metadata repository, (v) WordNet [23], a language ontology accessed via JAWS library and modified to an OWL (Ontology Web Language) file when the process completes.

Agents in the AOIS system are identified based on the consumer requests and the agents' own retrieval history. There are five types of agents employed in AOIS:

- Personal Assistant (PA)—Agent PA is used for upkeeping the new/updated record(s) in the system, propagate them to the next agent IF and get the requests from customers.
- Information Finder (IF)—Agent IF is used to pull out the responses against the user requests, restrict them depending on the pre-defined set of rules and do a semantic search within the local database.
- Information Pusher (IP)—Agent IP is used to move the updated/new record(s) to agent PA and keep track of the changes in the semantic repository.
- Directory Facilitator (DF)—Agent DF records new entrants into the system and addresses the queries regarding agent addresses raised by agent PA.
- Repository Manager (RM)—agent RM keeps an eye on reindexing whenever there is a change in the network, which in turn helps in semantic search procedures.

Agent PAs have the potential to access the topic ontologies and identify new topic terms. They are able to constr uct a derived ontology by accessing other users' ontologies as well enabling improved Web search based on the set of final topic terms. BitTorrent helps in bigger implementation of this multi agent system so that a huge number of users in the community can share the information files among them. Based on the list of topic terms referred against WordNet and stored in the topic repository, search index and semantic ontology get auto-updated by the agent RM. Clearance of the historical queries beyond a certain period of time is performed by agent IP after verifying the same with agent PA.

7.3.1.2 SCKE

Statistics and Collaborative Knowledge Exchange (SCKE) [24] is another multi agent system where each agent is represented by a hospital. Here the message is not forwarded at the same time to all the agents since the communication is only between two agents at a time. The author lists down four actions to be performed by each agent in this system:

- communicates to the next hospital agent
- receives the previous hospital agent's request
- semantic search for the previous hospital agent's request in the hospital metadata repository
- forward the semantic search output to the hospital agent.

Figure 7.2 depicts the two different flows followed in SKCE system—user query option and statistics retrieval option. For user query option, the hospital agent obtains the query and semantically searches if it is locally available in his repository first, otherwise does the same in all other hospital agent repositories. The user also feeds in the number of

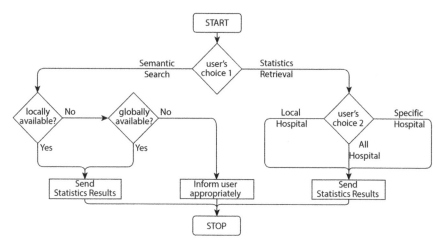

Figure 7.2 SKCE Multi agent system flowchart.

queries as an input before sending the actual queries. The requested agent finally collates the result and forwards it back to the user. For statistics retrieval option, the hospital agent questions the user if he would like to perform this activity on the local hospital or a particular hospital or on all hospitals in the network. For a particular hospital, the user also provides the hospital name. In all these cases, the agent collects the statistics and forwards it back to the user.

This system makes use of JADE environment for message traversal, Jena library for semantic search along the concepts and Protégé for diseases ontology development [25] which enlists the list of human diseases and extends a user interface for ontology maintenance. Nutch plug-in is used again in this system for online search along with Jena library to produce more meaningful results back to the user unlike conventional search procedures.

7.3.1.3   MASE

Multi-Agent SEmantic-driven framework (MASE) [26] is framed on epidemiology environment and has two layers—a user interface layer to analyze and update the data semantics and a registry layer to store the datasets and their semantic description files. This system is pilot run on decision support models based on geo-spatial information that lack efficient interoperability. Tasks in the user interface layer are listed as below:

- Specific MASE agents are invoked to initiate the system workflow.
- Basic epidemic information is stored in a local database so that user need not describe the context of the epidemic background and just provide the disease name, place and period to the MASE agent.
- Service Identification agent searches through Semantic Web for the requested information and updated the front end with the populated services. Design Engineering agent validates the service outputs if it complies all aspects of the user queries and forwards them to the front end user.
- The user collates the service outputs and transform them to the required results.

Registry layer deals with creating language ontologies semantically contributing to the identified services and datasets and repositories to publish Web Service accounts. Three ontologies are created and maintained in MASE system—one for epidemic data processing, one for abstract data model concepts management and one to provide spatial and temporal argument values to the existing geo-spatial records. Dataset Ontological insights in spatio-temporal systems play a crucial role in data annotations since a same location might coexist in many languages and time zones and might not represent any association between them semantically. Service Identification agent, Design Engineering agent and MASE agent together support and enhance the automatic decision making process in epidemiology scenario and produce results that are not so hard to interpret.

7.3.1.4   MET4

Interdisciplinary Healthcare Teams (IHT) are very complicated management groups that maintain clinical workflow processes starting from identification of suitable physicians and rules to choose apt practitioners for specifically delegated works. MET4 multi-agent system [27] helps in alleviating problems due non-compliance in these processes among the concerned management groups. This system makes use of five different models to convert system use cases in O-MaSE (Organization-based Multi-agent System Engineering) into final deployment. They are:

- Domain Model—builds ontologies for patients as well as physicians common to the given domain.
- Goal Model—showcases the nested relationships between layer-wise goals and their scope in the given domain.
- Agent Class Model—connects involved agents (like team supervisor, workflow administrator) with the external users and knowledge registries.
- Protocol Model—presents different types of message exchange protocols utilized among the agent classes.
- Plan Model—proposes suitable optimal algorithms to realize these established goals.

MET4 multi-agent semantic framework has been applied in patient care that improves the quality of life of patients facing terminal illness through early detection and pain treatment. Major two types of agents used in this system are—(i) Patient Representative (PR) agent who supports patients in reading through the therapies suggested by the practitioners in the system and (ii) Practitioner Assistant (PA) agent who could even lead the team managers and therapists in pain assessments and evaluations. PA agents are frequently deployed in team manager pickup process, team members addition/update process and therapy accordance process. Some MET4 systems employ additional agents like Workflow Executor agents, Data Synchronizer agents, etc. Also, PA agents could be divided into sub-agents like Evaluation Advisor agents and Proof Illustrator Agents.

This system is implemented using (i) WADE (Workflows and Agent Development Environment) derived from JADE environment and (ii) Microsoft Z3 solver API, that provides automated reasoning with semantic search using FOL (First Order Logic) in clinical workflows. This system is illustrated with Chronic Kidney Disease based prototype model proposed by the author [28]. FOL representation is very important to capture the platform changes effected by the workflow administrators or the task executors. Though physicians and practitioners are fixed within the team in most of the cases, MET4 admits them to get transferred to other teams by leveraging semantic interoperability feature enabled by language ontologies. The semantic principles executed in this system are modelled by three constituents—(i) a patient care ontology supporting IHT, (ii) obligatory filters against the evolving ontology structure and (iii) a concept store to populate ontology concepts along with their linkages.

7.3.2   Proposed Multi-Agent-Based Semantic Framework for Healthcare Instance Data

Among various types of healthcare data, this study concentrates on the instance data which deals with the list of tasks performed by medical resources in a specific medication procedure. For developing a semantic framework that translates different standards of data to the required target format with the help of RDF as information representation, there is also a requirement for efficient querying as well as rule based transformation mechanisms to handle RDF data in the required format. SPARQL (SPARQL Protocol and RDF Query Language) and STTL (SPARQL Template Transformation Language) satisfy this requirement for querying and rule based mapping processes respectively, which are used for effective data transformation. SPARQL is RDF query language for semantic data retrieval and updates whereas STTL is used for RDF transformation to different data forms. STTL has even been utilized with SPARQL in a Semantic Web MOOC online course framework [29]. Since STTL is derived from SPARQL's extension features [30], it uses the declarative property of rule-based RDF transformations.

Semantic Translation is in need of concept mapping between different data models in a structured pattern so that such data mappings could be automatically populated to a considerable extent in the translation process. Figure 7.3 displays the proposed semantic translation framework for healthcare instance data. Data model concepts from each data source are extracted and stored in the data dictionary and mappings database. Further, these data concepts can be exposed to domain experts who could create linkages in between such data concepts via a web application user interface. These mappings are again stored in the data dictionary database. The updated data concept mappings between the input and required output data mapping are then pulled. Input healthcare instance data are converted into RDF triple representation. RDF translator intakes the input RDF model, output data concept model and the crucial data concept mappings between the input and output data concept models. The output from RDF translator is again converted to RDF format of the output data concept model. There are many agents used in this proposed system—(i) Customer Agent (CA), (ii) Query Optimizer Agent (QOA) and (iii) Translation Agent (TA). Also, two types of ontologies are implemented—(i) Semantic web ontology and (ii) Decision Making ontology.

7.3.2.1   Data Dictionary

Corresponding to each and every input data source, the constituent data concepts get stored in the data dictionary. A data dictionary provides the relationships among different data elements, their concepts, concept values with their respective metadata.

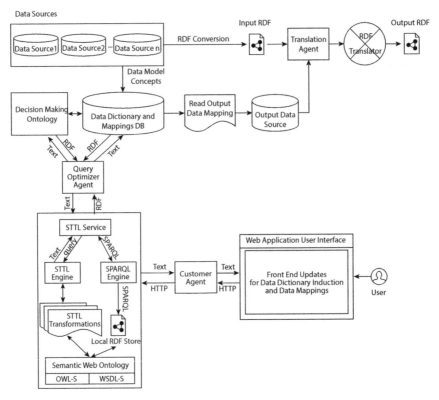

Figure 7.3 Semantic translation framework for healthcare instance data.

In the case of relational databases [31], a data dictionary comprises of the tables, their columns, default column values and relationships between them. In terms of data dictionary, these relational tables are populated as classes, columns as data concepts, default column values as data concept values. These terms control access and the updates to be performed on different database objects. Active data dictionary is always preferred since there should not be any time lag between the data dictionary details and the actual database object structures, whereas passive data dictionary is a private database that is saved only with metadata information, outside of the actual database structure. Users can only manipulate the actual database structure. They don't have any update rights on the data dictionary repository which is governed only by the metadata administrator. Figure 7.4 shows a sample data dictionary structure with its constituents—concept models, meta classes, concepts and concept values.

7.3.2.2 Mapping Database

The inner constituent of the data dictionary is a mapping database that aims at populating several mapping relationships among various input data sources. The mapping manager implements such linkages in different ways.

One of the options is to map the output data field against one or more input data fields which could be associated to numerous input data fields in priority order. Another option is to define field level value mappings from input data field values to output data field values.

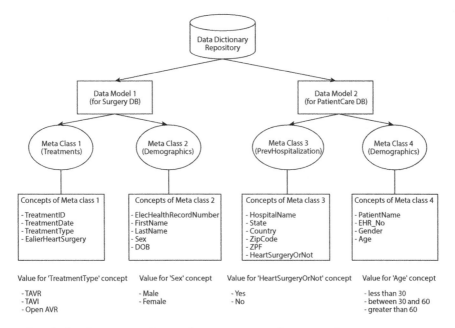

Figure 7.4 Sample data dictionary with meta classes, concepts and concept values.

A rule based mapping can also be defined to link a input field to its corresponding output field. These mappings provide the transformation instructions to link the content and structure of data fields between input and output data streams. Such mappings also enable interoperation among several input data sources that might look similar but not exact. Hence, data field mapping is an important task before the actual semantic translation takes place [32].

7.3.2.3 Decision Making Ontology

Decision making process among the results from semantic Web ontology services as well as SPARQL queries associated with STTL engine with the help of Query Optimizer Agent QOA needs to be presented in an ontology and the related strategies for this decision making process needs to be populated within this ontology. For this purpose, a decision making ontology is utilized which resolves the usage conflict on-the-fly dynamically depending on the nature of the request and the co-operation extended by the corresponding agents to agree upon the chosen strategy.

It is a light weight ontology used to send the appropriate result in RDF format to the next section, after different contentions between internal agents and other ontology service outputs. It is a trained ontology to organize the STTL transformed outputs in line with the domain ontology. This step is true for every agent communication during the user query handling process. Decision making mechanism can either be local or remote depending upon the nature of decision making strategy and availability of RDF represented set of data mappings. So, this is highly significant to devise a resolution process for ontology harmonization and arbitration. Decision making ontology along with data dictionary and mappings database represent the entire metadata repository of the proposed semantic framework.

Figure 7.5 depicts samples of concept level mappings between data dictionary elements populated from different data sources. Concept names represented in this figure are taken from the sample meta classes and concepts displayed in Figure 7.4. The concept 'EHR_No' of meta class 4 is mapped to the concept 'ElecHealthRecordNumber' of meta class 2. The concept 'HeartSurgeryOrNot' of meta class 3 is mapped to the concept 'EarlierHeartSurgery' of meta class 1. These two-concept level mappings are examples of direct mapping. The concept 'PatientName' of meta class 4 is mapped to the concepts 'FirstName' and 'LastName' concepts of meta class 2 based on a transformation rule that should be readable by the RDF translator explained in the next section. Transformation rule defined in this example is string concatenation with a blank space in between them i.e., FirstName || ' ' || LastName.

The concept 'Age' of meta class 4 is mapped to the concept 'DOB' of meta class 2 based on concept value level mappings since their default values don't match. Hence, three ranges in the concept 'DOB' are chosen based on which three categorical values for the concept 'Age' are mapped. Similarly, concept values of 'Sex' concept of meta class 4 are explicitly mapped against those of 'Gender' concept present in meta class 2 since they can't be directly mapped. There are also other types of concept mappings like conditional filter, adding extra concept values, etc.

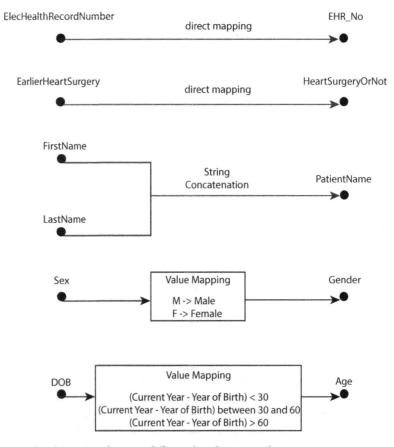

Figure 7.5 Concept level mappings between different data dictionary elements.

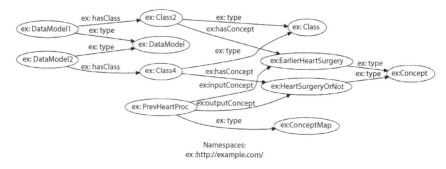

Figure 7.6 Sample RDF model of concept level mapping between different data models.

In this semantic translation framework, both data dictionary and mappings database are represented in RDF format. This helps in identifying the relationships among different data sources, which are otherwise disconnected. Figure 7.6 illustrates a sample RDF representation of the concept level mappings between different meta classes belonging to the data models 1 and 2 shown in Figure 7.4. It particularly displays the RDF linkage established between the concepts 'EarlierHeartSurgery' and 'HeartSurgeryOrNot' of the meta classes 'Treatments' and 'PrevHospitalization' respectively.

7.3.2.4 STTL and SPARQL-Based RDF Transformation

The RDF model based concept level mappings between input and output concepts are handled efficiently for querying and transformation tasks by STTL and SPARQL protocols [33]. This feature comes up with a SPARQL endpoint that supports SPARQL version 1.1 compatible RESTful web service. This enables an user to load the RDF based concept mappings defined in the previous step and make use of SPARQL queries and STTL templates to validate against them. STTL engine used in this framework takes care of RDF model of multiple sets of STTL templates defined for each rule based transformation. STTL RESTful web service that processes one or more STTL transformations should be able to get accessed by the RDF translator used in the next step. SPARQL query form enhances the process of RDF data extraction and transformation into the required output RDF model. STTL engine used in this framework is not restricted to any particular input RDF data format.

In the proposed semantic framework of healthcare instance data, STTL RESTful web service caters only to those STTL transformations directed from the local RDF model. Initially, a request from RDF model's STTL transformation is thrown at STTL engine in the form of URL closing with '/template' pattern whereas the query section of the same URL takes care of the specific RDF triple request, again in compliance to SPARQL version 1.1, appended at the end of URL. A sample URL that is tagged with specific 'st:qry' based STTL transformation on all triples of a RDF model is given below:

http://localhost:8080/template?query=SELECT*WHERE{?x?p?y}&transform=st:qry

Further, STTL transformation and the SPARQL query mentioned above can be clubbed into one feature called 'profile' which can replace the 'query' and 'transform' sections in the above URL. In other words, the URI of the profile key will hold the STTL service pointing to its 'SPARQL query' and 'STTL transform' properties. Since it is a plain RDF to RDF transformation within RDF data representation context, other context transformations like RDF-to-HTML, RDF-to-Turtle and RDF-to-XML transformations are not considered in this framework.

7.3.2.5   Query Optimizer Agent

STTL service explained in the previous section depending on the request type could point to SSTL transformation service or SPARQL query. Optimal performance of these SPARQL queries is achieved by Query Optimizer Agent (QOA) which rewrites them into efficient-to-execute queries to produce the same result. It also keeps an eye on the cycle time when the statistics need to be re-computed after RDF store updates. Sometimes, minor updates happen and will not trigger statistics re-compute task. Nevertheless, this would have potential to cause the statistics of a subsequent SPARQL query to be stale. In such cases, Query Optimizer Agent QOA would force recomputation of such statistics.

Also, even if all query statistics are gathered, resolving a optimally performing SPARQL query over a significant time is still a NP-hard challenge. To handle these issues, Query Optimizer Agent QOA would try to spot in the problematic section of the SPARQL query by analyzing the BGP (basic graph patterns) of several RDF triple patterns within the entire query. This would enhance the query turnaround time from the module of semantic Web ontology and the SPARQL engine to the module containing data dictionary and the decision making ontology.

7.3.2.6   Semantic Web Services Ontology

This type of ontology may just include single or collective ontologies that are distributed over the Web. No specific restriction on the use of intelligent agent type is applied on this semantic Web ontology. Either of OWL-S (Web Ontology Language for Services) ontology and its editor [34] or WSDL-S (Web Service Description Language for Services) and its editor [35] could be utilized for the creation of intelligent Web services where the former supports the ontology for relevant aspects of semantic Web Services and the latter provides WSDL extension properties for the related semantic relationships in WSDL constituents.

In addition to the conditional outputs and conditional effects of OWL-S ontology services, the extensible properties of WSDL-S service like 'modelReference', 'precondition', 'effect', etc., are used for service invocation as well as service discovery. These semantic Web services render to the requests from STTL transformations as well as SPARQL engine based on the nature of the request. In the proposed system, OWL-S Editor/WSDL-S editor protégé plugin is used along with semantic Web ontology. OWL file written with semantic description is populated for each requested OWL-S service. Otherwise, a corresponding WSDL file with syntactic description about various semantic operations required for the service is written and fed for STTL transformations or searched by SPARQL queries.

7.3.2.7   Web Application User Interface and Customer Agent

There is always a tradeoff between the domain experts and the framework consultants since their nature of work don't intersect. Information populated in the input data sources are administered by the framework consultants whereas the actual knowledge about the data concepts and their linkages are governed by the domain experts. Framework consultants work on the data models at the physical data sources level. The domain experts work on these data at the concept mappings level. This can be explained with an example. Healthcare and medical professionals will be able to differentiate between different heart surgery procedures like TAVR, TAVI and open AVR based on their valve replacement method. But, framework consultants will not be able to understand each of these terms and will consider each of their procedures as a data concept value and define how they are stored in the RDF model.

To bridge this task gap, a web application user interface and a Customer Agent (CA) are provided where the domain experts have the provision to define and update the mappings between different concepts and the framework consultants load them into the data models and technically link them. At the run time, the customer agent CA decides its goal to be pursued. It completely represents the user who has access to the user interface screen. The customer agent CA would interact with single or group of users would ascertain their goals regarding the set of mappings stored in the mappings database. Once these mappings are redefined, the results are pushed back to the user by the customer agent CA. Users will be able to view the data dictionary populated from several data sources in the user interface screen. They can either create new data concept mappings or alter the existing mapping definitions or both. This helps the framework consultants to cross validate the concept level mappings against those suggested by the domain experts.

7.3.2.8 Translation Agent

Translation Agent TA is another agent service that verifies and validates RDF translation compatibility between input and output RDF files. Sometimes the chosen output data model corresponding to the required output concept mapping may not match field by field to the input RDF file in which case Translation Agent TA helps. For example, it looks for the syntactic match between the data models' fields and tries to fix minor issues like data type manipulations if it does not require a totally different data type altogether. This agent conduces RDF translation by providing preprocessed input and output RDF files ready for translation.

7.3.2.9 RDF Translator

By referring the input data mappings in the converted RDF model and by reading the required output data mapping from the data mappings database in the RDF format, RDF translator executes the data translation process. Each input data source is unique and gets converted to the corresponding RDF model before being fed into RDF translator. This data to RDF conversion is performed on demand by RDF translator only for those particular data sources that are required for the current translation process. Data concepts level and concept values level mappings help in this semantic translation by providing seamless association between data sources and thereby conduces auto-code generation process to a considerable degree. This in turn makes the troubleshooting process easier by tracing the mapping definitions all the way back to the original input data source.

RDF translator enables coupling between different data models and their concepts. Mappings database records the novel term value mappings on the ground, which in turn links data sources on the top level. RDF translation happens as a one-to-one or one-to-many data term linkage depending upon the input and output data concepts. Also, the linkage can either be direct or derived from the original data concepts. Based on the order in which the data concepts are defined and the rule-based transformations between input and output data concepts, RDF translator will generate the semantic translation code.

The Web Services module is implemented in Java and Apache Axis2 framework with Protégé plug-in for semantic interoperability. The proposed multi-agent based semantic translation framework focusses on associating various healthcare instance data models. Plenty of domain data models, which are otherwise unable to get linked, leverage RDF translation technique based on data concept mappings. Data dictionary and the mappings database maintain an inventory of several data models, meta classes, data concepts, default values and their mappings. STTL and SPARQL protocols help in RDF querying and RDF transformation as per the requirement. STTL engine that runs on RESTful web service caters to every STTL transformation request against the corresponding rule based RDF transformation.

STTL transformation accepts requests from any RDF data format and SPARQL engine queries on the local RDF triple store. RDF Translator scans through the input RDF data models and validates them against the derived output RDF data mapping to produce the output RDF data model. A web application user interface helps to bridge the domain experts and the framework consultants on the concept level mappings maintenance and their storage in the repository. This framework takes complete advantage of schema independent and W3C recognized RDF representation of healthcare data and attains semantic translation among diverse data models. Further research on this framework could focus on handling unstructured data models and how to convert them into RDF data representation to obtain the required output data model.

7.4   Conclusion

In the current decade, succumbing to COVID-19 pandemic disease, huge demand has raised upon high quality and upto-date healthcare information all over the internet, available for a wide spectrum of healthcare stakeholders. This chapter caters to such demand by analyzing semantic Web ontology and various multi-agent based semantic interoperability systems. High level understanding on Semantic Web Ontology, RDF, RDFS, STTL and SPARQL are given. Multi-Agent based semantic translation framework proposed in this chapter discusses about data dictionary and data mappings database maintenance modules which access RDF formatted data and invoke appropriate STTL and SPARQL query based services to semantically transform the source data to the required output data mapping. The resultant output data is again available in RDF format.

Detailed study on the existing multi-agent systems—AOIS, SCKE, MASE and MET4 is presented and the proposed framework that integrates the intelligent agents and semantic descriptions of the data source elements is discussed. Heterogeneous interoperability among the data sources is a common feature in healthcare information domain and this system is able to deal with it by means of structured data mappings and domain ontology based semantic Web services. This translation framework outperforms the existing systems by yielding precise and more accurate information for effective healthcare data analysis and decision to be made on the impacted patients' health risk levels.

References

1. Healthcare Information and Management Systems Society, What is interoperability? [Online; accessed 30-July-2020] Available at: https://www.himss.org/resources/interoperability-healthcare.

2. Cyganiak, R., Wood, D., Lanthaler, M., *RDF 1.1 Concepts and Abstract Syntax*, W3C, Available at https://www.w3.org/TR/2014/PR-rdf11-concepts-20140109/diff-20131105.html, 2014.

3. Follenfant, C., Corby, O., Gandon, F., Trastour, D., RDF Modelling and SPARQL Processing of SQL Abstract Syntax Trees, in: *Programming the Semantic Web, ISWC Workshop*, Boston, USA, 2012.

4. Bizer, C., Lee, R., Pietriga, E., Fresnel—A Browser Independent Presentation Vocabulary for RDF, in: *Second International Workshop on Interaction Design and the Semantic Web*, Galway, Ireland, 2005.

5. Lanace, P., The role Big Data Ontology and Semantic Search will play to improve healthcare, Available at https://idm.net.au/article/0010742-role-big-data-ontology-and-semantic-search-will-play-improve-healthcare, October 22, 2015.

6. Sauermann, L. and Cyganiak, R., *Cool URIs for the Semantic Web*, Available at https://www.w3.org/TR/cooluris/, December 03, 2008.

7. Jacob, E.K., Ontologies and the Semantic Web. *Bull. Assoc. Inform. Sci. Technol.*, 29, 19–22, 2003.

8. Burstein, M., Bussler, C., Zaremba, M., Finin, T., Huhns, M.N., Paolucci, M., Sheth, A.P., Williams, S., A semantic web services architecture. *IEEE Internet Comput.*, 9, 5, 72–81, 2005.

9. Athanasiadis, I.N., A review of agent-based systems applied in environmental informatics, in: *MODSIM 2005: International Congress on Modelling and Simulation, Modelling and Simulation Society of Australia and New Zealand*, Melbourne, Australia, 2005.

10. Sengupta, R. and Sieber, R., Geospatial agents, agents everywhere. *T. GIS*, 11, 4, 483–506, 2007.

11. Cortés, U., Vázquez Salceda, J., López Navidad, A., Caballero, F., UCTx: A multiagent approach to model a transplant coordination unit. *J. Appl. Intell.*, 20, 1, 59–70, 2004.

12. Koutkias, V., Chouvarda, I., Maglaveras, N., A multiagent system enhancing homecare health services for chronic disease management. *IEEE Trans. Inf. Technol. Biomed.*, 9, 4, 528–537, 2005.

13. Cervantes, L., Lee, Y.S., Yang, H., Ko, S., Lee, J., Agent-Based Intelligent Decision Support for the Home Healthcare Environment, in: *Advances in Hybrid Information Technology. ICHIT 2006. Lecture Notes in Computer Science*, vol. 4413, M.S. Szczukaet, *et al.*, (Eds.), Springer, Berlin, Heidelberg, https://doi.org/10.1007/978-3-540-77368-9_41, 2007.

14. Corchado, J.M., Bajo, J., Abraham, A., GerAmI: Improving healthcare delivery in geriatric residences. *IEEE Intell. Syst.*, 23, 19–25, 2008.

15. Cortes, U., Annicchiarico, R., Urdiales, C., Barrue, C., Martinez, A., Villar, A., Caltagirone, C., Agent Technology and eHealth, in: *Whitestein Series in Software Agent Technologies and Autonomic Computing*, Ch. Supported Human Autonomy for Recovery and Enhancement of Cognitive and Motor Abilities Using Agent Technologies, pp. 117–140, Birkhäuser Verlag, Basel, Switzerland, 2008.

16. Tentori, M., Favela, J., Rodriguez, M., Privacy aware autonomous agents for pervasive healthcare. *IEEE Intell. Syst.*, 21, 6, 55–62, 2006.

17. Poggi, A. and Tomaiuolo, M., A DHT-Based Multi-Agent System for Semantic Information Sharing. In: Lai, C., Semeraro, G. and Vargiu, E. (eds), *New Challenges in Distributed Information Filtering and Retrieval. Studies in Computational Intelligence*, Vol. 439, pp. 197–213, Springer, Berlin, Heidelberg, https://doi.org/10.1007/978-3-642-31546-6_12, 2003.

18. Bellifemine, F., Poggi, A., Rimassa, G., Developing multi agent systems with a FIPA compliant agent framework. *Softw. Pract. Exp.*, 31, 103–128, 2001.

19. Bellifemine, F., Caire, G., Poggi, A., Rimassa, G., JADE: A Software Framework for Developing Multi-Agent Applications. Lessons Learned. *Inf. Softw. Technol. J.*, 50, 10–21, 2008.

20. Cohen, B., Incentives build robustness in BitTorrent, in: *Proceedings of the First Workshop on Economics of Peer-to-Peer Systems*, Berkeley, CA, USA, 2003.

21. Southern Methodist University, JAWS software, Available at https://www.freedomscientific.com/products/software/jaws/, 2011.

22. Nutch software, Apache Foundation, Available at http://nutch.apache.org, 2011.

23. Miller, G.A., WordNet: A Lexical Database for English. *Commun. ACM*, 38, 11, 39–41, 1995.

24. Alkahtani, N.H., Almohsen, S., Alkahtani, N.M., Almalki, G.A., Meshref, S.S., Kurdi, H., A Semantic Multi-Agent system to Exchange Information between Hospitals. *Procedia Comput. Sci., Elsevier*, 109, 704–709, 2017.

25. Patil, S.M. and Jadhav, D.M., Semantic Search using Ontology and RDBMS for Cricket. *Int. J. Comput. Appl.*, 46, 14, 26–31, 2012.

26. Li, S. and Mackaness, W.A., A multi-agent-based semantic-driven system for decision support in epidemic management. *Health Inform. J.*, 21, 3, 195–208, 2014.

27. Wilk, S., Kezadri-Hamiaz, M., Rosu, D., Kuziemsky, C., Michalowski, W., Amyot, D., Carrier, M., Using Semantic Components to Represent Dynamics of an Interdisciplinary Healthcare Team in a Multi-Agent Decision Support System. *J. Med. Syst.*, 40, 2, 1–14, 2016.

28. Wilk, S., Astaraky, D., Michalowski, W., Amyot, D., Li, R., Kuziemsky, C., Andreev, P., MET4: Supporting Workflow Execution for Interdisciplinary Healthcare Teams. In: Fournier, F. and Mendling, J. (eds), *Business Process Management Workshops, Lecture Notes in Business Information Processing*, 202, 1–12, Springer, Cham, https://doi.org/10.1007/978-3-319-15895-2_4, 2014.

29. Gandon, F., Corby, O., Faron-Zucker, C., Semantic Web and Web of Data—Session 1, Available at: https://www.fun-mooc.fr/courses/inria/41002/Trimestre_1_2015/about, 2015.

30. Corby, O. and Faron-Zucker, C., STTL: A SPARQL-based Transformation Language for RDF. *11th International Conference on Web Information Systems and Technologies*, Lisbon, Portugal, 2015.

31. Date, C.J., *Relational Database: Selected Writings*, vol. 1, Addison-Wesley, University of Michigan, 1986.

32. Aydar, M. and Melton, A., Translation of Instance Data using RDF and Structured Mapping Definitions, in: *International Semantic Web Conference (Posters & Demos)*, 2015.

33. Corby, O., Faron-Zucker, C., Gandon, F., A generic RDF transformation software and its application to an online translation service for common languages of linked data, in: *International Semantic Web Conference*, Springer, Cham, pp. 150–165, 2015.

34. Martin, D. *et al.*, *OWL Web Ontology Language for Services (OWL-S)*, W3C Submission, Available at: http://www.w3.org/Submission/OWL-S/, 2004.

35. Akkiraju, R., Farell, J., Miller, J.A., Nagarajan, M., Sheth, A., Verma, K., *Web service semantics—WSDL-S*, W3C submission, Available at: http://www.w3.org/Submission/WSDL-S/, 2005.

8

Detection, Prediction & Intervention of Attention Deficiency in the Brain Using tDCS

Pallabjyoti Kakoti*, Rissnalin Syiemlieh and Eeshankur Saikia

Department of Applied Sciences, Gauhati University, Guwahati, India

Abstract

Anodal transcranial direct current stimulation (tDCS) has been generally recognized as contributing to neuronal excitability and hence increased attention and lower reaction times but cathodal tDCS leads to inhibition of the neurons and leads to Attention deficient and increased reaction times. Here we have used Multi Fractal Analysis (MFA) on the EEG data of subjects classified according to age and gender to investigate the detection of attention level, who went through separate EEG sessions for anod Blink (AB) experiment. It is found and reported for the first time that the increase in fractality of the EEG is clearly registered during the tDCS sessions which leads to enhancement of attention and correctness of the AB task which showed during the tDCS session for some subjects and in post-tDCS session for other subjects. Also, age-specific features were found according to the increase or decrease of fractality during post-cathodal tDCS sessions which may lead to not only better understanding and prediction of the attention deficiency in the brain, and thus it is evident from our study that tDCS can be used as an effective tool for prevention and cure of attention deficiency through incorporating the features of MFA into Machine Learning model.

Keywords: Brain, cognition, EEG, transcranial Direct Current Simulation (tDCS), Multi Fractal Analysis (MFA), cognitive enhancement

8.1 Introduction

Attention is the perceptual function that helps pick and interpret knowledge that is significant or fascinating—which underpins all of our everyday behavior. A lot of psychological and neurological conditions such as Attention Deficit Hyperactive Disorder (ADHD) and hemiagnosis are both rooted in attention disruptions. It is therefore not surprising that the cognitive enhancement strategies centered mainly on attention. It has been found in several experiments that when two targets have to be identified in a fast stream of non-target information, most people have a surprisingly enduring effect—an attention blink (AB)—in recognizing the second target [1–3]. For many years, a key problem in probing attention was how long an object/entity remains to be in attentional range. The AB experiment confirmed

---

Corresponding author: pallabk@gauhati.ac.in

Sachi Nandan Mohanty, G. Nalinipriya, Om Prakash Jena and Achyuth Sarkar (eds.) *Machine Learning for Healthcare Applications*, (121–136) © 2021 Scrivener Publishing LLC

that attention persists few hundred milliseconds, indicating that the period is of higher magnitude than previously thought of [4]. The AB is normally acquired using continuous stream of alphanumeric stimuli that are introduced sequentially to learn the time-consolidation of attention and memory, and provide researchers with a tool to look into the human consciousness.

Transcranial direct current stimulation (tDCS) is a minimally-intrusive and well tolerated form of mental activation that uses electrodes to deliver low-amplitude direct current into the brain and to modulate the degree of cortical excitability, and which has been probed for various neuropsychological, psychophysiological and motor activity changes [5].

There have been increasing evidence through various tDCS stimulation experiments that specific changes in psychological, physiological and motor function may result from inducing tDCS on targeted brain areas [6, 7]. In addition, some desirable features of tDCS, such as, being minimally-intrusive and possibly the best-tolerated, transient and moderate adverse effects, have resulted in a rise in clinical trials, especially for psychiatric disorders such as depression, persistent and acute pain, trauma recovery, enhancing attention, drug addiction, and other neurodegenerative conditions [8–12]. In addition, several studies have shown a substantial correlation between impaired cognitive memory and hypoperfusion with right Dorsolateral Prefrontal Cortex (DLPFC) hypometabolism in neurodegenerative diseases such as Alzheimer and dementia [13, 14]. It was shown that anodal tDCS stimulation is successful when applied to the right DLFPC during an error recognition test. However, when left DLPFC is targeted, there was no change in results [15]. Anodal stimulation is considered to enhance excitability, whereas the excitability of the activated brain region is expected to be decreased by cathodal stimulation [5]. Important cytoarchitectural variations between motor neurons and frontal cortices plays an active role in motor and cognitive function differential sensitivity to change based on current flow direction. The impact of tDCS can also depend on the status of the original neuronal activation. While anodal stimulation may lead to a cognitive improvement by increasing neuronal excitability, which by default does not reach the threshold, it may not be sufficient for cathodal stimulation to substantially stop the firing of the already stimulated neurons by taking part in the cognitive task [16]. Also, previous studies have confirmed that cathodal tDCS leads to suppression of brain seizures, migraines and stroke rehabilitation [17–19]. It has been proposed that anodal tDCS can contribute and assist when the subject is confident in the task given, but such assistance is not present when performing a new task which the subject has never attempted before [20]. But in these cases, cathodal tDCS can contribute and assist by lowering the ambient background interference and enhancing attention by acting as a neural filter that decreases noise [21]. The principle is same as 'lateral inhibition', a process that can minimize neuronal activity as a result of inducing a noise signal along with the relevant signal, sharpening the evoked action potentials of the EEG and the response profile enhancing the output signal. Therefore, we cannot assume tDCS as a simplistic neuromodulatory system in which anodal tDCS enhances perception to cause cognitive enablement, and cathodal tDCS induces the reverse impact via repression.

Such association motivated us to research the multiple impacts of anodal & cathodal tDCS simulation on different age groups and subject class, and to explore their effects & fundamental variations on the overall degree of brain concentration. We will try to understand the underlying neural substrates of the brain of the tDCS simulation through Multi-Fractal Analysis (MFA).

MFA is an important non-linear dynamical method for studying the magnitude of fragmentation (or abnormality) in biological, synthetic, and statistical structures in non-linear systems. Fractal systems are defined by their self-similarity, their scaling autonomy, and their fractal dimension, an exponent obtained from a power or scaling law which can be used to identify and forecast any undesired events in the process being examined. It has been used for analyzing various real-life scenarios such as Internet traffic, DNA base sequences, climate forecasting, neurobiological mechanisms of human creativity to name a few [22–24]. However, all the complicated brain tissue, convoluted neural channels and EEG data gracefully demonstrate the common language of fractal analysis but couldn't be classified into Euclidean and other conventional geometries. Neuroscience experiments have contributed to the theory of nonlinear self-affinity hierarchical neuronal activation patterns from EEG signals which are non-stationary in nature. A study utilized MFA for differentiating EEG signals from awakening and various sleep states and to show their possible utility to automatically identify different consciousness states [25]. Although most natural self-reflecting systems display scaling law patterns defined by a mono fractal exponent, but Mandelbrot [26] described a more complex version of self-reflecting systems in which the system's fractal existence is represented better with a sequence of exponents or "Multifractal" exponent.

Here we used MFA on the pre-processed EEG data [27] obtained from 22 participants selected for the present study from 49 participants who performed an Attentional blink (AB) task before, during and after receiving tDCS either on anode and cathode on the right parietal and frontal cortex on each visit. The sample was composed of male and female participants in their early 20s and late 20s. Here we are trying to see if the effect of the polarity of tDCS invokes changes in fractality in the EEG and its impact on the level of attention in the brain, so that we can create personalized tDCS simulation for different subjects by age and gender to increase the level of attention.

8.2   Materials & Methods

8.2.1   Subjects and Experimental Design

22 subjects were chosen from a study consisting of 10 females and 12 males with their age ranging from 20 to 28 with a mean age of 22.3 who performed an AB task before, during and after tDCS [Table 8.1] on right parietal and frontal cortex as this is responsible for language and thought processing [28]. In daily tasks, the cognitive limitations of the human brain are observed, as many or rapidly changing pieces of sensory input must be treated simultaneously or in rapid succession. It is also imperative that the task-relevant visual input is accessible explicitly at the cost of the non-relevant input which requires cognitive functioning of working memory and attention. One method to analyze conscious awareness limitations entails overloading the visual attention system by displaying multiple visual objects related to the task concurrently or quickly, and determining the possibility of actively transmitting accurate information due to existence and/or temporal proximity of task-relevant information, which can be done by implementing the AB task [29, 30].

tDCS was introduced at an amplitude of 1 mA per 20 m (with a 1-minute ramp-up time before and a 1-minute ramp-down time after). The subjects visited the lab twice and received either anodal or cathodal tDCS during each session. Out of the 22 subjects, 11

Table 8.1 Age & Gender of Subjects.

SUBJECT	AGE	GENDER	ANODAL/CATHODAL ON FIRST VISIT
SUB-01	20 (L)	FEMALE	ANODAL
SUB-02	19 (L)	FEMALE	CATHODAL
SUB-06	20 (L)	FEMALE	CATHODAL
SUB-08	21 (L)	FEMALE	ANODAL
SUB-09	28 (H)	FEMALE	CATHODAL
SUB-10	20 (L)	FEMALE	CATHODAL
SUB-11	21 (L)	FEMALE	ANODAL
SUB-15	–	MALE	ANODAL
SUB-18	–	MALE	CATHODAL
SUB-17	20 (L)	MALE	ANODAL
SUB-19	26 (H)	FEMALE	CATHODAL
SUB-20	20 (L)	MALE	ANODAL
SUB-21	–	MALE	CATHODAL
SUB-23	19 (L)	MALE	ANODAL
SUB-24	20 (L)	MALE	CATHODAL
SUB-31	19 (L)	MALE	ANODAL
SUB-33	–	MALE	ANODAL
SUB-37	26 (H)	FEMALE	ANODAL
SUB-41	–	MALE	CATHODAL
SUB-47	21 (L)	MALE	CATHODAL
SUB-48	20 (L)	MALE	ANODAL
SUB-49	27 (H)	FEMALE	CATHODAL

subjects received anodal simulation on their first visit and other subjects received cathodal simulation. The latex tDCS electrodes were applied to the scalp using an electrically conducive paste and, since they were under the EEG headcap, a few of the EEG headcaps were blocked by the electrodes. The tDCS assembly consisted of a 7 × 5 mm electrode centered on F3 (long side parallel to midline) and a 7 × 5 mm electrode centered on the right forehead (approximately Fp2). Anodal or cathodal tDCS is defined according to the electrode over F3 [Figure 8.1].

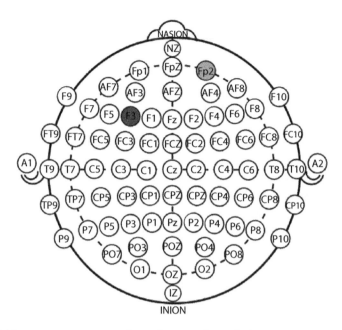

Figure 8.1 The tDCS montage was 7x5 mm electrodes centred over F3 (connector at posterior end) and Fp2 (connector at lateral end).

8.2.2   Data Preprocessing & Statistical Analysis

The EEG pre-processing was done using EEGLab in MATLAB. Spectral decomposition was done for all the channels and bad channels were removed by visual inspection of the spectra [Figure 8.2]. On the EEG data, a 1 Hz high-pass filter was applied to remove linear trends. AFz was chosen as reference electrode and channel locations were registered. The EEG timeseries was divided into 3 equal epochs of equal lengths for further analysis.

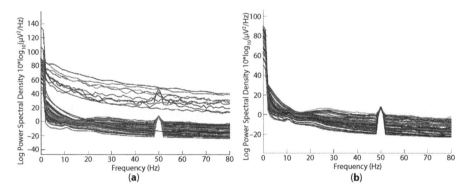

Figure 8.2 (a) Spectral Decomposition of EEG of Subject 8 which shows bad channels having greater Power Spectral Density. Bad Channels were identified and removed before further processing. 50 Hz spike due to interreference of AC signal is left unprocessed as its removal may lead to data-loss of the spectrum (b) Spectral Decomposition of EEG of Subject 8 after removal of bad channels.

8.2.3   Extracting Singularity Spectrum from EEG

Singularity spectrum is a continuous spectrum of exponents required to define the mono or multifractal dynamic system with a geometrical approach. By generating the output spectrum $f(\alpha)$ the range of points is quantified by a defined regularity exponent α known as the Hölder exponent [31], which is defined by:

$$\alpha = log\ \mu(box)\ /\ log\ \varepsilon$$

where $\mu(box)$ is the measure of the box, and ε is the dimension of the box. α values are similar to the respective fractal dimension of the dynamical system observed. Several points of the dynamical system can be characterized by similar magnitudes of α. We can count boxes having dimension ε for every α-value with its rough exponent of Hölder exponent equal to α and take the value as $N\varepsilon(\alpha)$, then Hausdorff dimension for α distribution is characterized as,

$$f_\varepsilon(\alpha) = -\frac{\log N_\varepsilon(\alpha)}{\log \varepsilon}$$

When $\varepsilon \to 0$, then $f_\varepsilon(\alpha)$ approaches the given threshold value $f(\alpha)$. Singularity Spectrum is the curve between the Legendre fractal dimensions $f_\varepsilon(\alpha)$ and the Hölder's exponent α, for which the width of the $\Delta\alpha_\varepsilon$ spectrum captures the form of the multi-fractal continuum of singularities and defines the distribution of probabilities and the Δf_ε dimension difference quantifies the self-similarity of the fractals [32]. The continuum converges in one-point source in case of monofractals, but transforms into a bell-shaped structure with downwards roots for a multifractal system. It is an excellent way of defining and evaluating the nonlinearity of undefined and irregular signals. The current study is based on the measurement in each point in the EEG time series of the regularity exponent of Hölder to calculate the singularity spectrum for each subject. The MFA has been done in FracLab package in MatLab for generating the Hölders exponents for the time-series and plotting the Legendre Spectrum [33].

Thus greater the value of $\Delta\alpha$, the likelihood of variability of the neuronal firings in the brain, since higher fractal dimension is a marker of richer geometry or texture, resulting in richer patterns suggesting uniformity at different neurological scales and therefore self-similarity is established in the EEG data considered. Although changes in the observed EEG signal can hardly be detected, the external stimuli will clearly show changes evoked by just a visual inspection of the $\Delta\alpha$.

8.3   Results & Discussion

The Hölder exponent α for all subjects was determined [Figure 8.3]. We categorized the subjects by age, gender and whether the subject was receiving anodal or cathodal tDCS during his first visit. In addition, to see the effects of tDCS on Attention Enhancement, in the AB experiment, we used the percentage of correct answers given

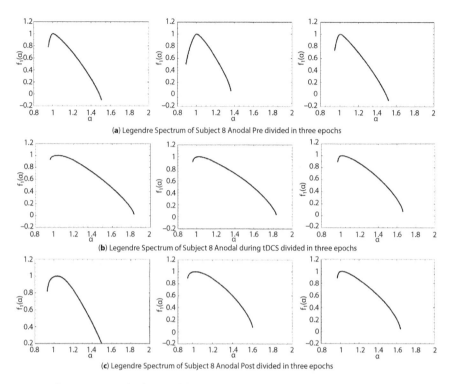

Figure 8.3 Legendre Spectrum of Subject 8 for Anodal Session.

by the subject during the first and second target questions [Table 8.2]. Firstly, it has been seen in nearly all the subjects $\Delta\alpha$ during the tDCS session is very significantly independent of the Anodal or Cathodal sessions [Figure 8.4]. The "Percentage of right responses" parameter also has similar Gaussian density distribution identical to $\Delta\alpha$ and can be used as a statistically acceptable replacement for it [Figure 8.5]. In addition, the increase was not the same and was different for each subject, suggesting that the effect of tDCS on the brain has temporal characteristics and that the necessary dose of tDCS can be measured over time by changing the $\Delta\alpha$. It was observed in the age-related comparison that the cathodal tDCS sessions can be used to mark differences between the subjects of high and low ages [Figure 8.6]. It was found that the high aged subjects in the pre-tDCS Cathodal session if $\Delta\alpha < 0.65$, then $\Delta\alpha$ and attention display no change in the post-tDCS session, which could be attributable to lower attenuation rates of the Default Mode Network (DMN) in the brain in some high aged subjects [34]. [Ref Subject: 19, 37].

In low-aged subjects, however, it has been observed that post-tDCS cathodal session leads to an increase in $\Delta\alpha$ and attention, even when $\Delta\alpha < 0.65$ [Ref Subject: 11].

If $\Delta\alpha$ decreases from pre to tDCS during the anodal session, the accuracy increases in male subjects, decreases in female subjects and increases slightly in both subjects during the cathodal session. [Ref Sub: 1, 17, 33].

In male subjects it was found that in the case of anodal sessions the tDCS sessions did increase in the $\Delta\alpha$ value and level of attention than their respective counterparts, whereas

Table 8.2 Percentage of Correct Answers in AB task and α of subjects according to Anodal & Cathodal Sessions.

SUB	SESSION	%	Δα	SUB	SESSION	%	Δα
1	ANODAL-PRE	59.12	0.65	20	ANODAL-PRE	66.83	0.65
1	ANODAL-DCS	57.02	0.63	20	ANODAL-DCS	68.62	0.97
1	ANODAL-POST	53.85	0.63	20	ANODAL-POST	72.66	0.84
1	CATHODAL-PRE	57.59	0.68	20	CATHODAL-PRE	60.56	0.73
1	CATHODAL-DCS	57.89	0.62	20	CATHODAL-DCS	57.42	0.75
1	CATHODAL-POST	56.43	0.56	20	CATHODAL-POST	63.67	0.73
2	ANODAL-PRE	85.60	0.64	21	ANODAL-PRE	50.73	0.64
2	ANODAL-DCS	84.34	0.69	21	ANODAL-DCS	50.41	0.87
2	ANODAL-POST	82.71	0.65	21	ANODAL-POST	51.49	0.73
2	CATHODAL-PRE	80.29	0.67	21	CATHODAL-PRE	60.05	0.67
2	CATHODAL-DCS	83.30	1.06	21	CATHODAL-DCS	53.29	0.77
2	CATHODAL-POST	81.37	0.71	21	CATHODAL-POST	58.71	0.82
6	ANODAL-PRE	81.33	0.59	23	ANODAL-PRE	58.41	0.67
6	ANODAL-DCS	75.71	0.64	23	ANODAL-DCS	56.11	0.74
6	ANODAL-POST	76.68	0.59	23	ANODAL-POST	60.50	0.68
6	CATHODAL-PRE	72.41	0.65	23	CATHODAL-PRE	57.21	0.71
6	CATHODAL-DCS	74.09	0.79	23	CATHODAL-DCS	58.11	0.82
6	CATHODAL-POST	75.22	0.76	23	CATHODAL-POST	58.62	0.72
8	ANODAL-PRE	68.55	0.62	24	ANODAL-PRE	63.37	0.67
8	ANODAL-DCS	62.37	0.9	24	ANODAL-DCS	64.59	0.74
8	ANODAL-POST	65.22	0.71	24	ANODAL-POST	63.75	0.59
8	CATHODAL-PRE	65.58	0.68	24	CATHODAL-PRE	52.71	0.61
8	CATHODAL-DCS	63.01	0.92	24	CATHODAL-DCS	62.64	0.73
8	CATHODAL-POST	63.49	0.79	24	CATHODAL-POST	63.47	0.63
9	ANODAL-PRE	67.73	0.51	31	ANODAL-PRE	66.04	0.71
9	ANODAL-DCS	64.78	0.62	31	ANODAL-DCS	60.43	0.84
9	ANODAL-POST	62.01	0.59	31	ANODAL-POST	61.75	0.72

(Continued)

Table 8.2 Percentage of Correct Answers in AB task and α of subjects according to Anodal & Cathodal Sessions. (*Continued*)

SUB	SESSION	%	Δα	SUB	SESSION	%	Δα
9	CATHODAL-PRE	62.82	0.69	33	ANODAL-PRE	80.34	0.68
9	CATHODAL-DCS	63.15	0.93	33	ANODAL-DCS	84.70	0.68
9	CATHODAL-POST	64.96	0.95	33	ANODAL-POST	84.75	0.7
10	ANODAL-PRE	67.16	0.76	33	CATHODAL-PRE	84.36	0.69
10	ANODAL-DCS	60.12	0.85	33	CATHODAL-DCS	81.82	0.81
10	ANODAL-POST	59.40	0.84	33	CATHODAL-POST	84.47	0.73
10	CATHODAL-PRE	61.95	0.74	37	ANODAL-PRE	66.93	0.57
10	CATHODAL-DCS	58.97	0.89	37	ANODAL-DCS	70.27	0.68
10	CATHODAL-POST	63.14	0.75	37	ANODAL-POST	64.67	0.52
11	ANODAL-PRE	58.95	0.59	37	CATHODAL-PRE	66.15	0.6
11	ANODAL-DCS	58.51	0.69	37	CATHODAL-DCS	59.20	0.69
11	ANODAL-POST	53.85	0.77	37	CATHODAL-POST	55.39	0.6
11	CATHODAL-PRE	65.44	0.59	41	ANODAL-PRE	42.51	0.62
11	CATHODAL-DCS	61.78	0.73	41	ANODAL-DCS	41.95	0.7
11	CATHODAL-POST	58.44	0.72	41	ANODAL-POST	48.20	0.71
15	ANODAL-PRE	53.13	0.69	41	CATHODAL-PRE	42.66	0.59
15	ANODAL-DCS	58.44	0.75	41	CATHODAL-DCS	42.39	0.78
15	ANODAL-POST	54.28	0.79	41	CATHODAL-POST	44.77	0.65
15	CATHODAL-PRE	54.96	0.66	47	ANODAL-PRE	43.20	0.48
15	CATHODAL-DCS	56.06	0.87	47	ANODAL-DCS	39.91	0.62
15	CATHODAL-POST	56.27	0.79	47	ANODAL-POST	37.75	0.55
17	ANODAL-PRE	75.00	0.40	47	CATHODAL-PRE	55.11	0.58
17	ANODAL-DCS	83.24	0.37	47	CATHODAL-DCS	58.93	0.74
17	ANODAL-POST	83.45	0.39	47	CATHODAL-POST	55.61	0.55
17	CATHODAL-PRE	77.54	0.65	48	ANODAL-PRE	59.01	0.62
17	CATHODAL-DCS	81.15	0.92	48	ANODAL-DCS	55.80	0.78
17	CATHODAL-POST	77.30	0.66	48	ANODAL-POST	57.22	0.68

(*Continued*)

Table 8.2 Percentage of Correct Answers in AB task and α of subjects according to Anodal & Cathodal Sessions. (*Continued*)

SUB	SESSION	%	Δα	SUB	SESSION	%	Δα
18	ANODAL-PRE	61.22	0.72	48	CATHODAL-PRE	60.72	0.65
18	ANODAL-DCS	60.34	0.88	48	CATHODAL-DCS	53.61	0.73
18	ANODAL-POST	61.61	0.69	48	CATHODAL-POST	54.99	0.74
18	CATHODAL-PRE	63.67	0.76	49	ANODAL-PRE	70.80	0.73
18	CATHODAL-DCS	64.71	0.84	49	ANODAL-DCS	65.33	0.74
18	CATHODAL-POST	65.81	0.67	49	ANODAL-POST	65.92	0.7
19	ANODAL-PRE	71.34	0.66	49	CATHODAL-PRE	59.54	0.68
19	ANODAL-DCS	69.06	0.75	49	CATHODAL-DCS	58.23	0.86
19	ANODAL-POST	64.12	0.76	49	CATHODAL-POST	59.60	0.82
19	CATHODAL-PRE	65.16	0.56				
19	CATHODAL-DCS	66.91	1.3				
19	CATHODAL-POST	64.87	0.52				

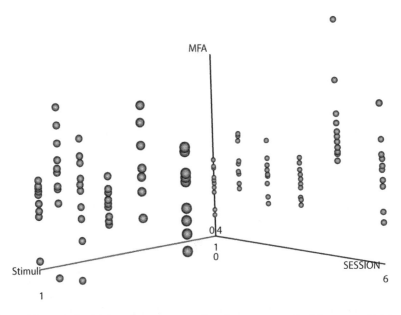

Figure 8.4 'Stimuli' is coded as '0' for subjects given at their first visit to Cathodal tDCS and '1' for Anodal tDCS, while 'SESSION' is coded as 1 to 6 for Anodal-Pre, Anodal-DCS, Anodal-Post, Cathodal-Pre, Cathodal-DCS, Cathodal-Post, respectively. During the tDCS process, attention of the subjects is shown to be substantially higher for both the Anodal and Cathodal Sessions, independent of Cathodal or Anodal intervention during their first visit.

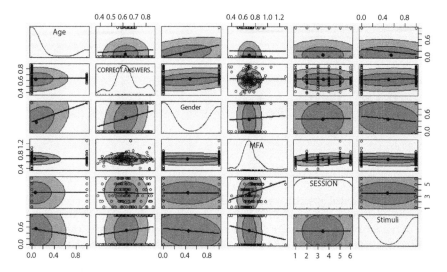

Figure 8.5 Relationships between pair of variables, in the form of a 6 × 6 matrix for 6 variables, highlighting individual density distribution along the diagonal. It confirms that "MFA" may be taken as a statistically permissible substitute for "Correct Answer", due to its similarity of Gaussian density distribution. Moreover, the spread of the data points, representing individual subjects, about the fitted line is also minimal for each pair.

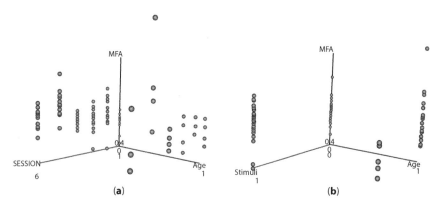

Figure 8.6 (a) While "SESSION" is coded from 1 to 6 for Anodal-Pre, Anodal-DCS, Anodal-Post, Cathodal-Pre, Cathodal-DCS, Cathodal-Post respectively, "Age" is coded in such a way that '0' denotes low and '1' denotes high age group. As it can be seen, the Cathodal Session in case of elderly subjects is significantly different from anodal, which may be used as a distinguishing parameter while classifying the subjects in different age groups using MFA. (b) "Stimuli" is coded as '0' for subjects who were given Cathodal tDCS and '1' for Anodal tDCS on their first visit. As it can be seen, while MFA increases in case of Cathodal intervention for the younger subjects, it decreases for the elderly subjects. This may be used as a confirmatory test to classify the subjects in different age groups.

in the case of cathodal sessions the $\Delta\alpha$ values and level of attention increased during the tDCS session and yet did not retain the values during the post-tDCS session [Figure 8.7]. This suggests that male subjects are less susceptible to tDCS simulation, resulting in faster attenuation of attention enhancement that can be controlled by changing the tDCS simulation's amplitude and time period.

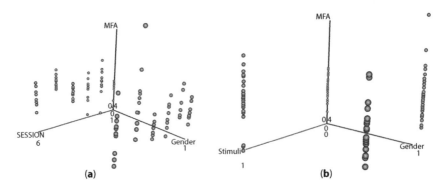

Figure 8.7 (a) "Gender" is coded in such a way that '0' denotes a Male and '1' denotes a Female subject. As it can be seen, the rate of attention enhancement from Pre to Post through the DCS phase during the Cathodal Session in case of Female subjects and Anodal Session in case of Male subjects is marginally higher than their respective counterpart sessions; and this may be used as a distinguishing parameter while classifying the subjects in different gender groups using MFA. (b) "Stimuli" is coded as '0' for subjects who were given Cathodal tDCS and '1' for Anodal tDCS on their first visit. It can be seen that while MFA increases in case of Cathodal intervention in first visit for the Female subjects, it decreases for the Male subjects. This may be used as a confirmatory test to classify the subjects in different gender groups.

This also shows that cathodal tDCS works differently than anodal tDCS as they are asymmetric and cathodal-inhibitory effects are effective in the muscle and sensory domains but questionable while examining cognitive functions [35], whereas anodal tDCS works on cortical excitability which in turns leads to the stability of the mental-state, but in case of attention enhancement, its effects are not directly seen in our study. It also emerged during the post-cathodal experiment that the female brain is more sensitive to tDCS simulation compared to male counterparts and helps with the overall increase in concentration during the AB experiment. Studies have shown that men and women tend to have different ways to store memories, emotions, remember words, resolve problems and make choices. Since the brain regulates perception and actions, these gender-related functional differences can be correlated with the gender-specific configuration of the brain since while women are believed to have higher percentage of gray matter, men are found to possess a higher percentage of white matter and cerebrospinal fluid than their respective gender counterparts [36].

8.4   Conclusion

In addition to challenging the existing understanding of cathodal tDCS as a tool leading to neuron inhibition, it has been found from the present study on 22 subjects that the tDCS effect is clearly reported in the increment in EEG fractality which directly correlates with the change in the level of attention in the case of post-cathodal tDCS but not in the case of post-anodal tDCS. Retention of tDCS simulation in post-anodal and cathodal sessions is specific for each subject, but classification into age and gender revealed some common features, such as male subjects showing attention-improvement during cathodal sessions but attention-inhibition during anodal sessions, which challenges the known fact that anodal tDCS leads to cortical excitability but does not automatically contribute to increased concentration which may be an significant finding in connection with potential cognitive applications. In addition, it has been found that high age subjects who do not reach the α threshold, the tDCS simulation does not result in any increase in α and attention due to the high tolerance of the DMN network which reduces the positive impact of tDCS. This can be addressed by using higher tDCS simulation amplitude and time-period that needs to be further tested by integrating the functionality into a machine-learning model. This would certainly find application in predicting age-related neuro as well as attention degeneration.

Compliance with Ethical Standards
All procedures performed in the study involved human participants and all procedures has been carried out in accordance with The Code of Ethics of the World Medical Association (Declaration of Helsinki) for experiments involving humans.

Informed Consent
Informed consent was obtained from all individual participants included in the study.

Acknowledgement

We are thankful to Leon C. Reteig, Lionel A. Newman, K. Richard Ridderinkhof, Heleen A. Slagter for sharing the data. PK & RS express gratitude to the Ministry of Human Resource Developement (MHRD), Govt. of India, for a fellowship under the World Bank funded project TEQIP-III.

Credit Authorship Contribution Statement
Pallabjyoti Kakoti: Methodology, Software, Formal Analysis, Investigation, Writing—Original Draft, Visualization. Rissnalin Syiemlieh: Software, Formal Analysis, Visualization. Eeshankur Saikia: Conceptualization, Validation, Resources, Writing—Review & Editing, Supervision, Project Administration, Funding acquisition.

References

1. Broadbent, D.E. and Broadbent, M.H., From detection to identification: Response to multiple targets in rapid serial visual presentation. *Percept. Psychophys.*, 42, 2, 105–113, https://doi.org/10.3758/bf03210498, 1987.
2. Raymond, J.E., Shapiro, K.L., Arnell, K.M., Temporary suppression of visual processing in an RSVP task: an attentional blink?, *J. Exp. Psychol. Hum. Percept. Perform.*, 18, 3, 849–860, https://doi.org/10.1037//0096-1523.18.3.849, 1992.
3. Weichselgartner, E. and Sperling, G., Dynamics of automatic and controlled visual attention. *Science* (New York, N.Y.), 238, 4828, 778–780, https://doi.org/10.1126/science.3672124, 1987.
4. Duncan, J., Ward, R., Shapiro, K., Direct measurement of attentional dwell time in human vision. *Nature*, 369, 6478, 313–315, https://doi.org/10.1038/369313a0, 1994.

5. Nitsche, M.A. and Paulus, W., Excitability changes induced in the human motor cortex by weak transcranial direct current stimulation. *J. Physiol.*, 527 Pt 3, Pt 3, 633–639, https://doi.org/10.1111/j.1469-7793.2000.t01-1-00633.x, 2000.

6. Fregni, F., Boggio, P.S., Nitsche, M., Bermpohl, F., Antal, A., Feredoes, E., Marcolin, M.A., Rigonatti, S.P., Silva, M.T., Paulus, W., Pascual-Leone, A., Anodal transcranial direct current stimulation of prefrontal cortex enhances working memory. *Exp. Brain Res.*, 166, 1, 23–30, https://doi.org/10.1007/s00221-005-2334-6, 2005.

7. Boggio, P.S., Alonso-Alonso, M., Mansur, C.G., Rigonatti, S.P., Schlaug, G., Pascual-Leone, A., Fregni, F., Hand function improvement with low-frequency repetitive transcranial magnetic stimulation of the unaffected hemisphere in a severe case of stroke. *Am. J. Phys. Med. Rehabil.*, 85, 11, 927–930, https://doi.org/10.1097/01.phm.0000242635.88129.38, 2006.

8. Iyer, M.B., Mattu, U., Grafman, J., Lomarev, M., Sato, S., Wassermann, E.M., Safety and cognitive effect of frontal DC brain polarization in healthy individuals. *Neurology*, 64, 5, 872–875, https://doi.org/10.1212/01.WNL.0000152986.07469.E9, 2005.

9. George, M.S. and Aston-Jones, G., Noninvasive techniques for probing neurocircuitry and treating illness: Vagus nerve stimulation (VNS), transcranial magnetic stimulation (TMS) and transcranial direct current stimulation (tDCS). *Neuropsychopharmacology: Official Publication of the American College of Neuropsychopharmacology*, 35, 1, 301–316, https://doi.org/10.1038/npp.2009.87, 2010.

10. Fregni, F. and Pascual-Leone, A., Technology insight: Noninvasive brain stimulation in neurology-perspectives on the therapeutic potential of rTMS and tDCS. *Nat. Clin. Pract. Neurol.*, 3, 7, 383–393, https://doi.org/10.1038/ncpneuro0530, 2007.

11. Nitsche, M.A., Boggio, P.S., Fregni, F., Pascual-Leone, A., Treatment of depression with transcranial direct current stimulation (tDCS): A review. *Exp. Neurol.*, 219, 1, 14–19, https://doi.org/10.1016/j.expneurol.2009.03.038, 2009.

12. Reteig, L.C., Talsma, L.J., Schouwenburg, M.R., Slagter, H.A., Transcranial Electrical Stimulation as a Tool to Enhance Attention. *J. Cognit. Enhancement*, 1, 1, 10–25, doi: 10.1007/s41465-017-0010-y, 2017.

13. Starkstein, S.E., Jorge, R., Mizrahi, R., The prevalence, clinical correlates and treatment of apathy in Alzheimer's disease. *Eur. J. Psychiatry*, 20, 2, 96–106, 2006.

14. Mendez, M.F., Anderson, E., Shapira, J.S., An investigation of moral judgement in fronto-temporal dementia. *Cogn. Behav. Neurol.: Official Journal of the Society for Behavioral and Cognitive Neurology*, 18, 4, 193–197, https://doi.org/10.1097/01.wnn.0000191292.17964.bb, 2005.

15. Harty, S., Robertson, I.H., Miniussi, C., Sheehy, O.C., Devine, C.A., McCreery, S., O'Connell, R.G., Transcranial direct current stimulation over right dorsolateral prefrontal cortex enhances error awareness in older age. *J. Neurosci.: The Official Journal of the Society for Neuroscience*, 34, 10, 3646–3652, https://doi.org/10.1523/JNEUROSCI.5308-13.2014, 2014.

16. Miniussi, C., Harris, J.A., Ruzzoli, M., Modelling non-invasive brain stimulation in cognitive neuroscience. *Neurosci. Biobehav. Rev.*, 37, 8, 1702–1712, https://doi.org/10.1016/j.neubiorev.2013.06.014, 2013.

17. Yook, S.W., Park, S.H., Seo, J.H., Kim, S.J., Ko, M.H., Suppression of seizure by cathodal transcranial direct current stimulation in an epileptic patient—A case report. *Ann. Rehabil. Med.*, 35, 4, 579–582, https://doi.org/10.5535/arm.2011.35.4.579, 2011.

18. Antal, A., Kriener, N., Lang, N., Boros, K., Paulus, W., Cathodal transcranial direct current stimulation of the visual cortex in the prophylactic treatment of migraine. *Cephalalgia: An International Journal of Headache*, 31, 7, 820–828, https://doi.org/10.1177/0333102411399349, 2011.

19. Khedr, E.M., Shawky, O.A., El-Hammady, D.H., Rothwell, J.C., Darwish, E.S., Mostafa, O.M., Tohamy, A.M., Effect of anodal versus cathodal transcranial direct current stimulation on

stroke rehabilitation: A pilot randomized controlled trial. *Neurorehabil. Neural Repair*, 27, 7, 592–601, https://doi.org/10.1177/1545968313484808, 2013.

20. Dockery, C.A., Hueckel-Weng, R., Birbaumer, N., Plewnia, C., Enhancement of planning ability by transcranial direct current stimulation. *J. Neurosci.: The Official Journal of the Society for Neuroscience*, 29, 22, 7271–7277, https://doi.org/10.1523/JNEUROSCI.0065-09.2009, 2009.

21. Antal, A., Nitsche, M.A., Kincses, T.Z., Kruse, W., Hoffmann, K.P., Paulus, W., Facilitation of visuo-motor learning by transcranial direct current stimulation of the motor and extrastriate visual areas in humans. *Eur. J. Neurosci.*, 19, 10, 2888–2892, https://doi.org/10.1111/j.1460-9568.2004.03367.x, 2004.

22. Likens, A.D., Amazeen, P.G., Stevens, R., Galloway, T., Gorman, J.C., Neural signatures of team coordination are revealed by multifractal analysis. *Social Neurosci.*, 9, 3, 219–234, 2014.

23. Grech, D. and Pamuła, G., Multifractality of Nonlinear Transformations with Application in Finances. *Acta Phys. Pol. A*, 123, 3, 529–537, 2013.

24. Gan, T.Y., Gobena, A.K., Wang, Q., Precipitation of southwestern Canada: Wavelet, scaling, multifractal analysis, and teleconnection to climate anomalies. *J. Geophys. Res.: Atmos.*, 112, D10, 2007.

25. Zorick, T. and Mandelkern, M.A., Multifractal detrended fluctuation analysis of human EEG: Preliminary investigation and comparison with the wavelet transform modulus maxima technique. *PLoS One*, 8, 7, e68360, https://doi.org/10.1371/journal.pone.0068360, 2013.

26. Mandelbrot, B.B., Iterated random multiplications and invariance under randomly weighted averaging, in: *Multifractals and 1/ Noise*, Springer, New York, NY, https://doi.org/10.1007/978-1-4612-2150-0_16, 1999.

27. Reteig, L.C., Newman, L.A., Ridderinkhof, K.R., Slagter, H.A., *EEG study of the attentional blink; before, during, and after transcranial Direct Current Stimulation (tDCS)*, https://doi.org/10.18112/openneuro.ds001810.v1.1.0, 2019b.

28. Monti, M.M., Parsons, L.M., Osherson, D.N., The boundaries of language and thought in deductive inference. *Proc. Natl. Acad. Sci.*, 106, 30, 12554–12559, 2009.

29. Dux, P.E. and Marois, R., The attentional blink: A review of data and theory. *Atten. Percept. Psychophys.*, 71, 8, 1683–1700, https://doi.org/10.3758/APP.71.8.1683, 2009.

30. Martens, S. and Wyble, B., The attentional blink: Past, present, and future of a blind spot in perceptual awareness. *Neurosci. Biobehav. Rev.*, 34, 6, 947–957, https://doi.org/10.1016/j.neubiorev.2009.12.005, 2010.

31. McCauley, J.L. and McCauley, J.L., Introduction to multifractals, in: *Chaos, Dynamics, and Fractals*, pp. 186–211, Springer Press, New York, NY, 1993.

32. Saha, R.K., Debanath, M.K., Saikia, E., Multifractal analysis of ZnO nanoparticles. *Mater. Sci. Eng.: C*, 106, 110177, 2020.

33. Véhel, J.L. and Legrand, P., Signal And Image Processing With Fraclab, in: *Thinking in Patterns*, https://doi.org/10.1142/9789812702746_0032, 2004.

34. Broyd, S.J., Demanuele, C., Debener, S., Helps, S.K., James, C.J., Sonuga-Barke, E.J., Default mode brain dysfunction in mental disorders: A systematic review. *Neurosci. Biobehav. Rev.*, 33, 279–296, https://doi.org/10.1016/j.neubiorev.2008.09.002, 2009.

35. Jacobson, L., Koslowsky, M., Lavidor, M., tDCS polarity effects in motor and cognitive domains: a meta-analytical review. *Exp. Brain Res.*, 216, 1, 1–10, https://doi.org/10.1007/s00221-011-2891-9, 2012.

36. Gur, R.C., Turetsky, B.I., Matsui, M., Yan, M., Bilker, W., Hughett, P., Gur, R.E., Sex differences in brain gray and white matter in healthy young adults: Correlations with cognitive performance. *J. Neurosci.: The Official Journal of the Society for Neuroscience*, 19, 10, 4065–4072, https://doi.org/10.1523/JNEUROSCI.19-10-04065.1999, 1999.

Detection of Onset and Progression of Osteoporosis Using Machine Learning

Shilpi Ruchi Kerketta* and Debalina Ghosh

School of Electrical Sciences, Indian Institute of Technology, Bhubaneshwar, India

Abstract

Osteoporosis, an immedicable and progressive decline of bone strength caused by reduction in bone mineral density, is widely prevalent among post-menopausal women and aging population. A timely and precise diagnosis of osteoporosis before a major breakage occurs is a challenging task. The prevalent techniques used for diagnosis of osteoporosis such as dual-energy X-ray and quantitative computed tomography, utilize ionizing signals and are time-consuming, expensive and non-portable. In recent times, biomedical estimation through microwave techniques aided by machine learning algorithms has produced some interesting outcomes. This article demonstrates the successful incorporation of microwave measurements along with machine learning algorithms to identify the various stages of onset and progression of osteoporosis. With the help of machine learning, it is possible to calculate the degree of bone mineral loss which can map the progression of osteoporosis. This will greatly assist the medical fraternity in treating the condition. The purpose of this article is to make a well structured and accurate machine learning technique for the early diagnosis of osteoporosis.

Keywords: Osteoporosis, machine learning (ML) algorithm, accuracy, classifier, microwave setup, KNN classifier, decision tree classifier, random forest classifier

9.1 Introduction

Osteoporosis is explicated as a relentless, elemental, skeletal ailment designated by low bone density and deterioration of micro-architectural of bone tissue with a subsequent elevation in bone fragility. Various dissertations have exhibited that the onset in the loss in the bone mass in both men and women commences from the age of 30 to 40. Meanwhile, type 1 or postmenopausal osteoporosis conventionally transpires in postmenopausal women, it has been predicted that within a year menopause is accompanied by an instantaneous decrement in bone mass density. This elevated rate of loss in bone density attains an equilibrium approximately after the 10 years of the menopause and then combines into a progressive age-related bone frangibility in both men and women which is termed as type 2 osteoporosis [1, 2].

**Corresponding author*: srk10@iitbbs.ac.in

Sachi Nandan Mohanty, G. Nalinipriya, Om Prakash Jena and Achyuth Sarkar (eds.) *Machine Learning for Healthcare Applications*, (137–150) © 2021 Scrivener Publishing LLC

India has 1.3 billion people and is considered the 2nd most populated nation in the world with nearly 10% of the people who are above the age of 50 [3]. Through a source of 2013, it has been estimated that in India 50 million people are either osteoporotic or have osteopenia. Due to a lack of nutrition, it occurs at a comparatively younger age. Further, the probability of occurrence of vertebral and hip fracture is 30% higher in older men as compared to women of a similar age [4, 5]. Here male osteoporosis is ignored and hence is misdiagnosed, untreated and is discovered only after a major breakage.

9.1.1   Measurement Techniques of BMD

The "gold standard" methodology for the quantization of the bone mineral density has been established through Dual-energy X-ray absorptiometry (DEXA) but has a major drawback of ionization. However, the high value, non-availability, and non-portability make it inaccessible to the majority Indian population, resulting in a few population-based osteoporotic research [6, 7]. Another prominent technique quantitative computed tomography (QCT) can differentiate between the cortical and trabecular bone through the geometrical and densitometry components providing a better sensitivity than DEXA. But on the other hand, it has a higher exposure than DEXA, is costly, non-portable, and not inapplicable to an immobile patient due to its prolonged examination duration. Meanwhile calcaneal quantitative ultrasound (QUS) is non-ionizing, cost-effective, compact size, easily portable, and can be operated by a layman. However, it cannot penetrate through the bone and lacks a screening threshold for quantification of bone quality [8, 9].

So microwave technique is found to be a convenient alternative to the standard DEXA and QCT methodology for bone quality assessment. Currently, electromagnetic techniques have acquired a substantial momentum in the healthcare applications as it can penetrate through various tissues, is non-ionizing, is cost-effective and has efficient computation methods. An extensive study by Gabriel recorded the different dielectric properties of bone, fat, muscles and other tissues [10]. Although few studies have been communicated towards the microwave-based bone analysis, detailed work on quantification and prediction is preferred [11, 12]. In one of the cases, a 3D microwave imaging setup was proposed to identify the fractured bone [13]. Another study was monitoring the healing process of broken bones [14]. But none of the microwave-based analyzers could classify the progression in osteoporosis.

9.1.2   Machine Learning Algorithms in Healthcare

In the past two decades, the medical experts are being greatly assisted by the computer-aided diagnosis, with the help of machine learning algorithms applied to the diagnosed samples. For making a good performance hypothesis, a substantial amount of diagnosed samples are recommended. Although a large number of samples could be collected through a regular health checkup, it is impossible for the health experts to make a diagnostic study for every acquired sample. If the diagnostic could be conducted immediately then the work of medical professionals could be made a lot easier [15, 16]. With the widespread of unhealthy habits among the youth, there is a huge spike in heart related disease and heart stroke at a young age. Through the assistance of various recorded data, factors such as age, sex, blood pressure, heart rate, cholesterol level, etc. and applying the ML algorithms helps the medical personals to predict the early heart-related diseases. Also, the disease like diabetic retinopathy, which can cause blindness is caused due to a high level of blood sugar. Implementation of ML algorithms on the substantial amount of retinal images enhance the early prediction of this eye disease. Similarly, tumors and breast cancer can be anticipated earlier by applying the ML through the imaging or on the various attributes of the tumor datasets. Further ML is also implemented to the thyroid ultrasound images or the thyroid attributes to detect thyroid-related diseases [17].

9.1.3   Organization of Chapter

In this article, a machine learning-based diagnosis method is proposed for the identification of progression of bone mineral density. In Section 9.2 the frequency analysis of microwave signals through biological tissue is presented. Using a pair of stubbed monopole antennas the changes in attenuation levels are recorded with bones of different masses in the frequency domain. As all humans have a differing wrist sizes, the transfer characteristics is also recorded by varying the human wrist tissue dimensions. The variation in the attenuation characteristics with each type of bone is recorded while varying each tissue individually and a large dataset is created with the recorded data. Section 9.3 discusses the ML algorithms, the implementation of ML algorithms to the assembled data, and the prediction of the solution. The ML predictive models such as KNN, Decision Tree, and Random Forest are utilized for the detection of onset and progression of osteoporosis from the data collected using microwave analysis. Finally, Section 9.4 summarizes the work and discusses the future aspects of this research.

9.2   Microwave Characterization of Human Osseous Tissue

For developing a system in healthcare utilizing microwave frequency sensing of the body, it is essential to understand the propagation of electromagnetic waves through the biological tissues. It is worth mentioning that the biological tissues are distinguished as highly permeable and conductive thus significantly attenuating the electromagnetic signal. This high permittivity and conductivity of the tissue causes the electromagnetic signal to severely degrade while propagating through the individual tissue. Meanwhile, the bone tissue is considered as an extremely anisotropic and inhomogeneous characteristic, as the bones are constituted of the bone minerals embedded with the soft tissues. Moreover, characteristics of the bone tissue change with the change in bone mineral density. The electromagnetic signal propagating through the bone will be reflected, refracted, and attenuated. The in-vitro permittivity and conductivity of an osteoporotic patient were reported by Amin *et al.* as demonstrated in Table 9.1 [18]. This estimation of relative permittivity and conductivity of the osteoporotic bone was incorporated in the simulation analysis of human wrist anatomy assisted by CST Microwave Studio. Here we have considered 6 levels of bone deterioration stage, first is the healthy bone, then osteopenia bone, the 4 different stages of osteoporotic bone, with each stage the bone mineral density decreases. This structure includes the bone tissue attached with the skin, muscle, and fat tissue as illustrated in Figure 9.1 [19]. Here the dielectric feature of the healthy bone, muscle, fat, and skin were considered from the inbuilt bio-tissue characteristic in

Table 9.1 Electrical properties of human tissue.

	Tissue	Relative Permitivity (E_r)	Loss Tangent	Conductivity (S/m)	Thickness/ Radius (mm)
Bone type	**Healthy**	9.4543	0.38487	1.2772	15
	Osteopenia	14	0.204	1	15
	Osteoporotic 1	18	0.2374	1.5	15
	Osteoporotic 2	23	0.2488	2	15
	Osteoporotic 3	28	0.275129	2.7	15
	Osteoporotic 4	32	0.30315	3.4	15
Muscle		47.801	0.33267	5.5818	4
Fat		4.9087	0.18965	0.32677	6
Skin		34.683	0.3424	4.1684	2

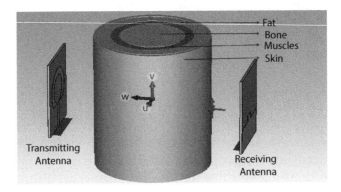

Figure 9.1 Human wrist characterization through the microwave setup.

CST Microwave Studio. All the tissue dielectric characteristics are analyzed at 6.3 GHz as tabulated in Table 9.1 [10, 20].

In this section a frequency domain study is conducted on the standard tissue size of the human wrist and again observe the changes in attenuation levels with different human wrist diameter by vtarying each tissue individually. A sample dataset of different level of attenuations are created through this human wrist variation.

9.2.1 Frequency-Domain Analysis of Human Wrist Sample

The microwave properties through the distinct biological tissues can be analyzed utilizing a pair of transmitting and receiving antennas. For this current objective, initially, a wideband stubbed monopole antenna [21] is used as a transmitter and the same type of antenna is used as a receiver to record the changes in attenuation levels through the bones of different

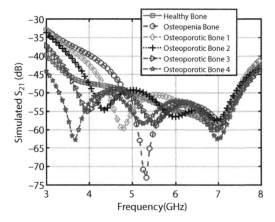

Figure 9.2 Transfer characteristics through the simulated wrist for standard size.

masses. This receiving antenna is placed opposite of the transmitting antenna as illustrated in Figure 9.1. For a standard-sized sample, the tissue parameters (dimension and dielectric characteristics) are tabulated in Table 9.1. This microwave setup is used to observe the transfer characteristics through the healthy bone, osteopenia bone and different stages of osteoporotic bones enveloped with the tissue layer of muscle, fat, and skin throughout the frequency band of 3 to 8 GHz. We observe a gradual shift in the transfer characteristics or S_{21} due to the loss in the bone mass as shown in Figure 9.2. This decrement in the bone mass density can be quantified by the increase of the electrical conductivity and permittivity as reported in Table 9.1.

By monitoring the transfer characteristics we can clearly observe a shift in the first resonance frequency with the lowering of the bone mass. However, the above characteristics is known to vary with the minor variations of tissue dimensions. For using the proposed method on actual samples, it is important to remember that such minor variations are quite common in the real human samples because each person under test will have differing body mass and fat layers. In order to generalize the above observations of change in the transfer characteristics due to change in bone mass, the additional parameters due to changing muscle, fat and skin have to be factored in the analysis. So for the purpose of quantification of the loss in bone mass, the transfer characteristics of bones of different bone masses is recorded by varying the size of each individual tissue i.e. bone, fat, muscle and skin tissue by 0.1 mm in each step.

9.2.2   Data Collection and Analysis

The transfer characteristics of the sample under test is collected by varying the bone mass density to signify healthy bone, osteopenia bone and differing levels of osteoporosis using the microwave setup as shown in Figure 9.1. No two human wrist sizes are same as tissues of every human vary in size. To address this difference, observations are taken by varying the tissue sizes. Each of the 4 tissues i.e. the bone, muscle, fat, and skin are varied individually by 0.1 mm each taking 10 cases with each tissue variation. The dataset details are tabulated in Table 9.2. The machine learning algorithm proposed in the subsequent section aims to identify the bone density stages irrespective of the variation in the dimension of the human tissues.

Table 9.2 Dataset creation.

Types of stages of bone mass density (healthy bone, osteopenia bone, osteoporotic bone 1,2,3,4)	6
Types of tissue (bone, fat, muscle, skin)	4
No. of variations of each tissue (0.1 mm to 1 mm)	10
No. of original readings (standard dimension)	6
Total no. of readings of transfer characteristics	$6 \times 4 \times 10 + 6 = 246$

Out of the 246 transfer characteristic, a few are shown for the entire measurement frequency spectrum of 3 to 8 GHz. Using the healthy bone, osteopenia bone, and different levels of osteoporotic bones while varying the bone, muscle, fat, and skin tissue sizes, 6 of the 246 transfer characteristics are shown in Figures 9.3–9.8. The figures show the changes in attenuation levels with the change in the degree of osteoporosis. Each figure shows that

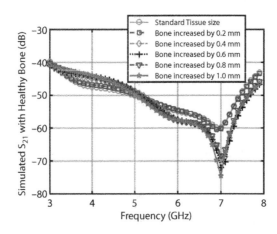

Figure 9.3 Simulated transfer characteristic with healthy bone by varying the bone tissue.

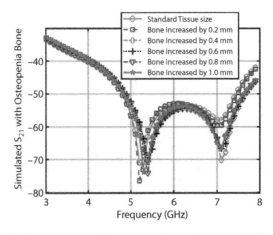

Figure 9.4 Simulated transfer characteristic with osteopenia bone by varying the bone tissue.

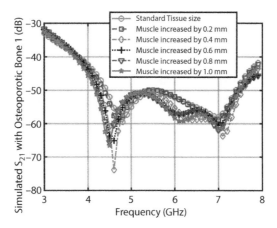

Figure 9.5 Simulated transfer characteristic with osteoporotic bone 1 by varying the muscle tissue.

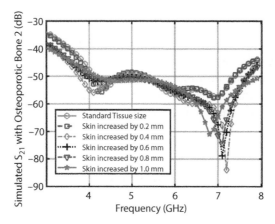

Figure 9.6 Simulated transfer characteristic with osteoporotic bone 2 by varying the skin tissue.

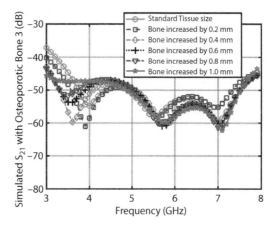

Figure 9.7 Simulated transfer characteristic with osteoporotic bone 3 by varying the bone tissue.

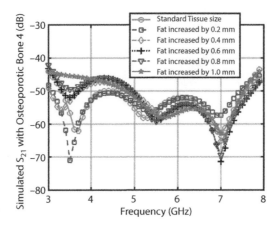

Figure 9.8 Simulated transfer characteristic with osteoporotic bone 4 by varying the fat tissue.

even slight changes in the tissue size there is significant change in the transfer characteristics. This implies that the identification of osteoporosis and its progression become a dependent variable of the human subject tissue variation. However, such dependence on external factors would render the identification of osteoporosis progression invalid. To counter this, the authors have proposed to apply machine learning algorithms on the collected data. In the absence of an accurate classification algorithm, it would be difficult to judge the stage of osteoporosis. Such a classification algorithm is able to identify the specific features attributable to the change in bone mass density while suppressing the effect of the change in the tissue sizes.

9.3 Prediction Model of Osteoporosis Using Machine Learning Algorithms

Recently, a considerable amount of effort has been devoted to the application of machine learning algorithms in healthcare applications for diagnostics. It is an effective way to anticipate the manifestation of an ailment in its initial stages. Machine learning (ML) provides a concise interpretation of the process of disease progression from which the disease can be anticipated from a given sample. Usually, ML algorithms are categorized into supervised, unsupervised, and reinforcement learning. The data samples collected through the frequency domain analysis described in Section 9.2 are analyzed using the different ML algorithms to evaluate the accuracy, precision, recall, F1-score, support, and confusion matrix of the system. In this work, Decision Tree, Random Forest, and KNN algorithms are utilized for the classification of different stages of bone mass density. These ML algorithms are implemented with the help of Sckit-Learn ML library using python programming language [22].

9.3.1 K-Nearest Neighbor (KNN)

KNN is one of the basic approaches to classify data samples. Here the measurement is executed through the different distances for the classifications of the data sample. KNN recognizes the no of samples in contrast to the training data found to be at the close proximity to the test sample data and designate it to the familiar class label.

9.3.2   Decision Tree

This is a type of supervised ML algorithm which consistently splits the data in accordance to the specific characteristic. This tree could be described by the two main entities with the decision nodes and the leaves. The nodes are the points where the data samples are divided and the leaves are considered as the final outcome or decisions.

9.3.3   Random Forest

As the name, Random Forest conveys that it comprises a huge no of distinct decision trees that acts as an ensemble. Each of these distinct trees is further divided into a class prediction and a class with a maximum no of votes to emerge as a model's prediction.

Here 60% of the data samples are used for training and 40% of the data samples are used for testing. With the help of the ML algorithm, the accuracy of the classifier could be determined. In this work, ML is utilized to compute the discrete efficiency metric as an illustration of confusion matrix, precision (P), recall (R), f1-score (F1), support (S), and accuracy [23].

The confusion matrices of Random Forest, Decision Tree, and KNN classifiers are illustrated through Figures 9.9, 9.10 and 9.11 respectively. Table 9.3 and Figure 9.12 compare the classification report of all the classifiers. Here the Random Forest classifier is found to be more efficient than the Decision Tree and KNN algorithms. Random Forest classifier gives an accuracy of 93% whereas the Decision Tree and KNN gave an accuracy of 89 and

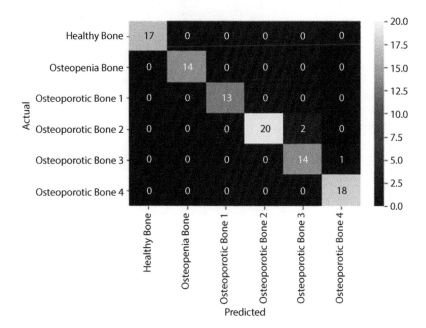

Figure 9.9 Confusion matrix for KNN.

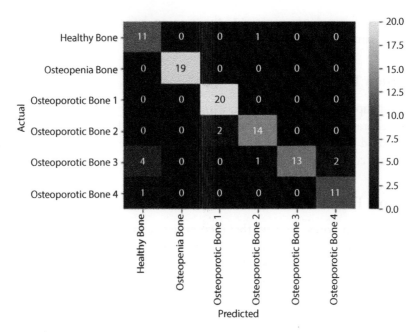

Figure 9.10 Confusion matrix for decision tree.

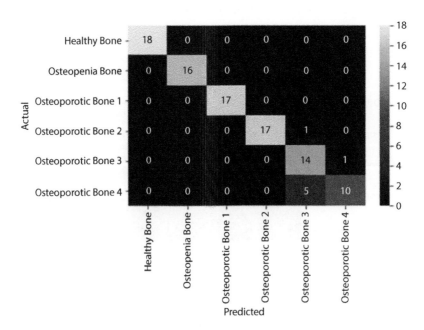

Figure 9.11 Confusion matrix for random forest.

Table 9.3 Tabular representation of Classification Reports using KNN, Decision Tree and Random Forest Classifiers [precision (P), recall (R), f1-score (F1), support (S)].

	KNN Classifier				Decision Tree Classifier				Random Forest Classifier			
	P	R	F1	S	P	R	F1	S	P	R	F1	S
Healthy Bone	0.75	1.00	0.86	15	1.00	1.00	1.00	16	1.00	1.00	1.00	18
Osteopenia Bone	1.00	1.00	1.00	18	0.95	1.00	0.97	19	1.00	1.00	1.00	16
Osteoporotic Bone 1	1.00	1.00	1.00	14	1.00	0.92	0.96	13	1.00	1.00	1.00	17
Osteoporotic Bone 2	1.00	0.74	0.85	19	1.00	0.88	0.93	16	1.00	0.94	0.97	18
Osteoporotic Bone 3	0.92	0.63	0.75	19	0.64	0.64	0.64	14	0.70	0.93	0.80	15
Osteoporotic Bone 4	0.65	0.93	0.76	14	0.78	0.86	0.82	21	0.91	0.67	0.77	15
Accuracy			0.87	99			0.89	99			0.93	99
Macro Avg	0.89	0.88	0.87	99	0.9	0.88	0.89	99	0.93	0.92	0.92	99
Weighted Avg	0.9	0.87	0.87	99	0.89	0.89	0.89	99	0.94	0.93	0.93	99

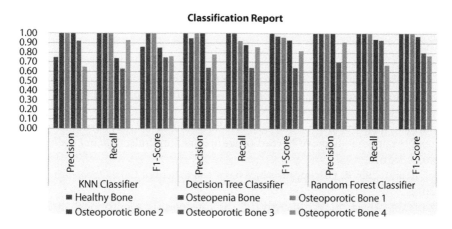

Figure 9.12 Graphical representation of the classification report.

87%. This illustrates that the proposed method is able to predict the degree of osteoporosis through microwave analysis. Needless to say that the accuracy and efficiency of the system will increase by collecting more data samples.

9.4   Conclusion

In this paper, an efficient ML-based bone diagnostic system is developed for detecting different stages of bone loss. A microwave system is proposed to differentiate the different stages of bone loss. Initially, a frequency domain analysis is evaluated in the standard human wrist tissue size, as the electrical parameters of the bone such as the permittivity and the conductivity enhances accordingly with the loss in the bone mass. As the bone mass density decreases a gradual shift the first resonant frequency is noted. Further, a dataset was created for various stages of bone loss along while human tissues such as fat, muscle, bone and skin are varied individually, to observe the variation in attenuation level for discrete diameters of human wrist samples. Various ML classifiers such as KNN, Decision Tree and Random Forest, have been utilized on this dataset of microwave-based diagnostic method. Here Random Forest classifier is found to be the most accurate of all and can clearly identify the different stages of the loss of bone mass density in the presence of tissue variations. Although further experimental work with human bone samples need to be conducted, it is clearly demonstrated through the findings of this work that the proposed system using microwave signals is an efficient bone mineral density analysis system that will help the medical personnel to evaluate the progression of osteoporosis.

Acknowledgment

The authors are thankful to the R&D Infrastructure Division, Department of Science & Technology, Government of India for funding and upgrading the Microwave and Optical Engineering Laboratory and to the HRD, Government of India for the Research Fellowship.

References

1. World Health Organization, *Assessment of Fracture Risk and Its Application to Screening for Postmenopausal Osteoporosis, Report of a WHO Study Group*, World Health Organization, Geneva, 1994.
2. Kadam, N.S., Chiplonkar, S.A., Khadilkar, A.V., Khadilkar, V.V., Prevalence of osteoporosis in apparently healthy adults above 40 years of age in Pune City, India. *Indian J. Endocrinol. Metab.*, 22, 1, 67–73, 2018.
3. Mithal, A. and Kaur, P., Osteoporosis in Asia: A call to action. *Curr. Osteoporos. Rep.*, 10, 245–247, 2012.
4. Sridhar, C.B., Ahuja, M.M., Bhargava, S., Is osteoporosis a nutritional disease? *J. Assoc. Physicians India*, 18, 671–676, 1970.
5. Cilotti, A. and Falchetti, A., Male osteoporosis and androgenic therapy: From testosterone to SARMs. *Clin. Cases Miner. Bone Metab.*, 6, 229–233, 2009.

6. Babatunde, O.M., Fragomen, A.T., Rozbruch, S.R., Noninvasive quantitative assessment of bone healing after distraction osteogenesis. *Hospital for Special Surgery (HSS) J.*, 6, 1, 71–78, 2010.

7. Kanis, J.A., Melton, L.J., III, Christiansen, C., Johnston, C.C., Khaltaev, N., The diagnosis of osteoporosis. *J. Bone Miner. Res.*, 9, 8, 1137–1142, 1994.

8. Zhou, T., Meaney, P.M., Pallone, M.J., Geimer, S., Paulsen, K.D., Microwave tomographic imaging for osteoporosis screening: A pilot clinical study. *2010 Annual International Conference of the IEEE Engineering in Medicine and Biology*, Buenos Aires, pp. 1218–1221, 2010.

9. Nayak, S., Olkin, I., Liu, H., Grabe, M., Gould, M., Allen, I., Owens, D., Bravata, D., Meta-analysis: Accuracy of quantitative ultrasound for identifying patients with osteoporosis. *Ann. Intern. Med.*, 144, 11, 832, 2006.

10. Gabriel, S., Lau, R.W., Gabriel, C., The dielectric properties of biological tissues: II. Measurements in the frequency range 10 Hz to 20 GHz. *Phys. Med. Biol.*, 41, 11, 2251–2269, 1996.

11. Jagan, G.M., Palanikumar, A., Christen, A., Miranda, V., Florence, E., Development Of A Planar Sensor For Monitoring Orthopaedic Health. *Proceedings Of 38th Irf International Conference*, 2016.

12. Cruz, A.S., da Silva, S.G., de Castro, B.H., Bone Density Measurement Through Electromagnetic Waves. *The 2013 Biomedical Engineering International Conference (BMEiCON-2013)*, 2013.

13. Meaney, P.M., Goodwin, D., Golnabi, A., Pallone, M., Geimer, S., Paulsen, K.D., 3D Microwave Bone Imaging. *6th European Conference on Antennas and Propagation (EUCAP)*, 2011.

14. Symeonidis, S., William, G., Whittow, Panagamuwa, C., Zecca, M., An Implanted Antenna System for the Monitoring of the Healing of Bone Fractures. *2015 Loughborough Antennas & Propagation Conference (LAPC)*, 2015.

15. Li, M., and Zhou, Z., Improve Computer-Aided Diagnosis With Machine Learning Techniques Using Undiagnosed Samples. *IEEE Trans. Syst. Man Cybern.—Part A: Syst. Hum.*, 37, 6, 1088–1098, 2007.

16. Haripriya, L. and Jabbar, M.A., Role of Machine Learning in Intrusion Detection System: Review. *2018 Second International Conference on Electronics, Communication and Aerospace Technology (ICECA)*, pp. 925–929, 2018.

17. Shailaja, K., Seetharamulu, B., Jabbar, M.A., Machine Learning in Healthcare: A Review. *2018 Second International Conference on Electronics, Communication and Aerospace Technology (ICECA)*, pp. 910–914, 2018.

18. Amin, B., Elahi, M.A., Shahzad, A., Parle, E., McNamara, L., Orhalloran, M., An insight into bone dielectric properties variation: A foundation for electromagnetic medical devices. *2018 EMF-Med 1st World Conference on Biomedical Applications of Electromagnetic Fields (EMF-Med)*, pp. 1–2, 2018.

19. Vendik, I.B., Pleskachev, V.V., Yakovlev, V., Tamilova, S., Microwave diagnostics of osteoporosis. *2018 IEEE Conference of Russian Young Researchers in Electrical and Electronic Engineering (EIConRus)*, pp. 1239–1242, 2018.

20. Andreuccetti, D., Fossi, R., Perrucci, C., *Calculation of the Dielectric Properties of Body Tissues in the frequency range 10 Hz–100 GHz*, IFAC-CNR, Florence (Italy), http://niremf.ifac.cnr.it/tissprop/htmlclie/htmlclie.php, 1997–2015.

21. Kerketta, S.R. and Ghosh, D., Bandwidth enhancement of monopole antenna using stubbed ground plane. *Int. J. RF Microw. Comput. Aided Eng.*, 29, e21868, 2019.

22. Pedregosa, F., Varoquaux, G., Gramfort, A., Michel, V., Thirion, B., Grisel, O., Blondel, M., Prettenhofer, P., Weiss, R., Dubourg, V., Vanderplas, J., Scikit-learn: Machine learning in Python. *J. Mach. Learn. Res.*, 12, 85, 2825–2830, 2011.

23. Kumar, D., Sarkar, A., Kerketta, S.R., Ghosh, D., Human Activity Classification Based On Breathing Patterns Using IR-UWB Radar. *2019 IEEE 16th India Council International Conference (INDICON)*, pp. 1–4, 2019.

Applications of Machine Learning in Biomedical Text Processing and Food Industry

K. Paramesha[1], Gururaj H.L.[1*] and Om Prakash Jena[2]

*[1]Department of Computer Science & Engineering, Vidyavardhaka College of Engineering,
Mysuru, India*
[2]Department of Computer Science, Ravenshaw University, Cuttack, India

Abstract

The evolutions of the World Wide Web (WWW) has witnessed proliferation of data and boom in technologies for extracting information out of the big data for marketing strategy and adds value to products, services and personalize the customer experience. Recently there has been a dramatic surge of interest in the era of Artificial Intelligence and Machine Learning (AI and ML), and more people become aware of the scope of new applications enabled by the ML approaches. The applications of ML ranging from household to healthcare, domestic applications to enterprise applications, agriculture to military applications, encompass all walks of life. In this book chapter, the main focus would be on applications of ML approaches in two different sub-domains which are connected to healthcare sector. The first application is on Sentiment Analysis (SA) of user narrated drug reviews and the second one is about engineering in food technology. As AI and ML techniques push the limits of scientific drug discovery, ML approaches are preferred over other approaches for two important reasons. The first one is that ML comes with distinctive learning strategies and its viability for many NLP tasks. The second is that its inherent ability to model many features which capture the aspects of sentiments in text. However, despite the fact that the results ML approaches produce are no human understandable, they may help us to achieve high accuracy. Food Engineering is an advanced branch of Engineering, which deals with production, Evaluation of quality of food, innovation in new recipes, nutritional level in the food and management of food. Most of the food engineering mechanisms involve classification and prediction algorithms. In this chapter two facets of food engineering technologies which use machine learning techniques are depicted using some case studies. Nowadays, malnutrition of a child is a major problem. The analysis of children's health by classifying malnutrition and nutrition using classification algorithms is also depicted in this chapter.

Keywords: Artificial intelligence, machine learning, deep learning, transfer learning, healthcare, food technology

*Corresponding author: gururaj1711@vvce.ac.in

Sachi Nandan Mohanty, G. Nalinipriya, Om Prakash Jena and Achyuth Sarkar (eds.) Machine Learning for Healthcare Applications, (151–168) © 2021 Scrivener Publishing LLC

10.1   Introduction

The healthcare sector is emerging as a prominent area for AI and ML research and applications which have the potential to transform many aspects related to healthcare [1]. ML poses some exciting opportunities in the healthcare space to swim through the vast amount of data currently untapped and leverage it to improve outcomes, optimize costs, and deliver a better quality of care. The landscape of AI-based startups in healthcare sector is vibrant with ever increasing scope for new technological innovations and solutions. The emerging startups in the space are leveraging AI and ML technology to develop AI-driven solutions to help individual consumers, pharmaceutical and bio-tech companies and hospital systems improve everything from fitness to clinical trials to diagnostics. The applications of AI-powered healthcare sector are setting ground breaking milestones with new reinventing and reinvigorating the multi-billion industry. Figure 10.1 depicts wide ranging AI-driven applications such as clinical trial management, privacy solutions, drug discovery, wellness, genome sequencing, hospital decision support system, imaging and diagnostics, predictive analytics and risk scoring, remote monitoring and virtual assistance, etc. in which startups are using ML and NLP to analyze and consolidate medical and health data from disparate sources.

As good food leads to fit and healthy life of individuals, food processing has a great influence on health of consumers thereby impacting the healthcare system. The food science degree is fundamentally multi-domain study which has potential direct benefits for healthcare sector and opens up a numerous of openings [3]. Among the most important upcoming experiments, the sustainable supply, storage and transport of energy, clean freshwater and adequate food for all mankind at an equitable cost will be influenced by food engineering technologies [4]. Reducing amount of the farmland and the increasing human population requires new ideas to feed the world and meet the consumer difficulties for food in the future. The industry and researchers working in the food process engineering and food packing engineering will give equal importance for hygienic environments, food security and also to access to sufficient, safe and nutritious food.

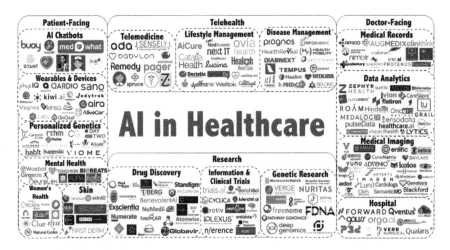

Figure 10.1 Industry landscape of AI in healthcare (Courtesy: Emily Kuo [2]).

10.2   Use Cases of AI and ML in Healthcare

The advancements in the fields of AI and ML, particularly deep learning, marked the dawn of new era in machine learning healthcare applications which has witnessed exponential growth in recent times. With all the new excitements in research communities, joint-ventures, investors and coupled with excellent techno-healthcare eco-system, hottest young start-ups are disrupting the space with deep learning algorithms and extending the horizons uncovering more extensive possibilities. Emerging use cases of ML and NLP are poised to redefine the paradigm and are expected to change the face of customer experience in the healthcare sector.

10.2.1   Speech Recognition (SR)

SR is matured NLP application which caters to the needs of many industries. SR in healthcare itself has many use cases to assist the clinicians and automated process such as e-records security, transcribe notes for useful Electronic Health Record (EHR) data entry and patient engagement in healthcare system through Interactive Voice Response Systems (IVRS). Deep learning models pre-trained on domain specific data work to detect and correct any errors in the transcription before passing it on for human proofing. Many ML industries, with integration of SR, digital dictation, and work flow management in the medical sector, offer complete document creation solution. SR has many emerging use cases on horizon as the underlying models are being leveraged to deliver state-of-the-art results [5].

10.2.2   Pharmacovigilance and Adverse Drug Effects (ADE)

It is related to all the activities involving the detection and analysis of adverse effects and related problems of drugs. It is concerned with the safety of drugs which have been launched to the market. It means assessment, monitoring, and prevention of professionally unreported potential side effects of drugs by analyzing widely available data from various internet sources. As per statistics, in the US alone, harmful side effects or ADEs have accounted for a third of total admissions to the hospitals in each year. In recent times, pharmacovigilance is gaining momentum and is vital for effective prevention of any side effects that the drugs may cause. As ADEs are considered to be the most frequent problems and preventable medical errors, analysis of drug reviews from different sources could play a key role concerning the safety of drugs once there were introduced to the market [6].

10.2.3   Clinical Imaging and Diagnostics

Computer-aided detection of symptoms and medical diagnosis of a specific medical conditions performed by using ML algorithms could leverage physicians to interpret medical imaging findings and initiate better decisions [7]. On the one hand humans are fatigued and could drastically reduce the interpretation quality, but on the other hand AI-enabled machines could work round the clock and are able to learn patterns that are beyond human perception. AI-integrated software serves as a valuable companion to medical professionals looking to enhance their productivity through accurate interpretations. AI-powered software that diagnose patients for diabetic retinopathy has shown precise and high success rate without the need for a second opinion from an expert.

10.2.4   Conversational AI in Healthcare

NLP-based chatbots could assist in providing answers to queries to many segments of healthcare. It has many roles ranging from creating awareness to providing suggestions to a plethora of questions and queries related to healthcare without the intervention of a physician [8]. A health chatbot learning independently over a period of time could actually handle queries as naturally as any physician does and provide immediate assistance at the touch of fingertips. Chatbots acting as personal assistant perform fixing up of consultations of patient with the doctor at convenient time and follow-up appointments. Assessing the symptoms of patients, a medical chatbot guides them to nearest and proper healthcare. The next generation chatbots relaying on deep learning render smart responses based on context for every single interaction.

10.3   Use Cases of AI and ML in Food Technology

AI and ML offer many opportunities to automate and optimize processes, save money and reduce losses, and reduce human intervention and errors for many industries. AI and ML can benefit retail food chains, bar and restaurants and cafe businesses as well as in food processing and manufacturing sector. Maintaining sanitation and hygienic conditions in places of food preparations could be ensured through video surveillance. In this section, we discuss a few interesting use cases related to nutrition and food technology.

10.3.1   Assortment of Vegetables and Fruits

In food processing plants, vegetables and fruit are not at all the same with respect to features. Even though a type of fruits and vegetables such as oranges, tomatoes and apples, look same but they differ in features. The major features in the food processing of plants are size, shape and color. Exploiting the various attributes of fruits and vegetables, TOMRA, which is one of the leading food sorting technologies, has developed the technology which is capable of viewing the food items in the same way that most purchasing consumers do and sort it based on that insight as depicted in Figure 10.2.

10.3.2   Personal Hygiene

In this pandemic situation food hygiene is of prime importance for each and everyone. For ensuring that food is safe, the kitchen should be hygienic and personal hygiene is also very much important [10]. KanKan is one of the top leading companies that maintains the hygiene of the individual food workers, by adopting systems which are capable of identifying objects and human faces to verify whether the workers in food industries are following professional practices such as wearing the cap, facial masks, hand gloves as required by food safety regulations. If it finds a violation, it extracts the screen images for further reviews.

Figure 10.2 Tomra—Tomato sorting and processing machines (Courtesy: Tomra [9]).

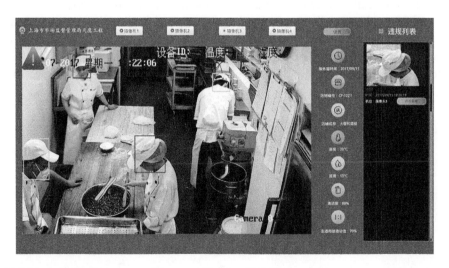

Figure 10.3 Kankan's Machine system (Courtesy: KanKan AI [11]).

According to the assessment of the system reported by the company, the performance accuracy of this technology is more than 96%. Figure 10.3 depicts the usage of KanKan's machine vision system which showcase correct (white box) and not correct (red box).

10.3.3 Developing New Products

Gastro graph AI implications enable the food industries to invent new products for the consumer markets. This technology leverages AI and ML for predictive analysis to come up with consumers' flavor preferences and predict that how they will receive and respond to new tastes. The food items can be categorized into demographic collections to assist food industries to develop new food products as per the preferences of their target consumers.

10.3.4   Plant Leaf Disease Detection

The life disease detection at the early stage makes the farmers to take necessary precautionary measures in such a way that the yield of the crop will not get affected. The farmers still even today go with the classical farming without knowing the status of the soil in which they will grow the crop neither the pesticides are required or not. Early detection of disease by taking the various samples of the plants leaf also improves the yield of the product. The detailed examination of the leaf disease can be done with the help of disease type, severity, and the future, may even recommend management practices to limit loss from a disease. The proper disease diagnosis of plants reduces the human effort wastage without knowing the disease in the crop. The satellite images and UAV images of the plots also provides better accuracy compared the images datasets of the plants as shown in Figure 10.4.

10.3.5   Face Recognition Systems for Domestic Cattle

The recognition of cattle faces in the dairy units will be solely monitored in all aspectual behaviors of the cattle, as well as body condition score and feeding. Lameness is a common disorder in the cattle dairy units which indirectly imparts the deficiency in the milk product of the cows. The detection of lameness in cows brings the conclusion whether the cow is willing to have more food or not. The lameness of the cattle is depicted in Figure 10.5.

Figure 10.4 Plant disease detection (Courtesy: Bitrefine [12]).

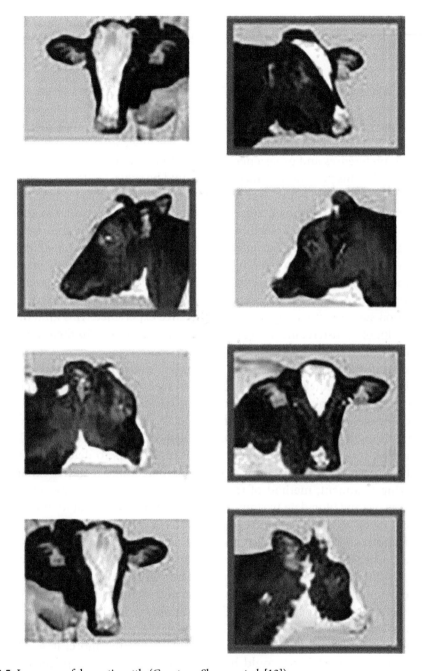

Figure 10.5 Lameness of domestic cattle (Courtesy: Shearer *et al.* [13]).

10.3.6   Cleaning Processing Equipment

Sanitation and Cleaning is also an important criterion which maintains better health of the society. Especially in this pandemic, cleaning is also an important need to maintain hygiene. SOCIP (Self-Optimizing-Clean-In-Place) is one of the major cleaning equipment technologies which imbibe the ultrasonic and optical imaging technology which senses the cleaned equipment and checks for the validity of the devices before into the execution. The researchers with respect to the SOCIP analyzed that it saves 100 million dollars per year.

10.4   A Case Study: Sentiment Analysis of Drug Reviews

Online consumers' review posting sites and opinion blogs and forums generate tons of data every day. It include a wealth of information regarding consumers' desires, needs and requirements, preferences and experiences over multiple products and services across various domains [14]. This publically available data could be subjected to data mining process to derive useful patterns and knowledge for planning business strategies. In this chapter, we investigate the reviews of consumer concerned with the pharmaceutical domain for understanding the sentiments on ADE. Online drug reviews contain useful information related to multiple aspects such as drug side effects and effectiveness of drugs, making automatic analysis very interesting but also challenging. However, extracting sentiments concerning the various aspects of drug reviews could render valuable insights and help decision making to improve monitoring on pharmaceutical care, and promoting pharmacovigilance and clinical decision support system by revealing collective experience. This kind of analysis is relevant for a lot of industries including pharmaceutical so as to help them understanding post-launch market research.

With the steep rise in internet usage, more online users have registered with health communities such as medical blogs and forums to seek and gather health-related information, to share experiences about drugs effects, clinical treatments, symptoms, diagnosis or to engage with other users with similar health conditions in communities. Processing information posted on social media networks such as Facebook, Twitter and patient.info have indeed fascinated medical NLP researchers to detect various medical abnormalities such as adverse reactions of drugs, ambiance and facilities extended to the patients during treatment, method of treatments and cost-effectiveness, etc. Sentiment analysis of reviews and blog data pertaining to healthcare systems could unravel the multiple forms of medical sentiments [15], which could be extracted from users' treatment, drugs medications and medical conditions has numerous benefits for their stakeholders. For instance, a healthcare center could take suitable measures to achieve the effective and better results to increase quality of healthcare centers upon sentiments expressed in the reviews and responses shared by the patients treated in that center [16]. Aspect-oriented SA of drug reviews could reveal detailed information but due to lack of labeled dataset, cross-evaluation using traditional statistical classifier with respect to different medical conditions and fields is not satisfactory [17]. Furthermore, it was concluded that the problems of portability could be solved by employing deep learning models. Aspect-oriented sentiment analysis is taken one step forward to another level by evaluating double BiGRU model [18] which exhibits improvements in performance as the model could capture bi-directional semantic information and incorporate domain knowledge by transfer learning. Using deep learning Bidirectional Encoder Representations from Transformers (BERT), models in [19] have achieved a new state-of-the-art results for on both the adverse drug effects detection and its extraction task. Extreme Learning Machine-Autoencoder (ELM-AE) trained on various diverse features including word embedding for analysis of patients' discharge summaries are key in outperforming many baseline models state-of-the-art classification approaches such as naive Bayes, logistic regression, Support Vector Machine (SVM), decision trees, random forest, Embeddings Language Models (ELMo), Long Short Term Memory (LSTM) based Convolution Neural Network (CNN) and Recurrent Neural Network (RNN) [20].

10.4.1   Dataset

For illustration of NLP tools and techniques in SA of drug reviews, a multi-labelled (Positive, Neutral and Negative) sentiment dataset [21] of reviews narrated by patients on different drugs is considered. Each review post is identified with a drug name which is the topic of discussion in the post. There could be many reviews of different sentiments for every single drug. The dataset is characterized by several challenging aspects such as the text is ridden with grammatical errors and noisy text, use of sarcasm, imbalanced distribution, discussion on multiple topics with different sentiments in single review, sentiments expressed on out of context topics, special characters and emojis, etc. The dataset consist of a total of 5,042 reviews with Positive (3,737), Neutral (592) and Negative (813) sentiment distribution.

10.4.2   Approaches for Sentiment Analysis on Drug Reviews

With the given dataset, several experiments have been carried out to assess the performance of the models which were reported in the literature for the same kind of tasks. A typical pipeline of processing steps is as shown in Figure 10.6 is in practice for ML based NLP

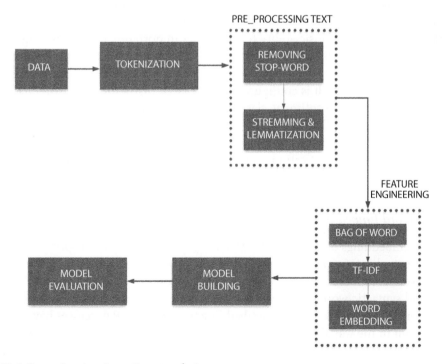

Figure 10.6 Processing steps in sentiment analysis.

tasks. In tokenization phase, the document is tokenized into sentences and each sentence is tokenized into words which form the vocabulary list. The pre-processing is applied to bring the text suitable for further processing by performing tasks such as removing noisy characters, eliminating stop words, spelling corrections, expanding contractions, stemming, etc. Furthering the processing, the feature engineering is performed to transform refined input text to numerical representation normally in vector format which ML models could able to understand. The performance of all the proposed models is evaluated by 10-fold cross-validations.

10.4.3   BoW and TF-IDF Model

The feature engineering phase creates the vector for ML models by extracting different aspects which capture sentiments [22]. The most primitive forms for word embedding are the Bag-of-Word (BoW) and Term Frequency-Inverse Document Frequency (TF-IDF) in which individual words are assigned a value based on its occurrence or relative frequency of the word in other documents resulting in sparse matrix. The model doesn't retain the ordering of the words thereby the resulting vector lacks the syntactic and contextual information. These models could capture the importance of the word as depicted by its value in the document. The models are trained on logistic and SVM classifiers to evaluate the performance.

10.4.4   Bi-LSTM Model

The Bi-directional Long Short Term Memory (Bi-LSTM) is improved version of sequential LSTM model. It can learn the word context based on its predecessors and following words in the sentence. LSTM models were developed to address the limitations in Recurrent Neural Network (RNN). It has intrinsic ability to remember important patterns for long duration of time. The LSTM model as shown in Figure 10.7 takes word embeddings of a sequence of text inputs and generates a consolidated vector which could be further used to predict the class label using a classifier. It is configured to operate in many-to-one for predictive tasks such as text classification, sentiment classification, etc. LSTM can provide effective solution when it comes to handling sequence. For evaluation of the model, pre-trained Global Vectors for Word Representation (GloVe) word vectors were used due to better coverage of words. For sentiment classification, fully connected dense layer with softmax classifier is employed.

10.4.4.1   Word Embedding

As the word embeddings of BoW and TF-IDF are primitive and do incorporate the semantic and contextual information, the evolved word embedding models based on a neural network have revolutionized NLP due to their ability to capture a large number of precise semantic and syntactic word relationships when trained with the sufficiently large corpus. The results and benefits of using word embedding models in NLP processes have brought a significant shift in the way the text processing frameworks are modeled and implemented. Work presented in ref. [23] have used word embeddings for various applications such as sentiment analysis, text classification NER, question and answering, sequence tagging, etc.

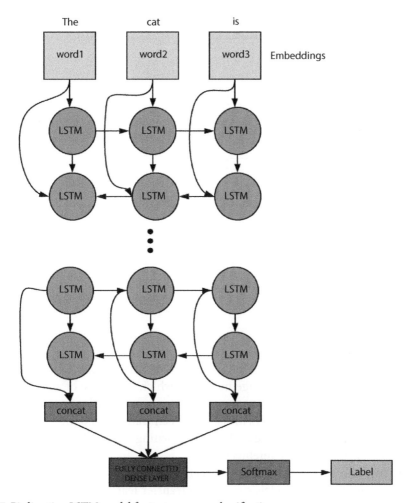

Figure 10.7 Bi-direction LSTM model for text sequence classification.

The notion of word embedding as depicted in Figure 10.8 gives the representation of word as dense vector factoring in all the contextual senses of the word in the training corpus. Unlike weighting scheme of words such as Tf-Idf and word count vector, which are relative to occurrence of words in other documents, word embedding is more advanced and inclusive representation of words containing many aspects. Word embeddings obtained by training large corpus using Word2Vec and GloVe frameworks have achieved state-of-the-art results in several downstream NLP tasks.

10.4.5   Deep Learning Model

Unlike Word2Vec and GloVe, deep learning language models such as BERT, Embeddings from Language Models (ELMo), Universal Language Model Fine-tuning (ULMFiT) trained on large corpus would obtain deep contextualized word representation that models both complex characteristics of word use in terms of syntax and semantics, and senses of words depending on the linguistic contexts. Deep Learning has been proven its potential viability

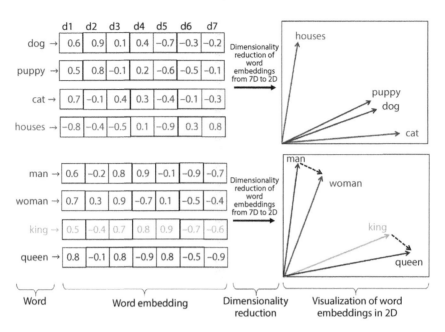

Figure 10.8 Word embedding representation in vector space (Courtesy: David Rozado [24]).

on many NLP tasks like text summarization, machine translation, sentiment analysis, etc. They are essentially built upon language modeling which has come of age due to tremendous research effort with great results to use neural networks for language modeling. As a result, many shallow architecture algorithms have been transformed into deep architecture models with multiple layers to create end-to-end learning and analyzing models resulting in applications smarter and more intelligent.

In recent years the NLP community has seen many breakthroughs in NLP, especially the shift to transfer learning. Models supporting transfer learning based on deep learning architecture such as BERT, ELMo, ULMFiT, Transformer and OpenAI's GPT have allowed researchers to achieve state-of-the-art results on multiple benchmarks and provided the community with large pre-trained models with high performance. Due to the lack of large labeled text datasets and issues that most of the labeled text datasets are not big enough to train deep neural networks because these networks have a huge number of parameters and training such networks on small datasets will cause overfitting, transfer learning technique in NLP would provide an alternative solution in two steps. First step is pre-training the language model in an unsupervised fashion on vast amounts of unannotated datasets, and then using this pre-trained model for fine-tuning for various NLP downstream tasks in second step.

In this chapter, we have focused on leveraging transfer learning capabilities of the pre-trained models like BERT on drug reviews labeled dataset and evaluating the performance. The process of training the pre-trained models is known as model fine-tuning which is required for domain adaptation. The transfer learning technique as depicted in Figure 10.10 has been reinforced in the BERT model which is big neural network architecture and has gained a lot of interest from researchers and industry alike, owing to the impressive accuracy it has been able to achieve on a wide range of tasks. With a huge number of parameters, which can range from 100 million to over 300 million, training a BERT model from scratch

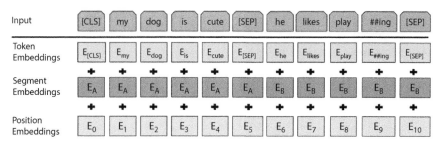

Figure 10.9 BERT input embeddings (Courtesy: Cheney [25]).

on a small dataset would result in over-fitting. So, it is better to use a pre-trained BERT model that was trained on a huge dataset, as a starting point. The inputs to the BERT as shown in Figure 10.9 for training and testing validation consists of three different types of embeddings to make a robust and efficient model. Different configuration of BERT models such as BERT without fine-tuning, with fine-tuning and ensemble BERT models were evaluated on the drug dataset to assess the performance.

The input reviews were pre-processed to extract the sentences mentioning the drug name. With the extracted sentences, lower cased all sentences, contraction phrases were expanded, stop words, emojis, URLs, punctuations, numbers and other special characters were filtered out. The pre-processed input text review sequences are tokenized using BERT tokenizer and subsequently converted to BERT word embeddings with encapsulation of [CLS] and [SEP] tokens which were used for sequence labeling tasks. The BERT$_{BASE}$ model with 12 layers was selected and configured to process input sequence of maximum length of

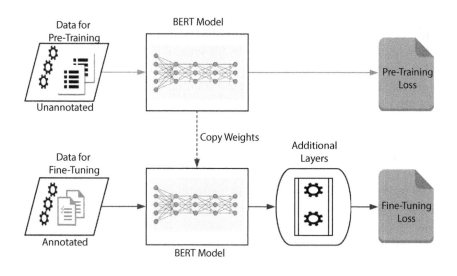

Figure 10.10 Fine-tuning of pre-trained BERT models.

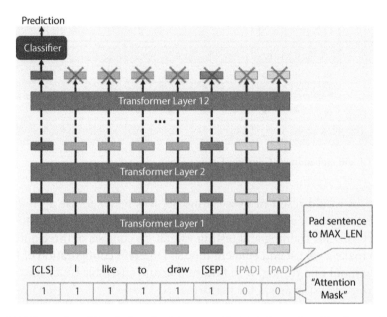

Figure 10.11 BERT layered model with classifier (Courtesy: Chris McCormick and Nick Ryan [26]).

512 tokens. The input sequences length less than 512 were padded with zeros. The dataset was evaluated on three different setting of BERT models: (1) BERT without fine-tuning, (2) BERT with fine-tuning and (3) BERT in ensemble mode. In the BERT without fine-tuning mode, input text is pre-processed and performed the sequence labeling. The architecture of the BERT model is shown in Figure 10.11. The output of the BERT model corresponding to the [CLS] token representing the sense of the input sentence is labelled using fully connected dense layer with softmax output. With fine-tuning mode, the BERT model is evaluated by 10-fold cross-validation process. In the ensemble model, a combination of three fine-tuned BERT models which were trained with different text samples were employed in voting ensemble mode. For accelerating the training of BERT models, the model were trained and tested on GPU platform available on Google Colab.

10.5   Results and Analysis

The results shown in Table 10.1 capture the performance of different NLP models. The dataset is experimented with both traditional and deep learning models. It is evident that the performance of the deep learning models is better than the traditional models. Although the BERT is pre-trained on huge corpus, without fine-tuning, it wouldn't be leveraged enough to perform well, whereas the fine-tuned BERT and ensemble BERT show comparatively better performance with the domain adaptation. With the challenging dataset, the improvements in the performance of deep learning models are attributed to many intrinsic features and capabilities of the models. BERT based on transformers could preserve the sequence of text and the sentence wide context, which is a key feature to enhance the language model thereby performance. Other important aspects of this model are the word tokenization and its supporting word embeddings which have factored in the different word senses. As BERT

Table 10.1 Performance of SA on drug reviews using ML models.

Model	Accuracy (%)	Macro-F1-Score
TF-IDF$_{SVM}$	63	0.30
TF-IDF$_{Logistic}$	61	0.29
Bi-LSTM$_{FCD+Softmax}$	70	0.46
BERT$_{Without\_Fine-Tuning}$	71	0.45
BERT$_{With\_Fine-Tuning}$	75	0.65
BERT$_{With\_Fine-Tuning\_Ensemble}$	76	0.66

has changed the NLP landscape with its start-of-the-art results, it is indeed a breakthrough in the use of ML in NLP for various tasks.

10.6   Conclusion

Recent advancements in the ML techniques have brought in many new opportunities in NLP applications. With many major breakthroughs, deep learning is a popular scientific research trends now-a-days achieving state-of-the-art results and bringing tectonic shift in way NLP models are being designed. It has proven its potential viability in various types of NLP tasks such as SA, text summarization, machine translation, etc. Deep learning models for NLP are essentially language models which have come of age due to tremendous research effort with great results to use neural networks for language representation. As a result, many shallow architecture models have been upgraded into deep architecture models with multiple layers with dropout features to create end-to-end learning and analyzing models resulting in smart and intelligent applications. With the advent of transfer learning technique, the problems faced in traditional NLP tasks such as lack of annotated datasets and portability issues are subsided, as a result, the language model which is basis for many NLP applications has undergone dramatic transformations in terms of word representation and domain adaptation. Another inherent leverage of transfer learning in NLP is pre-training followed by fine-tuning where in the pre-training is performed on a large corpus of unlabeled text and fine-tuning is carried out on suitable annotated dataset for the respective downstream NLP task. The knowledge of deeper and intimate understandings of natural language representation gained in pre-training is like a Swiss army knife that is useful for almost any NLP task. As the computation power is increasing exponentially and becoming cheaper and accessible to larger community, the future holds bright for the deep learning models with fine-tuning capabilities and set to be a de facto model for next generation NLP based healthcare applications. Food Engineering is a newer technology which has direct impact on health sector. It will be adaptable by everyone in the near future. In this pandemic situation, ML application could contribute to maintaining the hygienic which is very important to keep away the virus. As ML plays a key role in this changing technology, adapting in food science gives the better performance and efficient output benefiting the healthcare.

References

1. Devanport, T. and Kalakota, R., The potential for artificial intelligence in healthcare. *Future Healthc. J.*, 6, 2, 94–98, 2019.
2. Kuo, E., AI in Healthcare: Industry Landscape, techburst.io, 12 December 2017. [Online], Available: https://techburst.io/ai-in-healthcare-industry-landscape-c433829b320c.
3. Tahir, G.A. and Loo, C.K., An Open-Ended Continual Learning for Food Recognition Using Class Incremental Extreme Learning Machines. *IEEE Access*, 8, 82328–82346, 2020.
4. Min, S., Evrendilek, G.A., Zhang, H.Q., Pulsed electric fields: Processing system, microbial and enzyme inhibition, and shelf life extension of foods. *IEEE Trans. Plasma Sci.*, 35, 1, 59–73, 2007.
5. Santosh, K., Speech processing in healthcare: Can we integrate?, in: *Intelligent Speech Signal Processing*, pp. 1–4, 2019.
6. Sarker, A., Ginn, R., Nikfarjam, A., O'Connor, K., Smith, K., Jayaraman, S., Upadhaya, T., Gonzalez, G., Utilizing social media data for pharmacovigilance: A review. *J. Biomed. Inform.*, 54, 202–212, 2015.
7. Seetharam, K., Kagiyama, N., Shrestha, S., Sengupta, P.P., Clinical inference from cardiovascular imaging: Paradigm shift towards machine-based intelligent platform. *Curr. Treat. Options Cardiovasc. Med.*, 22, 3, 1–11, 2020.
8. Kidwai, B. and Nadesh, R., Design and development of diagnostic chabot for supporting primary healthcare systems. *Procedia Comput. Sci.*, Gurugram, 167, 2020, 75–84, 2019.
9. Tomra, *Tomato Sorting & Processing Machines By Tomra*, Tomra Systems ASA, 2017, [Online]. Available: https://www.tomra.com/en/sorting/food/your-produce/vegetables/tomatoes.
10. Tonda, A., Boukhelifa, N., Chabin, T., Barnabé, M., Génot, B., Lutton, E., Perrot, N., *Human and Machine Learning*, Springer, Cham, 2018.
11. AI, K., *Industry Applications*, KANKAN AI, 2016, [Online]. Available: https://www.kankanai.com.cn/en/case/production/.
12. BitRefine, *Plant disease detection*, BitRefine Group, 2016, [Online]. Available: https://bitrefine.group/industries/precision-agriculture/88-industries/agriculture-food/agriculture-solutions/184-plant-disease.
13. Shearer, J., Anderson, D., Ayars, W., Belknap, E., Berry, S., Guard, C., Hoblet, K., Hovingh, E., Kirksey, G., Langill, A., Mills, A., A record keeping system for capture of lameness and footcare information in cattle. *Bov. Pract.*, 38, 1, 83–92, 2004.
14. Paramesha, K. and Ravishankar, K., Optimization of cross domain sentiment analysis using sentiwordnet. *Int. J. Found. Comput. Sci. Technol.*, 3, 5, 35–41, 2013.
15. Yadav, S., Ekbal, A., Saha, S., Bhattacharyya, P., Medical sentiment analysis using social media: towards building a patient assisted system, in: European Language Resources Association (ELRA), Miyazaki, 2018.
16. Abualigah, L., Alfar, H.E., Shehab, M., Hussein, A.A., *In Recent advances in NLP: The case of Arabic language*, Springer, Cham, 2020.
17. Gräßer, F., Kallumadi, S., Malberg, H., Zaunseder, S., *Aspect-based sentiment analysis of drug reviews applying cross-domain and cross-data learning*, ACM, New York, 2018.
18. Han, Y., Liu, M., Jing, W., Aspect-Level Drug Reviews Sentiment Analysis Based on Double BiGRU and Knowledge Transfer. *IEEE Access*, 8, 21314–21325, 2020.
19. Fan, B., Fan, W., Smith, C. et al., Adverse drug event detection and extraction from open data: A deep learning approach. *Inf. Process. Manag.*, 8, 21314–21325, 2020.
20. Waheeb, S.A., Khan, N.A., Chen, B., Shang, X., Machine learning based sentiment text classi cation for evaluating treatment quality of discharge summary. *Information*, 11, 5, 281–296, 2020.

21. Shah, B., *AV-Innoplexus-Online-Hiring-Hackathon-Sentiment*, Innoplexus, 2019, [Online]. Available: https://www.kaggle.com/buntyshah/av-innoplexus-online-hiring-hackathon-sentiment/data#Analytics-vidhya-Innoplexus-Online-Hiring-Hackathon-Sentiment-Analysis.
22. Paramesha, K. and Ravishankar, K.C., Analysis of opinionated text for opinion. *Mach. Learn. Appl.: An International Journal (MLAIJ)*, 3, 2, 65–74, 2016.
23. Segura-Bedmar, I., Suárez-Paniagua, V., Martínez, P., Exploring word embedding for drug name recognition, in: Association for Computational Linguistics, Lisbon, 2015.
24. Rozado, D., Wide range screening of algorithmic bias in word embedding models using large sentiment lexicons reveals underreported bias types. *PLoS One*, 15, 4, 1–26, 2020.
25. Dong, C., *Cheney's blog*, Disqus, 27 November 2019, [Online]. Available: https://cheneydonc.cn/A-Review-of-Pretraining-General-Language-Representations.html.
26. McCormick, C. and Ryan, N., BERT Fine-Tuning Tutorial with PyTorch, 20 3 2020. [Online]. Available: https://mccormickml.com/2019/07/22/BERT-fine-tuning/.

Comparison of MobileNet and ResNet CNN Architectures in the CNN-Based Skin Cancer Classifier Model

Subasish Mohapatra, N.V.S. Abhishek, Dibyajit Bardhan, Anisha Ankita Ghosh and Shubhadarshini Mohanty*

Department of Computer Science and Engineering, College of Engineering and Technology, Bhubaneswar, India

Abstract

The deadliness of skin cancer cannot be overstated. A very common form of cancer, the disease's potential dangers lie in its numbers. The numbers tell a gloomy tale. At an ever-increasing rate of over 3 million skin cancer cases year after year and a rapidly declining ozone cover, a technological intervention is the need of the hour. The main cause of skin cancer related death rate is due to lack of early prediction. We are trying to address this through our machine learning model, Skin Cancer Classifier. The model has been trained on HAM10000 dataset (a huge repository of varied-sources dermatoscopic common coloured skin lesion images) using the concept of Convolutional Neural Network (CNN). The model tells us whether a skin lesion is cancerous or non-cancerous by giving an output of three most likely diagnosis of skin condition. The concept of deep learning used is then further leveraged by executing hyperparameter tuning on the model. Our next main focus has been to make a thorough comparative analysis of MobileNet and ResNet50 CNN architectures. The skin cancer classifier model is of tremendous value when it comes to saving precious human lives from the malice of skin cancer through an early diagnosis with the help of deep learning.

Keywords: Skin cancer, convolutional neural networks (CNN), skin lesion, machine learning, HAM10000, MobileNet, ResNet50

11.1 Introduction

The recent era of humanity is blessed with the gift of advancement in science and technology, so much so that the most frivolous and basic needs of ours are taken care of by technology and its many products. These days, with the help of Computer-aided diagnosis (CAD), important insights into medical images can be mined. One spectacular instance of this application can be seen in the form of mammogram which is being used to detect breast cancers in the United States of America [1]. In the field of medical research, CAD has

---

Corresponding author: smohapatra@cet.edu.in

Sachi Nandan Mohanty, G. Nalinipriya, Om Prakash Jena and Achyuth Sarkar (eds.) Machine Learning for Healthcare Applications, (169–186) © 2021 Scrivener Publishing LLC

become an indispensable toolkit to derive at important results, all the more so in imaging radiology [2–4] and diagnosis of medical images. The most effective use of CAD is in early stages when the diagnosis of a medical condition takes precedence over anything else. This inevitably results in lesser number of human fatalities. Skin cancer as a disease also relies heavily on early diagnosis in order for recovery to happen. Most often, skin cancer is a mixture of various interconnected illnesses. We saw more than 14 million new cases of skin cancer with 8.2 million mortalities due to cancerous lesions around the world. This tells us enough how skin cancer if detected early will help humanity's cause a lot.

The main focus of our project is to facilitate early diagnosis in skin cancer [5, 6]. One of the more frequent cases of skin cancer is found in body parts of people which are exposed to direct sunlight for long continuous hours. However, the other probabilities—skin cancer occurring in other body parts is never out of the window. One of the relief points about skin cancer is that it starts penetrating the human body from top, which means, from the outer skin layer called the epidermis. The upside to this being it is visible to the naked eye. Also, it clearly indicates that the CAD systems can come in handy here in order to go for an analysis without the disturbance or noise from any other piece of information. This can be termed as a preliminary early stage rough diagnosis [7, 8].

Most cancerous of all skin cancers in humans is the melanoma. The usual signs of melanoma are pigmented or coloured marks on the skin. Humans face a lot of skin cancer conditions but melanoma is the deadliest. Abnormal conditions in melanin producing cells or melanocytes cause melanoma. Extensive and repetitive use of tanning beds, a weak or dysfunctional or poor immune system, fair coloured skin tone or complexion, hereditary factors, continuous exposure to direct UV rays—all contribute to melanoma conditions. As per Refs. [9, 10], approximately 91,270 new forms of melanoma cases were identified in the last year, 2019. 9,320 fatalities have been reported due to melanoma in the same year.

Young women have especially shown a tendency to succumb easily to the dangers of melanoma. One of the most important factors again in case of melanoma is diagnosis at an early stage. Otherwise the skin lesion just grows and continues its journey spreading at a rapid pace, starting from the outer surface of human body, that is outermost skin layer and then gradually proceeding to affect the deeper surfaces or layers in which we find an intimate connection with the blood and other vessels such as lymph vessels [11, 12]. As in other cases of cancer, an early detection of skin cancer conditions can significantly reduce the fatality rate. This is a significant point to note. However, mostly the early diagnosis of skin cancer is a complex and costly process to undertake.

The main purpose now then is to enable diagnosis at an early stage. It's important to study the soreness of the skin lesion and most importantly, classify it as cancerous/melanoma [13, 14] or non-cancerous/benign. At present we have multiple techniques going on for diagnosis like Support Vector Machines (SVMs), Artificial Neural Networks (ANNs), genetic algorithms, Convolutional Neural Networks (CNNs), the ABCDE rule, etc.

These systems have garnered wide support in favor of using them and have been termed as tech-savvy, excellent in productivity and efficiency and over all, less cumbersome and excruciating than traditional medical methods and procedures. In any case, CNNs as well as profound learning are the decision methods in numerous PC vision issues.

Hence, we have clearly been informed now that an early diagnosis is the best way to tackle the menace of skin cancer. How early can we do it? A technological intervention is the need of the hour. One that's super-efficient, scalable and cost-effective. Our paper focused on this particularly. Our skin cancer classification system is a model of ML that has been trained on HAM10000 dataset (The huge repository of varied-sources dermatoscopic usual coloured skin lesion images) using the concept of Convolutional Neural Network (CNN) [15–17]. The model tells us whether a skin lesion is cancerous or non-cancerous by giving an output of three most likely diagnosis of skin condition [18]. The concept of deep learning used is then further leveraged by executing hyperparameter tuning on the model. Our next main focus has been to make a thorough comparative analysis of MobileNet and ResNet50 CNN architectures [19]. The skin cancer classifier model is of tremendous value when it comes to saving precious human lives from the malice of skin cancer through an early diagnosis with the help of deep learning.

11.2   Our Skin Cancer Classifier Model

Neural networks training for auto diagnosis of pigmented skin lesions is hampered by the less size and absence of assorted variety of accessible dataset of dermatoscopic pictures. Hence the HAM10000 ("Human Against Machine with 10,000 training images") dataset was released. HAM10000 is a publicly available dataset which contains nearly 10,000 dermatoscopic images. These images were collected from different populations, obtained and stored by different modalities [20]. It includes both training set and validation set which are dermatoscopic images obtained from different groups of people in different countries. The final dataset contains 10,015 dermatoscopic images to be used as training set for academic machine learning purposes. Cases include a representative collection of all-important diagnostic categories in the domain of pigmented lesions.

The dataset is grouping of all the critical demonstrative characterizations of pigmented bruises: Actinic keratosis and intraepithelial carcinoma/Bowen's ailment (akiec), basal cell carcinoma (bcc), accommodating keratosis-like wounds (sun oriented lentigines/seborrheic keratoses and lichen-planus like keratosis, bkl), dermatofibroma (df), melanoma (mel), melanocytic nevi (nv) and vascular wounds (angiomas, angiokeratomas, pyogenic granulomas and channel, vasc) are shown in Figure 11.1. Over half of wounds are bore witness to through histopathology, the ground truth for the remainder of the cases is either follow-up examination, expert accord, or affirmation by *in vivo* confocal microscopy.

Our proposed model was able to classify a given skin lesion image into one of the given seven categories and shown in Figure 11.2. CNNs were utilized for this picture classification task on the grounds that after the appearance of incredible GPUs and plentiful wellsprings of picture information, CNNs have given preferable outcomes over conventional picture classification algorithms.

On web application model was published. Solution follows two steps, first one is training model that yield perfect result then second is building up a web application which gave an intuitive stage to the clients to utilize the machine learning model.

It is quite clear that CNNs are one of the best techniques to decipher patterns and meanings in images. Our machine learning classification model trained on HAM10000 dataset uses CNN involving both MobileNet and ResNet architectures. MobileNet architecture has a predefined number of layers and weights in it whereas in ResNet we define the number of layers and also give the weight attributes required for training the learning architecture.

A comparative analysis of MobileNet and ResNet architectures has also been done in order to come to conclusion as to which architecture gives us maximum accuracy.

1	lesion_id	image_id	dx	dx_type	age	sex	localization
2	HAM_0000118	ISIC_0027419	bkl	histo		80 male	scalp
3	HAM_0000118	ISIC_0025030	bkl	histo		80 male	scalp
4	HAM_0002730	ISIC_0026769	bkl	histo		80 male	scalp
5	HAM_0002730	ISIC_0025661	bkl	histo		80 male	scalp
6	HAM_0001466	ISIC_0031633	bkl	histo		75 male	ear
7	HAM_0001466	ISIC_0027850	bkl	histo		75 male	ear
8	HAM_0002761	ISIC_0029176	bkl	histo		60 male	face
9	HAM_0002761	ISIC_0025068	bkl	histo		60 male	face
10	HAM_0005132	ISIC_0025837	bkl	histo		70 female	back
11	HAM_0005132	ISIC_0025209	bkl	histo		70 female	back
12	HAM_0001396	ISIC_0025276	bkl	histo		55 female	trunk
13	HAM_0004234	ISIC_0025396	bkl	histo		85 female	chest
14	HAM_0004234	ISIC_0025984	bkl	histo		85 female	chest
15	HAM_0001949	ISIC_0025767	bkl	histo		70 male	trunk
16	HAM_0001949	ISIC_0032417	bkl	histo		70 male	trunk
17	HAM_0007207	ISIC_0031326	bkl	histo		65 male	back
18	HAM_0001601	ISIC_0025915	bkl	histo		75 male	upper extremity
19	HAM_0001601	ISIC_0031029	bkl	histo		75 male	upper extremity
20	HAM_0007571	ISIC_0025836	bkl	histo		70 male	chest
21	HAM_0007571	ISIC_0032129	bkl	histo		70 male	chest
22	HAM_0006071	ISIC_0032343	bkl	histo		70 female	face
23	HAM_0003301	ISIC_0025033	bkl	histo		60 male	back
24	HAM_0003301	ISIC_0027310	bkl	histo		60 male	back
25	HAM_0004884	ISIC_0032128	bkl	histo		75 male	upper extremity

H ◄ ► H   HAM10000_metadata

Figure 11.1 A snapshot of HAM10000 dataset.

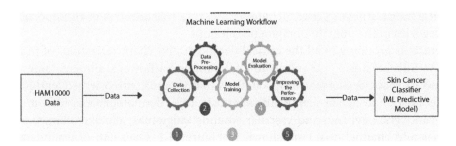

Figure 11.2 A high-level view of our classification model.

The respective output graphs have also been included. Lastly, we have incorporated the classification model into a fully functional web application that will empower specialists and lab technologists to realize the three most noteworthy likelihood analyses for a given skin sore. Henceforth, the model will be of tremendous assistance in rapidly recognizing high need patients and accelerate the procedural work process.

11.3   Skin Cancer Classifier Model Results

The first step of building any machine learning model is data pre-processing. In our case too, we performed data-pre-processing and after that we had 9,077 images for the purpose of training and 938 images for the purpose of validation by employing a standard 90:10 ratio (split) for training and validation of the ML model.

As appeared in the table over, our dataset contained a lot of skewness for example the class Dermatofibroma (df) had way less pictures when contrasted with the class Melanocytic Nevi (nv). This skewness should have been evacuated for the model to perform well. We utilized the method of picture enlargement to deliver new pictures for just the preparation set. In the wake of performing picture growth, we had the option to deliver a preparation set according to arrangement referenced beneath in Table 11.2.

Utilizing the methodology of move learning, we utilized the MobileNetV1 model's design to prepare our own model. Convolutional Neural Networks (CNN)s have moved various PC vision ventures in the previous decade and keep on drawing in enormous enthusiasm from scientists, who hope to alter and apply them for different use cases. We picked MobileNetV1 on the grounds that it has a light-weight engineering, which makes it perfect for web arrangement.

After the process of training our model, we underwent the process of testing our model on the validation set. The results of the testing process are as follows:-

1. Loss—We got 0.72 in the last epoch and 0.56 in the best epoch.
2. Categorical Accuracy—We got 0.80 in the last epoch and 0.84 in the best epoch.
3. Top 2 Accuracy—We got 0.92 in the last epoch and 0.92 in the best epoch.
4. Top 3 Accuracy—We got 0.95 in the last epoch and 0.96 in the best epoch.

After evaluating the performance, the classification report, shown below in Table 11.1, was generated.

The trained model was then saved and converted to JSON format using TensorFlow.js's command line tool. The generated model.json file was then used to build the backbone of our web deployment, using Tensorflowjs's in-built methods, to classify an uploaded image of a skin lesion, into the top three classes among the seven classes, on the basis of their confidence.

Table 11.1 Classification report of our machine learning model.

Class	Precision	Recall	F1-Score	Support
nv	0.91	0.97	0.94	751
bkl	0.86	0.08	0.15	75
mel	0.28	0.28	0.28	39
bcc	0.59	0.97	0.73	30
akiec	0.46	0.50	0.48	26
vasc	1.00	0.45	0.62	11
df	0.25	0.50	0.33	6
Macro Average	0.62	0.54	0.51	938
Weighted Average	0.86	0.85	0.82	938

11.4   Hyperparameter Tuning and Performance

In machine learning hyperparameter tuning refers to the process of adjusting various parameters to optimize the learning process. These parameters are different from the node weights because weights are the parameters that are learned while training the neural network whereas the parameters in question merely act as helpers in the learning process.

The various types of parameters used in this project are as follows:

- Optimizer: Optimizers play a crucial role in determining both the rate at which our model will reach the global minima and the net loss our loss function will incur at the end of the training phase. As discussed earlier, some of the famous optimizers include Adam, Adamax, SGD, RMSProp, etc. Adam is the most popular optimizer, used heavily by researchers across the world, due to the reason that it is specifically designed to train deep neural networks.

- Dropout Rate: Two of the most common problems that are faced almost every day while training any machine learning model are overfitting and underfitting. Dropout is a technique to tackle overfitting in deep neural networks by "dropping out" or ignoring a certain number of randomly chosen neurons from a particular hidden layer. These dropped neurons will no longer participate in the learning process, making the representation of the model less complex. Dropout rate is the metric that decides the proportion of neurons that will be dropped. If the dropout rate is too low then our model will still suffer from overfitting. If the dropout rate is too high then our model will suffer from underfitting, which is even worse. So, dropout proves to be a very handy approach while dealing with overfitting given that the dropout rate is chosen appropriately. If the dropout rate is 0.5, it means that 50% of the neurons in the hidden layer will be dropped randomly.

- Learning Rate: Every optimizer operates within the limits of a certain learning rate. Learning rate determines the extent to which our model should react to the error or loss generated each time the weights are updated. Learning rate needs to be set very cautiously. If the learning rate is too high the model will spiral outwards, away from the minima and will never reach a global minimum. If the learning rate is too low then the model will take a very long time to reach the minima. In the days where compute power doesn't come cheap, we wouldn't want our model to run forever. The figure given below accurately describes the three possible scenarios that might arise directly due to the learning rate.

- Epochs: An epoch refers to a point at which the whole dataset has been parsed completely, both from the forward and the backward directions. More epochs almost always give better results. But, as in earlier cases, the number of epochs that we can train our model on is limited by the compute power we possess.

11.4.1   Hyperparameter Tuning of MobileNet-Based CNN Model

- Optimizer: After analyzing the various optimizers on our dataset by keeping other parameters constant we found out that Adam optimizer performed the best among all. This can be attributed to the reasons given below. In all the further model evaluations Adam is taken as the default optimizer.
  Adam showed the lowest validation set best epoch loss of 0.5983.
  Adam showed the highest validation set best epoch top 3 accuracy of 0.9626.
- Dropout Rate: After evaluating the performances of both the values of 0.10 and 0.25, dropout = 0.25 gave comparatively better results in terms of top 3 accuracy and loss for validation set, by demonstrating lower proportions of overfitting. In the graph of training and validation loss for dropout = 0.25, we observed that the loss of validation data is closer to training data than that in the graph for dropout = 0.10.
- Learning Rate: After evaluating the various learning rate values, we concluded that an initial rate = 0.001 for our Adam optimizer proved to be the best fit for our problem. Initial rate = 0.01 proved to be overshooting the global minima and consequently taking more time to reach it. Initial rate = 0.0001 proved to be very slow and also took more time to reach the global minima.
- Epochs: As one might expect, we got the best results by training our model for 100 epochs. It gave the best epoch top 3 accuracy of 0.9616 and best epoch loss of 0.7640 for the validation set, better than other values for number of epochs.

11.4.2   Hyperparameter Tuning of ResNet50-Based CNN Model

- Optimizer: Adam optimizer outperforms all the other optimizers for many modern-day deep learning problems, which includes our specific problem of skin lesion image classification.
- Dropout Rate: After evaluating the performances of both the values, dropout = 0.40 gave comparatively better results in terms of top 3 accuracy and loss for validation set, by demonstrating lower proportions of overfitting. In the graph of training and validation loss for dropout = 0.40, we observed that the loss of validation data is closer to training data than that in the graph for dropout = 0.25.
- Learning Rate: After evaluating the various learning rate values, we concluded that an initial rate = 0.001 for our Adam optimizer proved to be the best fit for our problem. Initial rate = 0.01 proved to be overshooting the global minima and consequently taking more time to reach it.
- Epochs: As one might expect, we got the best results by training our model for 100 epochs. It gave the best epoch top 3 accuracy of 0.9658 and best epoch loss of 0.5521 for the validation set, better than other values for number of epochs.

11.4.3 Table Summary of Hyperparameter Tuning Results

Table 11.2 depicts summary of hyper parameter tuning.

Table 11.2 Summary of hyper parameter tuning.

ResNet50 Model		
	Validation loss	Validation top 3 accuracy
Optimizer = Adam	0.5983	0.9626
Dropout = 0.40	0.7596	0.9616
Learning Rate = 0.001	0.664	0.9552
Epochs = 100	0.5521	0.9658
Mobile Net Model		
	Validation loss	Validation top 3 accuracy
Optimizer = Adam	0.5983	0.9626
Dropout = 0.25	0.6281	0.9637
Learning Rate = 0.001	0.6281	0.9637
Epochs = 100	0.764	0.9616

11.5 Comparative Analysis and Results

After performing hyperparameter tuning on various parameters, we are now ready to do a comparative analysis of the two models used to perform the given image classification task. The specifications of the models used to analyze and compare are given below.

MobileNet:
Optimizer: Adam optimizer
Learning Rate: 0.001
Epochs: 100
Dropout: 0.25

ResNet50:
Optimizer: Adam optimizer
Learning Rate: 0.001
Epochs: 100
Dropout: 0.40

11.5.1   Training and Validation Loss

11.5.1.1   MobileNet

Figure 11.3 depicts training and validation loss of MobileNet Architecture.

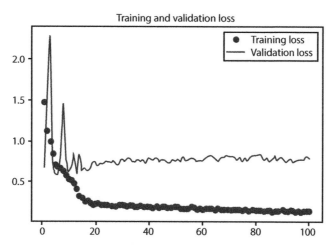

Figure 11.3 Training and validation loss MobileNet.

11.5.1.2   ResNet50

Figure 11.4 depicts training and validation loss of ResNet50 Architecture

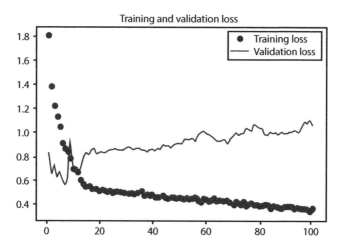

Figure 11.4 Training and validation loss ResNet50.

11.5.1.3   Inferences

Both ResNet50 and MobileNet have similar trajectories in terms of training loss. MobileNet has a better final epoch validation loss while ResNet50 has better best epoch validation loss.

11.5.2   Training and Validation Categorical Accuracy

11.5.2.1   MobileNet

Figure 11.5 depicts training and validation categorical accuracy of MobileNet Architecture.

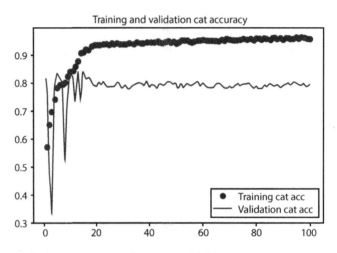

Figure 11.5 Training and validation categorical accuracy MobileNet.

11.5.2.2   ResNet50

Figure 11.6 depicts training and validation categorical accuracy of ResNet50 Architecture.

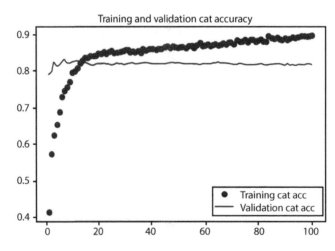

Figure 11.6 Training and validation categorical accuracy ResNet50.

11.5.2.3   Inferences

ResNet50 has a lot better categorical accuracy than MobileNet because of its more complex architecture.

11.5.3   Training and Validation Top 2 Accuracy

11.5.3.1   MobileNet

Figure 11.7 depicts training and validation top 2 accuracy of MobileNet Architecture.

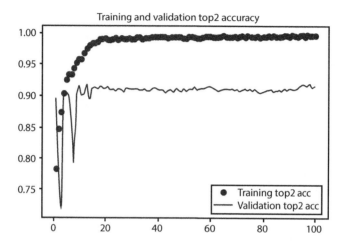

Figure 11.7 Training and validation top2 accuracy MobileNet.

11.5.3.2   ResNet50

Figure 11.8 depicts training and validation top 2 accuracy of ResNet50 Architecture.

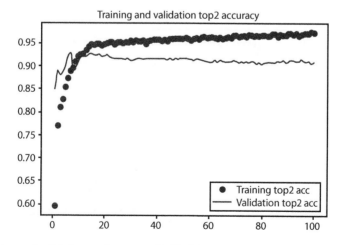

Figure 11.8 Training and validation top2 accuracy ResNet50.

11.5.3.3 *Inferences*

MobileNet has a better last epoch top 2 accuracy while ResNet50 has better best epoch top 2 accuracy.

11.5.4 Training and Validation Top 3 Accuracy

11.5.4.1 *MobileNet*

Figure 11.9 depicts training and validation top 3 accuracy of MobileNet Architecture.

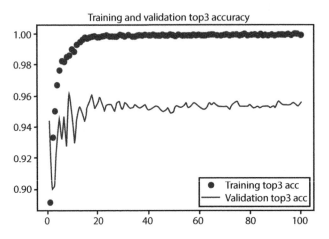

Figure 11.9 Training and validation top3 accuracy MobileNet.

11.5.4.2 *ResNet50*

Figure 11.10 depicts training and validation top 3 accuracy of ResNet50 Architecture.

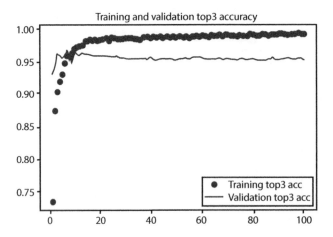

Figure 11.10 Training and validation top3 accuracy ResNet50.

11.5.4.3   Inferences

Both ResNet50 and MobileNet have similar trajectories in terms of training and validation top 3 accuracy. One key difference in both of these networks is that ResNet50 is larger as compared to MobileNet. Hence it would mean that MobileNet takes less time to train whereas ResNet50 is more robust towards overfitting.

11.5.5   Confusion Matrix

11.5.5.1   MobileNet

Figure 11.11 depicts confusion matrix of MobileNet Architecture.

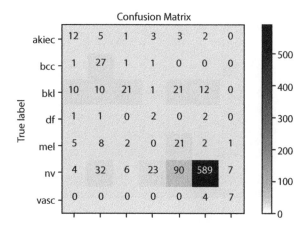

Figure 11.11 Confusion matrix MobileNet.

11.5.5.2   ResNet50

Figure 11.12 depicts confusion matrix of ResNet50 Architecture.

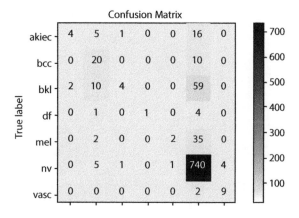

Figure 11.12 Confusion matrix ResNet50.

11.5.5.3   Inferences

One of the major drawbacks of using ResNet50 over MobileNet is that ResNet50 has a greater number of False Negative misclassifications for Melanoma (mel), which is the major type of cancerous skin lesions we are looking to classify. ResNet50 has a total of 37 false negative misclassifications for melanoma whereas MobileNet has only 18.

11.5.6   Classification Report

11.5.6.1   MobileNet

Figure 11.13 depicts classification report of MobileNet Architecture.

	precision	recall	f1-score	support
akiec	0.36	0.46	0.41	26
bcc	0.33	0.90	0.48	30
bkl	0.68	0.28	0.40	75
df	0.07	0.33	0.11	6
mel	0.16	0.54	0.24	39
nv	0.96	0.78	0.86	751
vasc	0.47	0.64	0.54	11
accuracy			0.72	938
macro avg	0.43	0.56	0.43	938
weighted avg	0.86	0.72	0.77	938

Figure 11.13 Classification reports MobileNet.

11.5.6.2   ResNet50

Figure 11.14 depicts classification report of ResNet50 Architecture.

	precision	recall	f1-score	support
akiec	0.67	0.15	0.25	26
bcc	0.47	0.67	0.55	30
bkl	0.67	0.05	0.10	75
df	1.00	0.17	0.29	6
mel	0.67	0.05	0.10	39
nv	0.85	0.99	0.92	751
vasc	0.69	0.82	0.75	11
accuracy			0.83	938
macro avg	0.72	0.41	0.42	938
weighted avg	0.81	0.83	0.78	938

Figure 11.14 Classification reports ResNet50.

11.5.6.3   Inferences

Accuracy

ResNet50 has a higher overall F1 score than MobileNet which shows that it has a greater balance on predictions of all the categories. But MobileNet has a greater F1 score than ResNet50 in case of Melanoma, which makes it more desirable in use cases where we have to perform a binary classification between cancerous and non-cancerous images. ResNet50 is a better fit for our particular use case where we have to classify images into seven different classes.

Macro Average

ResNet50 has a greater macro average precision than MobileNet whereas MobileNet has a greater macro average recall than ResNet50. From this we can infer that MobileNet has a higher number of false positives but a comparatively lower number of false negatives than ResNet50.

Weighted Average

ResNet50 has a greater weighted average recall than MobileNet whereas MobileNet has a greater weighted average precision than ResNet50. From this we can infer that ResNet50 has a higher number of false positives but a comparatively lower number of false negatives than MobileNet, with more weightage given to melanoma (mel).

11.5.7   Last Epoch Results

11.5.7.1   MobileNet

Figure 11.15 depicts last epoch results of MobileNet Architecture.

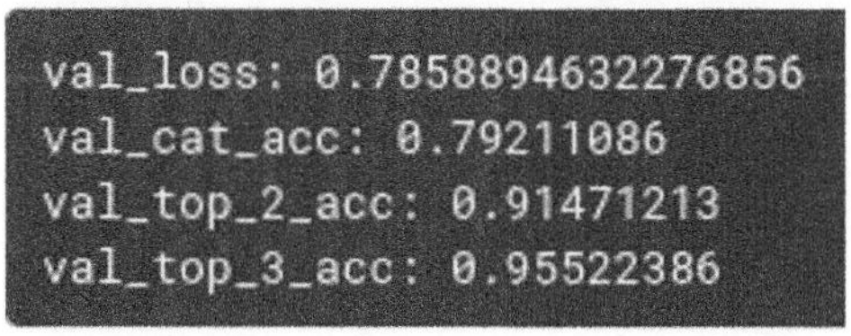

```
val_loss: 0.7858894632276856
val_cat_acc: 0.79211086
val_top_2_acc: 0.91471213
val_top_3_acc: 0.95522386
```

Figure 11.15 Last epoch results MobileNet.

11.5.7.2   ResNet50

Figure 11.16 depicts last epoch result of ResNet50 Architecture.

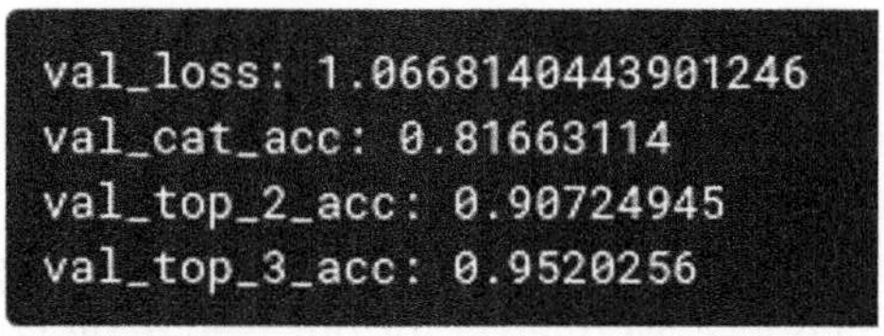

```
val_loss: 1.0668140443901246
val_cat_acc: 0.81663114
val_top_2_acc: 0.90724945
val_top_3_acc: 0.9520256
```

Figure 11.16 Last epoch results ResNet50.

11.5.7.3 Inferences

In the last epoch both ResNet50 and MobileNet had similar performances in terms of top 3 accuracy for validation set. MobileNet gave a lower loss as compared to ResNet50 whereas ResNet50 gave a higher categorical accuracy than that shown by MobileNet.

11.5.8 Best Epoch Results

11.5.8.1 MobileNet

Figure 11.17 depicts best epoch results of MobileNet Architecture.

```
val_loss: 0.7640448813545226
val_cat_acc: 0.7238806
val_top_2_acc: 0.8987207
val_top_3_acc: 0.96162045
```

Figure 11.17 Best epoch results MobileNet.

11.5.8.2 ResNet50

Figure 11.18 depicts best epoch results of ResNet50 Architecture.

```
val_loss: 0.5521315547003857
val_cat_acc: 0.8315565
val_top_2_acc: 0.9275053
val_top_3_acc: 0.96588486
```

Figure 11.18 Best epoch results ResNet50.

11.5.8.3 Inferences

As we can see ResNet50 outperformed MobileNet in terms of best epoch results. Even though the top 3 accuracies are similar the losses on the validation set are very much different, where ResNet50 incurred a loss of 0.5521 as compared to 0.7640 incurred by MobileNet. ResNet also outperformed MobileNet in terms of top 2 accuracy and categorical accuracy. It achieved a categorical accuracy of 0.8315, the highest seen so far.

11.5.9 Overall Comparative Analysis

ResNet50 is a larger network than MobileNet. This means that ResNet50 would take longer to train but will be more robust towards overfitting.

MobileNet architectures are specifically developed to be light-weight and mobile-friendly. So it is natural to choose MobileNet for our web deployment as ResNet50 would take a longer time to give out predictions.

MobileNet performs better than ResNet50 when we have to perform binary classification for cancerous and non-cancerous images specifically.

ResNet50 performs better than MobileNet when it is classifying an image into more than two classes. Hence, with this perspective, ResNet50 is a better fit to our problem as we have to classify images into a total of seven classes.

MobileNet has a lower number of false negatives associated with melanoma (mel) as compared to ResNet50. It is a very crucial advantage that MobileNet displayed over ResNet50 for our specific problem.

Using either of the two models depends on our use case. In the case of web application deployment MobileNet is a better fit. But if we need better performance and do not care about mobile deployments, ResNet50 is a better fit.

11.6   Conclusion

The skin cancer classification model aims at providing a preliminary diagnosis of the patient by classifying the skin lesion image into various types which includes cancerous and noncancerous being the broader categories. The convolutional neural network architecture was used as it is one of the best deep learning techniques to deal with image classification. The model was then successfully deployed into a web application so as to make the model usable and accessible to its various stakeholders like patient, lab personnel and medical professionals.

The comparative analysis of MobileNet and ResNet architectures clearly pointed out to the fact that ResNet50 is more robust to overfitting while MobileNet is light-weight architecture and hence very suitable for application development. MobileNet performs better than ResNet50 when we have to perform binary classification for cancerous and non-cancerous images specifically while ResNet50 performs better than MobileNet when it is classifying an image into more than two classes. Hence, with this perspective, ResNet50 is a better fit to our problem as we have to classify images into a total of seven classes. Using either of the two models depends on our use case. In the case of web application deployment MobileNet is a better fit. But if we need better performance and do not care about mobile deployments, ResNet50 is a better fit.

Here, we have made an attempt to battle the harm of skin malignant growth, for which early prediction is necessary. With expectation of an expansion in the occurrences of skin malignant growth because of expanded UV radiation infiltration because of an exceptionally exhausted ozone layer, being not too far off, this opportune innovative mediation would support oncologists and clinical crew in conveying their best work, and spare millions around the world through a beginning phase diagnosis.

References

1. Abdel-Zaher, A.M. and Eldeib, A.M., Breast cancer classification using deep belief networks. *Expert Syst. Appl.*, 46, 139–144, 2016.
2. Masood, A. and Ali Al-Jumaily, A., Computer aided diagnostic support system for skin cancer: A review of techniques and algorithms. *Int. J. Biomed. Imaging*, 2015, 1–2, 2013.

3. Doi, K., Computer-aided diagnosis in medical imaging: Historical review, current status and future potential. *Comput. Med. Imaging Graph.*, 31, 4–5, 198–211, 2007.

4. Mehta, P. and Shah, B., Review on techniques and steps of computer aided skin cancer diagnosis. *Procedia Comput. Sci.*, 85, 309–316, 2016.

5. Parás-Bravo, P., Paz-Zulueta, M., Santibañez, M., Fernández-de-Las-Peñas, C., Herrero-Montes, M., Caso-Álvarez, V., Palacios-Ceña, D., Living with a peripherally inserted central catheter: The perspective of cancer outpatients—A qualitative study. *Support. Care Cancer*, 26, 2, 441–449, 2018.

6. Smith, R.A., Andrews, K.S., Brooks, D., Fedewa, S.A., Manassaram-Baptiste, D., Saslow, D., Wender, R.C., Cancer screening in the United States, 2018: A review of current American Cancer Society guidelines and current issues in cancer screening. *CA: Cancer J. Clin.*, 68, 4, 297–316, 2018.

7. Pathan, S., Prabhu, K.G., Siddalingaswamy, P.C., Techniques and algorithms for computer aided diagnosis of pigmented skin lesions—A review. *Biomed. Signal Process. Control*, 39, 237–262, 2018.

8. Mohapatra, S., Abhishek, N.V.S., Bardhan, D., Ghosh, A.A., Mohanty, S., Skin Cancer Classification Using Convolution Neural Networks, in: *Advances in Distributed Computing and Machine Learning*, pp. 433–442, Springer, Singapore, 2020.

9. Esteva, A., Kuprel, B., Novoa, R.A., Ko, J., Swetter, S.M., Blau, H.M., Thrun, S., Dermatologist-level classification of skin cancer with deep neural networks. *Nature*, 542, 7639, 115–118, 2017.

10. Nylund, A., *To be, or not to be Melanoma: Convolutional neural networks in skin lesion classification*, KTH Royal Institute of Technology School of Technology and Health, Stockholm, Sweden, 2016.

11. Dubal, P., Bhatt, S., Joglekar, C., Patil, S., Skin cancer detection and classification, in: *2017 6th international conference on electrical engineering and informatics (ICEEI)*, 2017, November, IEEE, pp. 1–6.

12. Ridell, P. and Spett, H., *Training set size for skin cancer classification using Google's inception v3*, KTH Royal Institute of Technology School of Technology and Health, Stockholm, Sweden, 2017.

13. Pomponiu, V., Nejati, H., Cheung, N.M., Deepmole: Deep neural networks for skin mole lesion classification, in: *2016 IEEE International Conference on Image Processing (ICIP)*, 2016, September, IEEE, pp. 2623–2627.

14. Guo, Y., Liu, Y., Oerlemans, A., Lao, S., Wu, S., Lew, M.S., Deep learning for visual understanding: A review. *Neurocomputing*, 187, 27–48, 2016.

15. Ali, A.A. and Al-Marzouqi, H., Melanoma detection using regular convolutional neural networks, in: *2017 International Conference on Electrical and Computing Technologies and Applications (ICECTA)*, 2017, November, IEEE, pp. 1–5.

16. Hameed, N., Ruskin, A., Hassan, K.A., Hossain, M.A., A comprehensive survey on image-based computer aided diagnosis systems for skin cancer, in: *2016 10th International Conference on Software, Knowledge, Information Management & Applications (SKIMA)*, 2016, December, IEEE, pp. 205–214.

17. Krizhevsky, A., Sutskever, I., Hinton, G.E., Imagenet classification with deep convolutional neural networks, in: *Advances in Neural Information Processing Systems*, pp. 1097–1105, 2012.

18. ur Rehman, M., Khan, S.H., Rizvi, S.D., Abbas, Z., Zafar, A., Classification of skin lesion by interference of segmentation and convolotion neural network, in: *2018 2nd International Conference on Engineering Innovation (ICEI)*, 2018, July, IEEE, pp. 81–85.

19. Howard, A.G., Zhu, M., Chen, B., Kalenichenko, D., Wang, W., Weyand, T., Adam, H., Mobilenets: Efficient convolutional neural networks for mobile vision applications, Google.inc, arXiv preprint arXiv:1704.04861, 1–69, 2017.

20. Tschandl, P., Rosendahl, C., Kittler, H., The HAM10000 dataset, a large collection of multi-source dermatoscopic images of common pigmented skin lesions. *Sci. Data*, 5, 180161, 2018.

Deep Learning-Based Image Classifier for Malaria Cell Detection

Alok Negi[1], Krishan Kumar[1]* and Prachi Chauhan[2]

[1]Department of Computer Science and Engineering, National Institute of Technology, Srinagar, India
[2]College of Technology, G.B. Pant University of Agriculture and Technology, Pantnagar, India

Abstract

Malaria is now a lethal, contagious, mosquito-borne critical disease spawn by Anopheles mosquito bitten spread through Plasmodium parasites. Modern information technology, along with biomedical research and political efforts, plays an important role in many attempts to combat the disease. Automating the diagnostic process would allow for precise diagnosis of the infection and therefore holding the potential of providing quality healthcare to resource-scarce areas. Combined to open access resources, artificial intelligence (AI) will boost malaria treatment and a strong mix to improve society. Throughout this chapter, we also explore whether AI can be able to leverage for low-cost, reliable, and precise open sourced deep learning solutions to predict lethal malaria. We outline a few of the findings regarding the reasonably precise malaria-infected cells classification leveraging deep neural convolution (CNN) networks. We will discuss the strategies for assembling a pathologist-cured visual dataset to train deep neural networks, and also some data augmentation approaches used to significantly increase the dimensionality of the data, given the overfitting problem especially in deep CNN training.

Keywords: CNN, data augmentation, deep learning (dl), malaria, precision, recall, WHO

12.1 Introduction

Malaria is indeed a prevalent infectious disease which has currently asserted lives of millions of people worldwide of around 200 million cases and over 400,000 deaths annually. It is endemic where common disease areas involve Africa and South East Asia. The emergence of the disease in today's technology as per WHO is shown in Figure 12.1.

Malaria precipitated by Plasmodium parasites is indeed a blood dysfunction that is transferred through the bite of a woman called Anopheles mosquito. Parasites enter through the blood and proceed to damage red blood cells (RBCs) which always carry oxygen to produce fatal and lethal symptoms such as life-threatening illness, fever, headaches, vomiting and fatigue; It really can induce coma or perhaps death in extreme cases. The symptom usually begins in a couple of days or even weeks. The deadly parasites include *Plasmodium*

*Corresponding author: kkberwal@nituk.ac.in

Sachi Nandan Mohanty, G. Nalinipriya, Om Prakash Jena and Achyuth Sarkar (eds.) Machine Learning for Healthcare Applications, (187–198) © 2021 Scrivener Publishing LLC

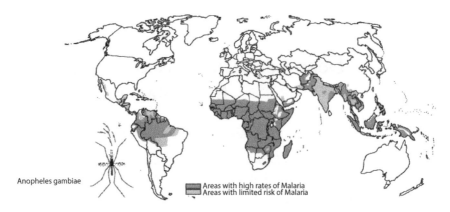

Anopheles gambiae

■ Areas with high rates of Malaria
■ Areas with limited risk of Malaria

Figure 12.1 Globally vulnerable areas affected by malaria.

falciparum, P. vivax, P. ovale, P. knowlesi, and *P. malariae.* Interestingly, *P. falciparum* may be kept alive inside human blood for even more than a year without any symptoms. So, early detection of malaria can end up saving many human lives.

The secret to diagnosing malaria is identifying the existence of parasites. Therefore, this is important to recognize the parasite organisms and the occurrence of potential infections, as well as to determine the growth phase of *P. falciparum* parasites within reference to that same extent of its illness. Collecting parasites to assess parasitemia rates is not only necessary to identify an epidemic and quantify its severity, this also enables patient supervision by assessing drug effectiveness and possible drug susceptibility. In several instances, just one obtainable approach to malaria treatment is a manual inspection of a microscopic slide [1]. RDT as well as microscopic diagnosis have always been two of the greatest effective methods of malaria successful diagnosis that contribute to the control of malaria today [10]. RDT is an appropriate screening method, as it requires no microscope or skilled professional and also provides a test of diagnosis in less than 15 min. Moreover, referring to WHO and some others, there are few limitations in RDT [11] which include lack of sensitivity, unable to determine the density of the parasite and distinguish between *P. ovale, P. vivax,* and *P. malariae,* increased cost relative to light microscope, and vulnerability to humidity and heat damages.

The best standard approach for in-field malaria diagnosis involves light blood film microscopy. All parasite organisms can be observed with microscopy. It makes possible to measure the degree of parasitemia, discharge an individual through an effective procedure and an assessment of drug resistance. It is also cost effective than many methods, as well as available commonly. Conversely, its major disadvantages seem to be the extensive training usually needed for a microscopist for becoming a skilled reader of the malaria slide, a massive cost with training and practicing, the maintenance of skills as well as the huge portion of manual labor work. Hence, comprehensive training and experience are necessary in attempt to provide an accurate diagnosis. Regrettably, in remote areas whereby malaria has a significant predominance, these skilled human resources are quite often restricted. Manual microscopy also becomes subjective, and lacks standardization.

This now encourages us to implement an automated detection for malaria through a deep learning (DL) method that leads to an accurate, quick, simple and effective diagnosis [2]. The automated system aims to perform the whole task without manual assistance and to provide an objective, consistent and efficient method to do so. Hospitals, clinics and some other medical practitioners will become the selected target category of the project: an adaptive system consisting of optimized imaging procedures for initial filtration and segmentation, a series of pattern recognition and machine learning applications for comprehensive detection of infectious cells in a lighting or complete slide [3] microscopic image. There is a tendency around the world to optimize the diagnosing system with the assistance of machine learning methods to improve health specialists make the correct diagnosis.

A deep learning view depends on the classification of malaria afflicted cells from red blood clots. Deep learning has identified amazing new applications in biomedicine [4], genomic medicine [5], bioinformatics and medical imaging analysis [6]. It really should be remembered that successful blood cell classification and malaria parasite recognition also can be seen to accommodate the counting. The segmentation of cells is the most well-researched field and tremendous output has already been recorded throughout many studies [7]. Previous work upon this detection of infected cells includes the image recognition methods and techniques [8], computer vision [9] and machine learning. However, very little work has been done to apply DL approaches for computer-aided identification of malaria infections.

In order to develop an effective malaria identification solution, we aim to develop a ConvNet model based on deep learning that is intended to be simpler and more computational compared to most state-of-the-art approaches that take reliable time for training.

12.2   Related Work

Poostchi et al. [2] surveyed on image processing and deep learning approaches to update the latest advances with data recognition and computer vision in the automatic malaria diagnostics. It is a quite active research field which has seen a large amount of literature in the last 10 years. With the advent of modernization, deep learning algorithms have already had a profound influence with research seeing an interesting new creation that is noteworthy. This would make many of the previous approaches to classification replaceable. In addition, as deep learning brings on the person's difficult challenge of building classification features, most of those handcrafted features found up to now may become worthless.

Masud et al. [12] evaluated a customized CNN-based deep learning model to enhance malaria identification on thinner blood stain images and demonstrated that its use of the stochastic learning rate routine with an automated learning rate finder in response to the need for a widely used regularization approach like batch normalization with dropout leads in successful malaria classification outcomes. The model obtained 97.30% accuracy throughout the classification of parasitized with uninfected cell image data to high level of sensitivity and precision. The method also presents a high MCC value (94.17%) compared with all many existing concepts under research implying a strong co-relation between expected labels and true facts. The reviewers discovered that the recommended improved method showed better results in terms of precision, accuracy, responsiveness, and MCC in identifying infected cells and healthy against malaria related to the modified and many CNN models (relates directly such as VGG16 and ResNet50).

Fuhad et al. [13] presented various classification models for the detection of malaria parasites that also hardly take into account classification accuracy and yet also attempt for being computationally efficient. Authors implemented a sequence of experiments throughout the process which include general training, extraction training, and auto encoder mentoring, likely to result in 10 different models being compared, and used an auto encoder-based learning approach on 2,828 images, with its best achieving model yielding an average of 99.5% from these. This procedure enables just about 4,600 flops, equivalent to more than 19.6 billion flops needed for the method observed in the work already under way. Practical model-efficiency testing was carried out via distributing the product in 10 separate mobile phones with differing computational capacities and then web apps backed up by servers. Data obtained from such environments indicate that the methods are used in both online (web service) and offline (mobile only) modes to perform inferences around 1 s per sample.

Rajaraman *et al.* [15] observed that model system using numerous DL models acquired impressive predictive output which could not be achieved by any human additive models parasitized cells detection of thin-blood smear images. A supervised method eliminates model variance by efficiently integrating multiple prediction performance and reduces sensitivity to training samples and algorithm details. Authors have built a web application while deploying the prediction method into a web browser to escape anonymity, low latency challenges and has cross-platform advantages. The method ensemble's output imitates real-world conditions to reduce uncertainty, over fitting, and contributes to greater generalization. The findings proposed are helpful to the creation of clinically useful approaches for the identification and differentiation of parasitized and non-infected cells within thin-blood smear photos.

Vijayalakshmi *et al.* [14] proposed Deep learning-based approach VGG19-SVM is achieved with a 93.13% accuracy score. The suggested solution convergence rate with finite amount of time and O (P ∗ MNmn) is their computational complexity. This is also able to be implemented with a modest infrastructure for computing. Therefore, it reduces the reliance of qualified technicians on immediate malaria diagnosis. Since there are four main types of malaria parasites, the new methodology is being trained to identify parasites of falciparum malaria infected and uninfected. In addition, the effectiveness of the suggested method can be enhanced by constructing from ground up a new CNN model that incorporates more images into the malaria corpus. Convergence of VGG19-SVM reveals dominance in all performance metrics such as sensitivity, accuracy and classification report (specificity, precision and F1-Score) against existing CNN models.

Var *et al.* [16] aimed to Malaria parasites (*Plasmodium* sp.) are automatically detected on images captured from dried blood smears in Giemsa. Although sizes are small, deep learning techniques offer limited output. Digital features can be extracted from broad general sets of data in data augmentation, and task-specific classification challenge can be effectively overcome in restricted relevant datasets with limited problems and applying image classification method in this research to identify and recognize malaria parasites. We are using a common VGG19 model of CNN pertained. The methodology on 1,428 P trained besides 20 epoch. Vivax, P.1425 ovale, P.1446 falciparum, from 1,450 *P. malariae*, and reports of 1,440 non-parasite. This model of transfer learning achieved f-measurement scores of 83, 86, 86, 79% and 80, 83, 86, 75% precision and on 19 test pictures.

12.3   Proposed Work

The aim of the proposed research is to build a model based on deep learning designed to be simpler and more computational than other methods with sufficient training time. This

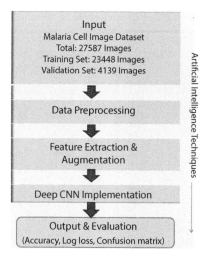

Figure 12.2 Block diagram for proposed work.

work also demonstrates the technical feasibility of a Deep Learning approach to allow for automated malaria cell detection by classifying the malaria disease between Parasitized and Uninfected. Figure 12.2 shows a block diagram of the work proposed.

12.3.1   Dataset Description

Malaria cell Images dataset from Kaggle is used for this work that includes images belonging to two classes: Parasitized and Uninfected. Further, Dataset is broken down into training set and Validation set with images respectively. Training set has images for Parasitized and images for Uninfected while Testing set has images for Parasitized and images for Uninfected. Figure 12.3 shows the sample images of the dataset and dataset distribution are given in Figures 12.4 and 12.5.

12.3.2   Data Pre-Processing and Augmentation

To prevent data leakage, images are resized to $224 \times 224 \times 3$ and data augmentation with Padding, horizontal flipping, padding, etc. are used to increase the variability of available data to training systems without certainly accumulating new data.

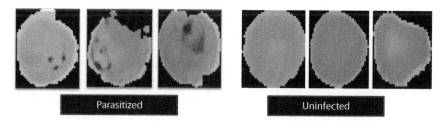

Figure 12.3 Dataset sample images.

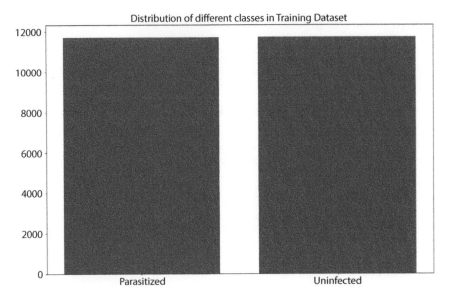

Figure 12.4 Classes distribution in training set.

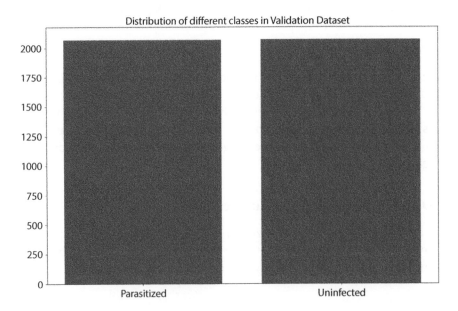

Figure 12.5 Classes distribution in validation set.

12.3.3 CNN Architecture and Implementation

In a broad variety of computer vision tasks, Convolutional neural networks (CNNs) have proved to be very successful. CNN is a deep neural network that typically takes images as input, trains features based on weights and bias, the value of which is randomly selected. Convolution begins to learn from records that are also correction-invariant, spatial hierarchical patterns so that they should learn various aspects regarding images. The pooling

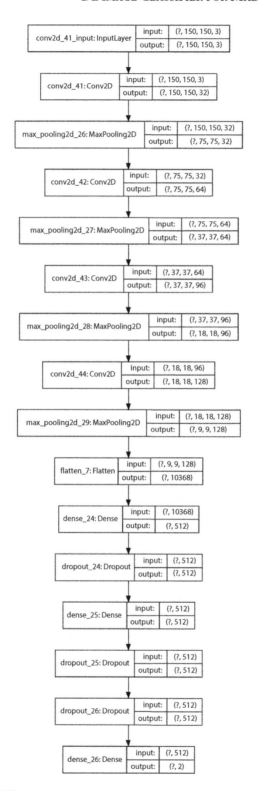

Figure 12.6 CNN architecture.

layers assist with down sampling and reduction of dimensions. Putting in dense layers only at later part of the system also helps to carry out all tasks such as classifying images.

Each feature vector passes via a sequence of kernels, pooling, fully connected layers and employs softmax activation to classify an entity with stochastic parameters from 0 to 1. Proposed model has four Convolution and pooling layers, consisting of two dense layers for regularization with dropouts and a final layer for image classification with softmax activation as shown in layered architecture in Figure 12.6.

12.4   Results and Evaluation

This work is implemented in ANACONDA 3.0 using TensorFlow on a single PC installed with an Intel(R) 2.30 GHz Core(TM) i5 3567 CPU, 64-bit operating system, 8 GB RAM and 2 GB of AMD Radeon R5 M330 graphics engine running on the Windows 10 operating system. Adam is used as the optimizer and Softmax, Relu are the activation functions. The model's efficiency is calculated using accuracy as shown in Equation (12.1).

$$Accuracy = (TP + TN) / (TP + TN + FP + FN) \tag{12.1}$$

As a metric, Categorical cross entropy is used and mathematics behind it is shown in Equation (12.2).

$$logloss = 1/N \sum_i^N \sum_j^M y_{ij} \log(p_{ij}) \tag{12.2}$$

During training, total parameter is 5,758,114 out of which 5,758,114 trainable parameters and there are 0 Non-trainable parameters. The experimental result recorded 96.11% training accuracy with logarithm loss 0.08 and the validation accuracy 95.70% with logarithm loss 0.31 in just 15 epochs as shown in Figures 12.7 and 12.8. For quantitative analysis, Normalized confusion matrix is shown in Figure 12.9 for our experiment.

Classification report (precision, recall, f1-score and support) for the experiment is shown in Table 12.1 and mathematics behind it is given by Equations (12.3), (12.4) and (12.5).

Precision is the ratio of relevant instances to the retrieved instances.

$$Precision = TP / (TP + FP) \tag{12.3}$$

Recall is the ratio of relevant instances that have been retrieved to the total amount of relevant instances.

$$Recall = TP / (TP + FN) \tag{12.4}$$

F1 Score is the weighted average of Precision and Recall and Support is the true instances that lie in that class.

$$F1Score = 2 * (Recall * Precision) / (Recall + Precision) \tag{12.5}$$

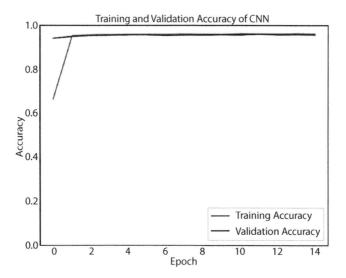

Figure 12.7 Accuracy curve.

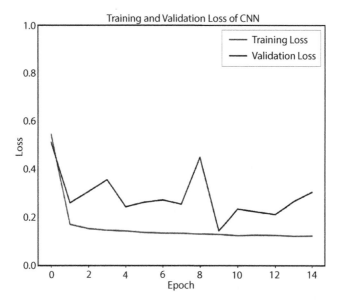

Figure 12.8 Loss curve.

Where,

TP (True positive) is the number of positive instances that are corrected classified.

TN (True negative) is the number of negative instances that are correctly classified.

FP (False positive) is the number positive instances that are classified.

FN (False negative) is the number of negative instances that are wrongly classified.

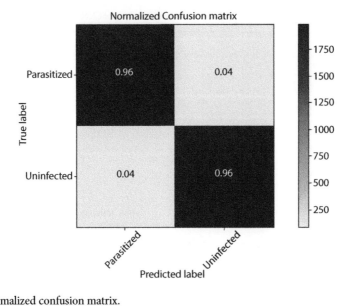

Figure 12.9 Normalized confusion matrix.

Table 12.1 Classification Report.

	Precision	**Recall**	**f1-score**	**Support**
Parasitized	0.9569	0.9569	0.9569	2067
Uninfected	0.9570	0.9570	0.9570	2072
macro avg	0.96	0.96	0.96	4139
weighted avg	0.96	0.96	0.96	4139

As shown in Table 12.1, for the proposed work, precision, recall and f1 score are recorded 96%, which are quite good and comparable with more complicated ones as described in the related work for the image processing and analysis.

12.5   Conclusion

Detection of malaria is not a straightforward task and functionality of trained staff across the whole world is a major problem in diagnosing and treating cases. The proposed work used medical imaging for malaria detection and recorded 95.70% accuracy with logarithm loss 0.31 in just 15 epochs and proved technical feasibility of approach based on a deep learning for malaria cell detection and classification. Qualitative and quantitative based analysis performed for the proposed work and we hope that our proposed work would make a significant contribution to healthcare sector.

References

1. Tek, F.B., Dempster, A.G., Kale, I., Computer vision for microscopy diagnosis of malaria. *Malar. J.*, 8, 1, 153, 2009.

2. Poostchi, M., Silamut, K., Maude, R.J., Jaeger, S., Thoma, G., Image analysis and machine learning for detecting malaria. *Transl. Res.*, 194, 36–55, 2018.

3. Cheng, W.C., Saleheen, F., Badano, A., Assessing color performance of whole-slide imaging scanners for digital pathology. *Color Res. Appl.*, 44, 3, 322–334, 2019.

4. Yue, T. and Wang, H., Deep learning for genomics: A concise overview, *CoRR*, arXiv preprint arXiv:1802.00810, 2018.

5. Leung, M.K., Delong, A., Alipanahi, B., Frey, B.J., Machine learning in genomic medicine: A review of computational problems and datasets. *Proc. IEEE*, 104, 1, 176–197, 2015.

6. Greenspan, H., Van Ginneken, B., Summers, R.M., Guest editorial deep learning in medical imaging: Overview and future promise of an exciting new technique. *IEEE Trans. Med. Imaging*, 35, 5, 1153–1159, 2016.

7. Yang, D., Subramanian, G., Duan, J., Gao, S., Bai, L., Chandramohanadas, R., Ai, Y., A portable image-based cytometer for rapid malaria detection and quantification. *PLoS One*, 12, 6, e0179161, 2017.

8. Mohanty, I., Pattanaik, P.A., Swarnkar, T., Automatic detection of malaria parasites using unsupervised techniques, in: *International Conference on ISMAC in Computational Vision and Bio-Engineering*, 2018, May, Springer, Cham, pp. 41–49.

9. Hung, J. and Carpenter, A., Applying faster R-CNN for object detection on malaria images, in: *Proceedings of the IEEE Conference on Computer Vision and Pattern Recognition Workshops*, pp. 56–61, 2017.

10. Makanjuola, R.O. and Taylor-Robinson, A.W., Improving Accuracy of Malaria Diagnosis in Underserved Rural and Remote Endemic Areas of Sub-Saharan Africa: A Call to Develop Multiplexing Rapid Diagnostic Tests. *Scientifica*, 2020, https://doi.org/10.1155/2020/3901409.

11. Obeagu, E.I., Chijioke, U.O., Ekelozie, I.S., Malaria rapid diagnostic test (RDTs). *Ann. Clin. Lab. Res.*, 6, 4, 275, 2018.

12. Masud, M., Alhumyani, H., Alshamrani, S.S., Cheikhrouhou, O., Ibrahim, S., Muhammad, G., Shorfuzzaman, M., Leveraging Deep Learning Techniques for Malaria Parasite Detection Using Mobile Application. *Wireless Commun. Mobile Comput.*, 2020, Article ID 8895429, 2020, https://doi.org/10.1155/2020/8896429.

13. Fuhad, K.M., Tuba, J.F., Sarker, M., Ali, R., Momen, S., Mohammed, N., Rahman, T., Deep Learning Based Automatic Malaria Parasite Detection from Blood Smear and Its Smartphone Based Application. *Diagnostics*, 10, 5, 329, 2020.

14. Vijayalakshmi, A., Deep learning approach to detect malaria from microscopic images. *Multimed. Tools Appl.*, 79, 21, 15297–15317, 2020.

15. Rajaraman, S., Jaeger, S., Antani, S.K., Performance evaluation of deep neural ensembles toward malaria parasite detection in thin-blood smear images. *PeerJ*, 7, e6977, 2019.

16. Var, E. and Tek, F.B., Malaria Parasite Detection with Deep Transfer Learning, in: *2018 3rd International Conference on Computer Science and Engineering (UBMK)*, 2018, September, IEEE, pp. 298–302.

Prediction of Chest Diseases Using Transfer Learning

S. Baghavathi Priya[1]*, M. Rajamanogaran[2] and S. Subha[3]

[1]Department of Information Technology, Rajalakshmi Engineering College, Chennai, India
[2]Data Science Consultant, Chennai, India
[3]Department of Computer Science and Engineering, Rajalakshmi Institute of Technology, Chennai, India

Abstract

People are being affected by pollution and irregular food habits day by day. This leads to the cause of many kinds of diseases, especially chest diseases such as Pneumothorax, Pneumonia, Effusion, Atelectasis, Nodule, Mass, Cardiomegaly, Edema, Lung Consolidation, Pleural Thickening, Infiltration, Fibrosis, and Emphysema. Machine learning, which is an important technique of artificial intelligence, has the ability to learn and predict the diseases automatically. The aim of deep learning in healthcare is its capability to extract the features from large number of datasets. Initially, pre-processing step is done to remove noise and to deal with blurred images from the database, which has training and testing datasets. Machine learning algorithms will learn the selected features from the training dataset and the gained experience will be stored as a separate data model that is recommended for predicting the chest diseases from the test dataset. The proposed method uses Convolutional Neural Network with InceptionV3 to predict the chest diseases. Transfer learning is used to extract the Inception V3 features from the pre-trained model and the predictions are given in terms of percentage. Thereby, the doctors can easily diagnose the diseases and save the lives of the patients.

Keywords: Chest disease, convolutional neural networks (CNN), inception, transfer learning, chest x-ray

13.1 Introduction

Disease occurs when cells in a healthy person are impaired due to infection or illness. Hereditary diseases, physiological diseases, infectious diseases, and deficiency diseases are the major diseases that are considered as life-threatening diseases. They are likely to be communicable or non-communicable diseases. Chest diseases affect the lungs of the human body either in a larger level or smaller level. A normal person can breathe nearly 25,000 times per day. If this count get reduces, it causes difficulty in breathing, which leads to lung disease. There are various types of lung diseases. A few of them are Pneumothorax, Pneumonia,

---

Corresponding author: baghavathipriya.s@rajalakshmi.edu.in

Sachi Nandan Mohanty, G. Nalinipriya, Om Prakash Jena and Achyuth Sarkar (eds.) Machine Learning for Healthcare Applications, (199–214) © 2021 Scrivener Publishing LLC

Effusion, Atelectasis, Nodule, Mass, Cardiomegaly, Edema, Lung Consolidation, Pleural Thickening, Infiltration, Fibrosis, and Emphysema. Due to rapid advancements in computer technologies, it becomes easy to predict any type of disease occurring among the common people. Artificial Intelligence plays an important role in the arena of Computer Science which makes machines mimic the human brain and to act intelligently. It makes machines to gain knowledge from the environment and its history. Machine learning, which is a subcategory of artificial intelligence, uses learning algorithms to build a model automatically and it will provide better results, by improving its learning from experience. One of the advancements in machine learning techniques is the concept of deep learning, where learning is achieved through examples. Prediction and classification of information can be achieved using multiple layers and parameters in the network. There are two widely used neural network architectures in Deep learning. Artificial Neural Network (ANN) mimics the biological neurons in the brain. Recurrent Neural Network (RNN) can be used for sequence-based classification and prediction of images. Shallow networks such as Back Propagation Networks and Competitive Neural Networks could not extract vital features from the given images [1]. CNN processes the input image which depends on its weights and biases, to classify and predict objects for different use cases. CNN is a mathematical model comprising of layers namely the convolution layer, pooling layer and fully connected layer. Feature extraction is performed by the first two layers and mapping of the extracted features into the final output is done by the third layer [16]. There are different pre-trained models in CNN for object classification. Among them, transfer learning is applied to predict the percentage of occurrence of chest diseases in the given Chest X-ray images.

13.2   Types of Diseases

13.2.1   Pneumothorax

Difficulty in breathing occurs due to Pneumothorax, which is also termed as a collapsed lung. Due to excess pressure on the outer part of the lung, it cannot be expanded normally. This occurs due to leakage of air in the lungs. In the X-ray images, the classification of Pneumothorax was achieved by the technique, named Support Vector Machines. Local Binary Pattern (LBP) was used to take out features from the input images [5].

13.2.2   Pneumonia

Pneumonia occurs due to bacterial, viral, fungal infection, or allergic reaction. The germs cause breathing problems, cough, fever, tiredness. It leads to respiratory failure and it can even be deadly. A deep learning technique was proposed to check pneumonia and cancer. To differentiate normal with pneumonia chest x-ray images, modified AlexNet (MAN) was implemented and it was compared with softmax [2].

13.2.3   Effusion

Pleural effusion is caused due to inflammation and infection on the lungs. This disease is commonly termed as "water on the lungs", as there is a huge collection of watery content in the cavity of the chest. Major parts of the human body are affected due to this disease. The root cause for this disease is not yet confirmed for nearly 20% of cases [8].

13.2.4 Atelectasis

A partial or complete collapse of the lungs leads to Atelectasis. Persons affected by this disease cannot get enough air and insufficient oxygen is supplied to the blood. It causes fluid buildup and excess pressure outside the lungs. Ultrasound was proposed to differentiate a complete atelectasis/consolidation from an incomplete one [17]. Causes, risk factors and symptoms of the above four diseases are mentioned in Table 13.1.

Table 13.1 Causes and symptoms for pneumothorax, pneumonia, pleural effusion and atelectasis.

S. No.	Name of the disease	Causes/Risk factors	Symptoms
1	Pneumothorax	Chest Injury at any level of risk, Prolonged smoking, Hereditary nature, Being tall and thin.	Sudden chest pain with coughing, Breathing problem, Bluish skin, Increased heartbeat, Tiredness, Widening of nostrils, Rigidity in chest.
2	Pneumonia	Risk factors-Weakness or suppression in the immune system, Chances of occurrence of severe diseases such as asthma, cancer, diabetes, heart failure, stroke, Exposure to chemicals, toxic fumes or pollutants, Prolonged smoking, and alcohol usage, Due to ventilators in Intensive Care Unit (ICU).	Vomiting and Diarrhea, Cough (with bloody or discolored mucus) and High fever, Breathing problem, Loss of energy and appetite, Chest pain and rapid pulse, Muscle pain, Nausea, Mental illness, Body shivering.
3	Pleural Effusion	Heart disease, Kidney disease, Liver infection, Pneumonia, Trauma, Tuberculosis, Lung cancer, Connective tissue disease, Lymphoma, Abdominal infections.	Dry cough, Fever, Hiccups, Trouble breathing or rapid breathing, Chest pain.
4	Atelectasis	Difficult to breathe or swallow, Injury in the spinal cord, Smoking, Obesity and Long-term bed rest, Consumption of oxygen using ventilators, Ageing (older age).	Feeling low consumption of oxygen, Cough, Chest pain, Rapid heart rate, Change in color (blue) in skin or lips.

13.2.5   Nodule and Mass

Lung nodule is a circular-shaped speck on the lung. It is a marble-like structure embedded in the lung tissue which can be round or oval and it surrounds the normal lung tissue. If the nodule size is smaller than 6 mm in diameter, there is a low risk of cancer. Nodules of a size larger than 10 mm in diameter are considered malignant and they must be removed or biopsied. Lung masses are referred to as the nodules with a size greater than 3 cm. So in general, the nodule size determines the occurrence or non-occurrence of lung cancer. Several CNN architectures were proposed for extracting the features and for classifying the lung nodules in the given images based on its severity [6]. Classification of Nodule in Computed Tomography (CT) images were performed using the Support Vector Machine algorithm [12].

13.2.6   Cardiomegaly

An enlarged heart is termed as cardiomegaly which is caused due to short-term stress. There may be chances for heart valve problems, abnormal heartbeat rate, or reduction in the strength of the myocardium. This disease can be either temporary or permanent, depending on the conditions of the body. Complications of the enlarged heart lead to blood clots, cardiac arrest, heart murmur, or sudden death. To differentiate pixel positions of each input image, a method called Adaptive Histogram Equalization was used [3].

13.2.7   Edema

Pulmonary edema is caused due to the filling of liquid in the air sac of the lungs. It affects the respiratory system, which leads to heart failure. It is also termed as lung water.

13.2.8   Lung Consolidation

When the air in the lungs is replaced with either a fluid or a solid, it leads to lung consolidation. Fresh air cannot enter the body and the used air cannot be removed from the body. So it causes shortness of breath. Also, it makes the skin bluish or pale due to oxygen deficiency. The consolidation was visible on a chest X-ray due to an exacerbation [7]. The causes and symptoms of the above mentioned diseases are listed in Table 13.2.

13.2.9   Pleural Thickening

The formation of rigid pleural scarring around the lungs is called pleural thickening. During breathing, the lungs become harder. The next stage of this disease is known as dyspnea in which the patients will be suffered from chest pain and shortening of breath. Pleural thickening causes irreversible damage with added impediments [14].

13.2.10   Infiltration

The diffusion of foreign elements or excess amounts of those elements in the body cells or tissues causes infiltration. Infiltrate are the materials collected in those cells or tissues.

Table 13.2 Causes and symptoms for nodule, mass, cardiomegaly, edema and consolidation.

S. No.	Name of the disease	Causes/Risk factors	Symptoms
1	Nodule and Mass	Cysts, Scars, Lung diseases caused by fungi, Inflamed lymph nodes, Pneumonia or tuberculosis, Formation of mucus in the lungs.	Coughing up blood, Breathlessness, Weight loss, Chest pain, Back pain.
2	Cardiomegaly	Red blood cells are decreased, Hemochromatosis (Excessive iron in the body), Thyroid disorder, Heart valve disease, Pericardial effusion, Cardiomyopathy, High blood pressure.	Swelling, Abnormal heart rhythm Shortness of breath.
3	Edema	Inflammation, Pneumonia, Trauma, Sepsis, Sudden hypertension, Cardiac attack, Kidney failure, Problems in heart valves.	Wheezing and cough, Chest pain, Irregular heart rate, Pale skin, Suffocation, and excessive sweating, Restlessness.
4	Consolidation	Pneumonia, Aspiration, Pulmonary Edema, Pulmonary hemorrhage, Lung cancer.	Dry cough, Chest pain, Chest murmur, Fever, Tiredness, Spitting up of blood or sputum, Rapid breathing.

It also refers to the deposition of amyloid proteins. It was proposed by Na'am et al., that this disease could be easily recognized by detecting the edges of objects in the images taken from infants using image processing techniques [11].

13.2.11   Fibrosis

When there is damage or scarring in lung disease, it leads to pulmonary fibrosis. Lungs will not work properly because of the stiffness in the tissue. The lung damage cannot be repaired, but lung transplantation can be done if needed.

13.2.12   Emphysema

Because of injured air sacs in the lungs, its inner walls get weakened and ruptured. It creates larger air spaces which reduce the area of the lungs. So, the quantity of oxygen reaching the bloodstream gets reduced. Lung densitometry has detected the severity of emphysema, which was not associated with a decrease in lung density [15]. Causes, risk factors and symptoms of the above four diseases are given in Table 13.3.

Table 13.3 Causes and symptoms for pleural thickening, infiltration, fibrosis and emphysema.

S. No.	Name of the disease	Causes/Risk factors	Symptoms
1	Pleural thickening	Chest Injury at any level of risk, Prolonged smoking, Hereditary nature, Being tall and thin.	Pain with coughing, Chest pain, Breathlessness, Shortness of breath, Difficulty drawing a deep breath.
2	Infiltration	Improper size of cannula, Puncture of the vein wall, Needle cannula.	Damp or wet dressing, Slowed/Stopped infusion, Inflammation with taut skin.
3	Fibrosis	Continuously coverage to toxins and pollutants, For lung and breast cancer, radiation therapy is used.	Aching muscles and joints, Shortness of breathe, A dry cough, Fatigue, Unexplained weight loss, Reduction of oxygen in the blood (Clubbing).
4	Emphysema	Long-term exposure to different kinds of smoke such as air pollution tobacco smoke, exposure to dust and chemical fumes, Genetic deficiency of a protein.	Shortness of breath, Bluish or gray lips or fingernails, Mental illness.

13.3   Diagnosis of Lung Diseases

The severity of lung disorders can be measured by checking the capacity of lungs for the easy flow of air and oxygen. For easy and quick diagnosis of lung diseases, any of the following tests can be taken at different stages, based on the occurrence level of the disease. They are Computerized Tomography (CT) scan, Chest X-ray, Bronchoscopy Thoracentesis, Pulse oximetry, Sputum culture, Magnetic Resonance Imaging (MRI), Positron Emission Tomography (PET), Pleural fluid analysis, and blood test. A segmentation technique in CNN is used for improving the quality and visualization of PET, MRI, and CT images [10]. Among many existing tools, ultrasound, CT, PET and MRI scans are more appropriate to collect substantial information for diagnosing the diseases [13]. In chest radiography, images were trained using CNN and RNN for image analysis and text analysis respectively [9].

13.4   Materials and Methods

The National Institutes of Health has released around 100,000 chest X-ray dataset for pulmonary diseases. A chest X-ray is a quick imaging test used for diagnosing diseases such as Pneumothorax, Atelectasis, Nodule, Infiltration, Effusion, etc. It produces chest images using electromagnetic waves. Pulmonary diseases can be identified using these images. Datasets are represented in the form of frontal view X-ray images. From that large collection, 40,000 images are considered to train the model and 10,000 images are taken to test the model. The sample input images containing few lung diseases are shown in Figure 13.1.

The histogram representation for the given dataset is illustrated in Figure 13.2. The first column denotes the occurrence or non-occurrence of diseases, which is labeled as No finding and the remaining columns contain different categories of pulmonary diseases. It is interpreted from the Histogram that around 9,000 images have the occurrence of infiltration, 3,000 images have the occurrence of Pneumothorax and 1,000 images have the occurrence of Emphysema. Likewise, all 14 lung diseases are used for data augmentation. It was proposed by Manuel *et al.* that few diseases could not be detected by Local Binary Patterns (LBP), as it depends only on texture information [4].

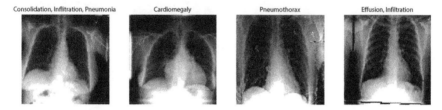

Figure 13.1 Sample input images of lung diseases.

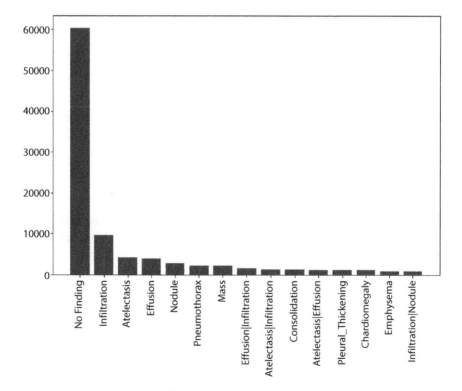

Figure 13.2 Histogram representation of the dataset.

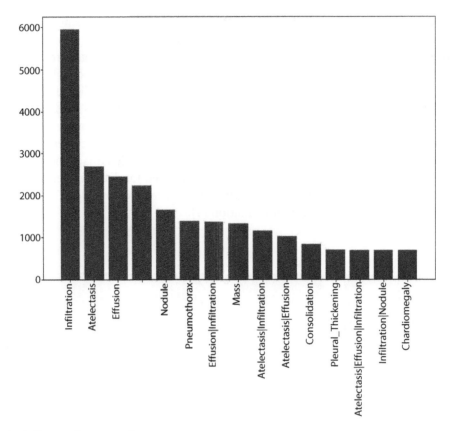

Figure 13.3 Output of augmentation process.

13.4.1 Data Augmentation

A method called augmentation is done to enhance the quality and dimension of the training images, by generating own data to the existing data. As there are few unique classes in the dataset, the augmentation process is performed to produce augmented datasets and it is represented in Figure 13.3. Those augmented datasets will be trained in the second round.

13.4.2 CNN Architecture

In neural networks, CNN shows a vital role in recognizing and classifying the images. Important characteristics namely height h, width w, and dimension d for each image matrix and a filter $(fh \times fw \times d)$ are taken into account. The output matrix is represented in Equation (13.1). For example, an image of $128 \times 128 \times 3$ matrix array of RGB and an image of $128 \times 128 \times 1$ matrix array of the grayscale image are taken as input.

$$(h - fh + 1) * (w - fw + 1) * 1 \tag{13.1}$$

In CNN, the input will be given via a set of layers namely, (i) convolution layer, (ii) pooling layer, (iii) dropout layer, and (iv) fully connected layer. Sigmoid activation function is applied for the classification of images with values ranging from 0 to 1. In CNN, many pre-trained models are available. An open-sourced model namely Inception V3 is used in this work and it can classify images into 1,000s of classes such as facial images, brain tumors, kidney stones, cancer detection, etc. From these classes, unique patterns can be identified using the model.

13.4.3   Lung Disease Prediction Model

In this work, the dataset images are fed to the Inception V3 model, and the lung disease prediction model is depicted in Figure 13.4. Through Inception V3, higher-level features are extracted and sent to the average pooling layer, which is used to decrease the dimensions of the parameters based on the pooling window size. The average value for one pigment on the features is computed using average pooling. This value is calculated using the parameters in the network with weight w and bias b and it is shown in Equation (13.2).

$$a_j^l = \sigma\left(\sum_k w_{jk}^l a_k^{l-1} + b_j^l\right) \tag{13.2}$$

The output pooled feature map is given as the input to the drop out layer, which avoids over fitting. It will drop 10–20% of features and the rest of 80–90% features will be given to the hidden layer (dense layer) which is fired using 512 neurons. Again, 10–20% features will be dropped and the rest will be given to the output layer, which is activated by sigmoid function and is given in Equation (13.3).

$$\emptyset(z) = \frac{1}{1+e^{-x}} \tag{13.3}$$

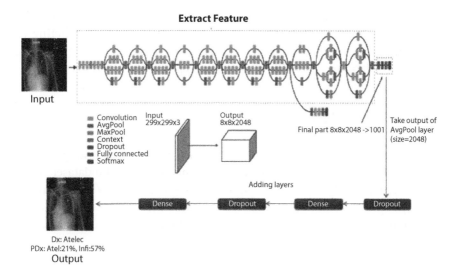

Figure 13.4 Lung disease prediction model.

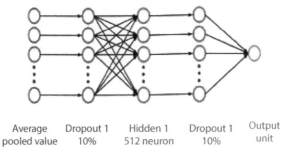

Average   Dropout 1   Hidden 1   Dropout 1   Output
pooled value   10%   512 neuron   10%   unit

Figure 13.5 The proposed layer construction.

Model: "sequential_2"

Layer (type)	Output Shape	Param #
inception_v3 (Model)	(None, 2, 2, 2048)	21802784
global_average_pooling2d_2	(None, 2048)	0
dropout_3 (Dropout)	(None, 2048)	0
dense_3 (Dense)	(None, 512)	1049088
dropout_4 (Dropout)	(None, 512)	0
dense_4 (Dense)	(None, 13)	6669

Total params : 22, 858, 541
Trainable params : 22, 824, 109
Non-trainble params : 34, 432

Figure 13.6 Calculation of model parameters.

Finally, the output dense layer contains 14 fired neurons for predicting the labels. The final predicted output holds the percentage of affected lung diseases. It is displayed in Figure 13.5.

The summary of the proposed architecture is represented programmatically and is presented in Figure 13.6. The hyper parameters are shown as trainable and non-trainable parameters. The trainable parameters are considered as features for predicting the class labels of the lung disease prediction model. Some values, which cannot be optimized with the existing training data, are treated as non-trainable parameters.

13.5   Results and Discussions

80% dataset is taken as training images and 20% dataset are taken as testing images for the prediction of chest diseases. In the initial round, the model trains the dataset, and thereby loss and accuracy will be calculated based on the training iterations. When the model learns the dataset properly, there will be a reduction in loss and thus the accuracy is increased by adjusting the values of weight and bias. The resultant cost function is given in Equation (13.4).

$$C = \frac{1}{2n} \sum_x \left\| y(x) - a^L(x) \right\|^2 \tag{13.4}$$

13.5.1   Implementation Results Using ROC Curve

After completing the initial round, the trained model validates the test dataset and accuracy is obtained as a result of the calculation of trainable parameters. The obtained accuracy in the initial round is 94%. Figure 13.7 depicts the results of the initial round.

To measure the performance of a model, a ROC curve (Receiver Operating Characteristic) is used. This curve is represented as a graph, having two parameters named True Positive Rate (TPR) and False Positive Rate (FPR). They are given in Equations (13.5) and (13.6) respectively.

$$TPR = TP(TP + FN) \tag{13.5}$$

$$FPR = FP(TF + TN) \tag{13.6}$$

ROC curves are appropriate when the observations are balanced between each class.

ROC curve of the first round with accuracy denoted as AUC is portrayed in Figure 13.8.

In the next round (final round), the model will be retrained with augmented data, which is the outcome of the first round. There will be a further reduction in loss and improved accuracy. The obtained accuracy in this round is 96% and is indicated in Figure 13.9.

Its corresponding ROC curve is presented in Figure 13.10.

Among the lung diseases, two classes namely Atelectasis and Infiltration are predicted as 21 and 57% respectively in Figure 13.11(a). Combination of Effusion (32%) and Infiltration (57%) image is illustrated in Figure 13.11(b). Occurrence of 10% Mass and 54% Infiltration in the given chest X-ray images are indicated in Figures 13.11(c) and (d) respectively. Similarly, the percentage of other diseases and its combinations are depicted in Figures 13.11(e), (f), (g) and (h).

The comparison of true labels and predicted labels for the final round is specified in Table 13.4. The final predicted output for 10,000 chest X-ray images closely matches the true label and it is given in percentage.

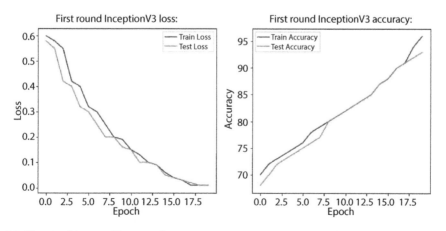

Figure 13.7 Training history of first round.

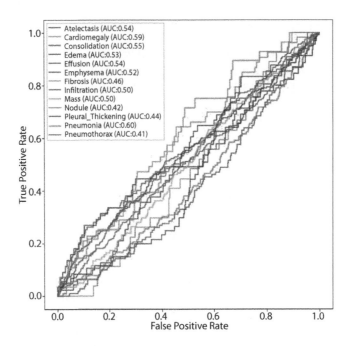

Figure 13.8 ROC curve of first round.

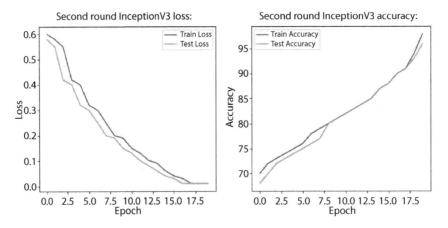

Figure 13.9 Training history of final round.

13.6   Conclusion

In this research work, the chest X-ray images are taken from the NIH datasets to predict the occurrence of lung diseases. The Lung Disease Prediction model (LDP) has been developed using Convolutional Neural Networks. One of the pre-trained models in transfer learning, named Inception V3 has been applied to extract the features from the dataset. Its output is

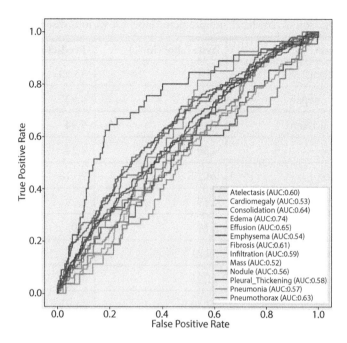

Figure 13.10 ROC curve of second round.

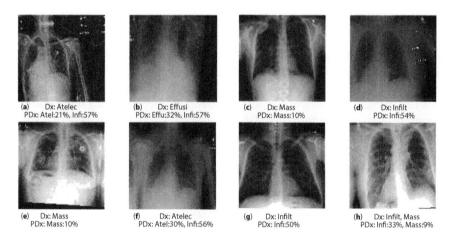

Figure 13.11 (a), (b), (c), (d), (e), (f), (g), (h) Prediction results—Lung diseases.

passed to the proposed layer construction. LDP model has trained the Inception V3 features and the various categories of lung diseases have been predicted. The occurrence of lung diseases in the given chest X-ray images is represented in percentage. Thereby, the doctors can easily diagnose the disease of patients and they can start the treatment at the earliest to save the lives of the patients.

Table 13.4 Comparison of true label and predicted label for various diseases.

S. No.	Disease	True label (in %)	Predicted label (in %)
1	Atelectasis	24.41	23.93
2	Cardiomegaly	5.18	4.92
3	Consolidation	10.55	9.94
4	Edema	4.39	4.24
5	Effusion	26.27	26.18
6	Emphysema	4.69	4.29
7	Fibrosis	2.64	2.05
8	Infiltration	37.21	36.67
9	Mass	11.91	10.15
10	Nodule	12.40	11.72
11	Pleural thickening	5.96	5.32
12	Pneumonia	2.73	2.52
13	Pneumothorax	11.04	10.85

References

1. Abiyev, R.H. and Ma'aitah, M.K.S., Deep Convolutional Neural Networks for Chest Diseases Detection. *J. Healthcare Eng.*, 2018, 1–11, 2018. https://doi.org/10.1155/2018/4168538.
2. Bhandary, A., Prabhu, G.A., Rajinikanth, V., Thanaraj, K.P., Satapathy, S.C., Robbins, D.E., Shasky, C., Zhang, Y.-D., Tavares, J.M.R.S., Raja, N.S.M., Deep-learning framewor k to detect lung abnormality—A study with chest X-Ray and lung CT scan images. *Pattern Recognit. Lett.*, 129, 271–278, 2020. https://doi.org/10.1016/j.patrec.2019.11.013.
3. Bouslama, A., Laaziz, Y., Tali, A., Diagnosis and precise localization of cardiomegaly disease using U-NET. *Inf. Med. Unlocked*, 19, 100306, 2020. https://doi.org/10.1016/j.imu.2020.100306.
4. Carrillo-de-Gea, J.M., García-Mateos, G., Fernández-Alemán, J.L., Hernández-Hernández, J.L., A Computer-Aided Detection System for Digital Chest Radiographs. *J. Healthcare Eng.*, 2016, 1–9, 2016. https://doi.org/10.1155/2016/8208923.
5. Chan, Y.-H., Zeng, Y.-Z., Wu, H.-C., Wu, M.-C., Sun, H.-M., Effective Pneumothorax Detection for Chest X-Ray Images Using Local Binary Pattern and Support Vector Machine. *J. Healthcare Eng.*, 2018, 1–11, 2018. https://doi.org/10.1155/2018/2908517.
6. da Nóbrega, R.V.M., Rebouças Filho, P.P., Rodrigues, M.B., da Silva, S.P.P., Dourado Júnior, C.M.J.M., de Albuquerque, V.H.C., Lung nodule malignancy classification in chest computed tomography images using transfer learning and convolutional neural networks. *Neural Comput. Appl.*, 32, 15, 11065–11082, 2018. https://doi.org/10.1007/s00521-018-3895-1.
7. Hurst, J.R., Consolidation and Exacerbation of COPD. *Med. Sci.*, 6, 2, 44, 2018. https://doi.org/10.3390/medsci6020044.

8. Karkhanis, V. and Joshi, J., Pleural effusion: Diagnosis, treatment, and management. *Open Access Emergency Med.*, 2012:4, 31–52, 2012. https://doi.org/10.2147/oaem.s29942.

9. Litjens, G., Kooi, T., Bejnordi, B.E., Setio, A.A.A., Ciompi, F., Ghafoorian, M., van der Laak, J.A.W.M., van Ginneken, B., Sánchez, C.I., A survey on deep learning in medical image analysis. *Med. Image Anal.*, 42, 60–88, 2017. https://doi.org/10.1016/j.media.2017.07.005.

10. Merjulah, R. and Chandra, J., Segmentation technique for medical image processing: A survey. *2017 International Conference on Inventive Computing and Informatics (ICICI)*, https://doi.org/10.1109/icici.2017.8365301.

11. Na'am, J., Harlan, J., Widi Nurcahyo, G., Arlis, S., Sahari, S., Mardison, M., Navia Rani, L., Detection of Infiltrate on Infant Chest X-Ray. *TELKOMNIKA (Telecommun. Comput. Electron. Control)*, 15, 4, 1943, 2017. https://doi.org/10.12928/telkomnika.v15i4.3163.

12. Rendon-Gonzalez, E. and Ponomaryov, V., Automatic Lung nodule segmentation and classification in CT images based on SVM. *2016 9th International Kharkiv Symposium on Physics and Engineering of Microwaves, Millimeter and Submillimeter Waves (MSMW)*, 2016, https://doi.org/10.1109/msmw.2016.7537995.

13. S.K., S. and Naveen, N.C., Study for Assessing the Advancement of Imaging Techniques in Chest Radiographic Images. *Commun. Appl. Electron.*, 4, 5, 22–34, 2016. https://doi.org/10.5120/cae2016652086.

14. Sen, S., Datta, A., Basu, N., Moitra, S., Pleural effusion with pleural thickening in a patient exposed to zinc chromate paints: A rare case report. *Int. J. Med. Public Health*, 5, 2, 200, 2015. https://doi.org/10.4103/2230-8598.153838.

15. Stolk, J., Putter, H., Bakker, E.M., Shaker, S.B., Parr, D.G., Piitulainen, E., Russi, E.W., Grebski, E., Dirksen, A., Stockley, R.A., Reiber, J.H.C., Stoel, B.C., Progression parameters for emphysema: A clinical investigation. *Respir. Med.*, 101, 9, 1924–1930, 2007. https://doi.org/10.1016/j.rmed.2007.04.016.

16. Yamashita, R., Nishio, M., Do, R.K.G., Togashi, K., Convolutional neural networks: An overview and application in radiology. *Insights Imaging*, 9, 4, 611–629, 2018. https://doi.org/10.1007/s13244-018-0639-9.

17. Yang, J., Zhang, M., Liu, Z., Ba, L., Gan, J., Xu, S., Detection of lung atelectasis/consolidation by ultrasound in multiple trauma patients with mechanical ventilation. *Crit. Ultrasound J.*, 1, 1, 13–16, 2009. https://doi.org/10.1007/s13089-009-0003-x.

Early Stage Detection of Leukemia Using Artificial Intelligence

Neha Agarwal* and Piyush Agrawal

Computer Science & Engineering, Jaipur National University, Jaipur, India

Abstract

Leukemia is tissue-forming cancer of blood including Bone Marrow. An increase in the number of White Blood Cells in blood cells is the main cause of leukemia. Leukemia and Lymphomas are most common forms of Hematological Malignancy. Many forms of leukemia exist, which are characterized by the production of access number of abnormal WBCs.

Artificial Intelligence is used to diagnosis acute myeloid leukemia (AML) which is the common type of blood cancer. It helps to detect this blood cancer with high accuracy. This approach is based on the activity of the gene in the blood cell.

The proposed approach promotes early stage identification of leukemia and allows early diagnosis of leukemia. This reduces the risk of development of leukemia cells inside the blood. The proposed work consists of four sections- Object Recognition, Image Enhancement, Pattern Recognition and Matching Probability and Results. These modules thus help us to implement the proposed technique and desired results are obtained.

This research has made an effort to detect leukemia and give a probability whether any person may suffer from it in coming years. Efforts by many authors have been analyzed and an efficient way is proposed with many positive intensions for future aspects of this technology.

Keywords: Leukemia detection, artificial intelligence, object recognition, image enhancement

14.1 Introduction

Leukemia is a type of blood cancer or cancer in bone marrow. Bone marrow is the type of tissue that generates blood cells. Leukemia can evolve due to problems with the development of these blood cells. It generally traps the leukocytes or white blood cells (WBCs). Although leukemia is more probable to develop in person crossing the age of 55 years and it is also most prevalent cancer for those whose age is below 15 years.

The National Cancer Institute already reported that 61,780 people have been diagnosed with leukemia. This has already been predicted that 22,840 deaths from leukemia will occur in 2019. Leukemia is mainly categorized into two states—Acute and Chronic. Acute leukemia is growing faster and increases rapidly, whereas the chronic one is getting terrible day by day.

*Corresponding author: meet2neha.261@gmail.com

Sachi Nandan Mohanty, G. Nalinipriya, Om Prakash Jena and Achyuth Sarkar (eds.) *Machine Learning for Healthcare Applications*, (215–224) © 2021 Scrivener Publishing LLC

14.1.1 Classification of Leukemia

- Acute Lymphocytic Leukemia
- Acute Myeloid Leukemia
- Chronic Lymphocytic Leukemia
- Chronic Myeloid Leukemia.

14.1.1.1 *Acute Lymphocytic Leukemia*

Acute lymphocytic leukemia (ALL), is a form of cancer in the spongy tissue inside bones where blood cells are produced. These blood cells are known as bone marrow. In ALL, the term "acute" is derived from the fact that the cancer develops rapidly and generates undeveloped blood cells instead of developed cells.

14.1.1.2 *Acute Myeloid Leukemia*

Acute Myeloid leukemia (AML) begins in the tissue that generates blood cells. These blood cells are the soft part which is present inside certain bones. In this part, the new cells (blood) are reproduced. But mostly, it moves suddenly within the blood. Sometimes, it might spread to other sections of the body, which include the spleen, liver, lymph nodes, and central nervous system (brain, spinal cord and testes).

14.1.1.3 *Chronic Lymphocytic Leukemia*

Chronic lymphocytic leukemia (CLL) is another form of leukemia. The word "chronic" in chronic lymphocytic leukemia is derived from the fact that it usually develops slowly than other leukemia types. In CLL, most of the patients do not have any symptoms when they are diagnosed. It occurs commonly in older persons.

14.1.1.4 *Chronic Myeloid Leukemia*

Another name for Chronic Myeloid Leukemia (CML) is Chronic Myelogenous leukemia. It is type of leukemia that begins in certain blood forming cells of the bone marrow. It takes place when the cells in the parts of the body begin to develop in an uncontrollable manner. Hence it starts spreading to the nearby cells. CML exists mainly in adults, but quite occasionally in babies.

14.1.2 Diagnosis of Leukemia

Leukemia is often diagnosed with the part of a routine blood sample that results in abnormal counts in the blood cells. When you have signs that indicate leukemia, the doctor tries to find out the cause of the disease. Then the doctor may ask about the medical history, both family history and personal history.

Leukemia can be diagnosed with the help of any following methods: biopsy and Bone marrow aspiration, Flow cytometry, Lumbar puncture, Complete blood count peripheral smears, Cytogenetics, Immunohisto-chemistry, etc. as shown in Figure 14.1.

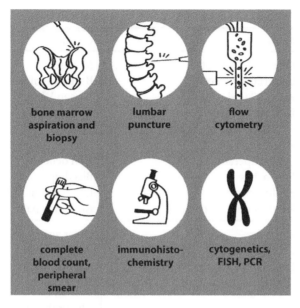

Figure 14.1 Various methods for detecting Leukemia.

14.1.3   Acute and Chronic Stages of Leukemia

The following Table 14.1 shows the difference between Acute Stage and Chronic Stage of Leukemia with respect to different parameters.

14.1.4   The Role of AI in Leukemia Detection

Artificial Intelligence (AI) is a machine-specific emulation of human knowledge processes, in particular of computer systems. One of the applications of artificial intelligence (AI) is Machine Learning (ML) which allows systems with the ability to automatically improve and learn from experience without programming explicitly. Machine learning contributes to the creation of computer programs that can access and learn data on their own.

Deep learning also performs a vital role in the field of artificial intelligence. It is the part of machine learning. It has systems that are capable of unsupervised learning from non-structured or non-labeled data. It is also referred as deep neural network or deep neural learning.

Further, a blood test that that is used to determine the overall physical health of a person is called as Complete Blood Count (CBC). It is used to diagnose a wide range of circumstance like leukemia, cancer and anemia. A CBC check tests many components and characteristics present in the blood like: Red Blood Cells (RBCs), which carry oxygen. Figure 14.2 shows the difference between normal blood and blood infected with leukemia.

Therefore Artificial Intelligence helps us to predict a new data. But for that we need to make our machine to program in following ways that it would give the exact prediction and saves many lives.

✓ Firstly, the machine should know the image pattern recognition to find the difference between the three cells.
✓ Secondly, should know how to compare his last dataset to new dataset.

Table 14.1 Difference between acute stage and chronic stages of leukemia.

Parameter	Acute	Chronic
Sign and Symptoms	Less WBCs Count Bacterial Infections Feeling Tired Difficulty in breathing Skin becomes pale Sweating Low temperature Joint aches Healing is slow Reddish dots over skin	Malaise Bacterial Infections Loss in Weight Appetite Loss Temperature Sweating at night Iron deficiency Bleeding Enlargement of Lymph nodes Abdomen pain
Risk Factors and Causes	Smoking Chemotherapy Exposure to high radiation Genetic abnormalities	Older age White-skinned Chemicals Exposure High radiation exposure
Treatment	Chemotherapy Targeted therapy Stem cell therapy Regular blood diagnosis Others(depends on type)	Chemotherapy Corticosteroids Monoclonal antibodies Blood transfusions Platelet transfusions
Images	Acute Lymphoblastic Leukemia Acute myeloid Leukemia 	Chronic Lymphocytic Leukemia Chronic Myeloid Leukemia

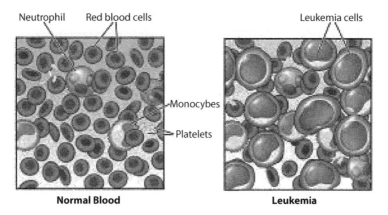

Figure 14.2 Normal blood and Leukemia infected blood.

14.2 Literature Review

There are various modern technologies implemented in order to detect leukemia. Leukemia is detected with the help of image processing and machine learning, MatLab, computer aided diagnosis.

Meesala and Wadhwa [1] introduced image processing technique as pattern recognition for analyzing and classifying cancer cells with the help of images microscopic blood cells images. Approaches like Genetic algorithm and fuzzy logic are used for optimization. To measure the performance, FAR and FRR parameters are used [3]. Auto encoders are stacked in the deep learning network [12] to form a hierarchical model in which inputs are compressed and structured and a high level functionality are extracted. This research considers that, direct digital nature is followed by most of the imaging techniques; these might help in upcoming challenges of broad data measures. It also describes analyzing process of cancer cell and also enlightens its importance in medical science. Some bacteria were discovered under blood cells [6] whose rate of growth help in detection and prognosis of cancer cell with the help of object recognition. This method helps in diagnosis of growth of the cells which is abnormal in any part of body. The sensitivity, specificity and accuracy of this research are 80, 91.04 and 96.4%.

Rajwa *et al.* [11] proposed another acknowledged technique named flow cytometry which is used to find out the progression of disease in acute myeloid leukemia. This study predicts the usefulness of nonparametric Bayesian's system and of change in progression of the disease using flow cytometry data accurately. The nonparametric Bayesian model is highly flexible and based on infinite Gaussian mixtures which further consist of infinite mixtures. These mixtures are used to model data from various flow cytometry (FC) samples for automatic identification of distinct functional cell populations and also local realizations, jointly. Author used 200 phenotypic panels of both diseased sample and non-diseased sample for training and testing of the system with additional leukemia cases gathered at multiple time points. This proposal got 90% accuracy for relapsing cases and 100% for others. They believe of this research is in accurate prediction by automated tools for monitoring diseases and response evaluation in a continuous manner. This research states that computerized monitoring and measurement of the therapeutic outcomes is critical not only for the objective assessment of disease levels, but also for the clear and concise assessment of treatment strategies.

Faivdullah *et al.* and Shafique [5, 10] implemented computer-aided diagnostic method for detecting and classifying leukemia from microscopic photographs of the blood. This microscopic images were then undergoes the process of reading, gradient, dilating and filling holes using MatLab [8]. It refers to the fact that a manual microscopic assessment of the stained sample slide is used to diagnose leukemia. But manual testing approaches are time consuming, less effective, and susceptible to error due to multiple human factors such as tension, exhaustion, and so on. As a consequence, various computer solutions have been introduced to fix errors in manual testing processes. Several computer-aided diagnosis techniques for leukemia have been introduced in the recent past. These procedures are more reliable, accurate and fast. It provides for the review of computer-aided diagnostic systems with regard to their methodologies. The methodology includes firstly enhancement, secondly segmentation, thirdly feature extraction then classification and finally accuracy.

Dharani and Hariprasath [2] used a ML classifier defined as Support Vector Machine (SVM) to classify of different types of leukemia. Various methods like linear contrast stretching, histogram equalization and a morphological technique are used to detect and count immature blast cells [4]. These researches describe the classifications of various leukemia cells and help in identification and detection of them. This helps in early detection of leukemia that prevents the transformation of Acute into Chronic State.

After using machine learning techniques, Select Most Informative Genes (SMIG) and Enhanced Classification Algorithm [13] were designed and implemented to enhance leukemia cancer classification. This technique is more accurate and it enhances the previous researches and also gave a milestone in the area of classification of Leukemia.

Desai and Shet [14] proposed a technique that aims at identifying images if leukemia easily and classifies them into their respective subtype. This was done with the help of MATLAB software with the help of image processing [7]. K-means method images are segmented by clustering algorithm and Artificial Neural Network (ANN) is constructed based on the extracted features. This neural network is equipped to recognize the images according to their form. It makes an ease in classification and detection in between different subtypes of Leukemia [9]. The main idea was that, ANN is the latest and fastest technology which has its many features too. ANN is also plays an important role in Computer Vision Algorithms too.

Besides of these many other authors also have a great contribution in this field, which initializes and clears path for many new technologies to be implemented in the same field. These researches enhance the medical treatment techniques and also connecting Computer Science to Medical Science.

14.3 Proposed Work

The ancient method for tracking the leukemia was done by using statistical parameters namely standard deviation and mean. This separates white blood cell which is present in the blood (erythrocytes and platelets) i.e. the count of WBCs. After that Image processing came in research. Our proposal is also related to Image recognition in which the machine is trained to process the given input image with the grid containing blood images of all blood types. This method gives an accurate probability and alerts the patient whether they are suffering from leukemia or might going to face it in coming years and in how many years. The accuracy of this method is much more than the statistical methods. The proposed work implements an algorithm for image processing and for calculating number of years by assuming the biological growth of cells. This parameter can be considered in normal case, if there is no catalyst like smoking, drinking or any type of drug.

Artificial Intelligence is used to detect the most common type of blood cancer that is acute myeloid leukemia (AML). It helps in detecting this cancer of the blood with high accuracy. This approach is based on the activity of the gene in the cells which is found in the blood. At the early stages, the symptoms of AML is same that of a severe cold but AML should be handled as soon as possible as it is a life-threatening disease.

14.3.1 Modules Involved in Proposed Methodology

The proposed methodology consists of four sections. Figure 14.3 shows the basic block diagram of proposed methodology. This includes:

a) Object Recognition
b) Image Enhancement
c) Pattern Recognition
d) Matching Probability and Results.

The following are the different modules that help us to implement the proposed technique and to obtain the desired results.

a) Object Recognition: Object recognition is one of the computer vision techniques. This technique is used to detect the object that is present in images and videos. In this stage, blood image of the patient is taken as an input. This image is the microscopic image of the blood cell. If the input image is not the blood image then the next input is taken into consideration.
b) Image Enhancement: Image enhancement is the process by which digital images are adjusted to make the results more appropriate to display or to make further image analysis. In this work, the image of the blood is enhanced. The pixel width and pixel height must be same in order to get accurate matching

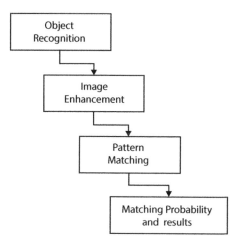

Figure 14.3 Basic Block diagram of proposed methodology.

of pixels. If the pixel width and the height are not same, it is enhanced to have same width and height.

c) Pattern Recognition: Pattern recognition is the process that categorizes the given input data into certain patterns based on key features. In this stage, each enhanced image is matched with the trained model. This process continues for the whole image of the blood cell.

d) Matching Probability and Results: This stage finds the probability of the affected blood cells which gives the result whether a person is suffering from cancer or not. It also finds the probability of cancer that a person might suffer in coming years.

14.3.2   Flowchart

The flowchart of implemented modules in Figure 14.4 describes how the samples are taken and analyzed.

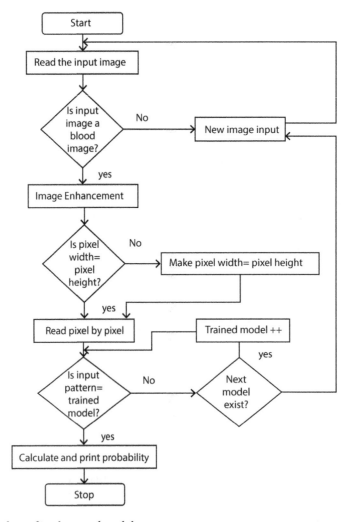

Figure 14.4 Flowchart of implemented modules.

14.3.3   Proposed Algorithm

Step 1: Input: Read the input images (I)
Step 2: Object recognition
      if (I = =Blood images)
          then (go to step 3)
      else (Take a new image as input)
Step 3: Image Enhancement
      Check every pixel of image
      if (pixel width = = pixel height)
          then (read blood image pixel)
      else (take every pixel with same width and height.)
      Read every pixel
Step 4: Pattern Recognition
      Check pattern through tensor flow library
      for (int i =0; i<=size; i++)
      {
          if (input pattern image = = train model)
              then (print probability)
          else
              train model = ++ arr [ ]
      }
      if (not matched)
          go to Step 1.

14.4   Conclusion and Future Aspects

Leukemia is a major global concern. The proposed method gives an ease in detection of Leukemia in early stages and helps in early diagnosis and may reduce the risk of development inside the patient as they know about it at early stage. Our research also gives a future aspect of Automatic detection Machines like ATMs by which people can easily get to know about their blood mutations and diseases like Leukemia. *Object Recognition, Image Enhancement, Pattern Recognition and Matching Probability and Results.* These different modules help us to implement the proposed technique and to obtain the desired results.

References

1. Meesala, S.K. and Wadhwa, S., An Artificial System for Prognosis Cancer Cells through Blood Cells Images Using Image Processing. *Int. J. Comput. Eng. Res.*, 09, 7, 01–06, 2019.
2. Dharani, T. and Hariprasath, S., Diagnosis of Leukimia and its types using digital image processing techniques. *International Conference on Communication and Electronics Systems (ICCES), IEEE*, 2018.
3. Sharma, N. and Sharma, S., An Efficient Method To Detect Leukemia Using Artificial Intelligence. *Int. J. Sci. Eng. Res.*, 09, 8, 777–783, 2018.

4. Himali, P.V., Modi, H., Pandya, M., Potdar, M.B., Leukemia Detection using Digital Image Processing Techniques. *Int. J. Appl. Inform. Syst., Found. Comput. Sci.*, 10, 1, 43–51, 2015.

5. Faivdullah, L., Azahar, F., Htike, Z.Z., Leukemia Detection from Blood Smears. *J. Med. Bioeng.*, 04, 6, 448–497, 2015.

6. Walter, J., Understanding Leukemia, in: *The Leukemia & Lymphoma Society*, 2012. https://www.lls.org/sites/default/files/file_assets/understandingleukemia.pdf

7. Chandrananda, S.S., Pathirage, S.H., Marapana, S.R., Amarathunga, N.M., Chandrasiri, S.S., Detection of Leukemia using Image Processing and Machine Learning. *Res. Gate*, 2016.

8. Mishra, S.J. and Deshmukh, A.P., Detection of leukemia using matlab. *Int. J. Adv. Res. Electron. Commun. Eng.*, 04, 2, 394–398, 2015.

9. Savvopoulos, S., Misener, R., Panoskaltsis, N., Pistikopoulos, E.N., Mantalaris, A., A Personalized Framework for Dynamic Modeling of Disease Trajectories in Chronic Lymphocytic Leukemia. *IEEE Trans. Biomed. Eng.*, 63, 11, 2396–2404, 2016.

10. Shafique, S. and Tehsin, S., Computer aided diagonsis of acute lymphoblastic leukemia. *Comput. Math. Methods Med.*, 1–13, 2018.

11. Rajwa, B., Wallace, P.K., Griffiths, E.A., Dundar, M., Automated Assessment of Disease Progression in Acute Myeloid Leukemia by Probabilistic Analysis of Flow Cytometry Data. *IEEE Trans. Biomed. Eng.*, 64, 5, 1089–1098, 2017.

12. Lin, M., Jaitly, V., Wang, I., Hu, Z., Chen, L., Application of Deep Learning on Predicting of AML with Cytogenetics, Age and Mutations, Clinical Oncology and Research, 3, 3, 1–6, 2020.

13. Nasser, E., Abd, A., Shaheen, M., Deeb, H.E., Enhanced leukemia cancer classifier algorithm. *Science and Information Conference, IEEE*, 2014.

14. Prasidhi, G., Desai, F., Shet, G., Detection and Classification of Leukemia using Artificial Neural Network. *Int. J. Res. Appl. Sci. Eng. Technol.*, 06, 4, 1316–1321 2018.

Part 3

INTERNET OF MEDICAL THINGS (IOMT) FOR HEALTHCARE

IoT Application in Interconnected Hospitals

Subhra Debdas[1*], **Chinmoy Kumar Panigrahi**[2], **Priyasmita Kundu**[3], **Sayantan Kundu**[4] **and Ramanand Jha**[5]

[1, 2]*School of Electrical Engineering, KIIT Deemed to be University, Bhubaneswar, Odisha, India*
[2,3,4]*School of Computer Science and Engineering, KIIT Deemed to be University, Bhubaneswar, Odisha, India*
[5]*College of Science, Mai Nefhi, Eritrea, East Africa*

Abstract

Health for All aims at providing equal access to healthcare system specifically in underdeveloped and remote parts of a country. However, it comes with diversified challenges of accessibility, availability and affordability. This is where the Internet of Things comes to the rescue. The extensive utilisation of IoT, notably the intelligent accouterments, would contribute significantly in developing the quality of service provided by the medical department, ensuring the convenience of the patients and boosting the level of management capability of the healthcare.

Notwithstanding, owing to the injunction of networking systems, there prevails a divided framework which will be able to associate each and every smart device in automatic health centres. This can be achieved with the help of the evolution of the Narrowband IoT. Keeping the system as the backdrop, a framework to associate smart device in automatic health centres established by using Narrowband IoT, and implement edge computing technology to be able to meet the requisite of dormancy in pharmaceutical proceedings can be brought to work.

In order to establish a automated monitoring system for healthcare, we introduce an Internet Of Things structured intelligent technology for edge computing. In this system, indispensable sensors, which we usually wear, broadcast information into the smart software gadgets - rapid active summarization for effective prognosis and exigency evaluated data alerts. These two software engines have been utilized and used in the Internet Of Things smart edge. The exigency index alerts engine gauges a cumulative criticality score whereas the RASPRO revamps the ample data collected by the sensors into scientifically allusive synopsis called personalized health motifs (PHMs). The IoT smart edge brings to use a risk-laminated covenant which consists of brisk assured push of PHMs and alerts straight to the medical practitioners, and the pull of itemized data, which was demanded, through the cloud by the finest effort. Both the performance appraisal and the clinical affirmation of this smart edge system has been done. The performance appraisal demonstrated noteworthy shrinkage in the energy (90%) as well as in the bandwidth (98%). Moreover, the clinical affirmation done on 183 patients brought about the fact that the IoT smart edge works persuasively well, when assessed according to three parameters, recall (0.83), F1-score (0.85), and precision (0.87), in the fields of warning which are to be given beforehand, detection of cardiac conditions, and remote monitoring. Thus, these assessments have succeeded in proving this as the best fit for the developing NB-IoT grids.

Corresponding author: subhra.debdasfel@kiit.ac.in

Sachi Nandan Mohanty, G. Nalinipriya, Om Prakash Jena and Achyuth Sarkar (eds.) *Machine Learning for Healthcare Applications*, (227–248) © 2021 Scrivener Publishing LLC

The proposed IoT smart edge system is an eloquent advancement en route to overcoming the obstacles to achieve the level of Health for All. However, we need to work upon the complications involved in bringing up a smart hospital by interlacing the intelligent things. We can also pave way to interconnected hospitals using edge computing to give the chief importance to the patient's convenience for availing the nearest serviceable ambulance in his locality during a medical emergency and related such issues.

Keywords: Smart hospital, machine learning, internet of things, LTE, information centric, cyber facility

15.1   Introduction

The Internet of Things (IoT) strives to achieve connection between every single gadget and the Internet in order to ensure accessibility of these devices at any place, at any time and through any route which implies through any network [1]. The Internet of Things (IoT) has already led its path to many noteworthy intelligent applications like smart phones, smart homes, smart refrigerators, smart washing machines, digital health, smart transport, smart cities and smart grids.

Health for All aims at ensuring good and proper healthcare facilities to be accessible to people from any of the smallest corners of the world. This becomes a major hurdle for the developing nations because the population of the people living in rural regions is quite large. There is a dearth of medical practitioners and diagnostic paraphernalia recognized in the remote regions which in overall points to paucity of proper healthcare facilities [2]. A large number of the medical practitioners do not wish to officiate in the rural regions. As its consequence, the already handful care centers established in these regions lack largely in the number of medical staff members [3]. It takes nearly a day for the population here to reach these health centers. For these daily wage earners, the regular check-ups come up as a hindrance to their livelihood. Even after the patients reach the care center, they suffer due to lack of proper examination time from the doctors owing to high load of patients.

The most propitious technological advancements which help to progress further in the way of achieving Health for All is the IoT or Internet of Things-based smart monitoring system for healthcare centers. A majority of the hospitals have started using mobile based applications for registering appointments with the doctors and for acquiring knowledge about the patients in the form of electronic medical records and consultation results. Moreover, many medical wearable gadgets help in perceiving and uninterrupted monitoring of physiological signs like blood oxygen (Sp02), electrocardiogram (ECG), blood sugar level, blood pressure (BP). Some of these smart gadgets include Bluetooth blood glucose meter, smart electrocardiograph (ECG) device, and 3G blood pressure meter. These monitored parameters can either be sent to the information platform for smart judgement backing devices to support the doctors for diagnosing real time problems or to keep a record of medical databases [4].

Adopting smart gadgets in the hospital environment can salvage the cost of the surgery, diminish the striving fervency of the clinical staff members and reinforce the medical affairs of the patients to a new level [5]. Nonetheless, the connection of these smart things using the perfect communication protocol still remains a great concern and threat to achieving the desired goals [6]. The wired communication does not comply with the needs for the mobile devices.

A large number of research workers have made an attempt to construct a framework for interlinking smart things using long range and short-range wireless communications. For tracking and supervising of medical records and patients in the hospital environment, Catarinucci *et al.* [7] brought out a three-layer network framework. The components included in this framework are: 1) RFID reinforced cellular sensor grid known as miscegenation sensing web structure, 2) Internet of Things intelligent portal and 3) Interfaces utilized by the user for resolving information with its administration. The miscegenation sensing web structure tracked sensor gadgets with RFID Gen2 labels and advance their data to the local area network or the Internet through the intermediate strata. By employing ZigBee and a long-range wireless transmission protocol, Boudra *et al.* brought in a supervising system for the patients. By employing both ZigBee and RFID, Alharbe *et al.* introduced a way to construct an information handling arrangement. In this arrangement, RFID was employed to identify objects without any user intervention and ZigBee was engaged for transmission of collected information to the centers of cloud. Using 5G communication means, Nasri and Mtibaa brought out a system of broadcasting data coming out of the terminals to smart phones which then receive additional treatment when directed to the cloud center. Zhanwei and Yongjian proposed a system where a number of smart gadgets are put on the patients to get the data on a cloud center by uploading it. Short range wireless networks are restricted by the media radius. These include Wi-Fi and ZigBee. Long range wireless protocols do not comply with the needs of the smart gadgets to be employed in a hospital environment owing to their excessive energy expenditure [8]. Narrowband IoT (NB-IoT) is a wireless protocol that functions nearly far and wide [9] and has the edge of low power expenditure and low cost [10, 11].

15.2 Networking Systems Using IoT

Radio-frequency identification: This system is customarily developed with the help of a radio-frequency identification label, radio-frequency identification reader consists of a coil that acts as an antenna for broadcasting and gathering signals. RFID labels make use of a backscatter technology to allow the radio wave to reflect back, hence handing over the data to the reader (Figure 15.1). Exclusive IDs on the labels pave way for each and every thing/object to be autonomously recognized and without the aid of human intervention [12]. RFID gadgets are further grouped into three divisions as illustrated below:

a) Active RFID tags: It makes use of batteries to transmit radio waves and ensures their gathering by the reader. The transmission ranges to a substantial radius which is dependent on battery power. One of the examples include the LoJack gadget which is affixed to a car and employs mobile technology as well as global positioning system (GPS) to help find the bereaved cars.

b) Semi-active RFID tags: This too employs battery use but on the contrary, its foundation lay on the precept just like the passive tags. It lengthens its communication distance by utilizing the battery.

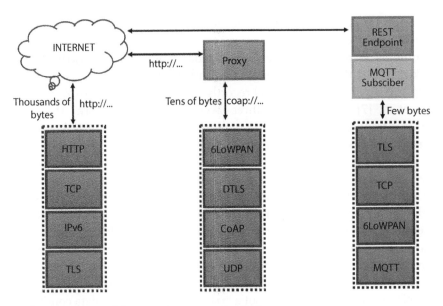

Figure 15.1 Complete layout of the network systems using IoT.

c) Passive RFID tags: These are entirely reliant on the reader's power fount. These are generally employed on not so expensive things. One of the examples may be gathering inventories of a huge pile of things in a shop.

A number of advantages of systems established on RFID in IoT are:

1. Its capability to concurrently look through numerous elements and not having to do so autonomously;
2. Its decreasing cost since the former years;
3. Its capability to systematically take up IDs of tags, on its own, from a certain range and not having any scrupulous contemplation for proceedings in the line-of-sight;
4. Its capability to look through tags rapidly.

Wireless Sensor Networks: This networking system is used by mankind for a significant amount of time as of now with a large number of disseminations of works. These are built up of minuscule nodes with sensors, battery, memory, and processor whose fundamental range of capability are discerning and broadcasting information. With worldwide focal attention on the Internet of Things, WSN could be promptly employed into the present IoT architecture with nearly nil [13].

WSN has primary assets associated with it which are illustrated below:

a) Wireless Sensor Network nodes further have some processing competency, which makes it advantageous in shrewd discerning and supervising, yet its calculation competency is restricted.

b) Scalability and competency to operate in severe and adverse ambience, particularly in industries.

c) Wireless Sensor Networks nodes work with the help of a battery with a lifetime of years paving way for them being energy-strained.

(LTE-A): Long Term Evolution-Advanced was made a standard by the 3rd Generation Partnership Project (3GPP) targets for accomplishing more advanced degree of structure accomplishment. The inclination is to furnish greater bit rates in a charge economical method [14]. The added lineaments in LTE-A are boosted employment of multiantenna approaches, a backing for relay nodes (RNs) and carrier aggregation. With these range of capabilities, it is appropriate for IoT, in consideration of the fact that gadgets might be employed for proposing services corresponding to relay systems and alternative higher ranked fog nodes or to end-gadgets too.

LoRaWAN: This is used for planning to the MAC and system layer of the OSI model. The low force wide region arrange innovation working in the ISM band is intended to permit low-fueled gadgets impart over long range, and can utilized in different IoT situations. LoRaWAN organizes for the most part convey a star-of-stars geography and involve dispersed GW which hand-off information between disseminated end-gadgets and a focal system server. Correspondence between the GW and end-gadgets is spread out on various information rates and recurrence channels, in this manner dispensing with obstruction. LoRaWAN has three classes that work at the same time specifically, Class A, Class B, and Class C. LoRaWAN information rates run from 0.3 to 50 kb/s and can deal with the information pace of end-gadgets utilizing the versatile information rate conspire. LoRaWAN has pulled in colossal consideration in territories of limit and throughput augmentation [15]. A numerical model was examined in which precisely assesses how bundle mistake rate relies upon the offered load.

Internet Protocol Version 6 (IPv6): The principle explanation behind acquainting IPv6 was with conquered inalienable inadequacies of Internet Protocol Version 4 (IPv4). IPv6 satisfactorily handles versatility by guaranteeing that an enormous number of things will have interesting locations. The IETF's Internet Protocol Next Generation working gathering was liable for normalizing the particulars. As referenced before, IPv6's primary inspiration is its enormous location space. With the expansion of IoT gadgets, address space will never again be a significant test, however the need to guarantee security to these gadgets. The IPv6 offers support for Internet Protocol Security [16]. The protocol was intended for increasingly proficient hubs as a top priority, and the apparently huge IPv6 addresses are progressively amiable to cross-layer pressure. Besides, the IPv6 bolsters neighbor revelation. This system empowers neighboring IPv6 hubs to impart, and furthermore dissuade mine the nearness of each other. This makes this convention truly reasonable in the IoT system, where FEC gadgets share reachability data, and deflect mine accessible FEC gadget through which data can be handed-off.

Sigfox: Sigfox21 is a system convention that is used for handling messages related to machine type, consequently limits the utilization of energy. It works in the two hundred kilo-hertz band of recurrence utilizing tweak of ultra-limited band. Sigfox is explicitly intended to fulfill the requirements related to longer gadget life-cycle, huge IoT applications, higher system limit, longer correspondence go and lower cost of gadgets [17]. An important component of this system is the arrangement of its product-based interchanges, in which all system as well as registering intricacy are overseen in the network cloud based systems. It would be able to inculcate superior valuable cores inside the Internet of Things layout because of t he capacity of gadgets to do a portion of its assignment adjacent to the system edge (Figure 15.2).

CARP: Channel-Aware Routing Protocol is a cross-layer appropriated directing convention explicitly intended for remote sensor systems. CARP misuses connect quality data for cross-layer transfer assurance, with hubs chose as transfers if past transmissions with neighboring hubs have been effective. Furthermore, the convention likewise mulls over force control systems for choosing vigorous connections [18]. The convention can be adequately sent inside the IoT area since it underpins lightweight bundles.

WSDL: Extensible Markup Language22 is used for structuring sentence in Web Service Description Language for addressing capacities as well as conjuring systems related to administrations in Web Systems. Generally, administrations comprise every physical item of a data, containing both nonfunctional and useful segments. Basically, it depicts Web administrations dependent on a theoretical design which the administration provides. Moreover, Web Service Description Language is protractible to permit portrayal of messages and their endpoints independent of organization or convention utilized for correspondence. Web Service Description Language is regularly sent along with straightforward item get to convention and a Schema of Extensible Markup Language22 to give Internet administrations throughout Web Network [19].

Simple Object Access Protocol: It is a convention which particularly endorses an unambiguous Extensible Markup Language22 message position. In this part, administration solicitations as well as reactions are epitomized in an Extensible Markup Language22-based way. This may involve solicitations to summon a technique on an assistance, reactions in

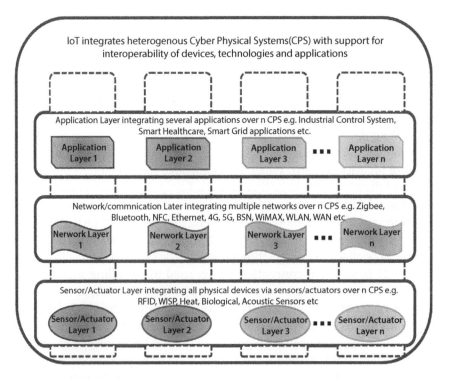

Figure 15.2 Network layer of IoT systems.

ACRONYMS	DEFINITION	ACRONYMS	DEFINITION
FP7	Framework Program7	IPv6	Internet Protocol Version 6
IoT	Internet Of Things	NDN	Normal Data Networking
LTE	Long Term Evolution	ICN	Information Centric Networking
GSM	Global System For Mobile Connection	LTE-A	LTE Advanced
M2M	Machine-To-Machine	MF	Mobility First
DPI	Deep Packet Inspection	FIA	Future Internet Architecture
CS	Content Store	GPRS	General Packet Radio Service
CONET	Content Network	SAIL	Stable and Adaptive Internet Solutions
PIT	Pending Interest Table	LRU	Least Recently Used
SIT	Satisfied Interest Table	IPv4	Internet Protocol Version 4
NSF	National Science Foundation	GUID	Globally Unique Identifier
FIA-NP	FIA-Next Phase	FIA	Future Internet Architecture

Figure 15.3 List of acronyms and their definitions.

distinction to a help strategy as well as mistakes. Simple Object Access Protocol is a vehicle skeptic informing framework which depicts the structure and information sorts of message payloads by utilizing the developing the World Wide Web Consortium Extensible Markup Language Schema standard. Simple Object Access Protocol solicitations as well as reactions travel utilizing Hypertext Transfer Protocol or some other vehicle system. Considering asset compelled Internet of Things systems, proposed a methodology to tie Simple Object Access Protocol to Constrained Application Protocol (Figure 15.3), hence bringing about a lightweight convention that can be promptly conveyed in the IoT structure [20]. This is because of the way that in profoundly asset obliged, the Hypertext Transfer Protocol and client convention datagram restricting might not yield wanted system execution.

15.3 What are Smart Hospitals?

This segment is divided into two components. The first component illustrates the backdrop of the smart hospitals, conferring significant stress on the delineation of the assigned name—"smart hospital", the ground rules associated with the surveillance of the information and the corresponding managerial architecture and the purposes of importing "smartness" in the backdrop of the hospitals. The second component places emphasis on the resources that bring in "smartness" in the hospital ambience and as they are acutely involved for the working of the smart hospitals, these are required to be secured and protected [21].

15.3.1   Environment of a Smart Hospital

The ambient objective of the automated healthcare centers is to give forth the most advantageous affection to the patients through the full utilization of the progressive ICT. The admittance to internal and external proficiency when required; having each and every pertinent information at one's disposal as and when needed; and competent and productive operation/examination proceedings which expedites accomplishing this target along with nominal glitch pace and cost productively.

The accessibility and application of the required inter-associated systems and gadgets is what attributes the term "smart" to the smart hospitals. While the systems of legacy can surely be an indispensable component of end-to-end smart procedures, this course will chiefly focus on advanced systems as well as specifically Internet of Things constituents. With reference to the word "traditional hospital" refers to the hospitals that are not falling under the division of smart hospitals which is delineated in Figure 15.4. The incentive

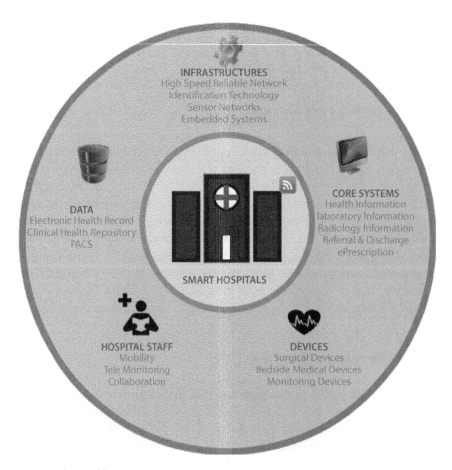

Figure 15.4 Smart hospital layout.

responsible for the idea of introducing a smart hospital ambience consisting of revamped/ computerized end-to-end processes and IoT constituents is established on the amelioration of current hospital processes and the influx of advanced potentials in the health maintenance of the patients. Nonetheless, this shift does involve extra considerations to be looked chiefly upon which is pertinent to the extensive dependence on ICT. Both of these, in combination, define the objectives of a smart hospital. As illustrated beneath, the category and scope of ICT utilization undoubtedly brings an impact upon the pertinent challenges and favourable circumstances along with the aims to achieve the goal: Improved exam native/ surgical capability: ICT not only enhances the current available procedures but also facilitates advanced procedures to ensure medical care (e.g. micro-surgery which is not achievable through surgeons can be done now by surgical robots). Progressively, hospitals are becoming more competent to unearth data related to patients which would further aid in making a choice for the best route to achieve good medical care or in medical examination. In addition, refined software fixes are conceding them to deftly tune their managerial procedures.

Seamless patient flow: Potent patient flow along with potent health management can be capable of shortening halting times and the time period of hospital detentions, dwindle glitches, boost up income and multiply the contentment of the patient (and staff member) [22]. ICT can be brought in use to distinguish, inspect and work out impediments and through this dispenses potent patient flow and health management. In addition to the potent patient flow and potent health management, the smart hospitals can be strengthened further by computerized refurbishments of medical data over information systems and the gadgets organized in a grid (Figure 15.5). The emanating accessibility of the data pertinent to the patients in each and every phase—starting with entrance to exit—as well as escalation procedures like admittance, scheduling and many more around it eventually lead to smooth flow of the patients.

Intelligent medical care: Among other purposes of bringing in IoT gadgets to the medical healthcare environment, one of the chief ones is the capability of IoT to stretch the hospital borders and ensure dispensation of medical care to rural regions [23]. A diversified number of medical gadgets like wearable gadgets, phone gadgets and wearable gadgets bring in the capability to accomplish patient supervision in real-time basis by means of measurement of primary essential signs and ensure that these measurements are easily accessible to staff members of the hospitals and systems by way of grid connections. These medical care abilities in remote regions are improved by various medical gadgets that display the capability to work on the patient counting on condition or by way of distant regulations. Thus, the admittance of the patients to hospitals can be restricted to only the essential cases, bringing diminished costs of patient care and upgraded patient involvement, since the patient can now take medication from one's individual home.

Reinforced patient safety: Reinforcing patient flow and the proper deliverance of healthcare conjointly escalate clinical and patient safety. However, it is to be clearly understood that the patient flow and the deliverance of the healthcare facilities should not advance in the risk of compromising with the safety (Figure 15.5). Gadgets gathering information pertinent to the life support supervising machines or the essentially important signs of the patient and the intake of the medicament, when correctly brought into use, can result into marked up safety of the patients provided these are banded together and are competent enough to render well-timed admonitions.

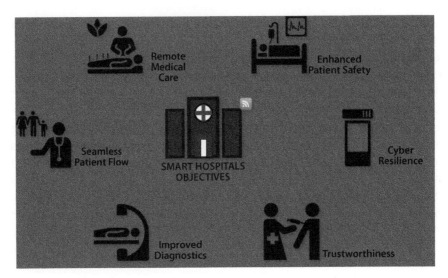

Figure 15.5 Objectives of smart hospitals.

Resilience towards Cyber facility: It pertains to the competency of a health center to make certain the accessibility and the durability towards dispensations that count upon Information and communications technology resources. More advanced Information and communications technology insertion surely paves its way to higher reliance on Information and communications technology, which is followed by a hike in the pertinence of data security for smart hospitals. The health division is envisaged to be a crucial foundation which is needed to be specifically secured. One who aids in the accomplishment of dispensing proper healthcare inclusive of the hospitals, require to foresee, be ready, reciprocate and acclimate to both unforeseen shifts and additive shifts. This is a matter of greater concern in smart hospitals as compared to traditional hospitals because the number of the constituents in the former that could be hampered by or result into dearth of service is in a large number (Figure 15.5).

Trustworthiness: To win the faith and achieve a good position, when there are many alternatives in making a choice between disparate providers, is a matter which involves great clashes and competition. Reliability also hampers devotion to medicament along with continuance of medical care, which has connotations for the consequences a health center will be able to realize. To be at the leading edge in terms of Information and communications technology utilization evidently furnishes leverage in securing a good position [24]. It is also to be taken care of that the safety and confidentiality of the patients is not exposed to danger in order to refrain from ruining the renowned regard achieved in the long race.

15.4   Assets

15.4.1   Overview of Smart Hospital Assets

Smart health center comprises of large number of assets that are indispensable for carrying out their jobs and hence, these are required to be properly secured. For instance, a few hospital assets are pertinent in the classical hospitals too, but the rest of them are the primary attributes of smart hospitals considering that they are shrewdly linked and capable of making resolutions independently [25]. Some of these assets are recognition systems, interlinked medical data systems and mobile consumer gadgets. In the succeeding section, the particular assets which distinguish smart hospitals are the chief center of attention.

a) Automated care system assets constitute the Information and communications technology environment which permits the automated hospitals for expanding its service and dispense health management facilities to patients who reside in rural regions:
  - Clinical accouterments for tele-diagnosis (like computations of ace of the heart, blood pressure, ECG, blood sugar computations and other minute corporeal computations, threshold-triggered alarm generators and so on) and tele-monitoring may come under the mould of implantable or wearable gadgets and so on.
  - Clinical accouterments for dispersion of medicament (automatic medicating accouterments) or to supervise medical care.
  - Tele-health accouterments, like sensors, telephone/internet linkages and cameras; telemedical system of computer for patients to list and record their corporeal computations themselves (inclusive of patient-side application/software provided that it is pertinent).

b) Networked medical devices whose comprehensive usage customarily distinguishes smart hospitals and also facilitates remote health monitoring of patients, which is a primary dispensation, as in comparison to traditional hospitals, which may cater healthcare administration at a national position. In addition to this, present-day implantable gadgets like pacemakers can be brought up to date, thereby diminishing the needs for reinstatement. Mobile along with stagnant gadgets have many at times been brought into application in the traditional hospitals (Figure 15.6). Anyhow, in the ambience of the smart hospital, they are shrewdly linked with medical data system and recognition constituents which thereby escalates the capability of arriving at decisions and the degree of automation. For instance, these can consist of:
  - wearable extrinsic gadgets (e.g. wireless temperature counters, compact and convenient insulin pumps);
  - mobile gadgets (e.g. blood sugar computation gadgets) [12];
  - Adjuvant gadgets (e.g. supportive robots).
  - implantable gadgets (e.g. cardiac pacemakers);
  - Stagnant gadgets devices (e.g. life support machines, chemotherapy furnishing stations, computer tomography (CT) scanners);

c) Identification systems are brought into application for recording and verification of staff members, hospital accouterments like beds or patients. In the ambience of smart hospitals, the biometric scanners in addition to reading the recognition systems, are also shrewdly put in a grid with the data systems and the gadgets. Furthermore, in smart hospitals, the systems to serve as the primary lead related to different parts like authentication and consequently

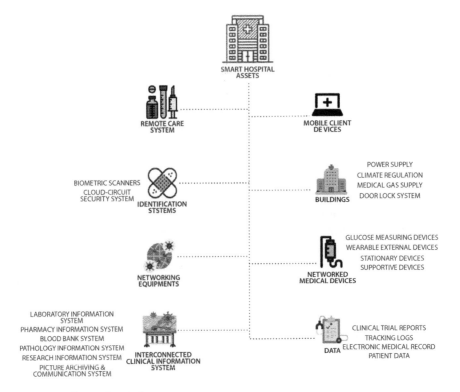

Figure 15.6 Assets of smart hospitals.

authorization [26] (e.g. permitting admittance to particular fields) are the closed-circuit security systems. The examples may comprise of:

- Supervise analogous shift of staff members/resources/patients and so on and RFID devices along with the support of location services to appraise.
- recognition systems components like bracelets, labels, smart badges (e.g. ultrasound facilitated) and tags.
- CCTV (video vigilance) along with identification/authentication abilities
- Biometric scanners;

d) Networking accouterments furnish the associability over a network foundation to back smart hospitals. The accouterments needed are nearly similar to the usual accepted accouterments brought into application in traditional hospitals. However, it is distinguishable by its embellished characteristics (e.g. bandwidth, transmitting protocols). The examples comprise of:

- Grid cards of interface;
- Network backbone gadgets;
- Internet of Things portals that will be to evaluate information gathered with the help of gadgets and transmit the signals to an Information center or Cloud networking systems;
- Transmission media

e) Mobile Client gadgets are shrewdly unified in smart hospitals to ensure the accessibility of the appropriate data in the appropriate place and at the

appropriate time. In addition to these, it helps to ease the maneuverability of the patients and the staff members (Figure 15.6). The examples comprise of:
- Applications developed for laptops, tablets and smartphones;
- Emergency connection applications for laptops, tablets and smartphones;
- Clients for mobile (e.g. pagers, smart phones, tablets, laptop computers);

f) Akin data systems for clinical purposes are set up within an intelligent healthcare center collectively along with clinical gadgets as well as recognition constituents to facilitate end-to-end smart processes related to patient care. Additionally, the medical data systems set up in a grid in smart hospitals are progressively becoming capable of taking decisions independently. The examples comprises of:
- Pathology information system;
- Hospital information systems (HIS).
- Laboratory information systems (LIS);
- Research information system;
- Picture archiving and communication systems (PACS);
- Blood bank system;
- Radiology information systems (RIS);
- Pharmacy information system (PIS);

g) Data are usually contemplated like essential resources from the viewpoint of data safety. The resolutions a smart gadget will make is chiefly established on the scrutiny of the gathered data. The examples comprise of:
- Medical and managerial patient information (e.g. tests outcomes, contact specifications, health records).
- Financial, hospital and other organizational information;
- Data pertaining Research Works;
- Information of staff members;
- Specifications pertaining vendors

h) Buildings and facilities, consisting of smart end-to-end processes which supervise diverse operations, are vital for the proper functioning of the smart hospitals. Some of the vital operations pertinent to the protection of the patients count upon the competence of shrewd amenity supervising systems (Figure 15.6). The examples comprise of:
- Temperature sensors;
- Smart patient room functioning and supervising systems, comprising of patient screens, medical staff members screens, smart boards etc.;
- Cclimate and power regulation systems, inclusive of smart ventilation systems;
- Smart system for door lock, administration for lock tokens as well as applications and administration software for lock system;
- Clinical gas supply.

15.4.2   Exigency of Automated Healthcare Center Assets

In a great environment known as smart hospital, each and every resource does not have equal exigency for the regular functioning and service offering. A resource is labeled as crucial when any disruption or impairment may result not only into a huge repercussion on the patients but also on the comprehensive functioning of the system as a whole. The resources which were depicted above were appraised on the grounds of the repercussions that would be evoked on the event of the disruption in offering the service which is termed as criticality.

The remarkably crucial resources, when seen in the ambience of smart hospitals, are the clinical gadgets set up in a grid and the interlinked medical data systems. This is attributed by their magnificent way of functioning in smart hospitals. The remarkably distinct transformations undergone in the process of digital transition of a hospital to a smart hospital is the existence of progressively independent clinical gadgets and shrewdly linked medical data systems. The presence of dependable medical data systems and clinical gadgets set up in grid contributes significantly to the accomplishment of the majority of the primary intentions pertinent to the smart hospitals. In addition, the IoT constituents and gadgets reinstate legacy systems which contribute essentially to the functioning of the smart hospitals with a aim to enhance diagnostic competencies and to improve clinical care facilities; this portrays them to be precisely crucial for the comprehensive functioning of the hospitals as well as for the safety of the patients. Accouterments needed to set up in a grid is contemplated as crucial because it acts as the foundation of the Smart Hospital; it is only with the help of solid grid framework that the escalated competencies in the backdrop of interoperable fixes or of bandwidth, functions accurately. To be more particular and precise, the data collected by end constituents or clinical gadgets are required to be scrutinized as well as unified with other clinical data. This is customarily grasped by the interlinked medical data systems of the hospitals along with the third parties too. Majority of the evaluation are conducted in a central system which is furnished with the scientific know-how to scrutinize and assemble data from various external as well as internal sources skilfully. These are not conducted by the medical data systems or by the clinical gadgets. The process of setting up a grid is imperative if we want to obtain the information from the clinical gadgets and the data systems to this system taking the decisive steps forward (crucial signals in a room of the smart hospitals pinpoints the necessity of the modification of the prescribed drugs). One among the various aims of the Smart Hospitals is to ensure the dispensing of medical care facilities to the remote places; in order to accomplish this, the connection between the hospital systems and the medical care systems in the remote places at the patient's side. The problem that creeps in, in this type of system, is that on the occasion of any impairment of disruption, the gadget/system would be revived by the corresponding dealer because it does not fall under the obligation of the hospital. This justifies minuscule rating in the cruciality matrix, in spite of the significance of the information these systems gather for prescribing drugs and for diagnosis. The data (data logs, research data, and so on), the mobile client dispensing services and the recognition systems come in the succeeding rankings. Even though these are exceedingly substantial resources which are used for the proper operation of smart hospitals because they do not back the crux operations (their usage may stretch over from awareness promoting intents to establishing diagnosis or having medical care facilities at one's disposal in remote regions), any interruption would not result to a serious brownout in the functioning and dispensing of the hospital facilities. The building and facilities occur at the last in terms of position. In these circumstances, the repercussion which would crop up would be very serious but since the possibility of something like that to happen is pretty small (in accordance with the official hazard administration term, a "blackswan" case), it turns out to be at the end of the rankings. Nonetheless, the research study has delineated that cyber-seizures on the systems of dispensing services (power procurement, climate regulation and so on) are not so often. This is because they need great proficiency and composure and consequently the outcome would not be of any beneficial importance in terms of finance to the deleterious attacker (as seen in the situation of ransomware).

15.5   Threats

15.5.1   Emerging Vulnerabilities

This segment nuances the most broadly perceived weaknesses that ought to be thought out by smart health centers. The summary isn't contained particularly by specific weaknesses yet connects with affiliations and social points of view. Perils consistently misuse weaknesses credited to ICT people and resources. Concerning people, the remarkably applicable gatherings are an affiliation's personnel and the board. As the employees and the board independently procure and oversee ICT assets, for instance frameworks and gadgets both the clusters are immovably connected. When in doubt, safety and protection must be broad something different assailants basically misuse the most delicate resources. There are nevertheless, a couple of real amenabilities that go with the regulation of IoT in therapeutic administrations that are arduous to conclude. A crucial point of smart hospitals is that singular data intelligence is observed as naturally much largely significant as budgetary data by crooks. Beside admittance to susceptible and crucial data, admittance to doctor suggested medicines may in like manner be seen as profitable by aggressors. While carrying out IoT procedures the segments are preferred for their negligible exertion and unequivocal abilities in any situation the limits are on a very basic level underneath what may be bolstered when the advantages guaranteed are safety and protection costs and the lives of the individuals may be a gigantic piece of value, or significantly more vital than the expense of the sections. Transcendent weaknesses nevertheless, don't simply empower toxic exercises they may in like manner improve the probability and repercussion of human blunders and structure disillusionments. IoT contraptions inclusive of composed clinical gadgets are profoundly interlinked and a couple of gadgets even can normally connect with various devices. In this way, security decisions made locally for particular contraption may have overall effects. Much of the time huge clinical devices were organized without the specific mean to be related with a framework (a portion of the time expressly proposed to persist as being bound)—that need arrived much after some time and was surged on. The correspondence amid keen contraptions and legacy systems can in like manner make openings and give space for malignant aggressors to increment of unauthorized admittance to data and structures. The introduction of fresh fragments displays an additional assault surface.

IoT devices are dispersed any place in the emergency clinics (from sensors in the patient rooms to CCTV and RFID peruses that offer get the chance to control). This infers physical security is basically incomprehensible for all parts. Guaranteeing the fringe is restricting this feebleness in any case more protection is required. Most clinical gadgets are designed intentionally to avoid threats showing works out. Contraptions are amassed subject to "proposed use" situations, and what a rational individual may do. Hacking and other framework carried disasters are "unintended use" or "abuse" cases. This position prompts different fundamental weaknesses and threats all through the social protection organic framework. There is a mass-scale game plan of homogeneous IoT devices which makes it appear to be valuable to look at sensible ambush ways. While device makers and security associations need to remove all weaknesses, convicts simply need to find one. It is basically hard to fix all weaknesses for all devices [16]. All the while, in any case, if a specific pitifully is ousted, it is ordinarily not difficult for hoodlums to find another down to earth assault way. In particular, for clinical contraptions, their future is a huge drawback to consider. Emergency clinics don't change CAT scanners or MRI machines like clockwork and when they buy the contraptions may starting at now be old (it takes practically three years from plan to examining and making of a clinical gadget reliant on EU order). The identical puts in if there should arise an occurrence of clinical facilities generally speaking IoT parts depend on the roof of the present establishment.

IoT gadgets execute embedded working structures and applications with minor if malware recognizable proof or contravention abilities. The little size and compelled planning power of a large number of related gadgets consistently controls measures, for instance, encryption or other healthy well-being endeavors. Furthermore, it is much of the time inconvenient or hard to reconstruct or refresh gadgets. There is an extending degree of reliance on IoT gadgets, which are unknown for existing as specifically solid. The reliance on related advancement is getting much more rapid than our capability to ensure about it—in locales hampering the lives of individuals and open security a superior nature of care is legitimized. This is specifically legitimate for a few medical devices that are importantly crucial for the continuance of patients. The certified customer has close to zero comprehension into the internal operation of the devices or the specific data streams they generate. Concerning clinical devices, medical members of the staff, IT staff and the patient have close to zero such understanding. Danger decisions taken by the generator are not revealed in any distinguishable way to the social protection provider, specialist, or patient. This makes seeing likely risks just as reacting in a helpful manner if there ought to be an event of a scene inconvenient. There is every now and again no sensible technique to alert the customer when a security issue rises. This may realize a safety and protection break that continues on for a longer time interval before being distinguished and remediated. It has recently been showed up, regardless, that subverted medical devices became employed as bridgeheads for extra malware augmentation in crisis medical centers. In social protection this is especially noteworthy, considering the way that the usual safety frameworks may "bomb shut" by refusing admittance—yet that may place calm patient in peril greater than "bomb open" which grants overall admittance.

Admittance management is noteworthy in the keen medical clinic condition as the dearth of approval game plan may allow unauthorized access by way of a terminal device to an elementary architecture. Problems may arise with validation or approval of members of the staff who manage medical devices; every now and then, the "have to-know" hypothesis or the apprehension of the propositions from the angle of digital security is missing. In spite of being all around groomed and cautious, the members of the staff may evade endeavors pertaining to security, for instance, preparatory measures and techniques in the occasion where they come out to be excessively inadequately arranged or ameliorating recede them furthermore. Considering the ambience of the emergency medical center, medical staff members may try to undertake some actions basically as a result of the pressure of time or on account of assertions with various targets inclusive of effective quiet stream/human services, charming treatment and care received by the patients or patient/ representative safety and security. Considering a Smart atmosphere, the patients and physicians can make use of individual gadgets (portable, wearable devices, etc.); dearth of an unmistakable and critical BYOD game plan can be incredible frailty. Reinforcing techniques agreeable to the medical center's information safety and protection game plan need to be made compulsory to be able to make use of any outer device. By and large, the division of IT does not bother about the fact that such devices or architectures are being made use of, whereas in various situations, the venture requirement of displaying one more architecture/device to aid the medical operation does not allot proper time for legitimate examination of the aforesaid architecture/device for keeping consistency along with the organization's preconditions.

Owing to medical requirements, it is practicable for architectures or devices to be made use of which is not able to meet the corporation or authoritative protocols. Considering situations like these, the IT office is typically conscious of the employment of the architecture or device. Large numbers of IoT devices that may be employed in the situation of the social insurance ambience do not comply suitably with the present hierarchical moves. With special emphasis regarding portraying IoT in the organization's ICT condition, the favoured extension pace might regularly exceed the competency of the division of IT to adhere to proper Asset and Change Handling forms that include safety and privacy audits of recent architectures/devices. Looking from a hierarchical angle, the stance of the users is crucial, which is a integral frailty especially owing to communal protection and security. The primary aim displays limits the patients and medical physicians will pick up each and every alternative needed in the moment to carry out this aim effectively. As a matter of usual practice, this signifies that workaround preparations shall be ensued. Considering a smart environment, where owing to the disperse notion of the backdrop, a security regulation is difficult to be accomplished, so one cannot take care of the cost of workaround preparations which may pose a threat to the degree of safety and protection achieved .However, the workarounds, as mentioned before, are not tested comprehensively and are also not reported intermittently and thus these pave their way to set up a center fragility. Owing to the dearth of suitable arrangement or the medical necessities, the arrangements of devices or architectures and the executive's forms might not be in conformity to the industrial or hierarchical norms. The dearth of classic arrangement for comparative devices in all cases leads to an ICT circumstance where normal viewpoint in correlation to safety and precaution susceptibility is not present because analogous devices may be disclosed for different reasoning thus leading to the application of remedial appraisals exceptionally problematic from the beginning to the end of the organization as well as the disclosure of the susceptibilities.

The already cited susceptibilities for almost the entire component are inclusive of specially designed viewpoints natural to the assets of the ICT. Apparently, a minor part of the susceptibilities are more and more pertinent to particular sorts of the assets of the ICT resources than any other; for instance, susceptibilities that are recognized with the dearth of legitimate regulation of safety and protection viewpoint (for instance unfounded or architecture/devices not up to the standard) are increasingly relevant for arranged mobile phones or medical devices. Competencies pertinent to constructed dwelling, for instance, architecture of an entryway bolt or the atmosphere and coercion instructions might be defenseless also because they increasingly rely on the assets of ICT.

15.5.2 Threat Analysis

T his area talks about potential attack, focuses and danger types dependent on the key resources and a progression of main drivers. The underlying drivers of dangers looked by shrewd emergency clinics are malignant activities, human mistakes, framework and outsider disappointments and common marvels. The danger scientific categorization is centered around digital security viewpoints with importance to Smart clinics, a considerable lot of which likewise sum up to any IT frameworks.

a) Malicious activities are intentional acts by an individual or an association. Albeit both undermine keen emergency clinics, it is imperative to recognize malevolent activities from other intentional activities that sidestep strategies and methods without malignant expectation. An individual doing a noxious activity might be an outer or an inner from the viewpoint of the influenced association

b) Control seizing may be executed at degree of the device or at the degree of organize (arrange/assembling seizing—HTTP/TCP). The former is of particular hugeness in respect of savvy emergency clinics; Lately, the phrase "medjack" was conferred by the TrapX Security to hint at the capturing of medical gadgets to form subordinate channels in medical clinic structures. Medical gadget altering is another basic danger. Arranged clinical gadgets might be reinvented, reconstructed by deactivating or by alternating gadget settings. Communal designing assaults (for example phishing, bedevilling) assume a specific job with regards to shrewd emergency clinics. Social assaults are famous as the human component is generally the most fragile connection in the guard of an association. Device and information burglary are furthermore pertinent in terms of hateful charges; When one scrutinizes the bulk that a segment of the medical accouterments might have, it comes out to be an unusual incursion. However, when one presents sensors, the bulk does not count as a problem any further and the chances of this incursion to be endorsed escalate. Erroneous data collection, erroneous scrutiny and thus, erroneous dynamic are the result of the lack of the proper establishment of each and every interlinked device.

c) Skimming is a hearing in incursion on the huge reoccurrence RFID tokens. It is a pretty undeniable incursion anyhow because RFID tags are employed customarily in the matter of shrewd clinics (sensors, tags and so forth). The aforementioned is extremely applicable and shall be contemplated since the protection and safety coming out of this type of incursions relies extra further on accouterments venture. Dismissal-of-administration assaults may impart an architecture or organization both inside and out unreachable, which may comprehensively disturb the procedure of consideration of a patient. Since keen emergency clinics shall customarily rely on the resources of cloud or web to a continually escalating degree, a DOS intrusion might, for instance, lead to inapproachability of the data of patients (for instance in the situation that data is locked up in a cloud domain or when their collection is established on the grounds of Internet for consideration intentions of distant patients).

d) Human mistakes happen during the setup or activity of gadgets or data frameworks, or the execution of procedures. Human mistakes are regularly identified with deficient procedures or lacking preparing. Models include: Medical framework setup mistake that may bargain either the activity or the cybersecurity stance of the framework, or both. Absence of review logs to take into account fitting control - for example of access to keen emergency clinic assets—as well as episode distinguishing proof and appraisal of restorative/improvement activities. Unauthorized get to control or absence of procedures is exceptionally appropriate to brilliant emergency clinics especially because of the affectability of patient information included and because of the way that the clinical procedures include jobs with an elevated level of specialization in various spaces. Non-consistence, particularly in the Bring Your Own Device (BYOD) worldview. This is particularly appropriate for brilliant emergency clinics that depend on versatile applications that can be open/introduced (for example as portable applications) in close to home gadgets not expressly endorsed (and accordingly tried or satisfactorily solidified) by the emergency clinic's IT office.

e) Supply chain interruption lies out and not in the explicit authority of the concerned institution because it customarily comes under the obligation of or hampers a third party. The breakdowns in the third parties have deep-seated results for the hospitals since the smart hospitals are very much reliant on the third parties. Illustrated below are some examples of third-party breakdowns which would probably hamper the proper working of the smart hospitals.

- Clinical gadget manufacturer in situations of non-liability or breakdowns;
- Cloud service providers hosting clinical information, systems, remote patient information assemblage points, applications, administrative information—and other Internet-established smart health applications and so on;
- Power suppliers, a high cross sector reliance that can be somewhat alleviated;
- Network providers, like Internet service providers (ISPs), which work on wide area network connectivity and thus, accessibility to patients in rural regions, cloud information, systems hosted exterior to the information center of the hospital inclusive of national systems (e.g. EHR or e-prescription).

f) Natural phenomena, owing to their interrupting or calamitous repercussion, specifically on the ICT foundation and on dispensing the medical care competencies of smart hospitals might also induce the occurrence of the incidents. In addition to these, if such a case arises where even though the natural phenomena might not be directed to or hampering the hospital but it may indirectly hamper the procurement of the medical care services in the rural regions (like for instance, in the case of breakdown of the grid framework in the metro-level on the occurrence of an earthquake). The examples comprise of:

- Flood;
- Fires;
- Earthquakes.

15.6 Conclusion

In this book chapter, we have tried to portray how smart hospitals can prove to be efficient and productive in the way of ensuring that people at each corner of the world receive the best possible healthcare facilities. The book has tried to illustrate the different network systems, the smart ambience of the interlinked hospitals, the resources of these hospitals and its criticality and the possible threats to these hospitals. We hope that this book chapter meet the expectations of the reader and is able to clearly explain the different concepts pertinent to the smart hospitals.

References

1. Prasad, B., Idrees, B.A., Lydia, L.E., Pavani, T., Efimova, V.V., Cloud Services for Remote Healthcare Monitoring System using the Internet of Things (IoT). *Int. J. Adv. Sci. Technol.*, 29, 9s, 2675–2683, 2020.
2. Arunpradeep, N., Niranjana, Dr. G., Suseela, Dr. G., Smart Healthcare Monitoring System Using IoT. *Int. J. Adv. Sci. Technol.*, 29, 06, 2788–2796, 2020.
3. A.Y.F., *et al.*, Detecting Treatment Pattern In Traditional Medicine Prescriptions. *Int. J. Adv. Sci. Technol.*, 28, 13, 431–439, 2019.
4. Jaiprakash, H., Singh, H.M.P., Mohanraj, J., Joshi, V., Achanna, S., Jegasothy, R., Standardization of Simulated patients: Assessing their efficiency and evaluating their Perception. *Int. J. Adv. Sci. Technol.*, 29, 7s, 678–685, 2020.
5. Kaur, P., Kumar, R., Kumar, M., A healthcare monitoring system using random forest and Internet of Things (IoT), Multimedia Tools and Applications. *Multimedia Tools Appl.*, 78, 14, 19905–19916, 2019.
6. Li, Q. and Cao, G., Providing Privacy-Aware Incentives in Mobile Sensing Systems. *IEEE Trans. Mob. Comput.*, 15, 6, 1485–1498, 2016.
7. Catarinucci, L. *et al.*, An IoT-aware architecture for smart healthcare systems. *IEEE Internet Things J.*, 2, 6, 515–526, 2015.
8. Kasem, E. and Prokopec, J., The evolution of LTE to LTE Advanced and the corresponding changes in the uplink reference signals. *Electrorevue*, 3, 2, 1–5, 2012.
9. Chen, J. *et al.*, Narrowband Internet of Things: Implementations and applications. *IEEE Internet Things J.*, 4, 6, 2309–2314, 2017.
10. Hamad, Y., Burhanuddin, M.A., Ghani, M.K.A., Elzamly, A., Doheir, M., Control Methods for Mitigating Electronic Human Resource Management (E-HRM) Issues Based Cloud Computing System for Healthcare Organizations. *Int. J. Adv. Sci. Technol.*, 29, 9s, 1469–1482, 2020.
11. Prasad, Dr. B., Sarkar, Dr.A., Laxmi Lydia, Dr. E., Sharmili, N., Pustokhin, D.A., Pustokhina, I., Disruptive Technologies for Smart Healthcare Systems using Artificial Intelligence for Hospital Management System. *Int. J. Adv. Sci. Technol.*, 29, 9s, 2684–2692, 2020.
12. R. R. D., *et al.*, Big data Analytics in Healthcare: Tools and Application Perspective. *Int. J. Adv. Sci. Technol.*, 28, 17, 910–918, 2019.
13. Pooja, B.R., Allan, M.G., C.C.N., A., Study On Different Clustering Based Routing Protocol To Increase Energy Efficiency In Wireless Sensor Networks. *Int. J. Control Autom.*, 13, 02, 50–54, 2020.
14. Pandey, A., A Voyage of Long Term Evolution-Advance (LTE-A): A literature Review. *Int. J. Adv. Sci. Technol.*, 26, 2, 19–32, 2019.

15. Liu, J., Zhang, S., Kato, N., Ujikawa, H., Suzuki, K., Device-to-device communications for enhancing quality of experience in software defined multi-tier LTE-A networks. *IEEE Network*, 29, 4, 46–52, 2015.

16. Dr. Savitha, G. and Deepika, S., An Energy Efficient Secured Trust-Based RPL Routing Protocol for Internet of Things. *Int. J. Adv. Sci. Technol.*, 29, 7, 8424–8446, 2020.

17. Koushika, C. and Anjaneyulu, G.S.G.N., Medical Image Retrieval Using Curvelet Transform And Diffusion Maps. *Int. J. Adv. Sci. Technol.*, 29, 12s, 380–387, 2020.

18. Yamini, G., Ganapathy, Dr. Gopinath, Reliability Metric based Patient Centred Activity Recognition for Smart Healthcare Monitoring. *Int. J. Adv. Sci. Technol.*, 29, 7s, 3133–3140, 2020.

19. Ahire, M.A., Rane, Dr. S.B., Gorane, Dr. S.J., Exploring Barriers in implementing Agile Supply Chain in Healthcare: An ISM & MICMAC Method. *Int. J. Adv. Sci. Technol.*, 29, 9s, 7869–7888, 2020.

20. Chawla, P., Juneja, A., Juneja, S., Anand, R., Artificial Intelligent Systems in Smart Medical Healthcare: Current Trends. *Int. J. Adv. Sci. Technol.*, 29, 10s, 1476–1484, 2020.

21. Sujatha, M., Prasanna Kumar, D., Vijaya Lakshmi, M., Asadi, S.S., Patient Perception of Healthcare Services and Role of CRM Tools to Enhance In Healthcare Sector. *Int. J. Adv. Sci. Technol.*, 29, 05, 2481–2491, 2020.

22. Verma, A., Agarwal, G., Gupta, A.K., Real Time Health Monitoring Systems: A Review on Disease Prediction and Providing Medical Assistance to the Patients by the Data Mining Techniques and Cloud IoT. *Int. J. Control Autom.*, 13, 4, 162–180, 2020.

23. Bhonde, S.B. and Prasad, J.R., Machine learning approach to revolutionize use of Holistic Health Records for Personalized Healthcare. *Int. J. Adv. Sci. Technol.*, 29, 05, 313–321, 2020.

24. S.A., *et al.*, Preserving Human Healthcare Records Based On Hybrid Learning Methods In Cloud Computing. *Int. J. Control Autom.*, 12, 6, 465–476, 2019.

25. Sam, D., Srinidhi, S., Niveditha, V.R., Amudha, S., Usha, D., Progressed IoT Based Remote Health Monitoring System. *Int. J. Control Autom.*, 13, 2s, 268–273, 2020.

26. Bharucha, F., Kothadiya, R.K., Malleswari, T.Y.J. Naga, Securing Medical Records for Insurance Claims using Blockchain Technology. *Int. J. Adv. Sci. Technol.*, 29, 3, 7273–7286, 2020.

Real Time Health Monitoring Using IoT With Integration of Machine Learning Approach

K.G. Maheswari[1]*, G. Nalinipriya[2], C. Siva[3] and A. Thilakesh Raj[4]

[1]*Department of IT, Institute of Road and Transport Technology, Erode, Tamil Nadu, India*
[2]*Saveetha Engineering College, Chennai, India*
[3]*Nandha Engineering College, Erode, India*
[4]*Sri Venkateswara College of Engineering, Chennai, India*

Abstract

Healthiness is the base for every human being. It is directly or indirectly influencing the mental ability of the person. It gives them the confidence to each action of the human. Sound health is necessary to do all our day to day works with the fullest hope. Nowadays all people are having more health-conscious than in the past years. Because of these reasons, there are different types of health check-ups, monitoring clinics are evolved, and they do a lot of monitoring processes like daily, monthly, and master check-ups. To provide multiple services, options, and facilities to their clients the technologies play a vital role in the current era.

The rapid development of information technology influences every person's life and health consciousness. These technologies are helping to monitor the status of a person and provide necessary tips then and there. Different methods of check-ups and monitoring process are available to get the information about a person. There are several IoT enabled sensors available to sense the patient complete details about a particular person's behavior, human anatomy, and physiology. This will lead the Big data. The Data gained over the sensors are uploaded to the internet, and connected to the cloud server. The affected person records could be saved in the webserver and physicians can get right of entry to the data anywhere in the world. Any unexpected variation in the data of the patient who is using the healthcare system, inevitably the data of the p atient will be uploaded to the concerned doctor with immediate notification. This type of healthcare system will be most useful in rural and remote areas. In this chapter, discuss the Machine learning techniques which are important to the build analysis models. Then how this model is integrated with IoT Technology and provide accurate data of individual person and also discuss the Cardiovascular problems based on real-time input data.

Keywords: Machine learning, IoT (Internet of Things), health monitoring system, raspberry Pi, GSM, analysis of patients health

*Corresponding author: kgmaheswari@gmail.com

Sachi Nandan Mohanty, G. Nalinipriya, Om Prakash Jena and Achyuth Sarkar (eds.) Machine Learning for Healthcare Applications, (249–260) © 2021 Scrivener Publishing LLC

16.1   Introduction

When people go for physical check-up, the doctor has not only considered the conventional based static and metabolic state measurements, but also consider current health condition of the person. This type of data provided by the IoT technology, are used for making decision about patient diseases. This is the type of technology used by the physician for diagnosis for a patient's diseases and early intervention of diseases, mainly used in improving the human life time [11]. This novel technology has an influence on healthcare industry and extremely reduction medical costs and increase the speed and accuracy of diagnoses. Based on up-to-date technological trends, one can voluntarily visualize repetitive physical investigation is preceded by a two–to three days of continuous biological one-to-one care using low-cost sensors [12]. Over this pause, the electronic sensors were used to record the vital symptoms of biological constraints and send the report to the doctor/patient and all the information's are stored in cloud server.

Due to the progress of advanced healthcare systems, Nowadays, a massive quantity of data is created by healthcare industries (i.e. like disease identification, patients present condition, etc.). These data are used for build predictive analysis model. Machine learning (ML) technique is used for analyzing data from various perceptions and constricting into valuable information. The most emerging application of ML is finding and forecast of diseases which was discussed in numerous research works. Hence, in this chapter, we discuss a various machine learning algorithm, then how they are predictable for the heart disease. Remaining part of this chapter arrangement is explaining the health monitoring system integrated with IoT with various functional sensors and Arduino microcontrollers. In this new technology, sensors are used to collect data from multiple place of body, analyze the data and afford two communication from patient to doctor anywhere in the world.

16.2   Related Work

In recent years, people have awareness in electronic sensors and devices which are commercially accessible for individual healthcare, capability, and movement. In addition to the part of capability provided to by current IoT technology, there are many research applications considered in the clinical area. One of the emerging applications is continuous health monitoring, recording and communicating the data who is in the remote place also.

Uddin *et al.* proposed an "intelligent based health monitoring system for patients' health condition through different types sensors connected networks". But the proposed system was developed for ICU patients in the hospital environment. Emergency information are sent to only clinical persons like doctor, nursing assistance [5]. Divakaran *et al.* [6] proposed the diagnostic system which provides dynamic information of a patient report send to the medical professional who have the web-enabled system. Kakria *et al.* discuss the "Online telemedicine systems". It is beneficial for the healthcare services and this system was based on advanced wireless and sensor technologies [7, 13]. But this system generates alert messages to the doctor in critical situations. The advantages of the system are two-way communication is possible between doctor and patient. But patient record data security is not maintained in this work. Cheng *et al.* [8], in their work, projected nonlinear controller of feedforward and feedback mechanisms. It was implemented in electronic controlled treadmill system and it was very useful for design of individuals the exercise materials. But dynamic model may be needed to describe at higher intensity exercises.

Wan *et al.* developed WISE, which is used in the real-time personal health monitoring [1, 15]. The proposed system includes many sensors to identify the diseases. Samie *et al.* represent the machine learning applications used in medical environment and they used in prediction and decision system of Internet of Things [4].

16.3   Existing Healthcare Monitoring System

The electronic healthcare system needs a set of events consider to maintain the health monitoring system. Many sensors are required to provide real time data, so structural integrity valuations are needed to integrated system. Yuehong *et al.* [9] discuss the several surveys in technologies especially medical environment. This is used to progress and support the present technologies of healthcare services. Among the various techniques IoT have played a vibrant role to communicate the available medical resources and provide smart healthcare services. They discuss the challenges of digital component and communication between the electronic device and human behavior. Liang *et al.* proposed problem of the sensor in an extensive sensor network and projected diagnostic and reconfiguration reasoning system [10, 14]. Jalapur *et al.* implemented the various machine learning techniques using Arduino-based microcontroller. Using the IoT and machine learning techniques, they proposed the predication and detection of heart diseases [11].

16.4   Methodology and Data Analysis

The novel healthcare monitoring system used to improve the traditional healthcare system in the patient information gathering is from the digital sensor and IoT device. Artificial Intelligence (AI) techniques are used to implement in the large dataset, which is used to predict disease and clinical intervention. Machine Learning algorithms are used in this method to build analytic models. These analytic models are used in the health monitoring system.

Based on the previous research work, three different ML algorithms were implemented on the Heart Disease related dataset. R programming tool is used to detect the probability of heart diseases analysis. Then a continual monitoring system proposal has been planned with an Arduino. System design methods of the proposed system and the workflow as mentioned below:

- Based on the different datasets to train several machine learning algorithms.
- Compare the performance of machine learning algorithms.
- Choose, best algorithm and develop an IoT-based prediction and monitoring application.
- Patient details are get from the sensors, and through the IoT application, the details are sent to the doctors. Based on the input values predicts the diseases present or not.

- Using Arduino microcontroller and sensors real-time patient physiological data (i.e.) Blood pressure, temperature, humidity, and heartbeat are collected and send to the predictive system. This is used to notice the serious condition of the patient.
- After receiving an alert note, the doctor will communicate patient's/take care person cation through IoT.

16.5   Proposed System Architecture

The block diagram of the proposed model is as exposed in Figure 16.1. It explains all the digital components like the Arduino microcontroller, which is used to relate to the internet of the system. Also explain the techniques and tools are used for developing the complete arrangement. To develop a prediction system, a software tool is used to train with real-time datasets and analysis with many machine learning algorithms. The high accuracy ML algorithm is selected, and implemented in the predictive system for detecting and disease like heart disease risk level. In the system, different digital components like various biomedical sensors, IoT device LCD, buzzer, etc. are connected.

16.6   Machine Learning Approach

Machine learning leads to intelligent approaches used to improve performance of the system using example data or previous experience(s) through learning. More exactly, ML algorithms developed models of behaviors using mathematical techniques on huge datasets. There are many tools publicly available to implement machine learning algorithms. Some recent open source tools are WEKA tool for data mining applications, MATLAB for mathematical applications and R programming for data science application used. Based on the previous research work, the following machine learning algorithms, Multiple Linear Regression Algorithm, Random Forest, Support Vector Machine are considered in this chapter.

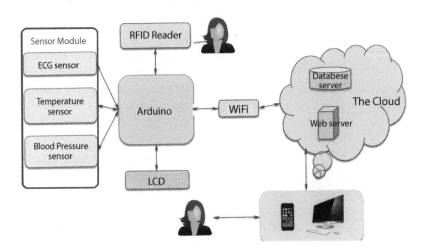

Figure 16. 1 Block diagram of the proposed model.

16.6.1   Multiple Linear Regression Algorithm

This algorithm is used to find the association between the variables and also find the predict the future. Predict the value of one dependent and predicted variable on the basis of other independent variables. The equation that denotes linear relationship between two variables a and b are:

$$b = \beta 0 + \beta 1 \alpha$$

When a = 0, then the value of intercept is the value of b. When $\beta 0 = 0$, then the b is directly proportional to a. When $\beta 1 = 0$: then Y is a constant, there is no relationship between b and a. Consider two or more quantitative and qualitative variable (a1, a2, a3 .... an) to predict a quantitative but dependent variable b. The output is the function model to predict the dependent variable with a new set of independent variables. A straight line is drawn, fit to the data. Find the relationship between the two or more quantitative and qualitative variable (a_1, a_2, a_3 .... X_n) and the dependent variable b to generate a regression model for predict the future values of b.

16.6.2   Random Forest Algorithm

This is the one of the most powerful and well-known learning algorithm in ML. This algorithm is also called Bagging or Bootstrap Aggregation algorithm. In order to valuation the sample data such as mean, the bootstrap is a very powerful statistical method. Using training data, frequent models are measured and for every data sample the models are created. For the prediction model, each prediction model is averaged and get an improved the output value.

16.6.3   Support Vector Machine

SVM is a supervised learning algorithm, used to perform classification and regression analysis model. They analyze the large amount of data and perform classification by making parallel lines between data. It splits the single line to generate flat and linear partitions also called hyperplane. These hyperplanes have the prime margin in a high-dimensional space to isolate given data into various classes. The margin between the two classes denotes the distance among the adjoining data points of the classes. So hyper-plane is used to create the classification of various the datapoints. Figure 16.2 shows the sample Classification can be made by the hyper-plane among the two classes. Select the hyper-plane which is used to isolates the two classes. Figure 16.2 shows the various available hyper-planes A, B and C and these are used to classify the datapoints into various modules.

16.7   Work Flow of the Proposed System

Figure 16.3 illustrates the work flow of our planned health monitoring system. It contains the various modules like Data resource, Analysis of ML algorithm, Sensor system, integration of IoT devices with cloud service and automatic health monitoring system.

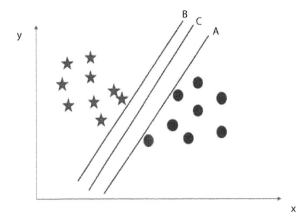

Figure 16.2 Classification using hyperplane.

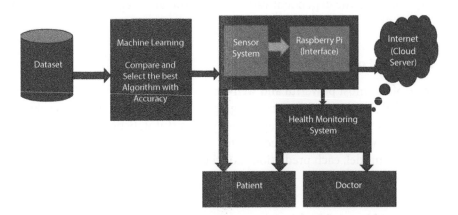

Figure 16.3 Work flow of the health monitoring system.

Data Source Module

In this work two datasets heart disease databases and Cleveland Heart Disease dataset [2] are used in this work because, they have same type of features. These datasets are combined to create new larger dataset. After the preprocessing implementation, 566 instances are used in this work for model validation. In this work, machine learning algorithm Multiple Linear Regression Algorithm, Random forest Algorithm and SVM Algorithms are used for classification of data and predictive model are created for the effective identification of Heart related diseases and the performance of algorithms were evaluated in terms of accuracy.

Attribute Documentation

In this work, attributes like age, sex, chest pain type etc. are consider for the implementation of prediction system of heart diseases. Patient's mobile number is used as a key attribute (*i.e.* unique identifier). Attributes play the important role to analyze the diseases.

Performance Analysis of Machine Learning Algorithms Module

Machine learning algorithms which are mentioned above are implemented in the R programming Environment on new renewed dataset. Using 10-fold cross validation method, the performances of all the algorithms are analyzed. The best five experimental results have been displayed in Figures 16.4, 16.5, 16.6 and 16.7. From the experimental, it has been observed that the SVM provides better results on the renewed dataset.

Comparative Analysis of Performance

Figure 16.7 shows the comparative of ML algorithm performance with metrics sensitivity, specificity and accuracy and the SVM Algorithm give the best results in R programming Environment.

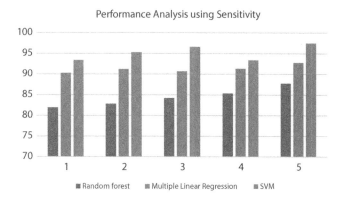

Figure 16.4 Performance analysis using sensitivity.

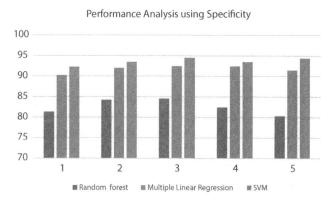

Figure 16.5 Performance analysis using specificity.

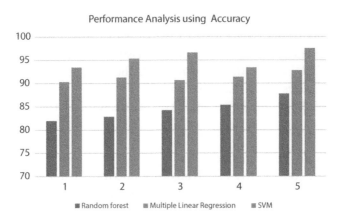

Figure 16.6 Performance analysis based on accuracy (%).

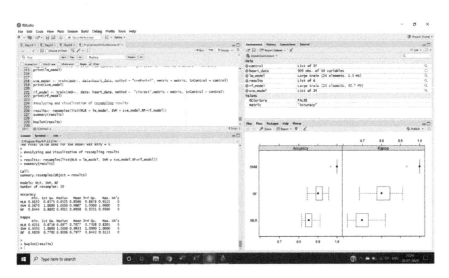

Figure 16.7 Comparative of performance analysis.

16.8 System Design of Health Monitoring System

Systems design explains the overview of proposed architecture and interfaces of the application and UML (Unified Modelling Language) is used to model system designs.

Figure 16.8 shows the complete hardware setup includes sensors like Heartbeat sensor etc. The microcontroller board Ardunio/Raspberry pi and GPRS modules are used to communicate with cloud server. For information sharing between patient and doctors, electronic device like mobile, LCD displays are used. Any abnormal value found in the data immediately notifies and communicates the doctor and patient via communication media. Table 16.1 shows the some of the example of about the condition of patient which is used to make the decision about the heat diseases.

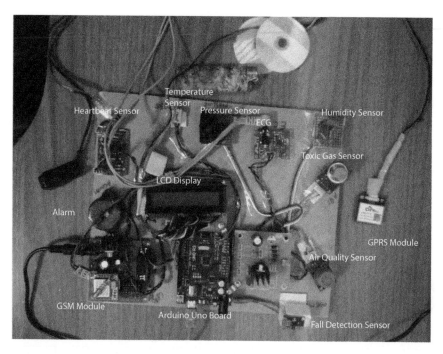

Figure 16.8 Overview of architecture and interfaces of a system.

Table 16.1 Patient's condition for decision making.

Temperature	Humidity	Human awareness	Pulse rate	Action taken	Risk level
<37°C	41–46%	Normal	60–100	Not Need	Normal
>38°C	41–46%	Abnormal for above 50 age persons	40–60 or 100–120	Notify to caretakers	Medium
>38°C	46–>52%	Abnormal body condition	40–60 or 100–120	Inform to doctor	High
>38°C	46–> 52%	Abnormal body condition	40–60 or 100–120	Need Emergence care	Emergency

16.9 Use Case Diagram

The Use Case Diagram includes actors, instances and their relationships. It represents all the scenarios, related to the application cooperates with users and other external systems related to application. Figure 16.9 shows the use case diagram of system design.

Sequence Diagram
Sequence Diagrams are also called interaction diagrams, which will give the detailed operations of the application. In the diagram vertical axis of represent time of messages are sent to the other objects. Figure 16.10 illustrates the sequence diagram of system design.

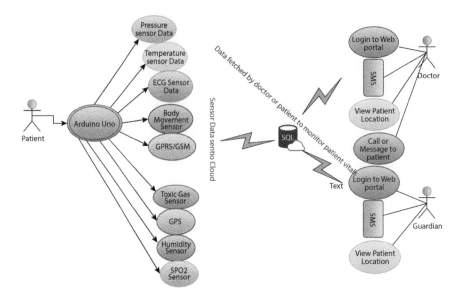

Figure 16.9 Use case diagram of system design.

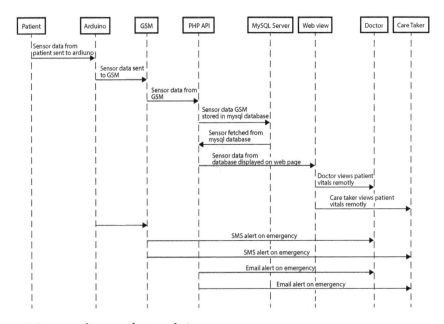

Figure 16.10 Sequence diagram of system design.

16.10   Conclusion

In the current pandemic COVID-19, effective and dynamic healthcare data analysis and decision is needed on patients' health record. ML Techniques are used to develop the analytic models and these models are integrated to IoT-based health monitoring system to improve the performance of the healthcare system. From the above analysis SVM algorithm, exposed better accuracy rates of more than 90%, this algorithm may be considered for medical applications to disease detection and prediction purpose. Normally the attributes will influence on the classification and prediction performance. But compared to the previous research work, even though the number of features is reduced, the SVM algorithm performance was good with renewed dataset. Therefore, it is significant that SVM is the most effective ML algorithm to be implemented on medical application system. Table 16.1 explains patient's condition for making decision of heart dieses and risk level. The normal and abnormal values of temperature, pluses, Humidity can be implemented to the proposed real-time IoT-based Health Monitoring system. Based on the real time data, it will send the alert message to the concern patient and doctor.

References

1. Al-awlaqi, J.W., Wang, J., O'Grady, M., Li, M.S., Munassar, A.A.H., Cao, N., Gu, X., Wearable IoT enabled real-time health monitoring system. *EURASIP J. Wireless Commun. Networking*, 298, 1–10, 2018.

2. UCI Machine Learning Repository: Heart Disease Dataset. http://archive.ics.uci.edu/ml/data sets/Heart+Disease.

3. UCI Machine Learning Repository: Statlog (Heart) Dataset, StatlogDatabase. https://data.world/uci/statlog-heart/workspace/file?filename=heart.dat.txt.

4. Samie, F., Henkel, J., Bauer, L., From Cloud Down to Things: An Overview of Machine Learning in Internet of Things. *IEEE Internet Things J. (IoT-J)*, 1–14, 2018.

5. Alam, J.B., Salah, M., Banu, S., Uddin, Real time patient monitoring system based on Internet of Things. *4th International Conference on Advances in Electrical Engineering (ICAEE)*, pp. 28–30, 2017.

6. Janani, P., Manukonda, L., Melinda Morais, M., Divakaran, S., Sravya, N., IOT Clinic-Internet based Patient Monitoring and Diagnosis System. *IEEE International Conference on Power, Control, Signals and Instrumentation Engineering (ICPCSI-2017)*, pp. 2858–2862, 2017.

7. Kitipawang, P., Kakria, P., Tripathi, N.K., A Real-Time Health Monitoring System for Remote Cardiac Patients Using Smartphone and Wearable Sensors. *Int. J. Telemed. Appl.*, Volume, 11 pages, 2015.

8. Celler, B.G., Cheng, T.M., Savkin, A.V., Su, S.W., Wang, L., Nonlinear modelling and control of human heart rate response during exercise with various work load intensities. *IEEE Trans. Biomed. Eng.*, 55, 11, 2499–2508, 2008.

9. Chen, X., Zeng, Y., Fan, Y., Yin, Y., The internet of things in healthcare: An overview. *J. Ind. Inf. Integr.*, 1, 3–13, 2016.

10. Fan, Z., Liang, D., Wu, L., Xu, Y., Self-Diagnosis and Self Reconfiguration of Piezoelectric Actuator and Sensor Network for Large Structural Health Monitoring. *Int. J. Distrib. Sens. Netw.*, 11, 4, 207303, 2015.

11. Badreldin, I., ElBabli, I., Ernest, K., Lamei, C., Mohamed, S., Shakshuk, M., A ZigBee-based telecardiology system for remote healthcare service delivery. *1st Middle East Conference on Biomedical Engineering (MECBME '11)*, pp. 442–445, 2011.

12. Abraham, A., Bajo, J., Corchado, J.M., Fraile, J.A., Applying wearable solutions in dependent environments. *IEEE Trans. Inf. Technol. Biomed.*, 14, 6, 1459–1467, 2010.

13. Bonato, P., Chan, L., Park, H., Patel, S., Rodgers, M., A review of wearable sensors and systems with application in rehabilitation. *J. Neuro Eng. Rehabil.*, 9, 1, 21, 2012.

14. Wu, F., Zhao, H., Zhao, Y., Zhong, H., Development of a wearable-sensor-based fall detection system. *Int. J. Telemed. Appl.*, 2015, 11, 2015.

15. Johansson, A.M., Lindberg, I., Söderberg, S., Patients' experiences with specialist care via video consultation in primary healthcare in rural areas. *Int. J. Telemed. Appl.*, 2014, 7, 2014.

Part 4

MACHINE LEARNING APPLICATIONS FOR COVID-19

Semantic and NLP-Based Retrieval From Covid-19 Ontology

Ramar Kaladevi* and Appavoo Revathi

Saveetha Engineering College, Chennai, India

Abstract

Advent of internet made abundant of medical data available in various formats. Emerging technologies like AI, big data, machine learning and sematic web are increasingly applied in various sectors. Healthcare is the essential field which requires technological support in order to administer healthcare workforce, to improve the quality of healthcare services in resource constrained region, to manage the chronic diseases and pandemics like Covid-19 and so on. The supply of precise data to the technical system plays a significant role in providing better healthcare support than the available unorganized data. With the help of ontologies, semantic web represents the conceptual relationship between data more precisely. The accurate semantic rule and query engine provides effective definition of rules and knowledge retrieval from ontologies. In the medical field ontologies are used to represent medical terms, interoperability between systems with lexically different but semantically similar terms. It enhances the reuse and sharing of medical information and patient data. Also increases the percentage of support to integration of data and knowledge. The proposed case study considered Covid-19 ontology with 158 classes and maximum depth of 12 levels. Information retrieval from the knowledgebase is done using Simple Protocol and RDF Query Language (SPARQL), and Semantic Web Rule Language (SWRL). Simple queries can be formulated using Natural language based template. Additional knowledge can also be generated from the available information. This chapter ensures the effective utilization of information thereby enrich interoperability, integration and information retrieval.

Keywords: Ontology, covid-19, corona virus, interoperability, information retrieval, semantic web, SWRL, SPARQL, NLP

17.1 Introduction

Technological advancement in medical field produces a high volume of document and data. It leads to tasks like maintaining the data, integrating data and how to relate, analyze and retrieve useful information from the data. Also medical domain is a rapidly growing field with complex medical terms and concepts. It is tedious to analyze and relate to these concepts which sometimes lead to an error. The medical terms are to be organized in a

Corresponding author: kaladevi@saveetha.ac.in

Sachi Nandan Mohanty, G. Nalinipriya, Om Prakash Jena and Achyuth Sarkar (eds.) Machine Learning for Healthcare Applications, (263–276) © 2021 Scrivener Publishing LLC

hierarchical manner in which general terms on top and specific terms are placed down accordingly. It is also necessary to specify the relation between various terms.

Due to the poor semantic support from HTML and URL in WWW, achieving semantic interoperability and integration among information systems are limited. The capability of the system to interchange information and to make use of it is termed as interoperability (IEEE 1990). The available information is in various formats, structures and meaning. This leads to the information heterogeneities between information systems. Ontology has been suggested as a method to represent information semantically by formal explicit specification of concepts (information) [1, 2].

For our case study, ontology has been developed for Covid-19 with the help of knowledge from World Health Organization (WHO), Indian Council of Medical Research (ICMR), Centre for Disease Control and Prevention (CDC), Domain ontologies, research articles and online sources. Covid ontology contains major classes like 'Microbiology', 'Etymology', 'Morphology', 'Species', 'Symptoms', 'Treatment' and its subclasses, object properties, data properties and instances.

The increased volume of data through internet also widens the gap between available and required information. Unfortunately the different structured data, ambiguity of words and high amount of information on the web makes the retrieval task more tedious [3, 4]. Conceptual retrieval techniques use semantic web-based technologies. For instance RDF, RDF Schema and OWL are used for knowledge representation. Semantic query languages such as RDQL-Query Language for RDF, SPARQL-Simple Protocol and RDF Query Language are used to retrieve information from ontologies. Semantic Web Rule Language (SWRL) is also used to deduce knowledge from ontology.

The proposed work is target to develop Covid-19 ontology with necessary concepts and properties thereby increases interoperability between similar systems, reusing of knowledge base, effective information retrieval from developed ontology using semantic query languages and Natural language queries.

The next section reviews the existing ontology based healthcare system and domain specific ontologies to assess the recent advancement in the field. The proposed work is demonstrated in the subsequent section with Covid ontology development from various sources. The result section shows the retrieval methods of knowledge from ontology. Finally conclusion section concludes the progress of our present work and suggests directions for future enhancement.

17.2   Related Work

Recent advancement in the medical field and computer technology paves way for new techniques. Semantic web is one among the technology which provides support to the medical field via ontologies [5, 6]. Ontology matching identifies the semantic relation between overlapping illustrations of the similar domain. The knowledge graph of ontologies enables data integration, data sharing and data quality. Ontology is a widely used technology to represent data mined from natural language text with their reasoning. Disease Ontology (DO) is a great platform for biomedical community to integrate disease and medical jargons through wider cross mapping. In this section, recent medical ontologies, its development, retrieval of information are analyzed.

Coordination of multi similarity and similarity calculation are considered as conventional technique for ontology mapping. Application of ASMOV tool is to analyze the text description features to compute concept similarity [7]. The algorithm takes lexical and structural characteristics of two ontologies. The different features and rules decide the weight distribution. Two different thesauri i.e. WordNet and UMLS (Unified Medical Language System) are experimented to build the model. The combination of lexical, structural and sematic verification proved greater accuracy.

Fuzzy rule-based ontology matching system exploits semantic and lexical details of entities and ontology's internal structure [8]. The model was experimented with two real world ontologies namely ACM topic taxonomy and DMOZ hierarchy. The Multi-layer Fuzzy Align model tested on OAEI, to analyze its performance for the criteria precision, recall and f-measure over general purpose ontologies. The proposed model was shown better results with some bench mark algorithms such as ASMOV [7], CODI [9] and SOBOM [10].

The ontology mapping tool YAM++ applies multiple strategies to accomplish ontology mapping between a pair of musical instrument ontologies [11]. YAM++ able to handle multi lingual ontologies. It applied machine learning technique to find mapping between two different ontologies by finding matchers at structural level. The similarity computed at element level and the transformation graphs of structural ontologies are combined using machine learning method. The system proved better performance and it was continuously proven from 2009 to 2013.

The disease ontology provides a wide coverage for various domain of disease [12]. The indications of healthy status and diagnostic criteria are covered with the help of Unified Medical Language System (UMLS).

The case study on UTM Clinic produced more relevant information on UTM clinic system by using ontology based information retrieval technique [13]. Web-based application programming interface for ontology and RDF schemas was developed with the help of data interchange model available on web. RDF model helps in evolution of new schemas and the software tool RAP is employed for query manipulation. The major achievement of the case study was presenting the result of single patient's details useful for information retrieval.

Infectious Disease Ontology (IDO) which interoperates with various domains, including clinical care, public health and biomedical research [14]. The relevant entities and relations are core part of IDO pathogen neutral ontology. Infectious disease research and all IDO extension ontologies are building blocks of IDO core. The focus on recent ontologies supports early stage data discovery of future pandemics.

Coronavirus Infectious Disease Ontology (CIDO) covers broad spectrum of domains in covid-19 disease which includes etiology, epidemiology, pathogenesis, diagnosis, hindrance, and treatment [15]. The logical representation of varied coronavirus details are available in CIDO repository provides a strong support in the field of COVID-19 and related diseases. The upper level architecture of CIDO is Basic Formal Ontology (BFO) which covers majority of general ontology classes.

The case-based reasoning (CBR) model employs NLP to create mini-ontology for each case [16]. The tokens of NLP are classified into special, temporal and thematic classes. The similarity of formalized features between new cases and the archived related cases reveals the result in early stages of the disease which helps to reduce the rate of contagion.

The application of Artificial Intelligence along with regression analysis to construct binary classification model considers multiple factors like temperature, humidity, population density of the place and wind speed to achieve better performance [17]. A case study was conducted by collecting dataset from 42 regions in China, South Korea, Italy and Japan.

The climate data was collected from the regions capital. The Group method of data handling algorithm is used in prediction. The analysis shows that the humidity and temperature have strong impact on Covid-19 confirmed cases.

The adaptive Neuro Fuzzy system applied two metaheuristic techniques to optimize accuracy of predicting coronavirus [18]. The neuro fuzzy inference engine is trained with the help of salp swarm method and flower pollination process is used to enhance the native search procedure. The proposed model aims to identify the corona affected patients in a short span of time. The model is shown optimal performance for different evaluation metrics such as root mean squared relative error, root mean square error, mean absolute and absolute % error.

The above mentioned ontology systems applied different types of retrieval techniques from various domain ontologies. Though few systems provide good results on Covid-19 ontologies a deep insight into the new pandemic is essential. NLP techniques can also be used to improve retrieval efficiency.

17.3   Proposed Retrieval System

17.3.1   Why Ontology?

Ontology is used to conceptually define the information system. Ontology is a hierarchical structure which includes key concepts of a particular domain, related sub concepts and description of each item's properties. Generally the terminologies and its associated properties are represented using ontologies [19]. The primary benefits of ontologies defined to have effective communication between users and also among similar systems, interoperability among related ontological system [20]. Meta data schemas, lexical terms of the annotations and the transformation of semantic annotations are the major components of ontologies. Semantic annotations are helpful in increasing the search accuracy of search engines. Web search engines can do better with the help of concepts used in ontology when compared with standard keyword based search. The shared and common domain related concepts in the ontologies allow machines to share syntax as well as semantics [21]. Sharing and reusing of domain knowledge results in mining of new knowledge which is viewed as important benefit of the ontological system.

The in depth domain specific words of medical system is not completely covered by WordNet and thesaurus. For example, 'Hersen tumor' is equivalent to brain tumor, this sense is not listed in WordNet. Similarly the meaning of 'Serology' is not available in WordNet. In addition continuous evaluation of new words and new senses assigned to existing words are not captured by Thesauri [22]. To overcome these issues and to achieve a conceptually efficient knowledgebase, ontology modeling is essential.

17.3.2   Covid Ontology

Covid-19 is a novel disease affects human by the type of corona virus belongs to SARS CoV-2 family. It has been reported from China in December 2019. The virus spread rapidly throughout the world from its origin. Few ontologies are available for Covid-19 and related coronavirus. There is a need to create an ontology which incorporates knowledge from the existing ontologies. The information regarding Covid-19 and corona virus are collected from various sources like World Health Organization (WHO), Indian Council of Medical Research (ICMR), Centre for disease control and prevention (CDC), upper ontologies, domain ontologies, central and state government portals, online sources and recent research papers on pandemics. Available naming convention and format of data is different across the sources. RDF and OWL provide a standard way to represent those data. The proposed work flow is shown in Figure 17.1.

Information sharing and information integration is supported with the help of reference ontology also called as background ontology. It acts as common repository of a domain to provide information for interoperability and integration. The background knowledge is improved with the help of WordNet, web, Linked Open Data (LOD), domain and reference ontologies [23].

In general more numbers of domain specific ontologies are available for reference. The AMC hospital's Medical Informatics group developed an ontology called DICE which contains around 2,000 classes defined by 5,000 terms. The medical terminologies are formalized using OWL DL. It utilizes more than 4,000 property links and different relation types to relate the classes. Gene ontology belonging to the bioinformatics domain represents gene product and gene attributes of all species. A more specific objective of this ontology proposal is to create and maintain knowledgebase of gene and its related attributes as well as create annotations for easy access, understanding of attributes. Assimilation of annotated data, tools to access data is provided by the ontology.

UMLS—Unified Medical Language System (UMLS) is the popular reference ontology used in biomedical domain [24]. It consists of more than 2 million lexical terms with 900,000 classes generated from 60 families of biomedical repositories and also has more than 12 million relations between classes. SNOMED CT (Systematized Nomenclature of Medicine—Clinical Terms) ontology contains medical related terms along with definitions, terminologies, codes, synonyms available in healthcare reports and documents [25].

Three main practices commonly used to acquire knowledge for domain or task specific ontologies includes: Incorporating existing ontologies, enhancing and enriching an available

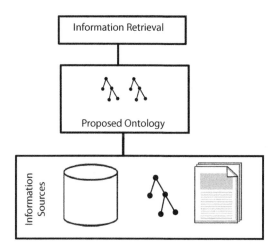

Figure 17.1 Ontology development and information retrieval process.

ontology using information derived from a specific domain, and the third approach is to focus on specific domain. Building an ontology requires domain knowledge, proficiency in ontology engineering and skillset to use ontology editor software. The six major subtasks to learn ontology include token identification, synonym representation, concept notification, taxonomic relation hierarchy, non-taxonomic relations, and rule acquisition [26].

Prior the construction of an ontology it is recommended to verify any duplication of classes, completeness of knowledge, concept consistency and extension of knowledgebase without changing the semantics of existing system. The ontology is structured in a hierarchal structural arrangement. Ontology creation follows top down approach in which the general classes appear in top level and the decomposed subclasses occupies successive levels. Multiple terms associated with the class is designated as synonym of the class and one preferred term among them will be the class name [27].

The primary concepts connected with Coronavirus are listed: 'Microbiology', 'Morphology', 'Etymology', 'Classification', 'Symptoms', 'Laboratory-tests', 'Treatment' and so on. Concepts of ancillary level are derived from primary concepts such as 'Family', 'Subfamily', 'Spices', 'Mild', 'Moderate', 'Serology', 'Hematology', etc. Continuing in this manner a complete concept hierarchy is built. The software tool "Protegé version 5.5" is employed to enrich domain knowledge with extracts of web portals and web sources. Protegé provides additional ontology management tools, supports OWL classes and contains rich set of knowledge modeling structures which makes it more suitable for the proposed ontology construction.

The proposed work spins around individuals also termed as domain objects and the binary relations on individuals called as properties. The customizable user interface has rich set of ontology authoring and management tools. This allows importing ontologies in various formats and extensible architecture enables integration with other applications. Java Application Programming Interface (API), inference using rules and queries are helpful in enhancing the ultimate purpose of ontologies. The snippet of concept hierarchy is shown in Figure 17.2.

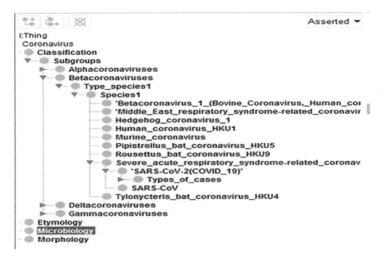

Figure 17.2 Snippet of concept hierarchy.

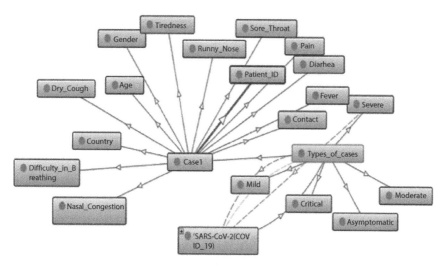

Figure 17.3 Visualization of concept hierarchy (sample case).

In ontology, properties are used to define relationships between individuals (or instance). Object properties such as *hasFamilyName, isPartOf, isa, hasGenomeSize, has-Symptom, hasOrder, hasShape, hasTreatment* are used to relate appropriate individuals. Similarly data properties are used to relate individual with values. For instance *hasTemperature* is related with corresponding °F or °C value. Similarly Genome size is assigned to 26 to 32 kilobases.

Researches on Covid-19 in various aspects like prevention, diagnosis, invention of Vaccine, information retrieval from related datasets and so on are carried out throughout the world. Kaggle is one such data repository consists of related datasets. Covid-19 patient dataset from the repository is imported into ontology. Figure 17.3 shows visualization of concept hierarchy of sample (patient) case. Similarly sample cases with different age group from the dataset are shown in Table 17.1.

17.3.3   Information Retrieval From Ontology

Currently, semantic web uses SWRL (Semantic Web Rule Language) to define rules and Semantic query language SPARQL (Simple Protocol and RDF Query Language) to retrieve knowledge from the ontology. SPARQL is a common query language for semantic web. It matches the graph patterns against RDF graphs. In addition SWRL is used to derive deductive knowledge from ontology. The Semantic Query-enhanced Web Rule Language (SQWRL) is a subsystem of SWRL that consists of Java based interface to derive the answer from SQWRL queries. SQWRL queries effectively return a two dimensional table containing the results of the query. Figure 17.4 demonstrates semantic and natural language based information retrieval from the knowledgebase.

A sample SWRL rule is defined for Covid-19 mild case with symptoms of fever above 39°C, cough and body pain. Also defined rule for severe case which considers aged person with symptoms like anosmia and breathing trouble is shown below.

Table 17.1 Sample covid-19 patient details with different age group.

Patient-Info	Patient 1	Patient 2	Patient 3	Patient 4
Patient-ID	P1	P2	P3	P4
Age	0–9	10–19	20–24	>60
Gender	Male	Male	Male	Male
Country	China	China	China	China
Fever	1	1	1	1
Tiredness	1	1	1	1
Dry Cough	1	1	1	1
Difficulty in breathing	1	1	1	1
Sore throat	1	1	1	1
Pain	1	1	1	1
Nasal Congestion	1	1	1	1
Running nose	0	1	1	1
Diarrhea	0	1	1	1
Contact	Yes	Yes	Yes	Yes
Severity-mild	1	1	–	–
Severity-Moderate	–	–	1	–
Severity-severe	–	–	–	1

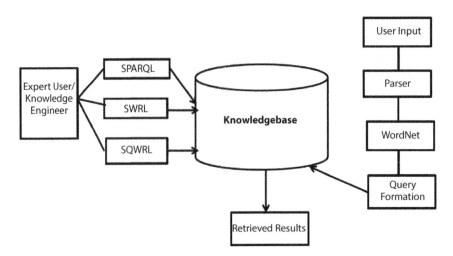

Figure 17.4 Information retrieval from knowledgebase.

Rule 1: Mild Case (with fever, cough and body pain)

Person(?p) ^ hasTempInCelcius(?p,?t) ^ swrlb:greaterThan(?t, 39) ^
hasCough(?p,?cough) ^hasBodypain (?p,?pain)→isMild(?p,?m)

Rule 2: Severe Case (with old age, Anosmia, breathing trouble)

Person(?p) ^ hasAge(?p,?a) ^ swrlb:greaterThan(?a, 60) ^ hasAnosmia (?p, ?An) ^
hasBreathingTrouble(?p, ?b) →isSevere(?p, ?s)

Sample SWRL rule

The SWRL is a rule language. SQWRL follows syntax of formal SWRL and replaces rule part with a retrieval composition. A sample SQWRL query is shown for the mild case and results are sorted based on temperature.

Person(?p) ^ hasTempInCelcius (?p,?t) ^ swrlb:greaterThan(?t, 39) ^ hasCough(?p,?c)
^hasBodypain (?p,?b)→sqwrl: select(?p, ?t) ^ sqwrl:orderBy(?t)

A sample SPARQL query for person with severe Covid-19 symptoms is given below. The selection is based on age, anomia and trouble in breathing and arranged using temperature value.

```
PREFIX rdf: <http://www.w3.org/1999/02/22-rdf-syntax-ns#>
PREFIX owl: <http://www.w3.org/2002/07/owl#>
PREFIX xsd: <http://www.w3.org/2001/XMLSchema#>
PREFIX rdfs:< http://www.w3.org/2000/01/rdf-schema#>
SELECT ?Person
WHERE{
?Person: hasTempInCelcius ?Temp.
?Person: hasCough ?Cough.
?Person: hasBodyPain ?Pain .
FILTER (? Temp >39)
}
```

Sample SPARQL Query

Existing semantic query languages such as SPARQL and SQWRL are completely depend on related syntax and structure of the ontology. Hence it is mandatory for the users to possess knowledge on query language syntax and domain knowledgebase structure. However, it is challenging for many users to have knowledge apart from the required queries. The essential and tedious task of any information system is to accept natural language queries aligned with ontology and to retrieve effective results [28, 29]. Though few systems address the issue, a complete solution is still a mile stone to be achieved. In order to address these issues, the user query is given to parser and parsed tokens are matched with WordNet to get synonyms. Finally the tokens are matched with knowledgebase to retrieve information. The following phases explain the process in detail.

Knowledgebase

Ontology is a conceptual representation of information using concepts, properties, instance, axioms of a domain collectively termed as knowledgebase and it is specifically for a certain domain i.e medical domain. It contains integrated knowledge from more sources.

User input
The end user or stakeholder enters a required query to the particular domain. The output of this entered query would be semantically similar entities from the knowledgebase. Finally, irrelevant results are removed based on their ranking.

Parsing of input query:
Given input query is divided into token based on noun, verb, and adjectives using parser for simplifying the search process. Parsing is the technique to process the given sentences or query into separate tokens syntactically, by determining the part of speech (POS) of each word from the query.

WordNet
The output from the previous phase is given as input to the WordNet to retrieve the related synsets of different tokens present in the query. WordNet can be given semantically similar words of the given tokens.

17.3.4   Query Formulation

The important process is to define a simplified query from the tokens separated by parser and synsets from WordNet. The user query can be converted into a structure called query template [30]. Query template covers most linguistic possible valid query options [31]. The objective is to identify the query interest and the relationship between interest and the input query. It leads to the form of finer query to retrieve result from knowledgebase. The query can be framed based on POS tags and its relevance with ontology components such as class (concept), instance and properties are shown below.

Class (D)—can be related to nouns such as NN, NNPS, NNP, and NNS
Instance (I)—can be related to nouns such as NN, NNS, NNP, NNPS
Relationship (R)—Verbs like VB, VBZ, VBG, VBD, VBN, and VBP
Modifier of class/instance (M)—Adverbs RB, RBS, RBR, adjective JJ, JJS, JJR

17.3.5   Retrieval From Knowledgebase

This segment is of more important in which the knowledge related to input user query is extracted from the ontology. The information from ontology is retrieved with the help of concepts and instance from natural language queries. If the match not found in ontology, then WordNet is explored with the parsed token to find a semantic equivalent. These semantics are matched against the concepts in the ontology to fetch more relevant knowledge. A bunch of semantically related collections are the end result of this process. Illustration of the process for two queries is given below:

Input query1: What are the symptoms of mild Covid-19 case?
Parser output: What_**WP**/<: are_**VBP** :>([the_**DT** symptoms_**NNS**]) of_**IN** ([mild_**JJ** Covid-19_**NNP** case_**NN**])?.

The basic and extended dependencies between token are shown using Stanford parser

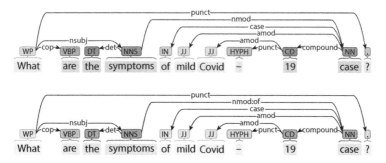

Refined output: Symptoms [D], Mild [D, I], Covid-19 [M], case [D, I]
Input query2: What is the serology tests used for Covid-19?
Parser output: ([What_**WP**]) <: is_**VBP** :> ([the_**DT** serology_NN tests_NNS])
<: used_**VBD** :> for_**IN** covid-19_**SYM**? _.
Refined output: serology [D, I], tests [D, I], used[R], Covid-19[D, I]

From the proposed ontology retrieval system, queries can be given using SPARQL and SQWRL and rules are formed using SWRL. This kind of retrieval is difficult for normal users. For such cases, user queries are simplified using refined output received from parser and extracted concepts, instance, relations. Then refined queries are given to knowledge-base for retrieval. The results of matched refined queries in the knowledge base are filtered and ranked to increase its indexing by the user.

17.4   Conclusion

Effective information management and retrieval is the ultimate goal of any information system. Covid-19 is the severe pandemic affected the entire world. Research towards the insight of the disease and related tasks are need of the hour. Health domain consists of complex medical terms, abbreviation and vocabulary. In order to meet the present requirements, Covid-19 ontology is developed with the knowledge of WHO, ICMR, online sources, research articles and existing ontologies. Semantic query language SPARQL and rule language SWRL are used to retrieve information from ontologies. To effectively handle user queries with insufficient knowledge on ontology and syntax of query language, retrieval using NLP based technology is suggested. Covid-19 patients dataset with various symptoms, severity (mild, moderate, critical) can be effectively used with instance based matching and case based reasoning (CBR) to improve efficiency of retrieval in future.

References

1. Gruber, T., A Translation approach to portable ontology specifications. *Knowl. Acquis.*, 5, 2, 199–220, 1993.
2. Uschold, M., Where are the semantics in the semantic web? *AI Mag.*, 24, 3, 25–36, 2003.

3. Ding, L., Finin, T., Joshi, A., Peng, Y., Pan, R.R., Reddivari, P., Search on the Semantic Web. *IEEE Comput.*, 10, 38, 62–69, 2005.

4. Horrocks, I., Semantic web: The story so far, in: *Proc. of the 2007 int. Cross-disciplinary conf. on Web Accessibility (W4A)*, ACM, Banff, Canada, pp. 120–125, 2007.

5. Zeshan, F. and Mohamad, R., Medical Ontology in the Dynamic Healthcare Environment. *The 3rd International Conference on Ambient Systems, Networks and Technologies (ANT), Procedia Computer Science*, vol. 10, pp. 340–348, 2012.

6. Kaur, P. and Khamparia, A., Review on Medical Care Ontologies. *Int. J. Sci. Res. (IJSR)*, 3, 12, pp 677–680, 2014.

7. Jean-Mary, Y.R., Shironoshita, E.P., Kabuka, M.R., Ontology matching with semantic verification. *J. Web Semant.*, 7, 3, 235–251, 2009.

8. Susel Fernández, R., Velasco, J., Marsa-Maestre, I., Miguel, A., Lopez-Carmona, Fuzzy Align: A Fuzzy Method for Ontology Alignment, in: *Proceedings of the International Conference on Knowledge Engineering and Ontology Development (KEOD-2012)*, pp. 98–107, 2012.

9. Huber, J., Sztyler, T., Noessner, J., Meilicke, C., *CODI: Combinatorial optimization for Data Integration—Results for OAEI Proceedings of the 6th International Workshop on Ontology Matching*, Bonn, Germany, pp. 134–141, 2011.

10. Xu, P., Wang, Y., Cheng, L., Zang, T., Alignment Results of SOBOM for OAEI 2010, *Ontology Matching OM-2010 ISWC Workshop*, pp 203-211, 2010.

11. Ngo, D. and Bellahsene, Z., YAM++: A multi-strategy based approach for ontology matching task. *Lecture Notes in Computer Science (Including Subseries Lecture Notes in Artificial Intelligence and Lecture Notes in Bioinformatics) LNAI*, vol. 7603, pp. 421–425, 2012.

12. Bodenreider, O., *Disease Ontology, Encyclopedia of Systems Biolog*, pp. 578–581, Springer, US National Library of Medicine, Bethesda, Maryland, USA, 2013.

13. Ibrahim, A.M., Hashi, H.A., Mohamed, A.A., Ontology Driven Information Retrieval for Healthcare Information System: A Case Study. *Int. J. Netw. Secur. Appl. (IJNSA)*, 5, 1, pp 61-69, 2013.

14. Babcock, S., Cowell, L.G., Beverley, J., Smith, B., The Infectious Disease Ontology in the Age of COVID-19, in: *OSF Preprints. Center for Open Science*, 2020.

15. He, Y., Yu, H., Ong, E. et al. CIDO, a community-based ontology for coronavirus disease knowledge and data integration, sharing, and analysis. *Sci. Data*, 7, 181, 2020. https://doi. org/10.1038/s41597-020-0523-6.

16. Oyelade, O.N., Ezugwu, A.E., COVID19: A Natural Language Processing and Ontology Oriented Temporal Case-Based Framework for Early Detection and Diagnosis of Novel Coronavirus. 2020050171, Preprints 2020.

17. Pirouz, B., Shaffiee Haghshenas, S., Shaffiee Haghshenas, S., Piro, P., Investigating a Serious Challenge in the Sustainable Development Process: Analysis of Confirmed cases of COVID-19 (New Type of Coronavirus) Through a Binary Classification Using Artificial Intelligence and Regression Analysis. *Sustainability*, 12, 6, 2427, 2020.

18. Al-qaness, M.A., Ewees, A.A., Fan, H., El Aziz, M.A., Optimization Method for Forecasting Confirmed Cases of COVID-19 in China. *J. Clin. Med.*, 9, 3, 674, 2020.

19. Gruninger, M. and Lee, J., Ontology—Applications and Design. *Commun. ACM*, 45, 2, 39–41, Feb 2002.

20. Uschold, M. and Jasper, R., A Framework for Understanding and Classifying Ontology Applications. *Proceedings of the IJCAI-99 workshop on Ontologies and Problem-Solving Methods (KRR5)*, Stockholm, Sweden, August 2, pp. 1–11, 1999.

21. Maedche, A. and Staab, S., Ontology learning for the Semantic Web. *IEEE Intell. Syst.*, 16, 2, 72–79, 2001.

22. Mao, M., *Ontology mapping: Towards semantic interoperability in distributed and heterogeneous environments*, Ph.D. dissertation, Pittsburgh Univ., Pittsburgh, PA, 2008.

23. Shvaiko, P. and Euzenat, J., Ontology matching: state of the art and future challenges. *IEEE Trans. Knowl. Data Eng.*, 25, 1, 158–176, 2013.

24. Niles, I. and Pease, A., Towards a standard upper ontology, in: *Proceedings of the 2nd International Conference on Formal Ontology in Information Systems (FOIS-2001)*, vol. 2001, pp. 2–9, 2001.

25. El-Sappagh, S., Franda, F., Ali, F., Kwak, K.-S., SNOMED CT standard ontology based on the ontology for general medical science. *BMC Med. Inf. Decis. Making*, 18, Article number: 76, 2018. https://doi.org/10.1186/s12911-018-0651-5

26. Buitelaar, P., Cimiano, P., Grobelnik, M., Sintek, M., Ontology learning from text. *Tutorial at ECML/PKDD*, Porto, October 2005.

27. Aleksovski, Z., Klein, M., Ten Kate, W., van Harmelen, F., Matching unstructured vocabularies using a background Ontology, in: *Proceedings of Knowledge Engineering and Knowledge Management (EKAW)*, pp. 182–197, 2006.

28. Lopez, V., Uren, V., Motta, E., Pasin, M., AquaLog: An ontology-driven question answering system for organizational semantic intranets. *Web Semant.: Science, Services and Agents on the World Wide Web*, 5, 2, 72–105, 2007.

29. Tablan, V., Damljanovi, D., Bontcheva, K., A natural language query interface to structured information, in: *The Semantic Web: Research and Applications, LNCS 5021*, pp. 361–375, Springer, Heidelberg, 2008.

30. Dasgupta, S., KaPatel, R., Padia, A., & Shah, K.,Description Logics based Formalization of Wh-Queries. *ArXiv*, abs/1312.6948, 2013.

31. Jaiswal, A. and George, V., A modified approaches for extraction and association of triplets. *International Conference on Computing, Communication & Automation*, 2015.

Semantic Behavior Analysis of COVID-19 Patients: A Collaborative Framework

Amlan Mohanty[1], Debasish Kumar Mallick[2], Shantipriya Parida[3] and Satya Ranjan Dash[2]*

[1]International Institute of Information Technology, Bhubaneswar, India
[2]School of Computer Applications, KIIT University, Bhubaneswar, India
[3]Idiap Research Institute, Martigny, Switzerland

Abstract

The world we live in today, where technology has become a very integral part of our lives, has new, untapped resources that can bring about massive changes in the health sector. The Internet and social media have become the flag bearers of the tech-savvy world. Some of the services provided by the various social media platforms like chats, comments, blogs, captions, as well as reviews are starting to get studied for Natural Language Processing (NLP) and Text Analytics. A generation that scrounges up even the silliest of answers on the internet, it is very common for people to search for their health-related queries on social media. In this book chapter, we intend to propose a model for extracting data complying with health records and health-related text documents of the COVID-19 patients from some of the top social media forums and present a semantic framework. Given the fact that social media allows a more open and direct form of communication, among health workers, patients, and even curious students and researchers, it is a reliable source for addressing public health problems. In these tough times, when the entire world is suffering from the deadly Coronavirus pandemic, we hope our work gets the perfect infrastructure to grow on.

Our book chapter puts forth a model to apply a semantic framework to retrieve healthcare data related to the Corona virus and COVID-19 pandemic from some of the social media forums available online and perform semantic analysis on the data. Social media can play a huge role in this aspect as people's experiences with the pandemic and patients affected by the virus from the root of information that is circulated online. This research work tries to provide a useful and reliable method of data retrieval and data extraction, which would catch data in its unstructured form like patient questions and discussions among doctors and patients, people who have had a close look on the virus, analyze the semantic nature of the data, and present it in a more structured manner so that it can be put to effective and immediate use. The sole purpose of our framework is aiming to help detect and predict the symptoms of Coronavirus through the textual data extracted from the various social media platforms.

Keywords: Natural language processing, semantic analysis, medical social media, COVID-19 patients healthcare data, naive bayes, decision tree

*Corresponding author: sdashfca@kiit.ac.in

Sachi Nandan Mohanty, G. Nalinipriya, Om Prakash Jena and Achyuth Sarkar (eds.) Machine Learning for Healthcare Applications, (277–288) © 2021 Scrivener Publishing LLC

18.1   Introduction

At a time when the world is hit by one of the worst pandemics of recent times, it is somewhat self-explanatory for an emotionally intelligent species like ours to bend our heads for guidance, inspiration, and even a solution to our problems, upon some greater power. Technology and science and the understanding of it is probably the messiah to look forward to in these times. One such learning that is new in its field and has immense potential, and can have our back in this pandemic is Natural Language Processing (NLP). The language we speak, our conversations, and even our expressions contain a lot of unstructured information that can be put to effective use by NLP. It is a pristine tool with a lot of potential to unearth, which can be a handy weapon in our arsenal in the fight against the Novel Coronavirus.

Speaking of the Novel Coronavirus, it has already affected almost all parts of the globe. A new strain of the already existing SARS-CoV-2, or as we call it the Novel Coronavirus was first identified in Wuhan, China reportedly in December 2019 before wreaking havoc across the world. The term COVID-19 refers to the Coronavirus Disease of 2019. Its symptoms are identical to flu and the common cold, which are common diseases, making it difficult to detect. Some patients are asymptomatic and show no possible symptoms of the virus. All this makes it more difficult to trace the virus and that is why testing becomes all the more important to detect a patient with COVID-19. The vaccine is still in its testing phase and therefore no practical cure for the virus is currently available. Smart lockdown of all the services and institutions except some and maintaining social distancing are the only two ways now to flatten the curve of the infection and curb the spreading of the virus.

The Corona virus has already affected 21 million people from across 215 countries and territories of the world with more than 5 million people being from the United States of America only. The low death rate does not show us the proper perspective of the virus. Apart from the health-related aspect of the virus, it has had a plethora of effects on all walks of life. The impact of the virus has been such on the economy that the IMF (International Monetary Fund) warns about the economy shrinking up to 3% this year, which is the most precipitous fall in the economy since the Great Depression of the 1930s [1]. Lockdown is beneficial for slowing down the rate of spread but lockdown also means restricting people to their houses, several businesses being shut, and abstaining from almost all economic activities. According to the World Economic Forum, "While the health challenges and economic consequences are potentially devastating, the political consequences are harder to foresee—but might be the most long-lasting" [2]. Sporting events have come to a halt and the Tokyo Olympics has been canceled. The only silver lining is the gift the virus bestowed on mother nature. Among the shutdown of the countries with huge polluting emissions, the Earth has found some time to heal itself. Researches show pollution levels going down by a notch in the cities and industrial areas, and several heart-throbbing videos of animals coming out of the wild into human settlements and fishes seen swimming again in the waters of Venice are flooding the internet. The lockdown also helped slow down our fast-paced life and spend some time with family, think about our future and play out old hobbies.

These days there is another thriving world unaffected by Coronavirus and lockdown, Social media—The virtual world. It is natural for people who are shut from the actual world to explore the world of social media. It is the ground zero for all types of conversations and information sharing from complex topics like politics and healthcare to films and entertainment and simpler things like posting pictures and conversing with friends. The Director-General of the World Health Organization (WHO) said in the Munich Security Conference "But we're not just fighting an epidemic; we're fighting an infodemic" [3]. The Internet is a huge source of information which can be put to good use in times like these. Awareness can be raised about the virus and information can be shared on the do's and don'ts during the lockdown. Apart from that, social media can be of colossal help to doctors, researchers, patients, and even common people who are confused about their symptoms. The medical data available online on COVID-19 can serve as useful information.

The information on social media is as vast as the sea but most of it is in unstructured form. This is where Natural Language Processing steps in. Natural Language Processing or NLP is a branch of Artificial Intelligence (AI) that tries to teach the machine to understand and interpret natural language. The language we speak, our expressions, and our behavior and all the other ways in which we communicate with each other can be termed as Natural Language. Everything we speak or express carries a huge amount of information. But it is complex and unstructured and difficult to manipulate for the machine. That is why NLP is required. NLP is a vast domain and is categorized into different groups and subgroups. The part of NLP we have tried to focus on in this book chapter is Semantic Analysis. It focuses on making the machines understand the meaning or logic behind a particular phrase or sentence. Natural language is complex and with the use of elements like sarcasm, puns, we don't always mean the exact thing we say. Semantic analysis tries to reduce this information gap and make the machines more capable of understanding our language and ways of communicating.

Sufficient and valid medical data is floating all around the Internet. Both patients and healthcare professionals provide valuable information in the social media groups and online forums, which are open to such discussions. These contain valuable information that can be used in the medical field of research. Social media allows open communication among patients, where they could disclose all their small, personal observations and health-related issues without being shy and having to worry about being mocked. Patients feel more comfortable sharing their experiences and awkward issues with other patients having similar grievances, which serves like a ground zero report. That means rather than reading about a particular disease and its symptoms, we get to know about the disease from the people who have experienced it or are going through it now. This is valuable information and can be used for research purposes.

Coronavirus pandemic is affecting lives worldwide and social media has gone wild about it. It has become the point of the topic in everyone's mouth. Such has been its effect that even in such a short period, social media is flooding with medical data of COVID-19. We aim to establish a model which would extract medical data related to Coronavirus and perform semantic behavior analysis on the extracted data. We wish this work will help humanity in the fight against Coronavirus by providing valuable information to the health analysts, data scientists, patients, and curious students and by helping save lives.

18.2   Related Work

18.2.1   Semantic Analysis and Topic Discovery of Alcoholic Patients From Social Media Platforms

This work tries to apply a semantic framework on healthcare documents available in social media groups and forums to extract and predict data related to alcoholic patients. Their model is based on the topic models of Latent Dirichlet Allocation (LDA) and Random Forest (RF). LDA is a probabilistic topic model that is widely used for text analysis and offers to represent the corpus in both the latent topic and predictive manner. Random Forest classifier is produced from many different decision trees. Bagging and feature randomness are used to design each particular tree. The main goal of this work is to show how the data extraction and information retrieval techniques work by extracting information from medical social networks [4]. One aspect of their work revolves around data retrieval from large amounts of patient questions from subjects revealing the experiences of the journey of their alcohol retrieval success story and asking doubts on how to go about the same. The pre-processed dataset was divided in such a manner that the testing set received 10% and the training set was handed 90%. The successful experimentation of their work throws light on how technology and social media can collectively be used to solve the health problems of patients.

18.2.2   Sentiment Analysis of Tweets From Twitter Handles of the People of Nepal in Response to the COVID-19 Pandemic

This work tries to show us the humongous impact social media has on all walks of life including science and technology, medicine, and even in fighting against this deadly world gripping Coronavirus pandemic. Sentiment Analysis is a bit nascent but is already recognized to have a lot of potential. This study uses Python programming with TextBlob library and Tweepy python library for sentiment analysis of the Twitter tweets of the people of Nepal [5]. The various tweets on the Coronavirus pandemic affecting Nepal and the world were collected from the people who accessed the Internet with their location as "Nepal" during May 2020. Text mining and semantic analysis were performed using Google Colab after the tweets were collected and pre-processed. There is one drawback to this study. All the research work has been performed on texts written in English when the majority of the population uses the native language.

18.2.3   Study of Sentiment Analysis and Analyzing Scientific Papers

Sentiment analysis teaches the machine to automatically understand the sentiment and emotions behind the lines of a text. Also known as "Opinion Mining", the name suggests how sentiment analysis has the power to understand and search for particular opinions. This makes the job so much easier for humans who would otherwise spend so much time searching for the same. This thesis focuses on using online reviews for sentiment analysis [13]. It has explained how people waste their time searching for essential sources of research for their work which also takes effort and costs paper. Instead, using online reviews and performing sentiment analysis on them will help them to automatically search research work which is helpful in their domain. This thesis proposes a new technique in the name of Sentiment Analysis of Online papers (SAOOP) [6]. SAOOP inspects the System score and the Sentiment score for the evaluation of the research papers. This approach uses the enhancement of the "Bag of words" model which solves the problem of low accuracy and manual evaluation. There are some challenges down this road like the creation of a big lexicon, evaluation, and extraction of keywords or topic features, world knowledge, and finally spams and fake reviews. But according to the comparison made among SAOOP and other famous techniques like NLTK and NLPS, it is seen that SAOOP is better than the other two by nearly 17%.

18.2.4   Informatics and COVID-19 Research

The Coronavirus has grabbed in its arms, millions of people around the world, and corona positive or not, the whole world is badly affected by the pandemic. Amid such horrible times, the aspect of the research has grown ten folds. While the whole world is sitting inside their respective homes, various creative ideas related to different research streams are gushing through our minds. Believe it or not but this pandemic has opened the gates for all types of research work and ideas. Even the search for the vaccine for the deadly virus is a research which is being taken up by several companies, scientists, and countries. The main idea behind this work is to highlight some of the research ideas related to the COVID-19 pandemic which have informatics at their core. The areas of work touched here are Bioinformatics, Clinical Informatics, Clinical Research Informatics, Consumer health informatics, and Public health informatics [7]. The idea is to throw light on some areas of informatics, which researchers can progress towards in this time of pandemic.

18.2.5   COVID-19 Outbreak in the World and Twitter Sentiment Analysis

The growth of social data has gone up rapidly in recent years and has made the access of data quite easier for everyone. The researchers find it easy to avail of the information on the web for academic or scientific research and commercial uses. The web contains detailed information on almost everything [15]. Whatever new happens in the world, the web updates us within seconds literally. During this pandemic, the government agencies and media organizations are trying hard to update the latest news regarding the pandemic using the Internet. Realizing the effect of the web in such a time, this study has extracted data from the Twitter handles of people using Tweepy Library and TextBlob library of Python programming language and performed sentiment analysis on the data. The graphical representation of the data has also been provided in the study. The data that was collected from Twitter was based on two hashtags—"COVID-19" and "Coronavirus" and the date of collection was a week from 9th to 15th March 2020 [8]. A visual presentation and its explanation are provided in the end.

18.2.6   LDA Topic Modeling on Twitter to Study Public Discourse and Sentiment During the Coronavirus Pandemic

The pandemic has done a lot of damage not only health or economy-wise but has also put a load on us mentally. Our mental health has gone for a ride in this pandemic. Staying inside the home all day has brought up all the past and ongoing issues of life and has had serious implications on our mental health. It is seen that people post about almost anything on social media, even their personal lives. So, it is obvious that they will try to share their feelings about their mental state and try to reach out for help. Keeping that in mind, this work tries to understand Twitter users' conversations and psychological reactions to the pandemic. Eleven keywords were used for the extraction of information. The outbreak of Coronavirus cases in New York City was acknowledged through tweets between 10th and 14th February 2020 [9]. The symptoms of Coronavirus and treatment options were also among extracted data but the main concern was on the mental and psychological health and mentality of the common mass during the lockdown and the ongoing pandemic.

18.2.7   The First Decade of Research on Sentiment Analysis

It has been almost a decade since the first research work on Sentiment Analysis was published. This paper tries to show us the journey of research of sentiment analysis through the decade with the help of statistics. Some of the most asked questions that this paper tries to answer include the kind of topics discussed under Sentiment Analysis, how its popularity changed with time and who were the leading researchers in this arena. The application of LDA (Latent Dirichlet Allocation) to the abstracts and titles of the research papers and statistical analysis of the keywords have been used to answer some of these questions. The step by step development of Semantic Analysis is presented in this work [10].

18.2.8   Detailed Survey on the Semantic Analysis Techniques for NLP

Computer science, Artificial Intelligence, and Linguistics together form the beautiful and vast domain of Natural Language Processing. Human and machine interaction is the main motive behind the subject. Natural languages or the processes used by us cannot be understood by the machine and NLP tries to bridge this communication gap between humans and machines. Human language is very complex and understanding it is difficult even for humans. This is what makes NLP a tough job. But scientists and researchers are going on improving day by day in this domain. This paper offers to help us explore the domain of Semantic Analysis by going through the different research done in this field with the help of an interesting survey. Two research fields are prioritized in the work. One being the Latent Semantic Analysis (LSA) model which is a prominent statistical model for information retrieval [11]. The other being Ontology, which is a branch of metaphysics and can be used to extract data in a structured way from the unstructured data.

18.2.9   Understanding Text Semantics With LSA

This paper focuses solely on Latent Semantic Analysis and how to use it in an attempt to understand the vast and complex arena of text semantics with a closer view of the subject. LSA is well-known as a statistical/mathematical model for the revelation and retrieval of latent or hidden associations of dependent use of words in a text document. The LSA model, which is also called a bag of words model is studied in this paper based on a single value decomposition [12]. It is used to search for the relations between keywords from the dataset consisting of different research papers related to NLP, semantic analysis, and all its applications. The importance of Latent Semantic Analysis and its varied and useful applications is discussed.

18.2.10   Analyzing Suicidal Tendencies With Semantic Analysis Using Social Media

Given the reach of social media these days, it is a stated fact that more than half of the population of the world uses social media to connect, communicate, learn, share, and live. Many people going through depression and living through a low point in life often find the heinous idea of "suicide" as the only solution to their problematic life. As we all know, suicide is not the solution, but another problem. This paper has tried to reach out to people having suicidal thoughts and help them through technology. The idea that such people might post stuff related to their mindset on social media which can be analyzed to reach out and help, is used here. Semantic analysis is performed on tweets and blogs to find out such texts that contain suicidal psychology. The Bag of Words model is used along with Parts of Speech using TextBlob to make it possible.

18.2.11   Analyzing Public Opinion on BREXIT Using Sentiment Analysis

Research proves that social media has given a rapid boost to the use of Sentiment Analysis. Social media is a platform that values each individual's opinion. Even people who are introverted in real life feel free to post their life and opinion on the Internet. Since social media is a very open and bias-free platform, it can be used to know people's opinions on public matters. This paper has tried to analyze public opinion on BREXIT by Sentiment Classification. A comparative study between Naïve Bayes Classifier Model and Python's TextBlob library by performing sentiment analysis on the data taken from Twitter [14]. The results have tried to lend a helping hand to both the British and Irish Governments to look profoundly into the matter and choose wisely.

18.2.12   Prediction of Indian Elections Using NLP and Decision Tree

Technology is progressively outgrowing itself in terms of its resources and functions. In simple words, technology is being used today to perform one miracle after another, things which humans never thought could be possible even before 10–15 years. This paper has tried to predict the General Elections of 2019 in India using the Sentiment Analysis and Decision Tree classifier. Social media is a huge library of information and contains a large corpus of raw data [15]. The social media platform of Twitter is used for this purpose. Tweets related to the General Elections were collected so that semantic analysis could be performed on the data. The data was trained and tested by using the Decision Tree classifier to be able to predict the results of the election. The details have been summarized in Table 18.1.

18.3   Methodology

Medical data and information shared by various healthcare professionals and patients online are both valuable and reliable. Social media, being the hub of all information these days, shares adequate information of all kinds at the doorstep of anyone who has an Internet connection. Given that the Prime Minister of India, Sri Narendra Modi, understands the value of the Internet and has taken it upon himself to make India digital in all sectors, it is not much longer before the Internet is available to every single individual in India.

Table 18.1 Related work table.

S. No.	Year of Publication	Title	Methodology
1	2019	A Collaborative Framework Based for Semantic Patients-Behavior Analysis and Highlight Topics Discovery of Alcoholic Beverages in Online Healthcare Forums	LDA model, Random Forest model classifier
2	2020	Twitter Sentiment Analysis During Covid-19 Outbreak in Nepal	Tweepy and TextBlob Library
3	2016	Analyzing Scientific Papers Based on Sentiment Analysis	Sentiment Analysis Of Online papers (SAOOP), text analysis, opinion mining
4	2020	Twitter Sentiment Analysis on Worldwide COVID-19 Outbreaks	Tweepy and TextBlob Library, Twitter tweets
5	2020	Public discourse and sentiment during the COVID 19 pandemic: using Latent Dirichlet Allocation for topic modeling on Twitter	Twitter tweets, mental health and psychology, LDA
6	2016	Research On Sentiment Analysis: The First Decade	LDA
7	2016	Techniques of Semantic Analysis for Natural Language Processing – A Detailed Survey	LSA
8	2017	Latent Semantic Analysis: An Approach to Understand Semantic of Text	LSA, singular value decomposition
9	2018	An approach to analyze suicidal tendency in blogs and tweets using Sentiment Analysis	Bag of words, part of speech, TextBlob

(Continued)

Table 18.1 Related work table. (*Continued*)

S. No.	Year of Publication	Title	Methodology
10	2018	Sentiment Classification of Current Public Opinion on BREXIT: Naïve Bayes Classifier Model vs Python's TextBlob Approach	Naïve Bayes Classifier Model, Python's TextBlob, Get public opinion on BREXIT
11	2019	Twitter Based Outcome Predictions of 2019 Indian General Elections Using Decision Tree	Decision Tree classifier

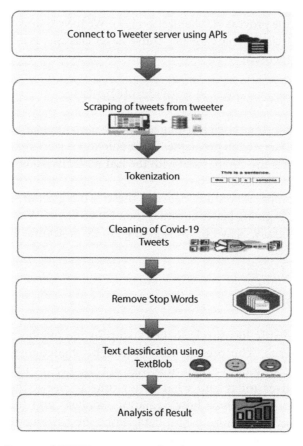

Figure 18.1 Data flow diagram of COVID-19 sentence classification.

Social media also contains reliable medical data in the form of social medical news and posts, personal chats, comments on medical posts, pictures and videos, health-related articles, and blogs. This information can be used for so many useful purposes. But unfortunately, this information is unstructured and scattered throughout. We need NLP and semantic analysis tools for smart extraction and better understanding and working with the data.

Our work is to analyze, implement and to do a brief comparison between two machine learning techniques—Naive Bayes and Decision tree collaborative framework after having performed semantic analysis on the data available on social media platforms published by doctors, health professionals, patients and even normal citizens who have shared their experience and expertise in the fight against the deadly Coronavirus on their social media handle [15]. Raw, unstructured, COVID-19 related medical data is collected from social media and semantic analysis techniques are applied to it, given in Figure 18.1.

The tweets related to COVID-19 which contain specific keywords are scraped from the Twitter server by tweet ids [16]. We have taken 1,000 COVID-19 related tweets and 1,000 Non-COVID-19 tweets for training purposes. Another 2,000 tweets specializing in COVID-19 and Non-COVID-19 are taken for testing purposes. The scrapped tweets are cleaned and tokenized by running filtration programs. The removal of stopwords from tweets is done during the process of tokenization [17]. We have trained two models—Naïve Bayes Classifier and Decision Tree classifier. Naïve Bayes classifier is a fast algorithm which is based on the Bayes theorem.

$$p(c \: / \: x) = \{p(x/c)p(c)\}/p(x) \tag{18.1}$$

Decision Tree is also a supervised learning technique used for decision-making purposes like Classification and Regression problems. The prediction starts from the root node of the tree. The first node starts the comparison with the leaf node. Based on the comparison, we go for leaf nodes for the decision.

We have done a comparative study between these two algorithms. We have observed that the Decision Tree is giving better accuracy than Naïve Bayes. Whenever Decision Tree is giving 93.9% of accuracy, Naïve Bayes is giving 76.7% of accuracy for classification of COVID-19 related tweets.

18.4 Conclusion

The COVID-19 pandemic has surely locked us up inside our homes but has not got the better of our spirits. The present time is tough, challenging us and testing us mentally, but without an iota of doubt, it brings out the best in us. Technology seems to be a part of our lives today and what better time to use it than a pandemic situation. Our main goal is to show how Semantic Analysis and information retrieval techniques can be used to acquire useful data about the Coronavirus pandemic from social media sites and prove how technology and social media can play an important role during this pandemic. We have tried to use NLP and semantic analysis to scrape COVID-19 related data from Twitter and use the data to help fight against

Coronavirus. A comparative study between Supervised Naïve Bayes classifier and Decision Tree has been done for the classifier to classify the tweets. So the machine automatically filters the profiles and tweets for keeping track of them. The key behind making a good accuracy system for Semantic analysis could be turning to encoder-decoder models which are more reliable systems for classifying the data by semantic analysis.

References

1. *Explained Desk: Explained How Covid-19 has affected the global economy*, The Indian Express, New Delhi, 2020, https://indianexpress.com/article/explained/explained-how-has-covid-19-affected-the-global-economy-6410494m/.

2. Scott, J., *The economic, geopolitical and health consequences of COVID-19*, World Economic Forum, 2020, https://www.weforum.org/agenda/2020/03/the-economic-geopolitical-and-health-consequences-of-covid-19/.

3. WHO Director-General, WHO, *Munich Security Conference*, 2020, https://www.who.int/dg/speeches/detail/munich-security-conference.

4. Jelodar, H., Wang, Y., Rabbani, M., Xiao, G., Zhao, R., A Collaborative Framework Based for Semantic Patients-Behavior Analysis and Highlight Topics Discovery of Alcoholic Beverages in Online Healthcare Forums. *J. Med. Syst.*, 44, 5, 3–8, 2020.

5. Pokharel, B.P., Twitter Sentiment analysis during COVID-19 Outbreak in Nepal. *SSRN*, 1–26, 2020, Available at SSRN 3624719.

6. Hussein, D.M.E.D.M., *Analyzing Scientific Papers Based on Sentiment Analysis*, pp. 1–102, Information System Department Faculty of Computers and Information Cairo University, Egypt, 2016.

7. Moore, J.H., Barnett, I., Boland, M.R., Chen, Y., Demiris, G., Gonzalez-Hernandez, G., Morris, J.S., …, in: *Ideas for how informaticians can get involved with COVID-19 research*, pp. 1–16, 2020.

8. Manguri, K.H., Ramadhan, R.N., Amin, P.R.M., Twitter Sentiment Analysis on Worldwide COVID-19 Outbreaks. *Kurdistan J. Appl. Res.*, 5, 3, 54–65, 2020.

9. Xue, J., Chen, J., Chen, C., Zheng, C., Zhu, T., Machine learning on Big Data from Twitter to understand public reactions to COVID-19, arXiv preprint arXiv:2005.08817. 1–23, 2020.

10. Ahlgren, O., Research on sentiment analysis: the first decade. *16th International Conference on Data Mining Workshops (ICDMW)*, pp. 890–899, 2016.

11. Rajani, S. and Hanumanthappa, M., Technique of Semantic Analysis for Natural Language Processing—A Detailed Survey. *Int. J. Adv. Res. Comput. Commun. Eng.*, 5, 2, 146–149, 2016.

12. Kherwa, P. and Bansal, P., Latent Semantic Analysis: An Approach to Understand Semantic of Text, in: *2017 International Conference on Current Trends in Computer, Electrical, Electronics and Communication (CTCEEC)*, pp. 870–874, 2017.

13. Madhu, S., An approach to analyze suicidal tendency in blogs and tweets using Sentiment Analysis. *Int. J. Sci. Res. Comput. Sci. Eng.*, 6, 4, 34–36, 2018.

14. Shekhawat, B.S., *Sentiment Classification of Current Public Opinion on BREXIT: Naïve Bayes Classifier Model vs Python's TextBlob Approach*, Doctoral dissertation, pp. 1–31, National College of Ireland, Dublin, 2019.

15. Joseph, F.J.J., Twitter Based Outcome Predictions of 2019 Indian General Elections Using Decision Tree, in: *2019 4th International Conference on Information Technology (InCIT)*, IEEE, pp. 50–53, 2019.

16. Chen, L., Lyu, H., Yang, T., Wang, Y., Luo, J., In the eyes of the beholder: Sentiment and topic analyses on social media use of neutral and controversial terms for Covid-19, arXiv preprint arXiv:2004.10225. 1–8, 2020.

17. Shoeibi, N., A Novel Recommender System Using extracted information from Social Media for doing Fundamental Stock Market Analysis. *ICCBR, Doctoral Consortium Proceedings*, pp. 32–36, 2020.

18. Hasan, A., Moin, S., Karim, A., Shamshirband, S., Machine learning-based sentiment analysis for Twitter accounts. *Math. Comput. Appl.*, 23, 1, 1–15, 2018.

Comparative Study of Various Data Mining Techniques Towards Analysis and Prediction of Global COVID-19 Dataset

Sachin Kamley

Department of Computer Application, S.A.T.I., Vidisha, India

Abstract

For the couple of days, Novel Corona Virus Infection Disease (COVID-19) is increasing day by day and it has become one of the main reasons of death in the modern world. At present, more than fifty lakh people have infected and over six lakh people have died due to this pandemic. Presently, no medicines have been developed to fight against this serious virus. There is a need of such kind of feasible automated system which helps medical professionals to take accurate decision on right time. However, data mining system would be very helpful to analyze COVID-19 dataset. This study presents a comparative study of various data mining techniques such as Support Vector Machine, Back Propagation Neural Network, Decision Tree and K-means clustering, etc. and analyzes their performance on COVD-19 dataset. The COVID-19 dataset from the Base lab and Worldometer data sources for the period of 31st December 2019 to 20th July 2020 is obtained for the study purpose. The Matlab R2017a machine learning tool is used to generate the experimental results. Finally, experimental results had stated that ANN method had recorded the highest performance accuracy and some new countries are identified which comes under in high risk category.

Keywords: COVID-19, data mining, prediction, the base lab, worldometer, Matlab R2017a

19.1 Introduction

Nowadays, Novel Corona Virus Infection Disease (COVID) has become a serious threat to the human society all over the world. The World Health Organization (WHO) has given its name as SARS-COV-2 and officially called COVID-19. Firstly, the virus was identified in Wuhan city, China on the last part of December 2019 when large no. of people having symptoms like Pneumonia [1,2]. However, the virus has diverse effects on the human body i.e. multi-organ and severe acute respiratory syndrome failure which can ultimately lead to a death of a person in a very short period of time [3]. Presently, there are more than 50 Lakh active Corona cases and over 6 Lakh deaths all over the world. Every day millions of people have been reported to be positive across the world. The virus primarily enters the

Email: skamley@gmail.com

Sachi Nandan Mohanty, G. Nalinipriya, Om Prakash Jena and Achyuth Sarkar (eds.) *Machine Learning for Healthcare Applications*, (289–308) © 2021 Scrivener Publishing LLC

human body by touching the contaminated surfaces, by physical contacts or by respiratory droplets in the air, etc. [4].

The main challenging aspect of this outbreak is that a person can possess a virus for several days without showing symptoms, so most countries in the world have implemented a partial or strict lockdown only in affected regions. Medical researchers of various countries are continuously involved to develop an appropriate antidote or vaccine but to date no medicine has been approved by WHO to kill the virus [5].

In this direction, data mining software and techniques have proven its importance to solve very sophisticated problems. The application areas of data mining include medical and healthcare, intelligent robots, Natural Language Processing (NLP), business applications, autonomous vehicle and many more.

These software and techniques have the ability to extract hidden or previously unknown patterns, relationships and knowledge from huge dataset [6]. Moreover, these patterns would be helpful for medical professionals or government to design strong policy and decision making in order to prevalence of COVID cases or deaths all over the world.

One of the most promising areas of data mining is forecasting where numerous researchers have applied various data mining techniques in this area including stock market, weather forecasting, diseases prognosis and diagnosis, etc. However, various classification and predictions techniques like Neural Network (NN), Support Vector Machine (SVM), Random Forest (RF), Regressions and Naïve Bays (NB), etc. have been widely applied in predicting the conditions of patients in future with a specified disease [7,8]. These studies include breast cancer, Cardiovascular Disease (CVD) prediction, etc.

Hence, implementing these systems using these techniques the patient will be benefitted or diagnosed at right time. The main concern of this study is to predict and analysis COVID-19 dataset based on the parameters like no. of infected cases, serious cases, death rate, recovery rate, case fertility rate, tests per million population, cases per million population and old age people, etc. for the next two to three weeks as well as categorized the countries based on risk measure i.e. low, medium and high respectively.

Moreover, this study would be helpful for medical professionals, government, police staff and business persons to take right decision on appropriate time in order to save the life of the people. Furthermore, various data mining techniques are compared based on their performance metrics.

After background discussions, some significant researchers work in brief is described by Section 19.2. Materials and methods of the study are described by Section 19.3. Experimental results analysis is described by Section 19.4. Conclusion and future scopes of the study is described by Section 19.5.

19.2   Literature Review

For the last couple of days, various researchers have contributed to predict the COVID-19 cases (serious cases, death rate, case fertility rate, etc.) from COVID dataset over the world. In this section, some significant researchers' works are presented in brief.

Car *et al.* [9] have adopted Multilayer Perceptron (MLP) model for finding maximum no. of patients across the world. For this purpose, dataset obtained from Johns Hopkins University, Maryland, USA, consisting of infected, recovered and deceased patients information of 406 locations over 51 days from the period of 22nd January to 12th March 2020. They have used 4 hidden layers with 4 neurons with Rectified Linear Unit (ReLU) activation function for study purpose. Finally, performance evaluation coefficient of determination (R2) and 10-fold cross validation method are used and they recorded the R2 scores of 0.98599 for confirmed, 0.99429 for deceased and 0.97941 for recovered patients respectively.

Pinter *et al.* [10] have suggested hybrid machine learning approach like Adaptive Network-based Fuzzy Inference System (ANFIS) and Multilayer Perceptron Imperialist Competitive Algorithm (MLP-ICA) for to predict no. of infected individually and mortality rates (death rate). Based on the experimental results, they have concluded that at the May last outbreak and mortality rate would be reduce substantially and they have achieved better accuracy for 9-day validation performance.

Gomathi *et al.* [11] proposed multi-disease prediction study using data mining techniques. Nowadays, data mining plays vital role in predicting multiple disease. This paper mainly concentrates on predicting the heart disease, diabetes, breast cancer, etc. Finally, they have concluded that by using the data mining techniques the number of tests can be reduced.

Rustom *et al.* [12] have utilized supervised machine learning techniques such as Linear Regression (LR), Least Absolute Shrinkage and Selection Operator (LASSO), Support Vector Machine (SVM) and Exponential Smoothing (ES) for forecasting the threatening factors of COVID-19. Therefore, they have made predictions based on the no. of deaths cases, no. of newly infected cases and the no. of recoveries in the next 10 days. At last, experimental results had shown that ES method outperformed than others in terms of death rate, no. of confirmed cases and in recovery rate scenarios on an available dataset.

Pujihari *et al.* [13] have presented application of data mining classification technique for finding the COVID-19 infected status individuals. For this purpose, they have used Naïve Bayes (NB) algorithm to classify the COVID-19 dataset to find out the negative or positive status of COVID-19 virus infection. However, dataset is downloaded from the Jeo website and Rapid miner 9.6 data mining tool is used for experimental purpose. Finally, experimental results stated that positive status of infected patients have recorded up to 55.48% highest while negative status is recorded up to 44.52% respectively.

Muhammad *et al.* [14] have developed data mining models for COVID-19 infected patients' recovery using epidemiological dataset of COVID-19 patients of South Korea. They have obtained epidemiological dataset of COVID-19 patients of South Korea for study purpose and Decision Tree, Support Vector Machine, Naive Bayes, Logistic Regression, Random Forest, and K-Nearest Neighbor techniques are applied on dataset. However, they have considered Python programming tool to design the proposed model and their experimental results had shown that DT method outperformed than others in terms of accuracy.

Russo *et al.* [15] have analyzed the first day of infections and predictions of COVID-19 cases in Italy. Based on the experimental results, they could be able to estimate the actual count of exposed cases of COVID-19.

Volpert *et al.* [16] have suggested the efficiency of quarantine model towards the spread of Corona virus infections using data analytics tool. Moreover, they have performed mathematical modeling in order to assess the placed quarantine people.

Sujath *et al.* [17] have performed the comparative study of various machine learning techniques like Multilayer Perceptron (MLP), Vector Auto Regression (VAR) and Linear

Regression (LR) to assess the epidemiological peak of COVID-19 in India. They have obtained the dataset from Kaggle data source and considered the death cases, recovered cases and confirmed cases across the India. Finally, they suggested that social distancing, lock-down, curfew, quarantine and isolation are important steps in order to stop the virus chain.

Shinde *et al.* [18] have considered various statistical, mathematical and medical (symptomatic and asymptomatic) parameters for study purpose. They have considered dataset from World Health Organization (WHO) and social media platform including daily death content, no. of carriers, incubation period, environmental parameters (temperature, humidity, wind speed), awareness about COVID-19, medical facilities available, social distancing, quarantine, age, gender, report time, transmission rate, etc. Finally they have concluded that rate of COVID-19 cases would be grow rapidly in future.

Finally, this study is enhanced by using Support Vector Machine (SVM), Decision Tree (DT), K-Means clustering and Back Propagation Neural Network (BPNN) respectively.

19.3   Materials and Methods

19.3.1   Dataset Collection

Dataset of 180 well-known countries from the Base lab and Worldometer repositories was jointly obtained for the period of 31st Dec 2019 to 20th July 2020 for study purpose [19]. The dataset consisting of variables like no. of infected cases, no. of cured, new deaths, serious cases, death rate, recovery rate, case fertility rate, etc. [18]. After data consideration, data pre-processing process i.e. removes missing, useless and some redundant information from dataset [6,20]. Table 19.1 shows COVID-19 dataset sample.

In order to predict and analysis the COVID-19 dataset in un-lock period following methods are used.

19.3.2   Support Vector Machine (SVM)

SVM model is firstly proposed by Cortes and Vapnik in 1995 [21]. However, the model is based on statistical learning theory and structure risk minimization concept and further model is modified by Vapnik in 1998 [22]. SVM model perfectly isolates the datasets in two decision boundaries i.e. classes under N dimensional space. SVM basically creates a hyper-plane which is used to separate the data points in such a way where all the data points in one side of class and rest data points in other side of the class [22]. The points which are closest to hyper-plane are called support vectors. Moreover, the hyper-plane is used to perform the data separation based on largest distance analysis to identify the classes as well as error minimization is denoted by largest margin classifier. Figure 19.1 shows a graph of two class problems with linear separable hyper-plane. Figure 19.2 shows a flowchart of the SVM model.

Table 19.1 COVID-19 Dataset Sample.

Country	No. of Infected (NOI)	Total Deaths (TD)	No. of Cured (NOC)	Death Rate (DR)	Recovery Rate (RR)	New Case (NC)	New Deaths (ND)
USA	3,900,434	143,316	1,802,550	3.67	46.21	1,884	27
Brazil	2,100,112	79,535	1,371,229	3.79	65.29	216	2
India	1,127,281	27,628	707,523	2.45	62.76	9,174	125
Russia	777,486	12,427	553,602	1.6	71.2	5,940	85
South Africa	364,328	5,033	191,059	1.38	52.44	0	0
Peru	353,590	13,187	241,955	3.73	68.43	0	0
Mexico	344,224	39,184	217,423	11.38	63.16	5,311	296

Serious Cases (SC)	Cases Per Million Population (CPMP)	Total Tests Per Million Population (TTPMP)	Old Age People (OAP)	Median Age People (MAP)	Hand washing Facility (HWF)	Population Density (PD)	Case Fertility Rate (CFR)
16,552	11,780	146,014	2.87	32.6	89.12	35.60	3.724
8,318	9,877	23,096	5.06	33.5	79.54	25.04	3.788
8,944	816	10,175	3.05	29.3	64.12	450.41	2.459
2,300	5,328	173,030	3.05	27.3	44	8.8	1.6

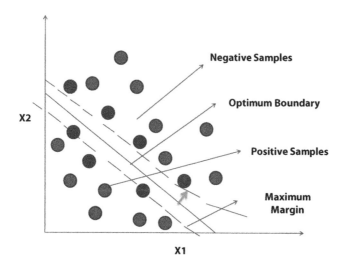

Figure 19.1 A graph of two class problem with linear separable hyper-plane [21,22].

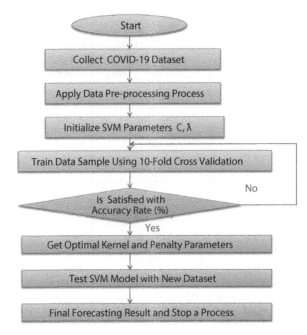

Figure 19.2 Flowchart of the SVM model [23].

19.3.3   Decision Tree (DT)

One of the well-known graphical and mathematical representations of a problem is used to generalize and categorize a given dataset and is named as Decision Tree (DT). A DT is a structure containing the topmost node called as root, where internal nodes represent the features of a dataset, branches represent the decision rules and each leaf node represents the outcome [6, 24]. However, an associate degree of an attribute is checked by each internal node, end result of a check is denoted by every branch, while category label is denoted by every leaf node. The main objective of DT model is to predict the value of a required variable based upon many input variables. Moreover, DT model also uses the prediction based rules classification. Finally, known label i.e. class level of test data is compared along with the classified result and accuracy is computed based on the split test data samples. Figure 19.3 shows flowchart of decision tree model.

19.3.4   K-Means Clustering

K-means clustering is a well-known and popular unsupervised cluttering algorithm which is used to classify the given data objects into n different size clusters over the iterative steps. However, it is a dividing-based clustering algorithm and convergent to a local minimum [25]. The method can be used in various practical applications and understood by each and every one. This method is verified to be a very effective way that can generate good clustering results and generated results i.e. clusters are minimized and independent. Flowchart of k-means clustering algorithm is shown by Figure 19.4.

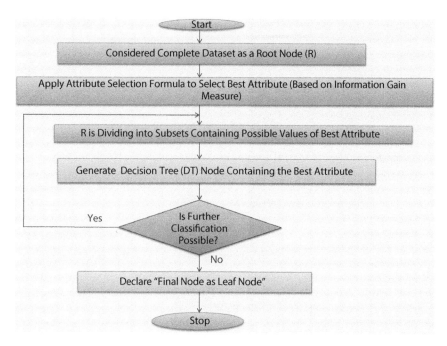

Figure 19.3 Flowchart of decision tree model [6,24].

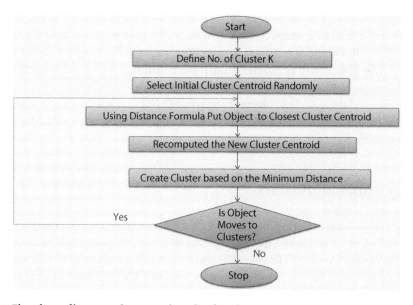

Figure 19.4 Flowchart of k-means clustering algorithm [6,25].

19.3.5   Back Propagation Neural Network (BPNN)

Back Propagation Neural Network (BPNN) is one of the most prominent and efficient supervised algorithm is used to train Artificial Neural Networks (ANNs) [26]. In this architecture, inputs are always transmitted from input layer to hidden layers where some activation functions like Sigmoid or Tangent is used and hidden layers to output layers

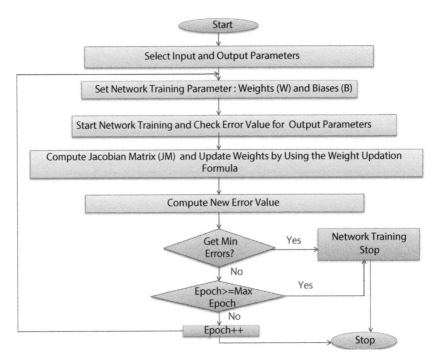

Figure 19.5 Flowchart of levenberg maquardt (LM) training algorithm [6,28].

where errors are calculated respectively. If errors are present then propagating in the "backwards" direction at hidden layers, so it is called as Back Propagation Neural Network (BPNN) [27]. This procedure is repeated until we could not satisfy with performance or errors are minimized. In order to solve small and medium size training problems, most popular BPNN method like Levenberg Maquardt (LM) is used in this study. However, LM method provides faster and stable convergence speed. Flowchart of LM algorithm is shown by Figure 19.5.

19.4 Experimental Results

In this study, real COVID-19 training dataset of different countries for the period of 31st December 2019 to 6th June 2020 and testing dataset from 7th June 2020 to 20th July 2020 is obtained for study purpose. However, Training dataset consisting of 120 samples and testing dataset consisting of 60 samples. In order to avoid instable operation results, 5-fold cross validation techniques is also utilized so each experiment is run out 5 times and finally, optimum classification accuracy is considered based on comparison. The aim of this research study is to predict and analyze worldwide COVID-19 cases using best classification algorithms. Therefore, four different classification algorithms like Support Vector Machine (SVM), Decision Tree (DT), k-means clustering and Levenberg Maquardt (LM) are used and Matlab 2017a machine learning tool is used for experimental purpose. Table 19.2 shows a sample of rise wise performance comparison of actual and predicted infected cases for SVM model.

Table 19.2 Sample of risk wise performance comparison of actual vs predicted infected cases for SVM model.

S. No.	Country	Actual Infection	Predicted Infection	Accuracy
1	USA	High	High	Correct
2	Portugal	Low	Low	Correct
3	--	Medium	Low	Incorrect
4	Singapore	Low	Low	Correct
5	--	High	Low	Incorrect
6	Egypt	Medium	Medium	Correct
7	Brazil	High	High	Correct
8	--	Low	High	Incorrect
9	--	Low	High	Incorrect
10	--	Medium	Low	Incorrect
11	Peru	High	High	Correct
12	Saudi Arabia	Medium	Medium	Correct
13	Austria	Low	Low	Correct
14	Mexico	High	High	Correct
15	Netherland	Medium	Medium	Correct
16	--	Low	High	Incorrect
17	Japan	Low	Low	Correct
18	India	High	High	Correct
19	Oman	Medium	Medium	Correct
20	Russia	High	High	Correct
21	--	Low	Medium	Incorrect
22	Columbia	Medium	Medium	Correct
23	Ghana	Low	Low	Correct
24	Italy	High	High	Correct
25	--	Medium	Low	Incorrect

Figure 19.6 shows accuracy comparison against no. of observations.

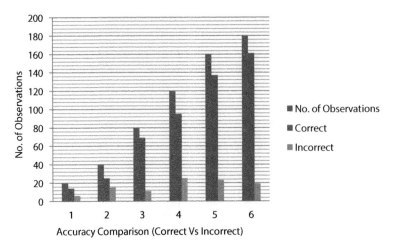

Figure 19.6 Accuracy comparison against no. of observations.

Figure 19.6 depicts that no. of observation increases then no. of correctly classified instances also increases as compared to incorrectly classified instances. Due to long size of Decision Tree (DT) generated here we have converted DT into rule based format which is shown by Table 19.3.

Table 19.4 shows classification of countries based on decision tree rule generation.

Table 19.5 shows cluster groups of k-means clustering algorithm.

Table 19.3 Sample of Rule Base Generation from Decision Tree.

S. No.	Rules
1	If OAP = High and HWF = Poor and DR = High Then NOI = High
2	If PD = High and CFR = Low and ND = Medium Then RR = Medium
3	If TTPMP = High and NOC = Low Then DR = High
4	If ND = Low and CPMP = High and MAP = Medium Then RR = High
5	If SC = High and TTPMP = Low Then CFR = High
6	If NC = high and RR = High and TTPMP = Medium Then DR = Low
7	If HWF = High and NOC = Medium and NOI = Low Then CFR = Medium
8	If NC = Medium and CPMP = Low and TTPMP = Medium Then CFR = Low
9	If PD = Low and NOI = High and RR = Poor Then ND = High
10	If SC = Low and TTPMP = High and NOC = Medium Then CPMP = Medium

Table 19.4 Classification of Countries based on Decision Tree Rule Generation.

S. No.	Country
1	UK
2	China
3	Spain
4	Turkey
5	France
6	Qatar
7	Poland
8	UAE
9	Belarus
10	India
11	South Africa
12	Chile
13	Germany
14	Philippines
15	Ecuador

Table 19.5 Cluster Groups of k-means Clustering Algorithm.

Attributes	Cluster1	Cluster2	Cluster3
No. of Infected (NOI)	67	23	11
Total Deaths (TD)	42	55	26
No. of Cured (NOC)	81	68	21
Death Rate (DR)	97	26	43
Recovery Rate (RR)	102	27	37
New Case (NC)	59	73	42
New Deaths (ND)	74	45	29
Serious Cases (SC)	70	37	69
Cases Per Million Population (CPMP)	79	81	20
Total Tests Per Million Population (TTPMP)	47	91	39
Old Age People (OAP)	105	55	19
Median Age People (MAP)	34	51	66
Hand washing Facility (HWF)	23	49	17
Population Density (PD)	107	21	34
Case Fertility Rate (CFR)	45	92	32

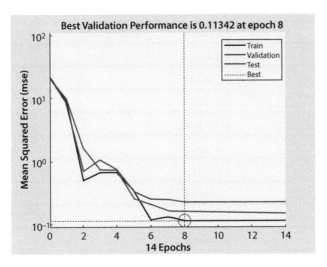

Figure 19.7 Training state of levenberg maquardt (LM) method.

Table 19.5 clearly states that very high no. of instances classified in clusters 1, 2 and 3 having attributes NOC, DR, RR, OAP and PD respectively. Training state of Levenberg Maquardt (LM) method is shown by Figure 19.7.

Figure 19.7 depicts that performance comparison between epochs and Mean Square Error (MSE) and during training state best validation performance got 0.11342 at epoch 8. In this study, effectiveness of all classifier are evaluated are based on the correctly classified instances and incorrectly classified instances as an accuracy. Table 19.6 shows classification accuracy of proposed algorithms.

Classification accuracy of the proposed algorithms is shown by Table 19.6. However, Back propagation algorithm has recorded the outstanding classification accuracy i.e. 96% which is better than other algorithms. Table 19.7 shows sample of classification of countries based on output variables Case Fertility Rate (CFR), Tests Per Million Population (TPMP), Cases Per Million Population (CPMP) and Serious Cases (SC).

Table 19.6 Classification accuracy of proposed algorithms.

Algorithm	Correctly Classified	Misclassified	Accuracy (%)
Support Vector Machine (SVM)	147	17	92%
Decision Tree (DT)	139	21	87%
K-Means	126	34	79%
Back Propagation (Levenberg Maquardt)	153	06	96%

Table 19.7 Sample of classification of countries based on output variables.

S. No.	Country	Actual CFR	Predicted CFR	Actual TTMP	Predicted TPMP	Actual CPMP	Predicted CPMP	Actual SC	Predicted SC
1	USA	3.72	3.78	146,014	139,879	11,780	9,840	16,552	21,321
2	Brazil	3.79	3.56	23,096	24,537	9,877	8,835	8,318	9,821
3	India	2.46	2.55	10,175	12,687	816	1,447	8,944	11,342
4	Russia	1.60	1.92	173,030	163,773	5,328	3,109	2,300	2,231
5	South Africa	1.38	1.21	41,651	40,341	6,139	5,852	539	443
6	Peru	3.73	3.60	62,534	61,992	10,717	9831	1,293	1,195
7	Mexico	11.38	11.40	6,372	6,342	2,668	1,926	378	675
8	Chile	2.57	2.47	73,416	77,832	17,304	15,432	1,764	2132
9	Spain	10.92	10.11	128,892	134,863	6,573	3,835	617	1,134
10	UK	15.37	15.41	195,768	167,883	4,341	4,345	142	321
11	Sweden	7.27	7.14	67,490	64,737	7,650	7,835	48	57
12	Ecuador	7.18	7.05	11,564	15,359	4,192	3,834	342	321
13	Belgium	15.34	14.92	124,642	102,371	5,512	5,434	28	41
14	Bolivia	3.61	3.24	10,993	10,556	5,101	3,519	71	63
15	Portugal	3.47	3.55	138,648	133,658	4,784	3,788	61	57
16	Netherlands	11.86	12.08	44,587	49,563	3,029	3,536	17	21
17	Romania	5.41	5.44	50,295	44,132	1,983	2,258	293	312
18	Switzerland	5.04	5.77	84,119	101,280	3,885	2,633	22	32
19	Poland	4.05	4.12	52,101	51,523	1,067	1,466	72	102
20	Japan	3.93	3.96	5,022	6,432	195	813	43	29
21	Sudan	6.32	6.16	9	7	250	525	15	12

(Continued)

Table 19.7 Sample of classification of countries based on output variables. (*Continued*)

S. No.	Country	Actual CFR	Predicted CFR	Actual TTMP	Predicted TPMP	Actual CPMP	Predicted CPMP	Actual SC	Predicted SC
22	Bulgaria	3.44	3.52	29,735	6,919	1,257	1,834	34	39
23	Finland	4.47	4.37	56,161	59,470	1,325	1,942	1	3
24	Hungary	13.76	13.60	32,102	38,718	449	1,405	5	14
25	Greece	4.84	4.83	39,420	35,675	385	356	13	25
26	Mali	4.89	4.78	986	16,471	122	212	3	9
27	Slovenia	5.70	5.68	58,816	54,964	939	965	3	13
28	Syria	5.04	5.41	400	789	30	50	4	11
29	Tanzania	4.13	4.15	335	697	9	31	7	22
30	Bahamas	7.19	7.05	6,723	6,554	389	724	1	4
31	Bermuda	5.88	6.10	261,447	287,612	2,457	1,956	2	5
32	Trinidad and Tobago	5.84	5.64	4,337	3,998	98	155	3	11
33	Niger	6.25	6.04	373	279	46	37	3	7
34	Monaco	4.59	4.43	973,329	111,155	2,777	3,579	4	14
35	Barbados	6.67	6.54	33,038	26,644	365	301	7	10
36	China	5.43	5.47	62,814	35,457	58	81	5	15
37	Denmark	4.64	4.72	230,232	108,895	2,289	2,099	3	11
38	Algeria	4.67	4.54	14,819	15,123	526	495	67	81
39	Iran	2.11	2.22	25,882	57,235	3,286	3,112	3583	4121
40	Italy	14.34	14.57	103,182	139,004	4,043	3,765	49	72
41	France	17.26	15.85	42,345	45,833	2,676	3,827	477	567

Table 19.8 shows risk measurement of output variables.

Table 19.8 Risk measurement of output variables.

Variables	Interpretation		
	Low	**Medium**	**High**
CFR	0–3.99	4–6.99	7–20
TPMP	0–10,000	11,000–50,000	≥50,000
CPMP	≤1,000	1,001–4,999	5,000–10,000
SC	0–199	200–999	≥1,000

Based on Table 19.8 values, countries are classified into three levels i.e. low, medium and high respectively. In this study, 180 well known countries are considered for study purpose, but here only few countries are represented due to long size of the table. Thus, some well-known countries are categorized. Sample of Classification of countries based on risk measurement is shown by Table 19.9.

Table 19.9 Sample of classification of countries based on risk measurement.

Case Fertility Rate (CFR)	Tests Per Million Population (TPMP)	Cases Per Million Population (CPMP)	Serious Cases (SC)
France	Bermuda	Chile	USA
UK	UK	USA	India
Belgium	Russia	Peru	Brazil
Italy	USA	Brazil	Iran
Hungary	Italy	Sweden	Russia
Netherlands	Spain	South Africa	Chile
Mexico	Portugal	Belgium	Peru
Spain	Monaco	UK	Spain
Sweden	Denmark	Spain	Mexico
Ecuador	Belgium	Ecuador	France
Bahamas	Switzerland	France	South Africa
Barbados	Chile	Portugal	UK
Sudan	Sweden	Italy	Ecuador
Bermuda	Peru	Monaco	Romania
Niger	Finland	Netherlands	Poland

(*Continued*)

Table 19.9 Sample of classification of countries based on risk measurement. (*Continued*)

Case Fertility Rate (CFR)	Tests Per Million Population (TPMP)	Cases Per Million Population (CPMP)	Serious Cases (SC)
Switzerland	Iran	Bolivia	Algeria
Slovenia	Slovenia	Iran	Italy
Trinidad and Tobago	Poland	Russia	Bolivia
China	Netherlands	Switzerland	Sweden
Romania	France	Romania	Portugal
Syria	Romania	Denmark	Belgium
Greece	South Africa	Bermuda	Bulgaria
Mali	Hungary	Finland	Switzerland
Denmark	Greece	Mexico	Japan
Algeria	China	Bulgaria	Greece
Monaco	Barbados	Poland	Tanzania
Finland	Brazil	India	Netherlands
Tanzania	Mali	Hungary	China
Poland	Ecuador	Slovenia	Hungary
Japan	Algeria	Japan	Monaco
USA	India	Bahamas	Slovenia
Peru	Bolivia	Sudan	Sudan
Brazil	Bulgaria	Algeria	Syria
Portugal	Bahamas	Greece	Trinidad and Tobago
Bulgaria	Japan	Barbados	Denmark
Bolivia	Mexico	Mali	Barbados
India	Trinidad and Tobago	Trinidad and Tobago	Mali
Chile	Syria	China	Niger
Iran	Tanzania	Syria	Bermuda
Russia	Niger	Niger	Bahamas
South Africa	Sudan	Tanzania	Finland
Red Color=Highest Risk Dark Blue Color= Medium Risk Green Color=Low Risk			

Hungry	Ecuador	Bahamas	Sudan	Trinidad and Tobago
Bulgaria	Syria	Tanzania	Niger	Belgium
Canada	Peru	Spain	Romania	Mexico
Greece	Mali	Algeria	Bolivia	Japan
Iran	Finland	Poland	Portugal	France
Monaco	Pakistan	Taiwan	Ireland	Afghanistan
Slovenia	Luxembourg	Greece	Barbados	Turkey
Egypt	Norway	Haiti	Nepal	Panama
UAE	Oman	Kuwait	Benin	Belarus

(High ↑ RISK ↓ Low)

Figure 19.8 Risk wise classification of other well-known countries.

Classification of countries form lowest risk to highest risk based on output variables i.e. CFR, TPMP, CPMP and SC is shown by Table 19.9. Countries France, UK, Belgium, Italy, Netherlands, Mexico, Spain, Sweden, Switzerland, China, Denmark and Poland are classified in high risk category while counties Romania, South Africa, Brazil, Greece, India, Japan and Syria have classified in medium and lowest no. of COVID tests performed. Similarly, Chile, USA, Peru, Portugal Iran, Russia and Belgium have classified in highest no. of COVID cases in cases per million population categories. Countries USA, India, Brazil, Iran, Russia, Chile, Peru and Spain have highest no. of serious COVID patients. Figure 19.8 indicates the rise wise classification of other well-known countries.

In Figure 19.8, some new counties are identified from highest level to lowest level respectively which are Hungry, Ecuador, Bahamas, Sudan, Trinidad and Tobago, Bulgaria, Syria, Tanzania, Niger, Greece, Mali, Algeria, Bolivia, Finland, Monaco, Taiwan, Afghanistan, Slovenia, Luxembourg, Barbados, Turkey, Egypt, Norway, Benin, Panama, Belarus, Oman, etc. If proper strategy and planning are not followed by the government then countries might be interchange their levels in the future i.e. low to high and high to low respectively. In this direction, government should implement the proper lock-down strategy, maintaining social distancing among people, compulsorily allow wearing surgical masks and keeping sanitizer for hand wash, weekly two to three days shutdown in order to prevent COVID-19 outbreak.

19.5   Conclusion and Future Scopes

In these days, world's almost countries have captured by Novel Corona Virus Infection Disease (COVID-19) outbreak and day by day it has become serious problem to the society. Data mining techniques have gained so much popularity in medical science field due to increasing no. of COVID-19 patients day by day over the world. In this direction, four most prominent data mining techniques like Support Vector Machine (SVM), Decision Tree (DT), K-means clustering and Back Propagation Neural Network (BPNN) are applied on COVID-19 dataset. However, performance of proposed techniques is measured based on correctly and incorrectly classified instances as an accuracy measure. The BPNN technique has recorded the highest classification accuracy i.e. 96%.

Based on the SVM results (Table 19.2), we have identified countries based on no. of infected COVID-19 patients which are USA, Portugal, Brazil, India, Mexico, Austria, Columbia, Italy, Ghana, Peru, etc.

In DT results (Tables 19.3 and 19.4), we have found some interesting rules and using rule we have recognized some countries as on risk like UK, China, Spain, Turkey, South Africa, Chile, Germany, Philippines, etc.

Similarly, in clustering results (Table 19.5), three clusters are formed and highly no. of instances classified in attributes like NOC, Death Rate (DR), Recovery Rate (RR) and Old Age People (OAP).

In BPNN results (Tables 19.7 and 19.9), we have predicted Case Fertility Rate (CFR), Tests per Million Population (TPMP), Cases Per Million Population (CPMP) and Serious Cases (SC) as an output parameters and finally, using parameters, we have categorized the countries based on risk level i.e. low, medium and high respectively. Some of well-known countries are identified in these levels are Belgium, France, Netherland, Iran, Russia, Japan, Sweden, Denmark, Poland, Greece, etc.

Apart from it, we have recognized some other new countries as on highest risk like Bahamas, Ecuador, Bulgaria, Syria, Tanzania, Niger, Canada, Romania, Mali, Bolivia, Monaco, Finland, etc.

In the future, countries shown in this study might interchange their levels i.e. low to high and vice-versa, if proper planning and policies would not be adopted by the government of these countries to fight against COVID-19 pandemic.

In this way, government should be come forward and take some preventive actions to stop COVID-19 infections like use inferred camera to maintain social distance, implementing curfew or lock-down rule in a two or four days in a week, compulsorily allow wearing surgical masks and manage automatic sanitizer machine in government offices, schools, colleges and public places to save the life of the millions of people.

This study would be fruitful for medical professionals, government, police staff and businesspersons in order to know the worldwide status of COVID-19 countries as well as helpful for government to manage the automatic sanitizers' machines, surgical masks, hospital beds, enhancing COVID test center and most important medical staff, so that proper strategy would be formed on right time to fight against this serious outbreak.

In the future, some other well-known and popular optimization machine learning techniques like Genetic, Neuro-fuzzy and Fuzzy-clustering will be implemented for better analysis and results.

References

1. Koh, G., Prime recommendation of report of the WHO–China joint mission on Corona Virus Disease 2019 (COVID-19), *F1000—Post-publication Peer Review of the Bio-medical Literature*, https://doi.org/10.3410/f737509210.793572110, 2020.

2. Read, J.M., Bridgen, J.R., Cummings, D.A., Ho, A., Jewell, C.P., Novel Corona Virus (COVID-19): Early estimation of epidemiological parameters and epidemic predictions, *Lancet*, 395, 1225–1228, 2020. https://doi.org/10.1101/2020.01.23.20018549, 2020.

3. Topcuoglu, N., Public health emergency of international concern: Corona virus Disease 2019 (COVID-19). *Open Dent. J.*, 14, 1, 71–72, https://doi.org/10.2174/1874210602014010071, 2020.

4. BBC: Corona virus sharp increase in deaths and cases in Hubei, https://www.bbc.co.uk/news/worldasiachina-51482994, Accessed on 12.05.2020.

5. Li, Q., Guan, X., Wu, P., Wang, X., Zhou, L., Tong, Y., Early transmission dynamics in Wuhan, China, of novel corona virus–infected pneumonia. *N. Engl. J. Med.*, 382, 1199–1207, 2020.

6. Han, J., Pei, J., Kamber, M., *Data mining: Concepts and techniques*, 3rd edition, Elsevier, USA, 2011.

7. Wang, C., Horby, P.W., Hayden, F.G., Gao, G.F., A novel corona virus outbreak of global health concern. *Lancet*, 395, 10223, 470–473, 2020.

8. Al-Turaiki, I., Alshahrani, M., Almutairi, T., Building predictive models for MERS-CoV infections using data mining techniques. *J. Infect. Public Health*, 9, 6, 744–748, 2016.

9. Car, Z., Šegota, S.B., Anđelić, N., Lorencin, I., Mrzljak, V., Modeling the spread of COVID-19 infection using a Multilayer Perceptron. *Hindawi: Comput. Math. Methods Med.*, 1–10, https://doi.org/10.1155/2020/5714714, 2020, 2020.

10. Pinter, G., Felde, I., Mosavi, A., Ghamisi, P., Gloaguen, R., COVID-19 pandemic prediction for Hungary: A hybrid machine learning approach. *Mathematics*, 8, 890–910, 2020.

11. Gomathi, K. and Shanmuga, P., Multi disease prediction using data mining techniques. *Int. J. Syst. Softw. Eng.*, 4, 2, 12–14, 2016.

12. Rustom, F., Reshi, A.A., Mehmood, A., Ullah, S., On, B.W., Aslam, W., Choi, G.S., COVID-19 future forecasting using supervised machine learning models. *IEEE Acess*, 8, 101489–101499, 2020.

13. Santoso, P.H., Fauziah, Nurhayati, Application of data mining classification for COVID-19 infected status using algoritma Naïve Method. *J. Mantik*, 4, 1, 267–275, 2020.

14. Muhammad, L.J., Islam, M.M., Usman, S.S., Ayon, S.I., Predictive data mining models for Novel Coronavirus (COVID-19) infected patients' recovery. *SN Comput. Sci.*, 1, 206, https://doi.org/10.1007/s42979-020-00216-w, 2020.

15. Russo, L., Anastassopoulou, C., Tsakris, A., Bifulco, G.N., Campana, E.F., Toraldo, G., Siettos, C., Tracing day-zero and forecasting the fade out of the COVID-19 outbreak in Lombardy, Italy: A compartmental modelling and numerical optimization approach, MedRxiv, *PLoS ONE, France*, 15, 10, 1–22, 2020.

16. Volpert, V., Banerjee, M., Petrovskii, S., On a quarantine model of corona virus infection and data analysis. *Math. Model. Nat. Phenom.*, 15, 24, 2020.

17. Sujath, R., Chatterjee, J.M., Hassanien, A.E., A machine learning forecasting model for COVID-19 pandemic in India. *Stoch. Environ. Res. Risk Assess.*, 34, 959–972, https://doi.org/10.1007/s00477-020-01827, 2020.

18. Shinde, G.R., Kalamkar, A.B., Mahalle, P.N., Dey, N., Chaki, J., Hassanien, A.E., Forecasting models for Coronavirus Disease (COVID-19): A survey of the state-of-the-art. *SN Comput. Sci.*, 1, 197, https://doi.org/10.1007/s42979-020-00209-9, 2020.

19. Data Source Available on http://www.worldometer.com and http://www.baselab.com, accessed on 22 May 2020.

20. Pujari, A.K., *Data Mining Techniques*, 10th Ed., Universities (India) Press Private Limited, Hyderabad (A.P.), 2006.

21. Cortes, C. and Vapnik, V.N., *The natural of statistical learning theory*, Springer, New York (U.S.A.), 1995.

22. Vapnik, V.N., *Statistical Learning Theory*, Wiley, New York (U.S.A.), 1998.

23. Friedman, H.T., *The Elements of Statistical Learning*, 2nd Ed., Springer Series in Statistics, California (U.S.A.), 2009.
24. Kumari, M. and Godara, S., Comparative study of data mining classification methods in Cardiovascular Disease prediction. *Int. J. Comput. Sci. Technol.*, 6, 304–308, 2011.
25. Yadav, J. and Sharma, M., A review of K-mean algorithm. *Int. J. Eng. Trends Technol. (IJETT)*, 4, 7, 2972–2975, 2013.
26. Bishop, C.M., Pattern recognition and feed-forward networks, in: *The MIT encyclopedia of the cognitive sciences*, vol. 13, No. 2, MIT Press, Cambridge (U.K.), 1999.
27. John, M. and Shaiba, H., Main factors influencing recovery in MERS Co-V patients using machine learning. *J. Infect. Public Health*, 12, 5, 700–704, 2019.
28. Sokolova, M. and Lapalme, G., A systematic analysis of performance measures for classification tasks. *Inf. Process. Manag.*, 45, 4, 427–437, 2009.

Automated Diagnosis of COVID-19 Using Reinforced Lung Segmentation and Classification Model

J. Shiny Duela and T. Illakiya*

SRM Institute of Science and Technology, Ramapuram Campus, Chennai, Tamil Nadu, India

Abstract

COVID-19 is a viral ailment and irresistible sickness brought about by a newfound coronavirus. This is disclosed by reverse transcription - polymerase chain reaction test or through Lung CT (Computed Tomography) imaging. The diagnosis made by a polymerase chain reaction test (PCR) has a lower sensitivity of 65% and above, where even when the patient is infected, test result is negative. To over through the discrepancies found in the values of PCR results, Lung CT imaging technique can be an important imaging modality in assisting the diagnosis of covid 19. This technique produces higher sensitivity, however lower specificity is assumed as a critical job in the determination and remedy of the illness. Predominant positions of the prime patterns found in posterior and peripheral lobe of the asymmetric lungs are difficult to segment and analyse. This difficulty could be addressed by introducing a Reinforced lung segmentation model that retrieves the affected portion which is present at the peripheral lobe of the asymmetric lungs. CT images with viral and Streptococcal pneumonia carries similar patterns such as ground-glass opacities pattern, crazy paving, pleural effusion etc. that are likely to be present in covid infected lungs. An efficient machine learning classification algorithm is chosen to carefully deal with this ambiguity so that successful segregation of covid cases from the other analogous lung diseases is possible. This model is proposed to increase the specificity and exactness of Covid-19 diagnosis from the lung CT image thereby, reducing the flawed prediction. This work facilitates in increasing the possibility of detecting patients infected with COVID-19 accurately, so that they can be quarantined and community spread can be reduced effectively.

Keywords: Lung CT segmentation, genetic algorithm, classification

20.1 Introduction

COVID-19 is a viral disease recognized as severe acute respiratory syndrome coronavirus 2. This can be diagnosed by PCR or through Lung CT (Computed Tomography) imaging. The diagnosis made by a PCR test has a lower sensitivity of 65% and above, where the test could be negative with infected patients. An analysis shows, out of 51 infected cases in China,

---

Corresponding author: illakiya29@gmail.com

Sachi Nandan Mohanty, G. Nalinipriya, Om Prakash Jena and Achyuth Sarkar (eds.) Machine Learning for Healthcare Applications, (309–322) © 2021 Scrivener Publishing LLC

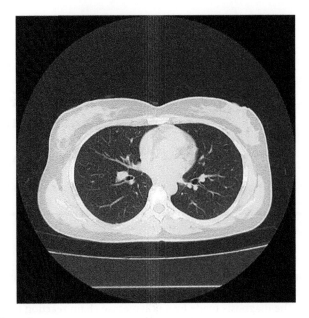

Figure 20.1 Lung CT scan image.

up to 15 cases are tested negative. Another study in United States returned multiple results at different times ranging from 75 to 95%. Further, the waiting time for the test results can take more than a day. To over through the discrepancies found in the values of RT-PCR results, Lung CT imaging technique can be an important imaging modality in assisting the diagnosis of COVID-19. X-beam figured tomography, registered hub tomography (CAT scan), is a clinical imaging strategy that uses PC prepared X-ray to deliver tomographic pictures or cuts of explicit parts of the body. These pictures are utilized for demonstrative and remedial purposes in different clinical orders. Figure 20.1 shows the computed tomography image of a lung.

20.2 Diagnosis of COVID-19

Analysis of lung issue includes 5 fundamental paces: 1. Pre-processing of Lung CT image, 2. Segmentation of Lung CT image, 3. ROI Extraction, 4. Feature derivation and 5. Classification.

20.2.1 Pre-Processing of Lung CT Image

It is a name for activities with images at the most reduced degree of deliberation. These pictures are of a similar kind as the first information caught by the sensor, with an intensity image generally given by a matrix of image function values (brightnesses). The point of pre-handling is an advancement of the image information that smothers reluctant parts or enhances some picture features significant for future preparing, albeit geometric changes of pictures (for example revolution, scaling, interpretation) are classified among processing methods here since comparable methods are utilized [18].

20.2.2   Lung CT Image Segmentation

The first and principal step in image examination is segmentation; in this progression, the organ is distinguished, and its anatomic limits are outlined, either consequently or physically. Mistakes in this part may create bogus data as to ensuing falsy prediction and different other clinical evaluations, so a precise segmentation is needed. This step is hard to accomplish because of the way that lung pathologies present different appearances not the same as the ordinary lung tissue.

20.2.3   ROI Extraction

Regions of interest (ROIs) are specimens inside an information collection distinguished for a specific reason. The principle objective of this progression is to decide the defects in clinical CT images. The imperfect tissues are generally considered as ROIs. The areas except ROIs are expelled from investigations.

20.2.4   Feature Extraction

Clinical images can be recognized by utilizing their shape and surface qualities. Many features including shape and surface descriptors are adjusted for portraying the ROIs. Feature extraction helps in classifying the images thus diagnosing of the lungs becomes easier [13].

20.2.5   Classification

The direction of classification is to decisively foresee the target class for each case in the data. In the underlying pace, classifier is worked by gaining from a learning set comprised of database tuples and their related class name. A few AI classifiers are accessible, for example, k-nearest neighbors classifier, SVM classifier, naive Bayes classifier, stochastic gradient descent classifier on lung CT images affected with cancer, random forest classifier, etc.

20.3   Genetic Algorithm (GA)

GA is an immediate strategy used in exploration and improvement that emulates the advancement of the creatures. They utilize the three fundamental standards of the evolution: reproduction, characteristic determination and enhanced species, kept up by the distinctions of every age with the past. Genetic Algorithm deals with individuals, which represent the solution to a problem. The ideal parent creates the next generation. Each chromosome serves as the solution of a problem. A group of different chromosomes shapes a generation. GA operators similar to selection, crossover and mutation create a new generation. In EA the choice of the optimal individual depends on an assessment of fitness function. The fundamental intention of selection is to incline toward good solution for more complex ones.

20.3.1   Operators of GA

When the initial generation is made, GA utilizes the following steps:

1. Selection Operator: The intention is to offer descent the individual by great fitness values and it is then pass the qualities to the forthcoming population.
2. Crossover Operator: Two individuals are chosen with selection operator are picked arbitrarily to make a totally new individual (offspring). Example— The common crossover methods can be listed as shown below:
   a. Single-Point Crossover
   b. Arithmetic Recombination
   c. Two-Point Crossover
   d. Uniform Crossover
   e. Davis' Order Crossover (OX1).
3. Mutation Operator: The intention is to update the gene in population to keep up the variety in populace to over through the untimely intermingling. For instance: Figure 20.3 shows the operation of mutation.

20.3.2   Applications of GA

Genetic Algorithms (GAs) have demonstrated incredible potential and capacity to take care of complex issues of optimization in various fields. The following list shows some of the applications of GA. Figure 20.2 shows the process of crossover.

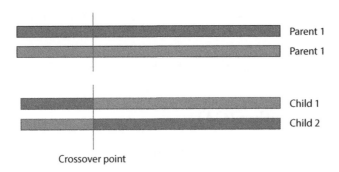

Figure 20.2 Crossover.

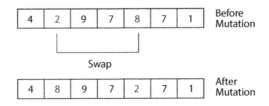

Figure 20.3 Mutation.

i. Optimization—utilized in optimization issues wherein we need to optimize the solution based upon the complications under a given arrangement of imperatives.

ii. Economics—used to portray different monetary models like the cobweb model, game theory equilibrium resolution, and so forth.

iii. Neural Networks—to prepare neural systems, especially recurrent neural systems.

iv. Parallelization—GAs likewise have generally excellent equal capacities, and end up being exceptionally powerful methods in taking care of specific issues, and furthermore give a decent zone to investigate.

v. Image Processing—utilized for different digital image processing (DIP) errands also like thick pixel coordinating.

20.4 Related Works

Numerous analyses have been done, in the goal of enhancing the diagnosis and treatment of lung problems breaking down all ordinary and deficient lung images from CT. This section shows some of the studies done in segmentation of Lung CT and its diagnosis. Elizabeth *et al.* presented a fuzzy classifier that utilizes the type 2 fuzzy logic system (T2FLS) which groups nodules from lung CT diagnosis framework [1]. Feature extraction technique dependent on GA is utilized to enhance the exhibition of false positive decrease the diagnosis of lung nodule in CT [8]. This methodology decides naturally the ideal amount of the features, and picks the pertinent features from an element group. Sanz *et al.* proposed an examination that is done among two strategies: the Work of breathing is determined by expecting groups of resistance R as indicated by generation, etc., while the CGA method gives a severe checking of GA steps so as to lessen vulnerability of outcomes [4]. Hybrid diversification operator developmental approach on tomographic picture recreation algorithm presents another and effective enhancement operator in the advancement to enhance the CT picture by utilizing SA, and law of mutation probability [16,17]. Qureshi *et al.* intended the perception that the convergence of a GA eases back down as it advances [13]. Fuzzy Cognitive Maps is prevailing with another information fuzzification technique for observables and improvement of addition of change work utilizing the transformative training in the development of FCM, results rose had few forecast mistakes in the analyzed information than delivered by the traditional GA methodologies [7]. Karnik and Mendel presented a vigorous fuzzy system, one that can deal with rule vulnerabilities. They utilized T2FLS [9]. The advancement of a fuzzy rationale framework has prompted an activity that we call type-decrease.

It is a feature extraction technique with GA that helps in enhancing the exhibition of false positive decrease in diagnosis. A combination with a classifier dependent with SVM was proposed [15]. So as to maintain a strategic distance from the restrictive running occasions acquired by an unpredictable utilization of math, they utilize the geometric properties of Bezier curves for sifting [10]. After rule-based classification, straight discriminant examination is utilized to additionally lessen the quantity of false positive (FP) objects [12].

An automated lung image segmentation was proposed using Robust Active Shape Model approach. It involves novel ASM matching method and constrained optimal surface finding approach [3]. An automated lung image segmentation was proposed using Contour Shape Model and Bayesian approach for nodule detection [2]. Main advantages are low segmentation errors, suitable for giant shape models, parallel implementation and works well with large shape models but juxtapleural nodules aren't segmented. An ideal strategy for division of lung nodule to distinguish bronchiectasis in lung scan image was proposed [6,14]. From the survey, it was regularly seen that an ideal thresholding is appropriate just in case that where PBR doesn't exist inside the border of the lung parenchyma. Our work is not the same as that talked about inside the literature in that it recreates the edge by utilizing the Bezier curve fitting algorithm.

20.5 Challenges in GA

Certain optimization issues can't be settled by GAs. This is a direct result of inadequately realized fitness functions which create chromosome issues. Because of the GA inheritance, it might be regularly slow in reaching the local optimum in the convergence area. One strategy to tackle this issue is to hybridize GA with other techniques which are able to do tweaking and enhancing the results created by the GA progressively exact and effective.

20.6 Challenges in Lung CT Segmentation

The prime features to be examined in the Lung CT image to confirm the presence of Covid-19 virus include the occurrences of: (a) ground-glass opacities pattern (GGO), (b) consolidation, (c) crazy paving, (d) pleural effusion, (e) Vascular dilatation (f) thoracic lymphadenopathy, (g) emphysema or fibrosis, and (h) Subpleural bands and Architectural distortion. Other irregularity, like cavitation, reticulation, interlobular septal thickening, calcification, and Traction bronchiectasis are also considered. Predominant positions of the above prime patterns found in posterior and peripheral lobe of the asymmetric lungs are difficult to segment and analyze. This difficulty could be addressed by introducing a Reinforced lung segmentation model that retrieves the affected portion which is present at the peripheral lobe of the asymmetric lungs.

20.7 Proposed Diagnosis Framework

The intention is to segment pathology bearing regions around the boundary of the lungs which are unbalanced and shift to a huge degree with their curved zone. By using the reinforced segmentation algorithm, the diseased part of the lung is automatically detected and points are extracted in the unaffected lung CT image. This automated diagnosis and detection is done by the following paces: 1. Pre-processing of image, 2. Segmentation of lung CT image, 3. Region of Interest Extraction, 4. Feature Extraction and 5. Classification. Figure 20.4 depicts the architecture of the diagnosis system.

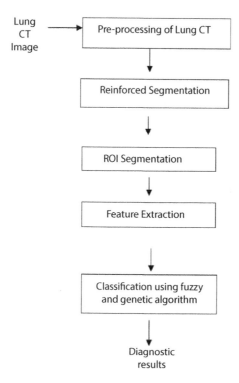

Figure 20.4 Proposed diagnostic system architecture.

20.7.1   Image Pre-Processing

The intention of this step is to upgrade lung CT scan image information with the goal that it smothers undesired mutilations and upgrades picture includes that are significant for diagnosis, for example, improve the appearance of pictures and improve the control of informational collections [19]. 2-D versatile noise expulsion method is utilized to expel the Gaussian commotion. White noise in the CT lung picture is dispensed by a piecewise Wiener filter.

20.7.2   Proposed Image Segmentation Technique

Segmentation of lung CT image is the way toward parceling an analyzed lung picture into different fragments. The point of segmentation is to disentangle and change the portrayal of a picture into progressively significant and simpler to dissect. The segmentation procedure utilized in this work includes the traditional optimal threshold and activities dependent on curved edge of the lung locale [11]. This method identifies the defect locales regardless of whether they are in the edge of the lung CT image.

In the proposed reinforced segmentation algorithm, affected and significant normal CT slice of a patient is taken for consideration. Affected portion of the lung is found by detecting the points. From the normal slice of the patient, extreme left, right, top and bottom points are plotted. The plotted points are extracted from the image and they are imposed into the affected slice of the patient. Thus the PBR's along the periphery of the lungs are segmented. Thereby the exactness of the classification automation gets improved. Figure 20.5 is the original CT slice, Figure 20.6 depicts the proposed segmentation work on the CT slice.

The proposed approach is used to segment the suspected pathological bearing regions along the edges of the lungs even if they are asymmetric.

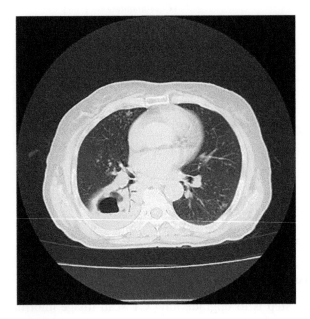

Figure 20.5 Original lung CT image.

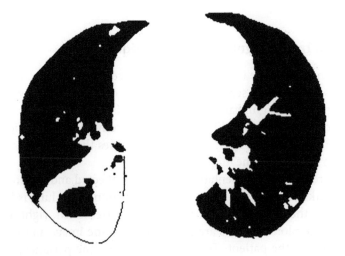

Figure 20.6 Segmentation—Proposed work.

Reinforced Segmentation Algorithm:
INPUT: lung CT image (Affected and Normal slice)
OUTPUT: Reconstructed Edge

i. Read Lung CT image img_aff(m, n) and img_nor (i, j)
ii. Set the value of L1 such that it splits the lungs image, img_aff(m,n) into two portions.
   a. Set $L1 = 0.5 * n$; $L2 = L1 + 1$;
   b. Left_lung = img_aff (m, L1);
   c. Right_lung = img_aff (m, L2);
iii. Find the threshold for the left and right image
   a. Threshold (Left_lung);
   b. Threshold (Right_lung);
iv. Count the black pixels from the left and right image and compare it to find which part has less black pixels. This step helps in determining which part of the lung is mostly affected.
      if(bwcount (Left_lung) < bwcount (right_lung))
      affected = Left
      else
   affected = right
v. Extract the extreme left black pixel, extreme rightmost pixel, topmost pixel and bottom most pixels in the affected lung image and retrieve co-ordinates of those points (p_0) from the image img_nor (i,j).
vi. Read the set of points (p_0), which is a 2D array matrix i.e., $p_0 = p_1, p_2, p_3, \ldots, p_n$
vii. Identify segnum = number of points − 1
   Case 1:
      if count of points <=1
      return error.
   Case 2:
      if count of points = 2 i.e., only straight line is possible.
      if (segnum==1)
      $3p_1 = 2p_0 + p_3$
      $p_2 = 2p_1 - p_0$
   Case 3:
      if number of points>=3 i.e., curve is possible.
      To find start point − $p_{start} = 0.5 * (p_0 + p_1)$
      To find end point − $p_{end} = 0.5 * (p_2 + p_3)$
viii. Impose the points (p_0) into the image img_aff (m, n). A Bezier curve is plotted between the points p_{start} and p_{end} using plot function.
   The CT image of the existing segmentation work is probable of not detecting any flaw in the lung, though it exists. Image segmentation through the proposed work is sure of detecting all the available flaws as this curve fitting algorithm extrapolates its range of analysis and thus it is unambiguous.

20.7.3   ROI Segmentation

ROIs are characterized as areas that has the objects of interest, and an efficient method is used for finding those regions. The key purpose of this phase is to establish the area of interest in the lung CT scan. The ROIs we consider here are problematic cells. ROI extraction is done by Pixel based segmentation.

20.7.4   Feature Extraction

A feature is a prime fragment of knowledge from a lung CT image that offers a comprehensive interpretation of the picture. Consideration is granted to GLCM characteristics such as contrast, correlation, entropy, homogeneity, etc. [6]. These features are used in classification of the particular nodule as affected or not affected.

20.7.5   Modified GA Classifier

Genetic algorithm helps to tune the type II internal fuzzy membership functions.

20.7.5.1   Gaussian Type—II Fuzzy in Classification

Type 2 Membership Function is a subset of a fuzzy set. T2FLSs were first presented by by Karnik and Mendel [9].

'P' is a Fuzzy set and used as,

$$P = \{((s, v), \mu_p (s, u)) \mid \forall s \in S, \forall u \in Js \subseteq [0, 1]\} \tag{20.1}$$

Here P is used by the $\mu_p(s, v)$, here $0 \le \mu_p (s, v) \le 1$. $S = \{s_1, s_2, \ldots s_n\}$,
An upper and a lower MF of a type 2 fuzzy system are stipulated as follows:

$$\mu`P(s) \equiv FOU`(P), \qquad \forall s \in S \tag{20.2}$$

$$\mu``P(s) \equiv FOU``(P), \qquad \forall s \in S. \tag{20.3}$$

The interval type 2 membership function is written as

$$\mu P(s, u) = 1, \qquad \forall u \in Js \subseteq [0, 1] \tag{20.4}$$

GA is used here to tune and overhaul the Gaussian T2MF. To build up the FOU of a IT2FS, the Gaussian characters are considered [5]. The boundary limits of a Gaussian membership function are written as follows.

$$a' = a + k_m \, sd, \; a'' = a - k_m \, sd, \text{ where } k_m \text{ is in the range } [0\text{--}1] \tag{20.5}$$

$$sd' = sd \times k_v, \; sd'' = sd / k_v, \text{ where } k_v \text{ is in the range } [0.3\text{--}1] \tag{20.6}$$

here, k_m and k_v are the limits for footprint of uncertainty, a' and a", sd' and sd" will be the limit furthest reaches of the mean and standard deviation of the IT2MF. Proposed GA used here, enhances the boundaries of the Gaussian T2MF.

20.7.5.2   Classifier Algorithm

Input: Feature Database

Output: Optimal k_m and k_v numbers.

Step 1: Read feature values from the feature database.

Step 2: Identify the number of samples and let it be X. Identify the normal mean and normal standard deviation.

Step 3: Find the Gaussian normal distribution for X using the formula,

$$f(x) = \frac{1}{\sigma\sqrt{2\pi}} e^{-\frac{(x-\mu)^2}{2\sigma^2}}$$

(20.7)

here f(x) is Gaussian normal distribution, σ and μ defines standard deviation and mean.

Step 4: The GA uses the chromosome arbitrary, with k_m in the range [0–1] and k_v in the range [0.3–1].

Step 5: Fitness of each chromosome is assessed.

Step 6: Individuals are selected based on the Roulette wheel selection

Step 7: The crossover is done with an amount of 0.25 followed by the mutation with the amount of 0.1.

Stage 8: Steps (5), (6) and (7) are rehashed till the ending condition is satisfied.

Step 9: The optimal k_m and k_v values are obtained. Find new mean and standard deviation with the values chosen by genetic algorithm.

Step 10: Find normal distribution and membership function. Upper, lower and normal distribution are plotted into the graph using Spline interpolation.

Step 11: Search operator helps in finding the curves does not intersect each other. fnzeros( ) is used here to accomplish this.

Step 12: The curve which correspond to the particular k_m and k_v value is chosen as the optimal k_m and k_v values.

GA gets the k_m and k_v that fulfills the fitness evaluation. The search operator utilizes the spline interpolation to analyze values that crosses the Gaussian curve of a component. The proposed operator recognizes the optimal fuzzy membership functions that make ideal appropriation in T2 FLS. This methodology decreases the untimely premature convergence in GA.

20.8   Result Discussion

The sectioned lung image with defected part is appeared in Figures 20.7 and 20.8. The improved GA utilized in this work is more proficient since it coincide to an ideal outcome

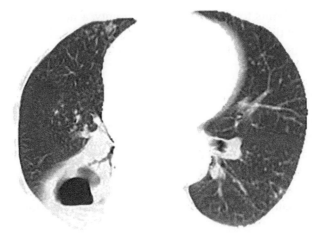

Figure 20.7 Lung CT image—segmented.

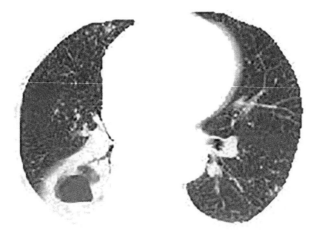

Figure 20.8 ROI segmentation.

inside a sensible measure of cycles paying little mind to the underlying populace size. Table 20.1 shows the ideal k_m and k_v esteems. This helps in getting the optimal Gaussian dissemination curve of a specific component that enhances exactness of the fuzzy classifier. The Reinforced lung segmentation model is developed that retrieves the affected portion which is present at the peripheral part of the asymmetric lung CT image.

Table 20.1 Values of k_m and k_v.

	k_m and k_v of proposed method		k_m and k_v of traditional GA	
Contrast	0.03	0.85	0.53	0.91
Correlation	0.67	0.79	0.55	0.36
Cluster shape	0.84	0.78	0.72	0.92

CT images with viral and Streptococcal pneumonia carries similar patterns such as ground-glass opacities pattern, crazy paving, pleural effusion etc. that are likely to be present COVID infected lungs. This machine learning classification algorithm can deal with this ambiguity so that successful segregation of COVID cases from the other analogous lung diseases is done. This approach increases the specificity and accuracy of COVID-19 diagnosis from the lung CT image thereby, reducing the erroneous prediction.

20.9   Conclusion

COVID-19 global pandemic is changing the life, work and well-being of every individual on this earth. While most businesses and individuals are working hard to survive the immediate crisis, it is expected that testing, treatments and vaccines will eventually allow the world to recover. To bring back the rate of survival, an Automated Diagnosis of COVID-19 using Reinforced Lung Segmentation and Classification Model is proposed to increases the specificity and exactness of COVID-19 diagnosis from the lung CT image thereby, reducing the flawed prediction. This model facilitates the possibility of detecting patients infected with COVID-19, so that they can be quarantined and community spread can be reduced effectively. Herewith, the proposed work, the unambiguous segmentation of computed tomography images could be successfully implemented in real time. Our approach definitely increases the diagnostics accuracy. The conclusion is the impact made on information quality shown by the system. This work elevates the True Positive and decreases the False Positive and False Negative, by that enhancing the accuracy of the existing diagnostic approaches.

References

1. Elizabeth, D.S., Kannan, A., Nehemiah, H.K., Computer-aided diagnosis system for the detection of Bronchiectasis is in chest computed tomography images. *Int. J. Imaging Syst. Technol.*, 19, 4, 290–298, https://doi.org/10.1002/ima.20205, 2009.
2. Chung, H., Ko, S., Jeon, J., Yoon, K., Lee, J., Automatic Lung Segmentation With Juxta-Pleural Nodule Identification Using Active Contour Model and Bayesian Approach. *IEEE J. Transl. Eng. Health Med.*, 6, 1–13, 2018.
3. Sun, S., Bauer, C., Beichel, R., Automated 3-D Segmentation of Lungs With Lung Cancer in CT Data Using a Novel Robust Active Shape Model Approach. *IEEE Trans. Med. Imaging*, 31, 2, 2012.
4. Sanz, J., Fernández, A., Bustince, H., Herrera, F., A genetic tuning to improve the performance of Fuzzy Rule-Based Classification Systems with Interval-Valued Fuzzy Sets: Degree of ignorance and lateral position. *Int. J. Approx. Reason.*, 52, 6, 751–766, https://doi.org/10.1016/j.ijar.2011.01.011, 2011.
5. Hosseini, R., Qanadli, S.D., Barman, S., Mazinani, M., Ellis, T., Dehmeshki, J., An Automatic Approach for Learning and Tuning Gaussian Interval Type-2 Fuzzy Membership Functions Applied to Lung CAD Classification System. *IEEE Trans. Fuzzy Syst.*, 20, 2, 224–234, 2012.
6. Elizabeth, D.S., Nehemiah, K.H., Raj, C.S.R., Kannan, A., A Novel Segmentation Approach for Improving Diagnostic Accuracy of CAD Systems for Detecting Lung

Cancer from Chest Computed Tomography Images. *ACM J.*, 3, 2, 4:1 to 4:16, https://doi.org/10.1145/2184442.2184444, 2012.

7. Papageorgiou, E.I. and Froelich, W., Application of Evolutionary Fuzzy Cognitive Maps for Prediction of Pulmonary Infections. *IEEE Trans. Inf. Technol. Biomed.*, 16, 1, 143–9, 2012.

8. Howarth, P. and Ruger, S.M., Evaluation of texture features for content-based image retrieval. *Proceedings of the 3rd International Conference on Conference on Image and Video Retrieval*, pp. 326–334, 2004.

9. Karnik, N.N. and Mendel, J.M., Introduction to type-2 fuzzy logic systems. *Proceedings of IEEE International Conference on Fuzzy System*, Anchorage, pp. 915–920, 1998.

10. Hanniel, I. and Wein, R., An Exact, Complete and Efficient Computation of Arrangements of Bezier Curves. *IEEE Trans. Autom. Sci. Eng.*, 6, 3, 399–408, 2009.

11. Otsu, A threshold selection method from gray-level histograms. *IEEE Trans. Syst. Man Cybern.*, 9, 62–66, 1979.

12. Ko, J.P. and Betke, M., Chest CT: Automated nodule detection and assessment of change over time—Preliminary experience. *Radiol.*, 218, 1, 267–273, https://doi.org/10.1148/radiology.218.1.r01ja39267, 2003.

13. Qureshi, S.A., Mirza, S.M., Rajpoot, N.M., Arif, M., Hybrid Diversification Operator-Based Evolutionary Approach Towards Tomographic Image Reconstruction. *IEEE Trans. Image Process.*, 20, 1977–1990, 2011.

14. Pu, J., Roos, J., Yi, C.A., Napel, S., Rubin, G.D., Paik, D.S., Adaptive border marching algorithm: automatic lung segmentation on chest CT images. *Comput. Med. Imaging Graph.*, 32, 452–462, 2008.

15. Boroczky, L., Zhao, L., Lee, K.P., Feature Subset Selection for Improving the Performance of False Positive Reduction in Lung Nodule CAD. *IEEE Trans. Biomed. Eng.*, 58, 85–90, 2011.

16. Jiao, L. and Wang, L., A Novel Genetic Algorithm Based on Immunity. *IEEE Trans. Syst. Man Cybern.*, 30, 552–561, 2000.

17. Licheng, and Wang, L., Quantum-Inspired Immune Clonal Algorithm for Global Optimization. *IEEE Trans. Syst. Man Cybern.*, 38, 5, 2008.

18. Itoh, S., Ikeda, M., Arahata, S., Lung cancer screening: Minimum tube current required for helical CT. *Radiology*, 215, 175–183, 2008.

19. Antonelli, M., Lazzerini, B., Marcelloni, F., Segmentation and reconstruction of the lung volume in CT images. *Proceedings of the ACM Symposium on Applied Computing*, pp. 255–259, 2005.

Part 5

CASE STUDIES OF APPLICATION AREAS OF MACHINE LEARNING IN THE HEALTHCARE SYSTEM

Future of Telemedicine with ML: Building a Telemedicine Framework for Lung Sound Detection

Sudhansu Shekhar Patra[1]*, Nitin S. Goje[2], Kamakhya Narain Singh[1], Kaish Q. Khan[1], Deepak Kumar[3], Madhavi[1] and Kumar Ashutosh Sharma[1]

[1]School of Computer Applications, KIIT Deemed to be University, Bhubaneswar, India
[2]IT Department, Faculty of Science, Tishk International University, Erbil, Iraq
[3]Department of Computer Applications, IFTM University, Moradabad, India

Abstract

Telemedicine is the supplementary service in the field of medical science related to medical information sharing tool. With the advancements and popularity of machine learning (ML) in several fields of the society, the study in the field of medicine has also geared up and researchers are working in the area of telemedicine to improve its capabilities and procedures to solve specific problems. The combination of ML and telemedicine will give the endless possibilities in the healthcare industry. The goal of this chapter is to construct a framework by examining the lung sound to predict respiratory issues. The proposed framework is trained through ensemble techniques. The experimental analysis shows the performance of the modified bootstrap aggregation is better than the ADA, XG and gradient boosting. The accuracy of the improved bootstrap aggregation is 99.02% and the framework of telemedicine is implemented with improved bootstrap aggregation.

Keywords: Telemedicine, machine learning, lung sound detection, ensemble learning

21.1 Introduction

Telemedicine is a mechanism [1] component of E-health through which the provider and the patient are connected to each other and it uses the information and communication technology (ICT) for delivering the healthcare services [2] and helps to overcome distances and is able facilitate the rural population where they can take the service from urban area. Tele-health isn't just for patient and treatment, but also shares knowledge and information about the equipment. The benefit of telemedicine is the ability to bypass the technique of traditional doctor's office visit. Instead of waiting for many hours in provider's office the acute patients can take the service of telemedicine from anywhere and whenever required. In the current scenario of COVID-19 pandemic the use of this mechanism is increasing day

---

**Corresponding author*: sudhanshupatra@gmail.com

Sachi Nandan Mohanty, G. Nalinipriya, Om Prakash Jena and Achyuth Sarkar (eds.) *Machine Learning for Healthcare Applications*, (325–342) © 2021 Scrivener Publishing LLC

by day as many patients are depending on telemedicine because of lock down and lack of availability of doctors because of their engagement to cure COVID patients.

For tele-consultation and for tele-education [3,4] telemedicine helps for effective delivery of medical care to suspected groups, remote people and the aging population. Remote follow-up and monitoring can also be successfully carried out through telemedicine [5]. But there must be an active ecosystem required that should comprise of care providers, patients, involvement of information technology and participating hospitals for the successful implementation of telemedicine mechanism. Proactive telemedicine governance and the machine learning techniques [6] build an efficient and effective healthcare delivery system and management system that improves the quality of healthcare. The areas in which the machine learning technique is helpful for providing services are as follows.

21.1.1 Monitoring the Remote Patient

These software are currently used for patient monitoring. They have been upgraded to a level where they simulate the in-person interface between the doctor and the patients. In the future, the need for direct meetings will reduce between them as advanced AI will help in monitoring the patient health conditions in their homes. Progresses in robotics and AI are going to evaluate the health criticality of patients without external aid.

21.1.2 Intelligent Assistance for Patient Diagnosis

Present-day technology helps the patients in monitoring vitals like blood pressure, heart rate and breathing. Many start-up companies use AI to filter and allot the patients so that practitioners can swiftly and competently form a diagnosis, and prescribe any needed medications from a remote telemedicine center [7]. AI collects data from a patient who is in the route for the emergency treatment helps in providing an initial treatment in the way, instead of reaching to the hospital emergency room.

21.1.3 Fasten Electronic Health Record Retrieval Process

The Annals of Internal Medicine study tells, that around 50% of a physician's time is spent working on electronic health records (EHR). But the growth in big data analytics and deep learning makes the EHR retrieval and analysis much faster. One system communicates through chat and collects patient data and stores it which is immediately retrievable. Another application with a biometric press on a smart phone yields a person's vital signs such as blood pressure and sends to cloud.

21.1.4 Collaboration Increases Among Healthcare Practitioners

The advancements in telemedicine will encourage the collaboration among health practitioners, and AYUSH doctor can conduct joint diagnosis in critical circumstances. Advances in ML will bring growth in medicine and all research and the findings will be more accessible to the medical practitioners. Big data analytics will bring a revolution in the field of pharmaceutical research by using pattern recognition [8].

There has been various research in the area of telemedicine for respiratory issues as this was the disease which was the fourth common reason for death rates is the world's and now the first common reason for death after COVID-19 pandemic. Recognizing the lung sounds and its analysis is the most crucial factor of pulmonary medical issues. Auscultation is the technique to classify and medicate a patient with the help of a stethoscope. For auscultation there is a need for medical expert and its practice also differs between medical practitioners. So there is need for computerized framework using ML for investigating the lung sound.

Lung sounds are of two types: regular and irregular breathing. When there is no lung disease the lung sound is normal and whenever there is a lung disease there is an irregular sound in the lung. The normal sound is not noticeable but the irregular sound is continuous. This chapter uses 3 ML algorithms to study the 7 types of respiratory sounds. Out of the 7 classes one is regular and the other 6 are irregular sounds.

The remaining chapter is organized as follows. Section 21.2 describes the different research work in adoption of ML techniques in telemedicine and lung sounds with different algorithms, Section 21.3 describes the strategic model for telemedicine, Section 21.4 proposes the methodology. Section 21.5 describes the experimental results and finally Section 21.6 concludes the chapter.

21.2 Related Work

Hayter *et al.* [9] have studied about Telemedicine infrastructure in 2015. They have designed an infrastructure for transferring video and voice data over LAN. Hwang *et al.* [10] have given a detailed study and methodology for medical data communication; the methodology was data centric. Wavelet transformation is used for data transformation. A compression for data technique is suggested by Ahmed *et al.* [11] for EEG data operation. Zajtchuk and Gilbert [12] have suggested the role of Telemedicine for modern day diseases and consultation. There are many research works that have been done in the area of detection of lung-sound detection and classification. Mondal *et al.* [13] have published an article for the feature extraction for pulmonary disorders. In this research, the correlation between the statistical features and the features has been studied and the differentiated lung sounds are identified. The features extracted are being evaluated by various supervised learning algorithms such as SVM, ANN and GMM (Gaussian mixture model).

Sengupta *et al.* [14] have published an article to extract the feature and develop a method for categorizing the lung sound disorder. The main aim of that study was accomplishing the features in the analyzing for the speech signal. The result of the experimental study shows the features they got from cepstral coefficient of mel-frequency (MFCC) gives better performance than wavelet transform and also from typical cepstral coefficient.

Chen *et al.* [15] suggested a system which helps the practitioners to predict the abnormal lung signals. They used MFCC to get the attributes from the signals of the lung sound. They used the K-means clustering to minimize the volume of information used in computation. In this they also used KNN method to categorize the sound. There are other literatures in this area where the researchers have used semi-supervised DL technique to differentiate the lung sounds. With a smart phone application they have collected the samples and by applying the SSDL method they achieve ROC of 87%. Tsallis entropy measure has also been used to identify the crack sounds. The simplified version of Boltzmann–Gibbs entropy is the

Tsallis entropy used for measuring lung sound and measures the crack sounds. This method delivers an accuracy of 95.5% with MLP along with 3-fold cross validation. The benefit is less computation required in this technique.

21.3   Strategic Model for Telemedicine

This model is a binary integer programming model that uses binary integer programming for the delivery system of telemedicine healthcare. The population staying in rural area $p \in N$, need of various health facilities $s \in S$. The intent of this model is to build adequate centers to get telemedicine services for any disease may be for lung disease by connecting them using communication links to currently running hospitals $h \in H$; and to equip a center with the offerings. The aim of the model is to cover the annual healthcare needs of the patients i.e., V_{ps} can be met. The model depends on various factors. The first is the healthcare functional cost. The binary decision variables y_k discover locations $k \in N$ of the telemedicine centers in the network, F_k is the fund required annually to operate them. The other cost δ_e is the cost incurred to purchase the telemedicine equipment $e \in E$ and the cost of building the data and the telecommunication channels $l \in L$ between the hospital of the patient's region and the health center k. The various other parameters which also affect the model are depicted as follows:

Notations	Meaning
A	Population of the region where telemedicine center has to set up
B	Nearby existing Hospital locations which may be joined to the network
C	Health services going to be given by the telemedicine center
D	Different categories of communication links
F_k	The cost incurred in opening a telemedicine centre at location k
W_{min}	The least number of patients must visit to the telemedicine center
D_{max}	The maximum distance a patient has to travel to reach to the center
V_{ps}	Probable visits/year from group of people p for services
A_{hs}	The accessibility of the service s at the hospital h
C_{ph}	The cost incurred for travelling from group of people in the population p to the hospital h
C_{pk}	The cost of traveling group of people p to telemedicine center k
D_{pk}	The distance of group of people in the population p to the telemedicine center k
T_{ph}	The cost incurred when a patient goes from population p to hospital h
α	opted choice in between hospital or telemedicine center
B_s	Required bandwidth required to get service s
B_l	Bandwidth capability of the communicating link l
d^l	Development cost of communicating link l
y_k	equals 1 if telemedicine center is operated at location k; else 0

a_{hs}^{p}	equals 1 if patient from location p gets health facility s from health center k; else 0
b_{hs}^{p}	equals 1 if patient from group of people p gets facility s from hospital h; else 0
w_{hk}^{l}	equals 1 if there is a communication link between hospital h and the healthcare center k; else 0
r_{hk}^{ls}	equals 1 if service between hospital h and healthcare center k uses link l; else 0
q_{ek}	equals 1 if eth equipment or the instrument is being used in health center k; else 0

Minimize,

$$\sum_{k \in N} F_K y_K + \sum_{l \in D} \sum_{h \in B} \sum_{k \in A} d^l w_{hk}^l + \sum_{k \in A} \sum_{e \in E} \delta_e q_{ek}$$
$$+ \sum_{k \in A} \sum_{e \in E} V_{ps} \left[\sum_{k \in A} C_{pK} a_{Ks}^p + \sum_{h \in B} \alpha(c_{ph} + T_{ph}) b_{hs}^p \right] \qquad (21.1)$$

Constraints are:

$$\sum_{k \in A} a_{ks}^p + \sum_{h \in B} A_{hs} b_{hs}^p = 1 \quad \forall p \in A, s \in C \qquad (21.2)$$

$$\sum_{p \in A} \sum_{s \in C} a_{ks}^p \leq |A||C| y_k; \forall k \in A \qquad (21.3)$$

$$\sum_{p \in A} \sum_{s \in C} a_{ks}^p \leq 1 - y_m; \forall k, m \in A \,|\, D_{pm} < D_{pk} \qquad (21.4)$$

$$\sum_{k \in A} D_{pk} a_{ks}^p \leq D_{max}; \forall p \in A, s \in C \qquad (21.5)$$

$$\sum_{p \in A} \sum_{s \in C} V_{ps} a_{ks}^p \geq W_{min} y_k; \forall k \in A \qquad (21.6)$$

$$\sum_{l \in D} \sum_{h \in B} r_{hk}^{ls} \leq y_k; \forall k \in N, s \in S \qquad (21.7)$$

$$\sum_{l \in D} \sum_{h \in B} A_{hs} B_l r_{hk}^{ls} \geq \beta_s y_k; \forall k \in A, s \in C \tag{21.8}$$

$$\sum_{s \in c} B_s r_{hk}^{ls} y_k \leq B_l; \forall k \in A, h \in B, l \in D \tag{21.9}$$

$$\sum_{s \in c} r_{hk}^{ls} \leq |C| w_{hk}^l; \forall k \in A, h \in B, l \in D \tag{21.10}$$

$$\sum_{p \in A} \sum_{s \in C} \eta_{es} a_{ks}^p \leq |A||C| q_{ek}; \forall k \in A, e \in E \tag{21.11}$$

$$a_{ks}^p, y_k, b_{hs}^p, r_{hk}^{ls}, w_{hk}^l, q_{ek} \in \{0,1\}; \forall k \in A, h \in B, p \in A, e \in E, l \in D \tag{21.12}$$

The goal of the telemedicine network is to minimize the total cost incurred which is depicted in Equation (21.1). In the equation the first part shows the cost incurred in opening the network. The second part shows the cost incurred in the setting up data communication link. The third part shows the installation as well as the procurement of the equipment in the telemedicine centers. The fourth part shows the travel cost of the patients. The model presented is used to develop strategic plans to establish the telemedicine networks for healthcare.

21.4   Framework for Lung Sound Detection in Telemedicine

The proposed framework has 4 stages:

1. Method to collect the Lung sound collection
2. Signal interpolation
3. Characteristics extraction
4. Classification.

Figure 21.1 shows the framework of the lung sound classification system. In the preprocessing stage the signals are de-noised and remove artefacts and heartbeats. In the extraction stage the most significant features are extracted. The features extracted can be passed to modified RF and other ensemble learning techniques to classify different sounds generated from the normal or abnormal lung.

21.4.1   Data Collection

The data collected in this study is from R.A.I.E [13]. It contains all the information of the lung sound such as the signal type, age, status, abnormalities type, length of the signal.

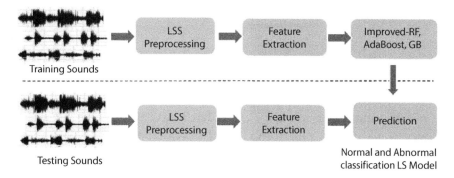

Figure 21.1 Stages for lung sound prediction.

It was mainly created for healthcare experts, doctors, students, researchers. The database contains around 50 samples collected from different age group of people.

21.4.2 Pre-Processing of Data

This step converts the raw data into prepared data. In this phase the data is separated into non-overlapping segments and then transferred to feature extraction phase to get the required features. The handling of null values, handling of categorical variables, one-hot encoding, standardization, multicollinearity are different steps involved in the pre-processing stage.

21.4.3 Feature Extraction

Feature extraction is an important work for recognizing the pattern for lung sound. The process involves in throwing off the unnecessary information and only considers the most effective signal features and creates a lower dimensional pattern feature vectors required for classification. But using the conventional method it is not possible to extract the feature, so MFCC and wavelet transform is considered in this chapter to extract.

21.4.3.1   MFCC

MFCC is a well-known technique to extract features from different applications including speech and sounds. It has the following phases:

Phase 1: Split the sound signals into various segments having a 50% intersection among the adjacent edges by using the Hamming window. A segment is denoted as $\{h(n)\}_{n=1}^{R}$ where R is the number of records in each segment.

Phase 2: Using N-pt Fourier transformation computer the energy of the windowed waveform of the sound signal.

$$E_i(k) = \sum_{t=1}^{R} e_i(t)h(n)e^{-j2\pi t/N}, k \in [1, K] \qquad (21.13)$$

Phase 3:

$$\rho(a) = \sum_{q=1}^{N} |S_i(q)|^2 \, X\varphi_i(q), a \in [1, R] \qquad (21.14)$$

Here ρ is the band pass, is triangular and ordered consistently in the mel-scale of filter group $S_i(q)$ is the sum of the energy band and the $\varphi_i(q)$ is the filter report.
Phase 4: The MFCC M_q is the discrete cosine transformation followed by a log and can be written as:

$$M_q = (2/R)^{1/2} \sum_{q=0}^{R-1} \cos\left[\tau.\left(\frac{2q-1}{2}\right)\frac{\pi}{R}\right].\log[\rho(q+1)] \qquad (21.15)$$

Here $\tau \in [1, T-1]$ where T is the predicted cepstral attributes.

21.4.3.2   Lung Sounds Using Multi Resolution DWT

Multi-resolution analytics (MRA) of wavelet is the most applicable method for analyzing the lung sounds that are non-stationary in nature.

21.4.3.2.1   DWT
From the definition of MRA

$$T_0 = T_1 \oplus W_1 = T_2 \oplus W_2 \oplus W_1 = T_3 \oplus W_3 \oplus W_2 \oplus W_1 = \wedge \qquad (21.16)$$

Here T_1 is the scale space and W_1 is the wavelet space, decompose T_1 to further approximation T_2 and wavelet space W_2. We have to repeat the process until all the approximations and details are not achieved at all arbitrary scales.
So we can mention any real function $r(t) \in T_0$ can be decomposed as

$$s_{j,k} = < r(t), \phi_{j,k}(t) >, \quad c_{j,k} = < r(t), \psi_{j,k}(t) > \qquad (21.17)$$

Here j is called the scale factor
k is the shift operator
$s_{j,k}$ is the approx. or scaling coefficients of space T_j
$\phi(t)$ is the scaling function
$\psi(t)$ is the wavelength function

For the arbitrary discrete sequence $x(n) \in T_0$ (n=[0,N], where N is the sequence length). Let $a_{0,k}$=x(n) be decomposed, then

$$s_{j+1,k} = \sum_{m} p(h-2k)s_{j,m}, \, c_{j+1,k} = q(h-2k)s_{j,m} \qquad (21.18)$$

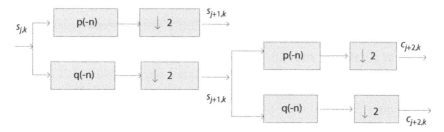

Figure 21.2 The circuit structure of the decomposition.

Here h = 2k + n

p(n) and q(n) are the low pass high pass filters coefficient respectively. p(n)'s mirror version is q(n).

Equation (21.18) shows that $s_{j+1,k}$ and $c_{j+1,k}$ in $T_{j+1,k}$ is derived respectively using the weighted sum of the $s_{j,k}$ in T_j through p(n) and q(n). Continue the decomposition procedure between $s_{j+1,k}$ and $c_{j+1,k}$ to get half the original signal iteratively until the p(n) and q(n) are becoming the same. The circuit structure of the decomposition is shown in Figure 21.2.

21.4.3.2.2   MRA

Selecting an appropriate wavelet and the number of iterations for the decomposition is very crucial in feature extraction. For 1-D lung sound signal, a smoother wavelet has to be selected. db4 is an appropriate one and can be selected. The features such as MOAV (mean of the absolute values), Mean, std. deviation and RAMV (ratio of absolute mean values) were used for time Vs frequency distribution of the lung sound signals. The db4 has been selected out of the four other kinds of wavelets coif4, db2, db12 and sym10. The performance of five wavelets with modified Random forest classifier for LSS datasets is shown in the following Table 21.1.

Table 21.1 Performance measures of different wavelet by Modified-Random Forest classifier.

Performance Parameter	db2	db4	Sym10	Coif4	db8
F-Measure	0.9761	0.9912	0.9682	0.9292	0.9825
PPV	0.9915	0.9957	0.9726	0,9356	0.9901
NPV	0.9657	0.9836	0.9547	0.9322	0.9725
Sensitivity	0.9752	0.9856	0.9626	0.9546	0.9768
Specificity	0.9875	0.9935	0.9653	0.9363	0.9867
Accuracy	98.1%	99.01%	96.42%	93.8%	98.12%

21.4.4   Classification

The extracted features are implemented by random forest and two other ensemble learning classifiers such as AdaBoost and GB. Ensemble learning is the combination of multiple models. Bagging and Boosting are the two techniques. Bagging is Bootstrap aggregation. Random Forest is one type of Bagging. Boosting AdaBoosting, GB, XG are the types of Boosting techniques. Decision tree [6] has two properties and they are low bias and high variance. Low bias says if we build the decision tree to its complete depth it will be properly trained for a training dataset and the training error is very less. High variance says that whenever we have our new test data, they prone to give larger amount of errors. In short we can say if we build a decision tree to its complete depth it leads to over fitting. Random forests (RF) is a popular tree-based ensemble machine learning tool that is highly data adaptive, which has low bias and low variance, uses multiple decision trees, combines them and predicts with respect to majority vote converts the decision tree feature of high variance to low variance and is able to account for correlation along with the interactions among the features. This makes RF particularly appealing for high-dimensional data analysis. Due to the strong robustness of the algorithm with respect to large feature sets, the technique shows good accuracy in its result in comparison to other ensemble-based classifiers. The methods implemented here are the potential to reduce the dimensionality of the training step.

21.4.4.1   Correlation Coefficient for Feature Selection (CFS)

The filter method checks the relevancy of the attributes which checks how much relevant is it to use in the training phase. IG, Chi-square and correlation coefficients are the measures for filtering the attributes of the dataset. The new random forest technique has been associated with CFS for the removal of non-associated attributes in the dataset.

21.4.4.2   Symmetrical Uncertainty

SU is a method for feature evaluator. It can be applicable for designing the Modified-RFC because it gives the symmetrical measure of correlation attributes and balances the bias of common information.

It is denoted as SU and can be defined as the ratio between the $Info_{gain}$ and En of two attributes a and b.

$$SU(a,b) = 2 * Info_{gain}(a|b) / [En(a) + En(b)]$$

Here $Info_{gain}$ is described as

$$Info_{gain}(a|b) = En(a) + En(b) - En(a,b)$$

Where En(a) denote the entropy and En(a,b) denote the joint entropy.

21.4.4.3   Gain Ratio

The information gain is the decrease in entropy after the dataset is split on an attributes. While constructing a decision tree we find out an attribute that gives maximum information gain or decrease in entropy. In decision tree gain ratio is the ration between information gain and intrinsic information.

$$GR(X, D_i) = [En(X) - En(X \mid D_i)] / En(D_i)$$

Here E(X) denotes entropy of decision and $En(X \mid D_i)$ denotes the entropy of decision with D_i.

The algorithm of the model modified RF model is as follows:

Algorithm 1: Modified-RFC
Input: D_{Train}: The training dataset i.e.,$\{x_1, x_2, \ldots x_n\}$
Output: classification accuracy

1. Select the attribute evaluator method and apply on EEG dataset and generate subset of attributes.
2. Apply illustration filter-Resample computation for subset of attributes for the EEG dataset and receive the EEG-Resample.
3. Select RF classification algorithm on EEG dataset resample to get the expected accuracy of the classification as Accuracy
4. Return classification_accuracy as Accuracy

21.4.4.4   Modified RF Classification Architecture

Figure 21.3 shows the architectural design of modified-RFC. The modified- RFC method selects the multi-class EEG dataset for classification. Feature evaluator method using CFS, SU and Gain Ration is considered and utilized on the training dataset to get the requisite features (line 1 of algorithm) for classification. After the application of feature evaluator, for the balance of class distributions in line 2 of algorithm illustration filter-resample is employed. In line 3 of the algorithm RF classification algorithm on EEG dataset is applied on the result obtained in line 2 of the algorithm. Line 4 finds the accuracy of the algorithm.

21.5   Experimental Analysis

Python is used for the analysis of the above algorithm for LSS. Intel i5 processors with 8 GB RAM is being used for classification. Scikit-learn library was used for accessing the pulmonary pathology classification. The modified RF classification algorithm is compared with the other classifiers such as AdaBoost and GB classifier and the matrices being used for the study of the effectiveness classifier are ACC (General Accuracy), SE (sensitivity),

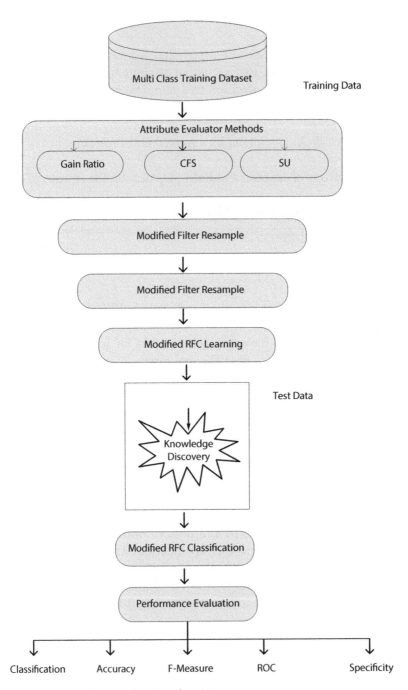

Figure 21.3 Modified random forest architecture for LSS.

SP (specificity), PPV (positive predictive value), NPV (negative predictive value) and FM (F-Measure). Every measure gives 4 possible results, TPV, FPV, TNV and FNV.

$$SE = \frac{TPV}{TPV + FNV}$$

$$SP = \frac{TPV}{FPV + TNV}$$

$$PPV = \frac{TPV}{FPV + TPV}$$

$$NPV = \frac{TNV}{FNV + TNV}$$

$$F\text{-Measure} = \frac{(2*PPV*SE)}{(PPV + SE)}$$

$$ACC = \frac{TPV + TNV}{TPV + FPV + FNV + TNV} * 100$$

Where TPV = True Positive Value
FPV = False Positive Value
FNV = False Negative Value
TNV = True Negative Value.

In the experiment we have taken 80% data as the training data and rest 20% is the testing ratio. The comparison of accuracies for proposed modified RF classification algorithm with AdaBoost and GB classifier are shown in Table 21.2. The symbols used in the tables are N, MW, SC, FC, SQ, PW and ST are Normal, Monophonic wheeze, Coarse crackle, Squawk, polyphonic wheeze, Fine crackle and stridor. Table 21.2 shows that the classification accuracy in each case using modified RF algorithm with db4 feature extraction is better in terms of confusion matrix as compared to the other algorithms. Table 21.3 shows the comparison of accuracy of db4 feature extraction with different classifiers for LSS dataset and Table 21.4 shows comparison of accuracy of MFCC feature extraction with different classifiers for LSS dataset.

Table 21.2 Accuracy comparison with db4 feature extraction using modified RF algorithm.

Classifiers	Predicted Output	Actual Output							Class accuracy
		N	CC	PW	ST	FC	MW	SQ	
Modified RF	N	984	2	0	1	0	0	1	99.56%
	ST	1	1	0	85	0	0	0	97.67%
	SQ	0	0	0	0	1	0	87	98.82%
	CC	2	140	0	2	0	0	0	97.23%
	FC	1	1	0	0	125	0	0	98.41%
	MW	0	0	1	0	2	169	0	98.2%
	PW	0	0	171	0	0	0	1	99.42%
AdaBoost	N	964	11	7	3	1	1	2	97.56%
	ST	1	1	0	85	0	1	0	96.65%
	SQ	0	1	0	0	1	0	87	94.82%
	CC	5	140	0	1	0	1	1	94.23%
	FC	1	2	0	1	125	0	1	96.01%
	MW	2	0	2	2	2	169	1	95.12%
	PW	3	2	171	0	4	2	1	96.42%
GB Classifier	N	943	23	9	4	2	2	5	95.46%
	ST	1	0	1	82	0	0	0	94.65%
	SQ	0	1	2	0	1	0	83	96.82%
	CC	2	135	0	2	0	3	0	93.73%
	FC	1	1	0	0	122	1	0	94.61%
	MW	2	2	1	0	2	163	0	96.25%
	PW	3	0	169	0	0	2	1	95.41%

Figure 21.4 shows the various performance with db4 and MFCC feature extraction of the classification Modified-RF, AdaBoost, GB classification algorithms with LSS. The comparative analysis shows that the proposed db4 RF is performed well as compared to the other classification algorithms having MFCC feature extraction. Figure 21.5 shows the performance of the Modified-RF, AdaBoost, GB classification algorithms with db4 and MFCC feature extraction.

Table 21.3 Comparison of accuracy of db4 feature extraction with different classifiers for LSS dataset.

Parameter Measure	Modified-RF	AdaBoost	GB
Accuracy	99.03%	96.62%	95.12%
F-Measure	0.9913	0.9787	0.9557
Sensitivity	0.9875	0.9656	0.9585
Specificity	0.9956	0.9657	0.9461
NPV	0.9825	0.9525	0.9453
PPV	0.9972	0.9734	0.9524

Table 21.4 Comparison of accuracy of MFCC feature extraction with different classifiers for LSS dataset.

Parameter Measure	Modified-RF	AdaBoost	GB
Accuracy	98.74%	96.38%	94.72%
F-Measure	0.9883	0.9771	0.9524
Sensitivity	0.9834	0.9621	0.9525
Specificity	09923	0.9624	0.9356
NPV	0.9787	0.9545	0.9436
PPV	0.9935	0.9746	0.9574

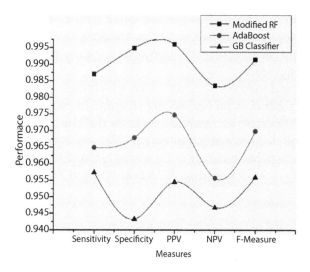

Figure 21.4 Various performance measures with db4 and MFCC feature extraction of the classification Modified-RF, AdaBoost, GB classification algorithms.

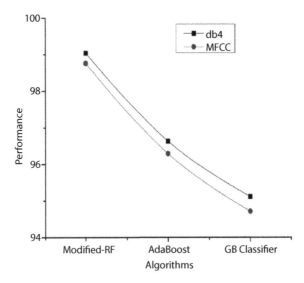

Figure 21.5 Performance of the Modified-RF, AdaBoost, GB classification algorithms with db4 and MFCC feature extraction.

21.6   Conclusion

Telemedicine is emerging as a tool to give health aid to the residents of the rural and inaccessible areas without access to the doctors and the practitioners who are mostly based in urban settlements. The telemedicine health centres can help them connect with the doctors those are in urban areas. Now in the pandemic this is a best tool to help the patients during the period of lock down and shut down.

The current clinical challenges surrounding Lung Disease can be met with the telemedicine device integrated into the computer-aided devices. Lung disease is a primary disease and should be attended to properly. Lung sound signal techniques are useful if we are able to classify different categories of signals as well as straight-forward. Acoustic signals generated through the lung at the time of inspiration and expiration generate useful information for the study of the lung's status.

Though the traditional method of classification which uses wavelet-based method and MFCC are satisfactory but cepstral features are computationally faster and take less computational overhead. The result we received concludes that the telemedicine model of prototype gives an efficient diagnosis of pulmonary problems using LSS with cepstral features and modified RF classifier. The accuracy of the model is found to be 99.03%. The execution time is also less than that of GB Boosting, ADA Boosting and XG algorithms.

References

1. World Health Organisation, *A health telematics policy in support of WHO's Health-For-All strategy for global health development: Report of the WHO group consultation on health telematics, 11–16 December, Geneva, 1997*, World Health Organization, Geneva, 1998.

2. Ajami, S. and Lamoochi, P., Use of telemedicine in disaster and remote places. *J. Educ. Health Promot.*, 3, 26, 2014, [PMC free article] [PubMed] [Google Scholar].

3. McLean, S., Protti, D., Sheikh, A., Telehealthcare for long term conditions. *Bmj.*, 342, d120, 2011, [PubMed] [Google Scholar].

4. World Health Organization, *Telemedicine, Opportunities and developments in member states. Report on the second global survey on eHealth*, World Health Organization, Geneva, 2010.

5. Wilson, L.S. and Maeder, A.J., Recent directions in telemedicine: review of trends in research and practice. *Healthc. Inform. Res.*, 21, 4, 213–222, 2015.

6. Russell, S. and Norvig, P., *Artificial intelligence—A modern approach*, Prentice-Hall, New Jersey, 1995.

7. Pacis, D.M.M., Subido, E.D., Jr., Bugtai, N.T., Trends in telemedicine utilizing artificial intelligence, in: *AIP Conference Proceedings*, vol. 1933, No. 1, AIP Publishing LLC, p. 040009, 2018.

8. Peterson, M.C., Holbrook, J.H., Von Hales, D., Smith, N.L., Staker, L.V., Contributions of the history, physical examination, and laboratory investigation in making medical diagnoses. *West. J. Med.*, 156, 2, 163, 1992.

9. Hayter, G., McGarraugh, G.V., Naegeli, A.H., Mazza, J.C., Feldman, B.J., U.S. Patent No. 7,768,386, U.S. Patent and Trademark Office, Washington, DC, 2010.

10. Hwang, W.J., Chine, C.F., Li, K.J., Scalable medical data compression and transmission using wavelet transform for telemedicine applications. *IEEE Trans. Inf. Technol. Biomed.*, 7, 1, 54–63, 2003.

11. Ahmed, S.T., Sandhya, M., Sankar, S., An optimized RTSRV machine learning algorithm for biomedical signal transmission and regeneration for telemedicine environment. *Procedia Comput. Sci.*, 152, 140–149, 2019.

12. Zajtchuk, R. and Gilbert, G.R., Telemedicine: A new dimension in the practice of medicine. *Dis. Mon.*, 45, 6, 197–262, 1999.

13. Shi, Y., Li, Y., Cai, M., Zhang, X.D., A Lung Sound Category Recognition Method Based on Wavelet Decomposition and BP Neural Network. *Int. J. Biol. Sci.*, 15, 1, 195–207, 2019.

14. Sengupta, N., Sahidullah, M., Saha, G., Lung sound classification using cepstral-based statistical features. *Comput. Biol. Med.*, 75, 118–129, 2016.

15. Chen, C.H., Huang, W.T., Tan, T.H., Chang, C.C., Chang, Y.J., Using k-nearest neighbor classification to diagnose abnormal lung sounds. *Sensors*, 15, 6, 13132–13158, 2015.

A Lightweight Convolutional Neural Network Model for Tuberculosis Bacilli Detection From Microscopic Sputum Smear Images

Rani Oomman Panicker[1]*, S.J. Pawan[2], Jeny Rajan[2] and M.K. Sabu[1]

[1]Department of Computer Applications, Cochin University of Science and Technology, Kochi, India
[2]Department of Computer Science and Engineering, National Institute of Technology Karnataka, Surathkal, India

Abstract

This chapter describes a lightweight convolutional neural network model that automatically detects Tuberculosis (TB) bacilli from sputum smear microscopic images. According to WHO, about one-fourth of the population in the universe is infected with TB, and every day five thousand people are killed due to TB disease. There are well-known recommended diagnostics are available for TB detection, among them sputum smear microscopic examination is a primary and most efficient recommended method for most of the developing and moderately developed countries. However, this manual detection method is highly error-prone and time-consuming. In this chapter, we proposed a lightweight CNN model for classifying Tuberculosis bacilli from non-bacilli objects. We adopted a Convolutional Neural Network (CNN) architecture with a skip connection of variable lengths that can identify TB bacilli from sputum smear microscopic images. The performance of the proposed model in terms of accuracy is close to the state-of-the-art. However, the number of parameters in the proposed model is significantly less than other recently proposed models.

Keywords: Tuberculosis, convolutional neural network, skip connection, sputum smear images, image processing

22.1 Introduction

Tuberculosis or TB, is an infectious disease, caused by a small rod-shaped, non-motile bacterium called *Mycobacterium tuberculosis*. Bacteria length ranges from 1 to 10 μm and it divides every 16 to 20 h [1]. TB is an airborne pathogen and mainly infects the lungs (known as pulmonary TB). But it can also spread outside the lungs such as the brain, kidney, lymphatic system, bones, joints etc. and is collectively known as extrapulmonary TB (Lymph node TB, Miliary TB, Pleural TB, Tuberculosis Meningitis, etc.) [9]. When people with TB cough, sneeze, spit, talk or sing, the bacteria is expelled into the air through tiny

---

*Corresponding author: oommanrani@yahoo.co.in

Sachi Nandan Mohanty, G. Nalinipriya, Om Prakash Jena and Achyuth Sarkar (eds.) Machine Learning for Healthcare Applications, (343–352) © 2021 Scrivener Publishing LLC

droplets and the disease can affect anyone nearby through the breathing process. According to the WHO 2019 TB report, 10 million people are infected with TB disease globally, among them 1million died due to TB in 2018 itself [3]. The highest burden is in adult men (57% of the total) [3]. The infected people have to take medications properly for many months for eradicating the TB infection from their body. According to the WHO 2019 report, the majority of TB cases and deaths were found in developing countries of South-East Asia, Africa, etc. [9]. TB can be mainly classified as active TB and latent TB (inactive TB) [2, 9]. Among them, active TB is quite dangerous and may cause to death if proper treatment is not given. Persons with latent TB are not infectious, but if left untreated some of them may end up in getting active at some point in their lifetime. Even though active TB can be effectively treated with drugs, there exists drug-resistant TB types [4].

Nowadays different diagnostic technologies are recommended by WHO for detecting different types of TB. Among them, active TB can be detected using culture-based method, the rapid molecular test, and sputum smear microscopy; while inactive TB can be detected using Interferon Gamma Release Assay (IGRA) and Tuberculin Skin Test [3]. Xpert MTB/ RIF and rapid line probe assays are used for detecting drug-resistant TB cases [5, 9]. Among them, sputum smear microscopic examination is the widely used method (gold standard) in the majority of the developing countries for detecting active TB cases. This is mainly because sputum smear microscopic examination is less costly, less time consuming and easy to use than other above detection techniques [5, 6]. Usually, sputum smear microscopic examination can be done with the help of either conventional microscope with Ziehl–Neelsen (ZN) staining procedure or fluorescent microscope with Auramine-O staining procedure [6]. Although fluorescent microscope provides better sensitivity than conventional microscope, majority of the developing countries with poor resource limited settings do not prefer fluorescent microscope due to its high maintenance cost and also needs well trained technicians for its operation [6].

Early detection and timely treatment of TB is required for reducing the number of cases. Manually identifying the bacteria with the help of a microscope is a difficult task, which needs expert technicians, and lots of mental concentration for focusing the microscope to an exact field of view [6]. Also, this process takes lots of time. From 1998 onwards, many automatic TB detection methods and systems have been put forward by various researchers. Among them, "TBDX" (A computerized TB detection system based on fluorescent microscopy) [7], detects the presence of TB bacilli automatically from sputum smear images. Main advantages of such systems are (i) patient record use, (ii) free from physical and mental strain, (iii) multi-head visualization and (iv) automatic decision making [2, 6, 9]. These systems can also be used in rural and urban areas, where poor resource settings (lack of well-trained clinicians and lab technicians) are available.

Annotated datasets are also required for developing machine learning based methods. However, not many public datasets are available for TB classification. Recently, Shah et al. [15] (ZNSM-iDB) and Costa et al. [16] made two datasets available in the public domain and these images can help the researchers for developing automatic TB detection techniques. Sample sputum smear TB images and its ground truth from the dataset [15] and [16] are shown in Figure 22.1, in that single bacilli are marked as a circle, touching bacilli is marked as square and doubtful bacilli are marked as a polygon. When compared to the performance of the traditional image processing and machine learning approaches, the methods based on CNNs are giving better performance. This is evident from the recently

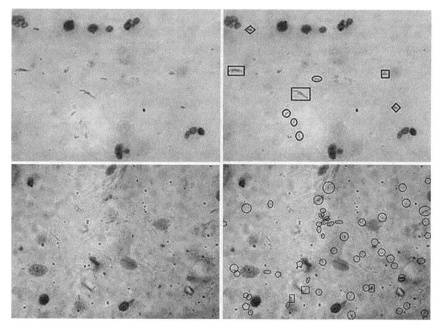

Figure 22.1 Sample sputum smear TB images and its ground truth (taken from Refs. [15] and [16]).

published papers. However not many CNN-based methods for TB bacilli detection from conventional microscopic images are proposed in the literature. The recently proposed CNN-based methods are discussed in the next section.

22.2   Literature Review

First automatic TB detection work based on conventional sputum smear microscopic images was published in 2008. When we analyze all the studies from 2008 to 2020, only very few papers followed convolutional neural network approach. Lopez *et al.* [8], put forward a convolutional neural network-based model for classifying a single patch as TB positive or TB negative. The authors trained three CNN models with RGB, R-G and grayscale image patches and tried the model with regularization and without regularization techniques. In Ref. [8], they found that the model with regularization techniques produces much better ROC curves than without regularization techniques. For experimental purposes, they utilized the public dataset of Costa *et al.* [16] and got a better performance (ROC curve = 99%) with RGB and R-G images than the grayscale images. Another CNN based TB classification method was proposed by Panicker *et al.* [9] in 2018; in their study, they used a two-stage approach such as an image binarization stage and a classification stage. Image binarization was done by using the Otsu method and their model got a recall of 97.13%. For their experiments, they took around 1,800 samples (900 bacilli and 900 non-bacilli samples) with different backgrounds from the Costa *et al.* [16] dataset and compared their results with studies that used similar dataset. The main advantage of [16] is that it automatically classified single bacilli and touching bacilli from sputum smear microscopic images. A drug-sensitive TB detection methodology using deep neural networks was performed in Ref. [10]. Their method utilized a simple five-layered CNN architecture to classify a patch as TB or not TB. In Ref. [10], they used the public dataset of Shah *et al.* [15] and did not apply any image enhancement or noise removal techniques, and their method got a recall of only 83.78%.

A subgraph-based TB detection was suggested by Hu *et al.* [13] in the year 2019. In their method, the authors used their own dataset and partitioned the sputum smear images into subgraphs. They experimented with three CNN models such as Inception V3, ResNet, and DenseNet for determining the performance and mentioned that the Inception V3 model performed better (98%) than the other two models. A faster Region-based Convolutional Neural Network (RCNN) methodology for identifying TB was proposed by El-Melegy *et al.* [14]. Here, a combination of region proposal method (bounding box facility) and CNN was applied for detecting and classifying the bacillus objects present in the TB image. The authors used 500 images from a public dataset such as ZNSM-iDB database [15] for their experiment and considered around 2,000 training objects. Their method attained a recall of 98.3%, precision of 82.6%, and F-score of 89.7%.

In this chapter, we propose a lightweight CNN model for TB bacilli detection. This method is an improvement over the one proposed in Ref. [9]. With the proposed architecture, we reduced the number of parameters in the model significantly when compared to the parameters in the model proposed in Ref. [9]. Section 22.3 presents the methodology and the experimental results are discussed in Section 22.4. Finally, conclusions are drawn in Section 22.5.

22.3   Proposed Work

(i) Datasets

This section discusses the datasets from where we created the samples. The first dataset is provided by Costa *et al.* [16] in 2014 and the other is provided by Shah *et al.* [15] in 2017. In Ref. [16], there are two databases such as an *autofocus database* and a *TB classification database*. They used Canon PowerShot A640 digital camera and Zeiss Axioshop 40 microscope for acquiring the images. The TB classification database contains 120 images; all are of 2,816 × 2,112-pixel resolution and the ground truth of each image is also marked by an expert clinician. In Ref. [15], there are mainly three databases: *auto-stitching database*, *auto-focusing database*, and a *classification database*. Classification database of Ref. [15] includes 1,900 images of single bacilli, no bacilli, overlapping and over stained bacilli of different backgrounds. We created around 2,220 samples (patches) from the classification databases in Refs. [15] and [16] (around 1,110 bacilli and an equal number of non-bacilli samples). Sample patches used for training and testing are depicted in Figure 22.2.

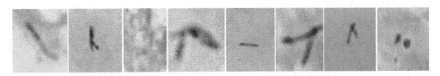

Figure 22.2 Sample bacilli patches used for training and testing. Bacilli images with different backgrounds and a non-bacilli image (last image) can be seen in the figure.

(ii) Methodology

Convolutional Neural Networks are predominant in the field of computer vision due to their innate ability to automatically encode features with the help of gradient descent optimizer or its variants. However, CNN incurs a large number of trainable parameters that cause challenges such as memory and computational overhead. So, it's imperative to develop an efficient and lightweight CNN model with less number of trainable parameters with better or competitive performance. In the below paragraph we discuss how we optimized the benchmark model [9] by adding skip connections.

The benchmark model proposed by Panicker *et al.* [9] is shown in the first part of Figure 22.3. This architecture consists of six convolutional layers, and two fully connected (FC) layers. The first 2 convolutional layers consist of 32 filters of shape 3 × 3 followed by 3 convolution layers with 64 filters of shape 3 × 3 and finally 1 convolution layer with 128 filters of shape 3 × 3 which is followed by a FC layer of 128 neurons which is connected to a neuron with sigmoid activation function. The total number of parameters in this model turned out to be 193,761. As a part of reducing the trainable parameters, we reduced the number of filters in the convolutional layers which are directly responsible for the overall performance degradation; to compensate for the performance loss we adopt skip connections of variable lengths. Designing a CNN architecture by incorporating the skip connections is a standard practice. Generally there exist 2 types of skip connections. 1) Long skip connections and 2) Short skip connections. Long skip connection is intended for extracting global information whereas, the Short skip connection focusses on local information. An architecture with skip connections renders many advantages as opposed to the counterpart. In sequential architecture, there will be a single path for the data to flow in the network that may often suffer from vanishing gradient or degradation problem; whereas, with the help of a skip connection, the network can possess multiple paths that provide a conducive environment for the stable data flow in the network [17]. A CNN with skip connections can be viewed as an ensemble of architectures. Skip connections also enable feature reuse by passing the same features to multiple subsequent blocks or layers. To this end, we adopted a CNN architecture with a skip connection of variable lengths that can extract both global and local features of TB bacilli, which helps in the detection of TB bacilli more effectively.

The proposed network architecture is portrayed in the second part of Figure 22.3. The model accepts image patches of shape 224 × 224 × 3 and generates a probability score predicting the confidence level of a given patch belonging to bacilli or non-bacilli. The model was developed using the dataset mentioned above by dividing it into 80% training (out of which 20% was used for validation) and 20% testing. We arrived at the proposed model after conducting an ablation study. The first convolutional block (block-1) of the proposed architecture consists of a convolutional layer with four filters of shape 3 × 3. The resultant feature map is propagated into the second block (block-2) of the convolutional layer having four filters of shape 3 × 3. The feature maps of block-1 and block-2, are concatenated with the help of a short skip connection to expedite local features. This type of short skip connection followed between every consecutive convolutional block throughout the network (block-i and block-i + 1). Further, the feature map of block-2 is passed to the block-3 of convolutional layer with 8 filters of shape 3 × 3 and we concatenated the feature map of block-1 and block-3 by using a learnable long skip connection to facilitate global information.

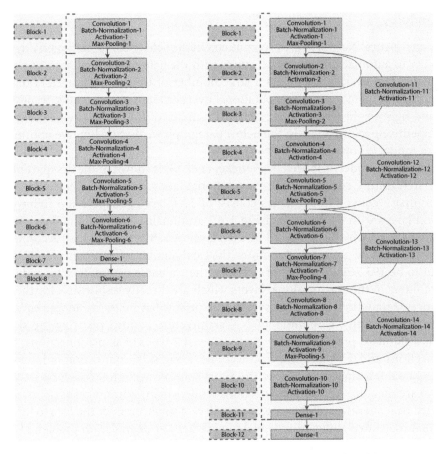

Figure 22.3 Architecture of the benchmark model (left) and the proposed model (right).

In block-4, we use convolutional layer with 8 filters of 3 × 3 shape and in the rest of the blocks, we use convolutional layer with 16 filters of 3 × 3 shape.

We follow this pattern throughout the network; where a long skip connection connects two blocks (block-i and block-i + 2) by bypassing the intermediate block (block-i + 1). The output of the final convolution layer is fed into a dense layer with 16 neurons followed by a classification layer with one neuron. Convolutional blocks are succeeded by 2 × 2 max pooling operations to reduce the data dimension and thereby introducing invariance. Batch Normalization is used to facilitate faster training and by reducing the internal covariate shift. ReLU activation is used throughout the network except for the classification layer that uses the sigmoid activation function.

We trained the proposed model on the samples using the Binary Cross-Entropy (BCE) loss function which is given below:

$$L = -(t \log (a) + (1 - t) \log (1 - a)). \tag{22.1}$$

where 't' is the actual output and 'a' is the predicted output. BCE aims at minimizing the loss to achieve optimum performance. We used Adam optimizer for training, with β1 = 0.9,

$\beta 2 = 0.99$, and $\varepsilon = 10^{-7}$ with the initial learning rate of 0.001. Further, to facilitate the training process and also to prevent possible overfitting we performed domain-specific augmentation (rotation, vertical and horizontal reflection) techniques. We used a batch size of 32 and the model was trained for 70 epochs.

22.4   Experimental Results and Discussion

We conducted all the experiments (the proposed model and the benchmark model) on a workstation with 64-bit Ubuntu, 64 GB of RAM and NVIDIA Quadro P5000 GPU with 16 GB dedicated memory. The model was implemented in Keras with TensorFlow [18] as the backend We ran both models for 70 epochs. For more reliable results, we conducted a 10-fold cross-validation with both models and the mean (of 10 experiments) are shown in Figure 22.4. To avoid data imbalance, we took the same number of samples for bacilli and non-bacilli (1,110 each). The accuracy that we obtained for each fold and the average is shown in Table 22.1.

When we analyze the Table 22.1, the performance of the proposed model and the benchmark model is very close to each other. However, the number of parameters in the proposed model is almost 90% less than the benchmark model (Table 22.2). The main objective of this work was to design a model that retains the performance of the benchmark model but with less number of parameters. By designing a model with the skip connections as shown in Figure 22.3 we managed to retain the accuracy of the benchmark model and reduced the number of parameters to a large extent.

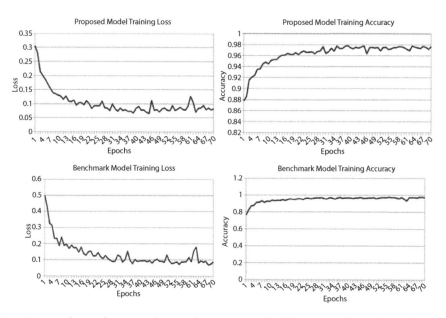

Figure 22.4 Training loss and accuracy (mean of 10 experiments) of the proposed model (row 2) and the benchmark model (row 1).

Table 22.1 Quantitative analysis of the proposed model and the benchmark model.

Data	*Benchmark*		*Proposed*	
Data	Train	Valid	Train	Valid
Metrics	Accuracy	Accuracy	Accuracy	Accuracy
Fold1	99.49	98.19	98.54	98.19
Fold2	99.69	98.19	98.69	97.29
Fold3	99.69	96.84	99.04	98.19
Fold4	99.09	95.49	98.29	95.49
Fold5	99.84	96.84	99.09	97.29
Fold6	99.74	97.29	98.39	97.74
Fold7	99.74	98.19	98.44	99.09
Fold8	99.64	97.74	98.34	99.09
Fold9	99.69	98.64	98.99	97.29
Fold10	99.84	99.09	98.54	98.64
Average	**99.64**	**97.65**	**98.63**	**97.83**

Table 22.2 Number of trainable parameters in the benchmark and the proposed model.

Model	Number of parameters
Benchmark Model	193,761
Proposed Model	18,213

22.5   Conclusion

In this chapter we propose a lightweight CNN model for TB bacilli detection from conventional microscopic images. With the proposed architecture, we reduced the number of parameters in the model significantly when compared to other state-of-the-art methods. The proposed model has only 18,213 parameters and gave an accuracy of around 97%. Other recently published CNN models have nearly 2 lakhs parameters. The model was trained and tested on benchmark datasets (Costa *et al.* [16], Shah *et al.* [15]). We used around 2,220 samples for developing the model.

References

1. Jindal, and editor-in-chief SK, *Textbook of Pulmonary and Critical Care Medicine*, p. 525, Jaypee Brothers Medical Publishers, New Delhi, 2011, Archived from the original on 6 September 2015.

2. Panicker, R.O., Soman, B., Sabu, M.K., Tuberculosis Detection from Conventional Sputum Smear Microscopic Images using Machine Learning Techniques, in: *Hybrid Computational Intelligence Research and Applications (HCIRA)*, pp. 63–80, Taylor & Francis, CRC Press, Boca Raton, 2019.

3. Global Tuberculosis Report 2018, https://apps.who.int/iris/handle/10665/274453. Last Accessed June 2020.

4. Tuberculosis (TB) TB drug resistance types, https://www.who.int/tb/areas-of-work/drug-resistant-tb/types/en/. Last Accessed July 2020.

5. Global tuberculosis report 2019, https://www.who.int/tb/publications/global_report/en/. Last Accessed July 2020.

6. Panicker, R.O., Soman, B., Saini, G., Rajan, J., A review of automatic methods based on image processing techniques for tuberculosis detection from microscopic sputum smear images. *J. Med. Syst.*, 40, 1, 1–13, 2016.

7. Signature Mapping TBDx—A Computer Aided Detection Solution for TB, signaturemapping.com, https://www.youtube.com/watch?reload=9&v=Wn6k5YxhFjU. Last Accessed June 2020.

8. Lopez, Y.P., CostaFilho, C.F.F., Aguilera, L.M.R., Costa, M.G.F., Automatic classification of light field smear microscopy patches using convolutional neural networks for identifying *Mycobacterium tuberculosis*, in: *Proceedings of IEEE CHILEAN Conference on Electrical, Electronics Engineering, Information and Communication Technologies*, Pucon, pp. 1–5, 2017.

9. Panicker, R.O., Kalmady, K.S., Rajan, J., Sabu, M.K., Automatic detection of tuberculosis bacilli from microscopic sputum smear images using deep learning methods. *Biocybern. Biomed. Eng.*, 38, 3, 691–699, 2018.

10. Kant, S. and Srivastava, M.M., Towards Automated Tuberculosis detection using Deep Learning. *IEEE Symposium Series on Computational Intelligence (SSCI)*, Bangalore, India, 2018.

11. Mithra, K.S. and Emmanuel, W.R.S., Gfnn: Gaussian-fuzzy-neural network for diagnosis of tuberculosis using sputum smear microscopic images. *J. King Saud Univ. Comp. Info. Sci.*, 2018, Article in Press, https://doi.org/10.1016/j.jksuci.2018.08.004.

12. Mithra, K.S. and Emmanuel, W.R.S., Automated identification of *Mycobacterium bacillus* from sputum images for tuberculosis diagnosis. *Signal Image Video Process.*, 13, 8, 1585–1592, 2019.

13. Hu, M., Liu, Y., Zhang, Y., Automatic Detection of Tuberculosis Bacilli in Sputum Smear Scans Based on Subgraph Classification. *IEEE International conference on Medical Imaging Physics and Engineering (ICMIPE)*, Shenzhen, China, 2019.

14. El-Melegy, M., Mohamed, D., El Melegy, T., Automatic Detection of Tuberculosis Bacilli from Microscopic Sputum Smear Images Using Faster R-CNN, Transfer Learning and Augmentation, Pattern Recognition and Image Analysis. *9th Iberian Conference, IbPRIA. Madrid, Spain, July 1–4, 2019. Proceedings, Part I*, Springer, 2019.

15. Shah, M.I. *et al.*, Ziehl–Neelsen sputum smear microscopy image database: A resource to facilitate automated bacilli detection for tuberculosis diagnosis. *J. Med. Imaging (Bellingham, Wash.)*, 4(2): 027503, 2017.

16. Costa, M.G.F., Costa Filho, C.F.F., Junior, K.A., Levy, P.C., Xavier, C.M., Fujimoto, L.B., A sputum smear microscopy image database for automatic bacilli detection in conventional microscopy, in: *Proc. of 36th Annual International Conference of IEEE Engineering in Medicine and Biology Society (EMBC)*, pp. 2841–2844, 2014.

17. Veit, A., Wilber, M., Belongie, S., Residual networks behave like ensembles of relatively shallow networks. *NIPS'16: Proceedings of the 30th International Conference on Neural Information Processing Systems*, pp. 550–558, 2016.

18. *Keras tutorial: Practical guide from getting started to developing complex deep neural network*, https://cv-tricks.com/tensorflow-tutorial/keras/. Last Accessed June 2020.

Role of Machine Learning and Texture Features for the Diagnosis of Laryngeal Cancer

Vibhav Prakash Singh* and Ashish Kumar Maurya

Motilal Nehru National Institute of Technology Allahabad, Prayagraj, India

Abstract

Laryngeal cancer is one of common cancer that has a high mortality rate and squamous cell carcinoma (SCC) is the primary malignant tumor that affects larynx and causes this cancer. To reduce patient mortality and morbidity, early-stage diagnosis of laryngeal cancer is of essential importance. However, early-stage diagnosis is very challenging due to small modifications of the mucosa and late-onset of symptoms. These changes are also unnoticed by human eyes. Machine learning is a growing field, which is being widely used in the healthcare sectors for the early diagnosis of diseases. Using machine learning with low-level pre-processing and feature extraction, we can design a computer-aided-diagnosis (CAD) system. This CAD system can play a vital role in the diagnosis of laryngeal cancer by providing clinical supports to the radiologists and doctors in their clinical decisions. The main objective of this chapter is to explore the background of laryngeal cancer and discuss the utilization of texture features with state-of-the-art machine learning algorithms for the implementation of a CAD system. Further, a case study has discussed for the detection of SCC, where we have analyzed the patches of narrow-band imaging (NBI) endoscopic videos, taken from 33 patients belonging to the four classes of laryngeal tissues.

Keywords: Laryngeal cancer, SCC, NBI, texture features, supervised learning, CAD system

23.1 Introduction

Cancer, also known as malignancy, is an uncontrolled growth of irregular cells. Today, many types of cancers are identified, including laryngeal cancer, skin cancer, and breast cancer, etc. As per the studies conducted between the years 1999 and 2017 on persons aged 45–64, cancer has higher mortality rates than heart disease [1,2]. Laryngeal cancer is a critical predictive disease related to high mortality and is one of the cancers which makes someone very weak and infirm. It is the 20th most serious cancer known globally in terms of estimated deaths and the 21st most frequent cancer in terms of predicted new cases in 2020 [3]. According to Ref. [4], the mortality of laryngeal cancer is expected to be at 1.66 demises per year per 100,000 people. Laryngeal cancer is the cancer of the voice box or larynx, or in other words,

---

Corresponding author: vibhav@mnnit.ac.in

Sachi Nandan Mohanty, G. Nalinipriya, Om Prakash Jena and Achyuth Sarkar (eds.) Machine Learning for Healthcare Applications, (353–368) © 2021 Scrivener Publishing LLC

it is a disease where malignant or cancerous cells grow in larynx's tissues. Larynx is a tube-shaped organ located at the top of the throat that comprises the vocal cords and involved in phonation, breathing, and protecting the lower respiratory tract. Larynx is anatomically divided into three parts: supraglottis, glottis, and subglottis. Subglottis is the lower portion of the larynx and placed above the windpipe or trachea. Glottis is in the mid-region of the larynx and comprising the true vocal cords. Supraglottis is the upper portion of the larynx, which encompasses epiglottis (it helps in swallowing food and keeps food out of the lungs) and false vocal cords [4]. The malignant cells may grow in any region of the larynx, and further, it may expand to other close tissues. Mostly, laryngeal cancer develops in the larynx's glottis region. Laryngeal cancer symptoms include the change in the quality of the voice, coughing up blood, hoarseness, neck swelling, breathing difficulties, sore throat, growth of mass in the neck, and pain in the mid-portion of the neck sometimes when a person eat or swallow food. It is not surely known that what causes laryngeal cancer, but there are several factors which increase the possibility of getting this cancer, for example, regularly consuming huge quantities of alcohol or smoking tobacco damages the DNA of the cells lies within the larynx, having a family history of neck and head cancer, having age over 50 years. The other common factors comprise acid reflux, low immunity, unbalanced diet, regular exposure to some chemicals or wood dust or coal dust or paint fumes, HPV (Human Papilloma Virus) infection.

Laryngeal cancer is identified in both men and women, but in comparison to women, men have a four times higher probability of getting laryngeal cancer. This cancer is treatable when identified and diagnosed timely. For the diagnosis of laryngeal cancer, firstly the doctor physically examines the neck and throat of the patient then, if needed, he may go for some other tests like laryngoscopy, endoscopy, CT (Computed Tomography) scan, MRI (Magnetic Response Imaging), biopsy, barium swallow, FNA (Fine Needle Aspiration) biopsy, and PET (Positron Emission Tomography) scan [5]. In laryngoscopy, the larynx is examined with a laryngoscope. In endoscopy, a procedure is performed to check the functioning of tissues and organs inside the body. CT scan takes several body images from various angles and processes them by a computing machine to generate cross-sectional images of scanned body parts, it is also known as CAT (Computed Axial Tomography) scan. MRI scan generates thorough images of organs, tissues, and bones of the body by using magnetic fields, radio waves, and a computer. In a biopsy, cells or tissues are removed for examination to determine the cause of cancer. In a barium swallow test, the patient first takes a barium compound with liquid which coats the stomach and esophagus, then a series of X-rays are taken. FNA is a quicker and less painful biopsy procedure which includes removal of tissues or cells from a lump in the neck by inserting a thin needle into it and then determining under a microscope whether the lump is cancerous. PET scan is an imaging test that helps to know whether a tumor has affected other parts of the body by injecting some radioactive sugar (glucose) into the vein [5]. After the diagnosis of laryngeal cancer, some tests are performed to know whether malignant cells spread outside larynx or not. This process of identifying the stage of laryngeal cancer is known as staging. It is essential to identify the stage of cancer before going for the treatment. The tests discussed above for the diagnosis of laryngeal cancer may also be used to know the cancer stage.

Current methods for the treatment of laryngeal cancer are becoming intricate, as elegant approaches have been designed to preserve vocal function. Due to this, many alternatives are present for the treatment of laryngeal cancer, and patients are often confused while choosing the best treatment method among available treatment options. Radiation therapy, chemotherapy, and surgery are three common methods for the treatment of laryngeal cancer. The patients may choose any one method for the treatment or combination of these methods. But generally, the treatment is considered based on the stage, size, location of the tumor, and age and health condition of the patient. In radiation therapy, high radiation X-rays are sent toward the tumor to kill malignant cells or control them from developing. This treatment may give a positive result in a patient who quits smoking before starting treatment [6]. In chemotherapy, medications are used to prevent the development of the malignant cells by killing them or by stopping them from dividing. These medications are frequently given via mouth or injected through a needle into a vein or muscle and can reach malignant cells throughout the body [6]. Surgery is a well-known treatment method in which tumors or cancer cells are removed through operation, and it can be applied in any stage of laryngeal cancer. Depending on the size and stage of tumor, many types of surgery may be used to remove the tumor such as cordectomy (treats very small tumors of a vocal cord), endoscopic laser surgery (uses laser beam to remove the tumor in the larynx), laryngectomy (removes part or all of the larynx), thyroidectomy (removes part or all of the thyroid), and neck dissection (removes lymph nodes in the neck) [7].

SCC is the utmost widely recognized malignant growth of the larynx tract emerging from 95 to 98% of all instances of laryngeal cancer. The most significant cause of vocal fold cancers is smoking and alcohol [8,9]. To bring down the death rate and protect both vocal fold function and anatomy of laryngeal it is known that an early-stage diagnosis of SCC is required. Presently for diagnosis, a histopathological checkup of tissue samples taken out through biopsy is considered as a benchmark. The little alterations of the mucosa and the late onset of symptoms, which can pass unnoticed to the natural eye, make the recognition of suspected tissues during the endoscopic evaluation challenging and difficult. Images were extracted using narrow-band imaging (NBI) endoscopy [8]. Figure 23.1 shows a pictorial view of four patches trimmed from an NBI outline [9]. This figure shows four patches, which are manually cropped from the image. These four patches are marked with blue, green, red, and yellow color tissues, where these colors show intraepithelial papillary capillary loop-like vessels (IPCL), healthy tissue (He), tissue with hypertrophic blood vessels (Hbv), and tissue with Leukoplakia (Le), respectively.

IPCLs show trademark morphological changes as indicated by the cancer infiltration and basic abnormality of esophageal epithelium. Tissue with Leukoplakia (Le) is a strongly connected white patch on a mucous layer which is related to an expanded danger of the

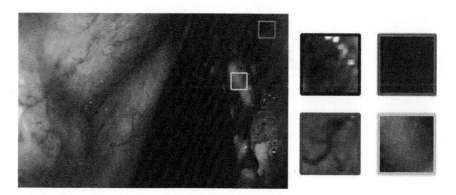

Figure 23.1 Four patches manually cropped from the image.

disease. There are changes in the lesion with the passage of time and the lesion edges are abrupt. Tissue with hypertrophic blood vessels (Hbv), a hypertrophic vessel is a condition portrayed by huge amounts of collagen deposits which is responsible for raised vessels. In the presence of dot-like vessels and longitudinal hypertrophic vessels, the major modifications happen to the mucosa vascular tree is known as IPCL. Changing in the characteristics of epithelium is not associated with the vascular tree for instance risk of developing SCC is related to whitening and thickening of the epithelial layer. Figure 23.2 shows four classes of laryngeal tissues. The first four samples in green frames illustrate tissues with hypertrophic vessels; the next four samples in red frames show healthy tissues, the next four samples in sky frames indicate tissues with IPCL-like vessels, and the last four samples in orange frames indicate tissues with leukoplakia [9,10]. From this figure, it is cleared that there are intra-class dissimilarities in all four classes. These dissimilarities increase the challenges of computer vision techniques in accurate and reliable diagnosis.

In the recent years, few researchers have worked in this area for the diagnosis of laryngeal cancer using low-level image pre-processing, segmentation, and reliable feature extractions with high-level image analysis based on machine learning and deep learning approaches [9–15]. By inspiring these studies, we in this chapter investigate whether texture-based approaches can classify laryngeal tissues in NBI images. If so, this can give reliable results

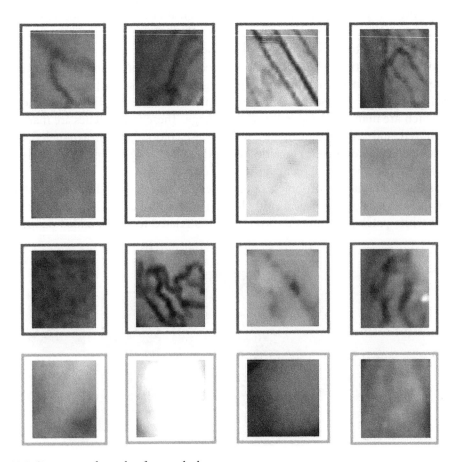

Figure 23.2 Sixteen sample patches from each class.

and can be utilized for initial stage diagnosis. Further, we explore the classification of laryngeal tissues in NBI images by using textual information and machine learning techniques. This chapter explores the possibility to predict first stage laryngeal cancer using laboratory test results. The main objective is to build a predictive framework that can be embedded in healthcare organizations' clinical decision support systems.

In this chapter, we have analyzed and discussed a case study of laryngeal tissue for the detection of cancer. In the next section, we elaborate on the role of texture features for the detection of laryngeal tissue, which includes gray level co-occurrence matrix (GLCM) [16], local binary patterns (LBP), and statistical features. Further, a CAD system is proposed for the diagnosis of SCC cancer using variants of these texture features with different machine learning approaches. The CAD system consists of the feature extraction and classification cum detection using machine learning techniques. All the working steps of the case study are shown in Figure 23.3. In this study, interesting frames are taken from the NBI videos, and section or part of interest is cropped from the frame for further study.

Further, texture features are extracted using the feature extraction techniques discussed in Section 23.2. Then all seven possible combinations of the feature vector are tested by splitting the dataset between the training set and testing set with 70% data in the training set. Several classification models which are reported in the Section 23.3 is trained using the training set, and then for validation purposes, the testing set in the form of query is given to the trained model and the confidence estimation of that classifier is calculated using the metrics like precision, recall, and accuracy from the confusion matrix. Section 23.4 gives fruitful outcomes of the extensive analyses and discussion, and finally Section 23.5 concludes the chapter with the final remarks.

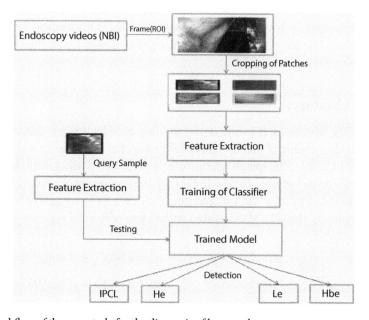

Figure 23.3 Workflow of the case study for the diagnosis of laryngeal cancer.

23.2   Clinically Correlated Texture Features

As laryngeal endoscopic images are shot from different perspectives and under various lighting conditions, the features that encode the data of the texture of tissues ought to be rich to the lighting conditions just as to the posture of the endoscope. This section includes the brief description and utilization of the clinical support descriptors for the analysis of laryngeal tissues.

23.2.1   Texture-Based LBP Descriptors

LBP is ge nerally viewed as revolutionary texture-based global descriptors for the examination of textures of images related to the medical field [9,17,19,20]. LBP gives low-complexity and is invariant of gray-scale, well coordinating the prerequisites of this project. The first articulation of LBP (R, P) presented in the writing needs characterizing, for a pixel c = (Cx, Cy), a spatial round-about neighborhood of span R with P similarly divided neighbor points ({pn} n $\in$ (0, P−1)):

$$LBP_{P,R} = \sum_{n=0}^{P-1} 2^n S(G_{Pn} - G_c) \qquad (23.1)$$

where G_c represents the pixel c's gray value, G_{Pn} denotes the gray value of nth neighbor of pixel c, and S is described as follows,

$$S(x) = \begin{cases} 0 & X < 0 \\ 1 & else \end{cases} \qquad (23.2)$$

The uniform rotation-invariant $\left(LBP_{R,P}^{riu2}\right)$ is the most frequently used LBP variation. Because the endoscope posture is continuously changing during the examination of the larynx, the uniform rotation-invariant of LBP is appropriate for his project. From $LBP_{R,P}^{riu2}$, the computed histogram ($HLBP_{riu2}$) is normalized using the L2 norm, and the resultant is used as the feature set extracted using LBP.

23.2.2   GLCM Features

For assessment, GLCM is tried. It is one of the top two broadly utilized descriptor and computes how frequently a couple of pixels in a predefined spatial relationship and having definite values in a picture [9,16,18]. The spatial relationship is determined using d and θ, where d is the distance and θ is the angle between i and j. In GLCM, the amount of quantized image intensity gray-levels is represented by its width (w) and height (h), where w is equal to h. For w is equal to h intensity gray-levels, the GLCM calculated with values of θ and d is described as follows,

$$P_{\theta,w}(h,w) = \begin{cases} 1, & I(c) = hand\ I[C_x + d.\cos(\theta), C_y + d.\sin(\theta)] = w \\ 1, & I(c) = hand\ I[C_x - d.\cos(\theta), C_y - d.\sin(\theta)] = w \\ 0, & otherwise \end{cases} \qquad (23.3)$$

A feature set (F_p) extracted from the normalized $P_{\theta,d}$, which conveys the likelihood of occurrences of gray-level and procured by dividing each and every $P_{\theta,d}$ record to the summation of total records. As given in Equation (23.3), various features are taken out from the matrix P.

Homogeneity: It shows uniformity of pixels in mammogram and defined in Equation (23.4).

$$Homogeneity = \sum_{i,j} \frac{P(i,j)}{1+|i-j|} \tag{23.4}$$

Energy: It shows the uniformity of texture in mammograms and defined in Equation (23.5).

$$Energy = \sum_{i,j} P(i,j)^2 \tag{23.5}$$

Contrast: It indicates change in the intensity with its neighbouring pixels in mammograms and defined in Equation (23.6).

$$Contrast = \sum_{i,j} |i-j|^2 P(i,j) \tag{23.6}$$

Correlation: It gives a correlation of neighboring pixels in the mammogram and defined in Equation (23.7).

$$Correlation = \sum_{i,j} \frac{(i-\mu i)(j-\mu j)P(i,j)}{\sigma_i \sigma_j} \tag{23.7}$$

23.2.3 Statistical Features

Statistical texture features based on spatial distributions, capture the transient intensity changes of medical images [21]. The useful statistical features for the detection of laryngeal cancer are listed in Table 23.1.

23.3 Machine Learning Techniques

This section contains a brief description of the classifiers used in this project.

23.3.1 Support Vector Machine (SVM)

It is an algorithm of machine learning that processes data for regression and classification analysis [22]. It is a type of supervised learning method that analyzes the data and arranges

Table 23.1 Statistical texture features.

Statistical Feature	Equation	Description
Mean	$$\mu = \frac{\sum_{i,j} X_{i,j}}{N}$$	Denotes average intensity
Standard Deviation	$$\sigma = \sqrt{\frac{\sum_{i,j}(X_{i,j} - \mu)^2}{N}}$$	Shows the deviation of intensity from mean
Skewness	$$\frac{\sum_{i,j}(X_{i,j} - \mu)^3}{N\sigma^3}$$	Shows the symmetries around the mean
Kurtosis	$$\frac{\sum_{i,j}(X_{i,j} - \mu)^4}{(N-1)\sigma^4}$$	Kurtosis is the flatness of intensity
Entropy	$$-\sum_{i=1}^{N} X_i \log_2 X_i$$	Represents the uniformity of the pattern

it into one of the given categories. The algorithm creates a hyper plane or a line dividing the data into different classes and from all the classes it discovers the points nearest to the line. These points are known as support vectors. Then, it computes the distance between the support vectors and the line. This distance is known as the margin. The objective of the algorithm is the maximization of the margin. The optimal hyper-plane or the optimal line is the one whose margin is maximum. The algorithm tries to create a decision boundary in a way so that the partition between classes is as wide as possible. SVM is preferred as it defeats the scourge of-dimensionality that arises while investigating our high-dimensional feature vector [23,24].

23.3.2 k-NN (k-Nearest Neighbors)

k-NN is a non-parametric, slow learning calculation [25]. The motivation behind this algorithm is to utilize a record wherein the data points are dispersed into a few classes to anticipate the classification of another sample point. The k-NN calculation presumes that alike things happen in close vicinity. It catches the notion of similarity (occasionally called closeness, proximity, or distance) with nearly calculation of the distance between points on a graph. Though, the Euclidean distance or straight-line distance is the most frequently used option. After the distance is calculated, it selects k nearest points and classifies the new data point according to the majority class in the set of k nearest points.

23.3.3   Random Forest (RF)

It is an ensemble learning technique for regression, and classification, also known as random decision forest. It works by generating numerous decision trees at time of training the model and yielding the mean prediction in case of regression and class in case of classification [26,27]. Random forest, as the name suggests, comprises many decision trees which function as an ensemble. In this classifier, each decision tree in the random forest brings about a class prediction and the class which receives the maximum votes becomes the model's prediction. In random forest, many comparatively uncorrelated models (trees) which work like a group can perform better than any of the individual constituent models.

23.3.4   Naïve Bayes

A Naive Bayes (NB) classifier is a machine learning algorithm that uses Bayes' theorem to classify objects [28,29]. This classifier presumes naive, or strong, self-sufficiency between properties of data points. Medical diagnosis, spam filters, and text analysis are well-known uses of the Naive Bayes classification algorithm. It is a probabilistic machine learning model that is utilized for the classification.

Bayes Theorem:

$$P(A|B) = \frac{P(B|A)P(A)}{P(B)} \tag{23.8}$$

Using Bayes theorem, the Naive Bayes algorithm can obtain the likelihood of A occurring, considering that B has already happened. Here, A is the hypothesis, and B is the evidence. The presumption made here is that the features are not dependent on each other i.e. existence of one specific feature doesn't influence the other. Therefore, this algorithm is called naive.

23.4   Result Analysis and Discussions

In this chapter, we have taken SCC dataset, formulated by Moccia *et al.* [9] and collected from 33 NBI endoscopy videos of 33 distinct patients. A total of 330 in-focus pictures (10 for each video) were physically chosen from the recordings so that the separation between the tissue and the endoscope could be viewed as steady and approximately equivalent to 1 mm for all the pictures. For each and every 330 images, 4 patches were manually trimmed from the pictures each having a dimension of 100×100 pixels, forming a dataset of 1,320 images, which were allocated equally amongst the four considered classes (tissues with hypertrophic vessels, tissues with leukoplakia, healthy tissues, and tissues with IPCL-like vessels). Each patch was trimmed from a part of tissue corresponding with any of 4 classes that are being considered here. So each of the four classes has an equal distribution of 330 images. For verification and comparison, the performance of different classifiers, for example, Naive Bayes (NB), k-closest neighbors (k-NN), and Random Forest (RF), are additionally examined. Before classification, the feature vectors are preprocessed and normalized.

In particular, the feature vectors are preprocessed scaling to unit variance and eliminating the mean (centering).

We divided 70% off the dataset for training purposes of the machine learning models and the left 30% of data was used for validating the models. Several feature extraction techniques like the LBP, GLCM and statistical features were utilized to extract features from the images. For tissue classification, several state of the art machine learning algorithms like random forest, Naive Bayes, Support Vector Machines (SVM), and k-Nearest Neighbors (k-NN) were used. We analyzed the model using a combination of features extracted using different feature extraction techniques stated above and used hybrid features to train the model.

Besides these descriptors, we tested all possible combinations of feature vectors constructed from combining one or more of the feature vectors obtained from $H_{LBPriu2}$, F_{GLCM}, and Stat. Thus, giving us the hybrid feature vectors namely ($H_{LBPriu2}$ + Stat), (F_{GLCM} + Stat), ($H_{LBPriu2}$ + F_{GLCM}), and ($H_{LBPriu2}$ + F_{GLCM} + Stat).

For the feature extraction techniques described, total nine combinations of the $LBP_{R,P}^{riu2}$ were computed using all possible combinations of (R; P), with R ϵ {1, 2, 3} and P ϵ {8, 16, 24} and the corresponding $H_{LBPriu2}$ sets from these nine combinations were concatenated to form the final feature vector of $H_{LBPriu2}$. This was done to give a progressively precise elucidation of the texture of pictures. Total twelve combinations of $GLCM_{\theta,d}$ was calculated using every conceivable mix of (θ, d), with d ϵ {1, 2, 3} and θ ϵ {0 deg, 45 deg, 90 deg, and 135 deg}, and the corresponding F_{GLCM} sets from these twelve combinations were integrated to build the final feature vector of F_{GLCM}. In this study, $H_{LBPriu2}$, a normalized histogram of rotation-invariant uniform LBPs; F_{GLCM}, GLCM-based features and Statistical (Stat) features are taken. All the computed features vectors and their associated number of features are given in Table 23.2.

All seven possible combinations of the feature extracted using three different techniques namely LBP, GLCM, and Statistical features were given to the above mentioned four classifiers and the accuracy was evaluated. After this, for validation purposes all predicted testing samples constituted a confusion matrix, holds true negative (TN), and true positive (TP), false negative (FN), and false positive (FP). Further, using this confusion matrix, other metrics like precision, recall, and accuracy were calculated.

Precision: It shows the discrimination ability for other images and their classes.

$$Precision(P) = \frac{TP_j}{TP_j + FP_j} \tag{23.9}$$

Recall: Also known as sensitivity. We calculated the class wise Recall, class j $\in$ [0, j = 3]) for the assessment of the detection performance of the classifiers for abnormal cases.

Table 23.2 Number of features in each combination of feature vectors used.

Features	$H_{LBPriu2}$	F_{GLCM}	Stat	$H_{LBPriu2}$ + Stat	F_{GLCM} + Stat	$H_{LBPriu2}$ + F_{GLCM}	$H_{LBPriu2}$ + F_{GLCM} + Stat
Dimensions	162	48	15	177	63	210	225

$$\text{Recall (R)} = \frac{TP_j}{TP_j + FN_j} \tag{23.10}$$

Accuracy: Accuracy is defined as the number of images that are correctly detected for the positive and negative cases. It is calculates as:

$$\text{Accuracy} = \frac{TP_j + TN_j}{TP_j + TN_j + FP_j + FN_j} \tag{23.11}$$

Where FN_j is the number of images of the jth class, which are incorrectly classified to any class other than j. The number of false-positives images of jth class is represented as FP_j. TP_j is the number of abnormal images of jth class that are rightly detected. TN_j is the number of healthy images of jth class that are correctly detected. Further, we calculated the accuracy of the classifier for a given combination of feature vector using the confusion matrix of the validation set where accuracy is given by the number of images rightly categorized upon the total quantity of images in the testing set.

F-Measure is a balanced metrics, defined as:

$$\text{F} - \text{Measure} = \frac{2 * P * R}{P + R} \tag{23.12}$$

The weighted average of recall regarding the amount of data in each class label for all the combination of feature vector and classifiers is tabulated in Table 23.3.

The weighted average of precision regarding the amount of data in each class label for all the combination of feature vector and classifiers is tabulated in Table 23.4.

The accuracy scores of each classier with each combination of the feature vector is reported in Table 23.5 below.

For the SVM, the grid-search space for C and γ was set to $[10^{-3}, 10^3]$ and $[10^{-7}, 10^{-1}]$, respectively, with six values divided uniformly on a *log10* scale in both cases. The kernel used is "Gaussian" kernel. From Tables 23.2, 23.3 and 23.4 it has been observed that the

Table 23.3 Average recall for the variants of feature sets.

-	$H_{LBPriu2}$	F_{GLCM}	Stat	$H_{LBPriu2}$ + Stat	F_{GLCM} + Stat	$H_{LBPriu2}$ + F_{GLCM}	$H_{LBPriu2}$ + F_{GLCM} + Stat
SVM	0.93	0.89	0.75	0.94	0.88	0.95	**0.97**
Naive Bayes	0.67	0.42	0.71	0.61	0.42	0.68	**0.71**
KNN	0.89	0.86	0.78	0.85	0.85	0.90	**0.90**
Random Forest	0.93	0.90	0.84	0.93	0.92	0.94	**0.95**

Table 23.4 Average precision for the variants of feature sets.

	$H_{LBPriu2}$	F_{GLCM}	Stat	$H_{LBPriu2}$ + Stat	F_{GLCM} + Stat	$H_{LBPriu2}$ + F_{GLCM}	$H_{LBPriu2}$ + F_{GLCM} + Stat
SVM	0.93	0.87	0.63	0.94	0.87	0.95	**0.97**
Naive Bayes	0.70	0.62	0.78	0.64	0.63	0.73	**0.79**
KNN	0.89	0.87	0.72	0.85	0.83	0.89	**0.89**
Random Forest	0.93	0.90	0.83	0.94	0.92	0.94	**0.95**

Table 23.5 Average accuracy for the variants of feature sets.

-	$H_{LBPriu2}$	F_{GLCM}	Stat	$H_{LBPriu2}$ + Stat	F_{GLCM} + Stat	$H_{LBPriu2}$ + F_{GLCM}	$H_{LBPriu2}$ + F_{GLCM} + Stat
SVM	0.926	0.893	0.747	0.944	0.876	0.946	**0.967**
Naive Bayes	0.669	0.424	0.724	0.611	0.419	0.679	**0.712**
KNN	0.893	0.856	0.775	0.845	0.845	**0.901**	0.896
Random Forest	0.929	0.898	0.843	0.929	0.916	0.941	**0.946**

LBP feature gives the accuracy, precision, and recall of 0.926, 0.93, and 0.93, respectively on the validation set. GLCM features give maximum accuracy, precision and recall of 0.893, 0.87 and 0.89, respectively and statistics features give the maximum accuracy score, precision and recall of 0.747, 0.63 and 0.75, respectively. The combination of LBP, and statistical features give accuracy, precision, and recall of 0.944, 0.94, and 0.94, respectively. The combination of GLCM, and statistical features give maximum accuracy score, precision and recall of 0.876, 0.87 and 0.88, respectively. The combination of LBP, and GLCM features give maximum accuracy score, precision, and recall of 0.946, 0.95, and 0.95, respectively. The combination of LBP, GLCM, and statistical features give maximum accuracy score, precision and recall of 0.967, 0.97 and 0.97, respectively. This study claims that the combination of texture features will give significantly encouraging detection performances as compared to the individual features.

Using k-NN on dataset after feature extraction, various neighbors are retrieved with a grid-search space set to [2, 10] with nine values divided uniformly. The metric used is "Minkowski" and the value of "p" is set to 2 in order to utilize the "Euclidean" distance to measure distance between neighboring points in the dataset. k-NN achieved accuracy, precision and recall of 0.901, 0.90 and 0.89, respectively for the combination of LBP, and

GLCM features. Also the combination of all features achieves the approximated the same detection performance.

Using Random Forest on dataset after feature extraction, the number of trees in the forest for the Random Forest algorithm with a grid-search space set to [40, 100] with six values divided uniformly. The criterion used is "Entropy". Random forests achieved maximum accuracy, precision and recall of 0.946, 0.95 and 0.95 for the combination of LBP, statistical textures, and GLCM features, respectively.

Using Naïve Bayes, we have achieved maximum accuracy, precision and recall of 0.712, 79, and 0.71 respectively for the combination of LBP, statistical textures, and GLCM features, respectively.

From all these analyses, it is evident that detection performances of SVM with hybrid features are significantly encouraging than other classifiers. This experimental analysis also reflects that the combination of LBP, statistical features, and GLCM perform significantly encouraging than other subsets of feature sets for the maximum classifiers.

Confusion Matrix of the testing set obtained using SVM classifier and hybrid features (combination of LBP, GLCM, and statistical features) is shown in Table 23.6. Class-wise precision and recall and F1-score of the hybrid features (combination of LBP, statistical features, and GLCM) using SVM are also given in Table 23.7. The performances of this approach are outstanding for healthy tissues. Also, the detection performances for the abnormal tissues are significantly encouraging. For Le, Hbv, and IPCL, maximum of four samples are misclassified to other cancerous classes. From these tables, we can see that no abnormal cancerous tissue is misclassified into a healthy class. This study reflects that SVM with hybrid texture features outperform as compared to the other classifiers and features sets for the early diagnosis of laryngeal cancer.

Table 23.6 Confusion matrix for the four classes using SVM.

–	He	Le	Hbe	IPCL
He	224	0	0	0
Le	1	104	3	0
Hbv	1	2	43	2
IPCL	0	2	2	12

Table 23.7 SCC detection performance for SVM.

Classes/Measures	Precision	Recall	F1-score	Support
He	0.99	1.00	1.00	224
Le	0.96	0.96	0.96	108
Hbv	0.90	0.90	0.90	48
IPCL	0.86	0.75	0.80	16

23.5 Conclusions

This chapter started with the discussion about laryngeal cancer, its causes, symptoms, diagnosis, treatment, and assessed an inventive way to the computer-aided categorization of laryngeal tissues in NBI laryngoscopy for the early diagnosis of cancer. The role of the CAD system is quite useful for the fast, automatic, and reliable diagnosis of cancer. This system increases the confidence of the radiologist and assisted the doctors. For the designing of an effective CAD system, distinct variants of textural features were tried to explore the best feature vectors to classify healthy and malignant laryngeal tissues. The best results were given by the classifiers when the hybrid features extracted using LBP, GLCM, and Statistical textures are combined with the equal weights. SVM has demonstrated similar execution as for RF and k-NN, while huge contrasts were found regarding NB. SVM was the best performing classifier with hybrid features for the accurate diagnosis of laryngeal cancer. For future work, it would be interesting to exploit the use of Deep learning models for feature extraction and classification of the laryngeal tissues.

References

1. Curtin, S.C., Trends in cancer and heart disease death rates among adults aged 45–64: United States. *Natl. Vital Stat. Rep.*, 68, 5, 1–9, 1999–2017, 2019.
2. Martins, S.M., Death from Cancer and Cardiovascular Disease between Two Brazils. *Arq. Bras. Cardiol.*, 114, 2, 207–208, 2020.
3. https://seer.cancer.gov/statfacts/html/common.html.
4. Nocini, R., Molteni, G., Mattiuzzi, C., Lippi, G., Updates on larynx cancer epidemiology. *Chin. J. Cancer Res.*, 32, 1, 18, 2020.
5. https://www.cedars-sinai.org/health-library/diseases-and-conditions/l/laryngeal-cancer.html.
6. https://www.cancer.gov/types/head-and-neck/patient/adult/laryngeal-treatment-pdq.
7. https://www.cancer.ca/en/cancer-information/cancer-type/laryngeal/treatment/?region=on.
8. Kraft, M., Fostiropoulos, K., Gürtler, N., Arnoux, A., Davaris, N., Arens, C., Value of narrow band imaging in the early diagnosis of laryngeal cancer. *Head Neck*, 38, 1, 15–20, 2016.
9. Moccia, S., De Momi, E., Guarnaschelli, M., Savazzi, M., Laborai, A., Guastini, L., Mattos, L.S., Confident texture-based laryngeal tissue classification for early stage diagnosis support. *J. Med. Imaging*, 4, 3, (034502) 1–10, 2017.
10. Araújo, T., Santos, C.P., De Momi, E., Moccia, S., Learned and handcrafted features for early-stage laryngeal SCC diagnosis. *Med. Biol. Eng. Comput.*, 57, 12, 2683–2692, 2019.
11. Marioni, G., Marchese-Ragona, R., Cartei, G., Marchese, F., Staffieri, A., Current opinion in diagnosis and treatment of laryngeal carcinoma. *Cancer Treat. Rev.*, 32, 7, 504–515, 2006.
12. Barbalata, C. and Mattos, L.S., Laryngeal tumor detection and classification in endoscopic video. *IEEE J. Biomed. Health Inform.*, 20, 1, 322–332, 2014.
13. Turkmen, H.I., Karsligil, M.E., Kocak, I., Classification of laryngeal disorders based on shape and vascular defects of vocal folds. *Comput. Biol. Med.*, 62, 76–85, 2015.
14. Xiong, H., Lin, P., Yu, J.G., Ye, J., Xiao, L., Tao, Y., Hu, W., … Computer-aided diagnosis of laryngeal cancer *via* deep learning based on laryngoscopic images. *EBioMedicine*, 48, 92–99, 2019.
15. Zhang, Y., Wirkert, S., Iszatt, J., Kenngott, H., Wagner, M., Mayer, B., Maier-Hein, L., Tissue classification for laparoscopic image understanding based on multispectral texture analysis. *J. Med. Imaging*, 4, 1, 015001, 2017.

16. Maurya, R., Singh, S.K., Maurya, A.K., Kumar, A., GLCM and Multi Class Support vector machine based automated skin cancer classification, in: *2014 International Conference on Computing for Sustainable Global Development (INDIACom)*, 2014, March, IEEE, pp. 444–447.

17. Nanni, L., Lumini, A., Brahnam, S., Local binary patterns variants as texture descriptors for medical image analysis. *Artif. Intell. Med.*, 49, 2, 117–125, 2010.

18. Haralick, R.M., Statistical and structural approaches to texture. *Proc. IEEE*, 67, 5, 786–804, 1979.

19. Singh, V.P., Srivastava, S., Srivastava, R., Effective mammogram classification based on center symmetric-LBP features in wavelet domain using random forests. *Technol. Healthcare*, 25, 4, 709–727, 2017.

20. Singh, V.P. and Srivastava, R., Automated and effective content-based mammogram retrieval using wavelet based CS-LBP feature and self-organizing map. *Biocybern. Biomed. Eng.*, 38, 1, 90–105, 2018.

21. Singh, V.P., Srivastava, S., Srivastava, R., Automated and effective content-based image retrieval for digital mammography. *J. X-ray Sci. Technol.*, 26, 1, 29–49, 2018.

22. Lin, Y., Lv, F., Zhu, S., Yang, M., Cour, T., Yu, K., Huang, T., Large-scale image classification: Fast feature extraction and SVM training, in: *CVPR 2011*, 2011, June, IEEE, pp. 1689–1696.

23. Bosch, A., Zisserman, A., Munoz, X., Image classification using random forests and ferns, in: *2007 IEEE 11th International Conference on Computer Vision*, 2007, October, IEEE, pp. 1–8.

24. Hsu, C.W., Chang, C.C., Lin, C.J., *A practical guide to support vector classification*, 2003. (https://www.csie.ntu.edu.tw/~cjlin/papers/guide/guide.pdf)

25. Zhang, Y.D. and Wu, L., An MR brain images classifier *via* principal component analysis and kernel support vector machine. *Prog. Electromagn. Res.*, 130, 369–388, 2012.

26. Breiman, L., Random forests. *Mach. Learn.*, 45, 1, 5–32, 2001.

27. Zhang, S., Li, X., Zong, M., Zhu, X., Cheng, D., Learning k for knn classification. *ACM Trans. Intell. Syst. Technol. (TIST)*, 8, 3, 1–19, 2017.

28. Bhuvaneswari, R. and Kalaiselvi, K., Naive Bayesian classification approach in healthcare applications. *Int. J. Comput. Sci. Telecommun.*, 3, 1, 106–112, 2012.

29. Dey, L., Chakraborty, S., Biswas, A., Bose, B., Tiwari, S., Sentiment analysis of review datasets using naive bayes and k-nn classifier, arXiv preprint arXiv:1610.09982. *IJIEEB*, 4, 54–62, 2016.

Analysis of Machine Learning Technologies for the Detection of Diabetic Retinopathy

Biswabijayee Chandra Sekhar Mohanty[1], Sonali Mishra[1] and Sambit Kumar Mishra[2]*

[1]Dept. of CSE, Siksha 'O' Anusandhan Deemed to be University, India
[2]Dept. of CSE, SRM University AP, India

Abstract

In Today's world, disease diagnosis plays a vital role in the area of medical imaging. Medical imaging is the method and procedure of making visual descriptions of the interior of a body for clinical investigation and clinical mediation, as well as visual depiction of the function of some organs or tissues. Medical imaging also deals with disease detection. We can get a better view of detecting the disease by using machine learning in medical imaging. So Now what is Machine Learning (ML)? ML is an artificial intelligence (AI) utilization that presents the system with the capacity to learn and develop itself. It mainly focuses on the development of computer programs that can access the data and use it for themselves. In this chapter we will focus on detection Diabetic retinopathy using machine learning. Diabetes is a type of disease that result in too much sugar in blood. There are three main types of diabetes. Diabetic retinopathy is one of them. Diabetic retinopathy is an eye infection brought about by the inconvenience of diabetes and we ought to recognize it right on time for effective treatment. As the disease advances, the sight of a patient may begin to break down and lead to diabetic retinopathy. Thus, two groups were recognized, in particular non-proliferative diabetic retinopathy and proliferative diabetic retinopathy. We should detect it as soon as possible as it can cause permanent loss of vision. By using ML in medical imaging we can detect it much faster and more accurately. In this chapter we will analyze about different ML technologies, algorithms and models to diagnose diabetic retinopathy in an efficient manner to support the healthcare system.

Keywords: Diabetes, retinopathy, machine learning, artificial intelligence

24.1 Introduction

Nowadays, diabetes is a very common disease. It goes under the group of metabolic ailment wherein the individual who is influenced has high glucose since his body either doesn't deliver enough insulin or the body doesn't react to the insulin created by his body. Mainly two types of diabetes are found in humans. One is type 1 and the other is type 2 diabetes. At the point when our body doesn't create enough insulin, then we get influenced by type 1 diabetes and this of diabetes mostly found in youngsters and youthful grown-ups. In type

---

Corresponding author: skmishra.nitrkl@gmail.com

Sachi Nandan Mohanty, G. Nalinipriya, Om Prakash Jena and Achyuth Sarkar (eds.) Machine Learning for Healthcare Applications, (369–382) © 2021 Scrivener Publishing LLC

2 diabetes the insulin propagated by our body is not enough or our cell doesn't react to the insulin produced by our body. Mostly middle aged person and older persons get affected by the type 2 diabetes. Type 2 diabetes can also occur in children. Due to diabetes our body can develop disease like heart disease, kidney disease, eye disease, dental problem, nerve problem, etc. Diabetic retinopathy is one of the eye diseases which is developed by our body due complication of diabetes. From an epidemiology study it is found that one in three persons having diabetes has a sign of diabetic retinopathy. In this disease a person can lose his vision permanently. It is a disease which is mainly found in middle aged persons. The main cause of this disease is the damage to the blood vessel in the eye. Mainly two types of diabetic retinopathy are found in humans. One is Non-Proliferative Diabetes Retinopathy (NPDR) and the other is Proliferative Diabetes Retinopathy (PDR). The first stage of diabetic retinopathy is NPDR. In first stage the blood vessels in the retina leaks blood and fluid which causes swelling and blurriness in the eye. The more advance stage of diabetic retinopathy is PDR. In this stage a person can lose his vision permanently due to the increasing swelling in the eye. If we don't detect this disease in early stage, then it can cause permanently vision loss.

Medical imaging is one of the techniques that are used to diagnose diabetic retinopathy. It is a technique in which visual representation of interior of body is produced and processed. The internal structure of the body which is covered by the skin and bones can be revealed by medical imaging which can further help us in the diagnosis of the disease. The database of normal anatomy and physiology which is established by the medical imaging can also help us in identifying the abnormalities. Wound care and dermatology use visible light medical imaging. We can improve the accuracy of disease detection by using machine learning in medical imaging.

The detailed study of computer algorithms that can learn and improve themselves automatically through their own experience is known as machine learning. Computer algorithms which are also known as machine learning build a mathematical model based on the data provided by humans and is also known as training data in order to predict or make decision on their own without programmed by the humans explicitly. Machine learning is mainly divided into three main categories. There are many applications of machine learning like agriculture, computer vision, bioinformatics, brain-machine interfaces, citizen science, medical diagnosis, DNA sequence, structural health monitoring, software engineering, etc. Our topic comes under medical diagnosis. The term medical diagnosis which is also known as computer-aided diagnosis (CDA) is used to diagnose disease using medical imaging [9].

The rest of the book chapter is organized as follows. Section 24.2 describes the literature survey for the detection of diabetic retinopathy. Section 24.3 outlines the various datasets used for the detection of the disease followed by methodologies used in Section 24.4. A detailed discussion on the analysis of the results is described in Section 24.5. Finally, the concluding remark is referenced in Section 24.6.

24.2　Related Work

Medical imaging is a very effective and promising field of research for machine learning. This is because we can check whether artificial intelligence can improve the result of disease detection and patient survival. There are many types of medical imaging like X-Ray, ultrasound, CT scan, MRI, etc. From decades many researchers are researching on ML applications in medical imaging. Diabetic retinopathy is a type of eye infection which is generated by diabetics. It has two stages. The minor stage is NPDR and the more advanced stage is PDR. First we collect dataset from various sources. Then we process them. In this portion we will discuss two things i.e.

1. Pre-processing of image
2. Diabetic retinopathy detection.

24.2.1   Pre-Processing of Image

There are different approaches to find effective image to train the machine and also testing. In this topic we will discuss about them in detail. First we will take image of the retina. By using the fundus camera, we can detect the exudates and micro aneurysms present in the retina. Micro aneurysms appear as red dots. Exudates are of two types one is soft exudates and another is hard exudates. Fundus camera is under power microscope with an appended camera whose optical design is based on an indirect ophthalmoscope. After the image is taken, the image is pre-processed so that the image can be used to training the model and also for testing the model.

To detect Diabetic Retinopathy, it is necessary to locate retinal vessels because if we can effectively detect retinal vessels position then we can say whether the patient has diabetic retinopathy or not. Numerous vessel detection techniques are there but mainly they are divided into 5 categories [1]. The fundus images which are taken have different types of resolution and contrast. Scaling is done to the image to resize them to have similar height and width [2,3]. Different techniques like gray scale transformation, DWT, green channel, adaptive histogram equalization and many more are used for pre-processing of image. Gray scale is used to convert the color image to gray scale image. The method which is used to increase the contrast of the image is known as Adaptive histogram equalization. It makes the image brighter. The image contains much information. Without changing that information to reduce the size of the image we use discrete wavelength transformation. To reduce the amount of noise in the image we use matched filter. FCM is a technique used to divide the data into different clusters. We use this technique to detect the blood vessels in the image. Green component and thresholding are used to detect the hemorrhages or exudates. Fundus images are taken in RGB form. The exudates appear brightest in green channel so the green channel of RGB is extracted. Thresholding is used to produce uniformity region within an eye using some maximum allowable limit or some minimum acceptable point [4]. To improve the image brightness and luminosity illumination correction is applied. Gaussian filter is used to remove the noise from the image. The resolution of image is suppressed by resizing the image and also taking care of the consistent of the image with the system. By applying augmentation, we can eliminate the variance in image varied classes [7]. The dataset used may contain many features out of which some of them may contain extreme values. In this case Normalization is used to label the whole dataset. Standardization is used to rescale different attribute so that they can have mean value of 0 and a standard deviation of 1 [5]. The dataset may contain many features which may takes more computational time for detection. So for better selection features selection is applied. There are many features selection techniques. Some of them are Univariate Selection, Correlation matrix with heat map. Feature importance is one of those techniques. It is a built-in function of the model. In this technique each feature has a score. The more the scores the more important is the feature [5]. There are many features in an image so we need to identify those features for further use in our research. Shape feature is used to identify the micro aneurysms are based on space and boundary of the lesion disk space. Color feature is used to detect the arduous and exudates. Mathematical approaches based features are known as Statistics-based features. The feature that is based on the red and green values of image is known as intensity based feature. It is used to detect arduous and exudates [7]. Image cropper, image augmentation and image resizer is also used for preprocessing of image. Image cropper is used to mask the pixels to hide patient details to protect confidentiality and privacy. Image resizer is used to resize the image to avoid computational overhead and also for effective training. Augmentation is applied on the dataset to increase the amount of healthy images in the data. The dataset is augmented by applying rotation and flipping on the images [8]. After pre-processing of image some of the image is then used for train the model while other images are used for testing the model. After testing if the model's prediction accuracy score is good, that model is used for detection of diabetic retinopathy [6, 10].

24.2.2   Diabetic Retinopathy Detection

Detection of diabetic retinopathy is a complex task. At higher level detection of DR is categorized into 2 tasks, namely lesion-based detection and image-based detection [11]. In the first category, the severity of diabetic retinopathy is determined by detecting every lesion and determining their location because the number of lesson and their locations are important for detection. After the image processing the image is used in different ml models for training and testing purpose. There are many machine learning techniques that are being used to detect diabetic retinopathy. ANN is a type of computing system in which working phenomena is based upon the working system of the biological neural network that is working in the animal's brain. Neural networks learn and improve themselves by processing the data that are provided by us. Nowadays ANNs are used for medical applications in different fields especially in cardiology. We also use ANN for detection of many eye diseases. Diabetic retinopathy is one of them. In this chapter we will focus on the methodologies used for detection of the disease using ML techniques. There are many techniques that are used for machine learning. We will discuss some of them in the subsequent section.

a) SVM

Support vector machine is a type of technique that is used to detect diabetic retinopathy and an example is shown in Figure 24.1. It comes under the category of supervised learning and consists of associated learning algorithm that analyzes the provided data for classification of the disease. It can find the hyper-plane or the decision boundary that is defined by the solution vector w which separates the training data and also performs well against the unknown test data. By determining the maximum margin between the classes SVM selects the decision boundaries [1]. Generally, the input space is divided into two parts by the SVM in which the first part consists of the vectors of class −1 and the other part is made of the vectors of class +1 [4]. In some cases, where the number of features is more, SVM sometimes perform better than the Regression model and Neural Network [5]. Li *et al.* found that the accuracy score for the five class classification task of diabetic retinopathy is 86.17% and for the binary class classification the accuracy score is 91.5%. The names of

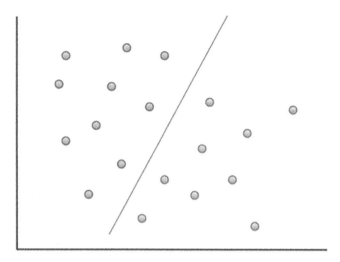

Figure 24.1 An example of SVM.

the five class classifications are normal, NPDR0, NPDR1, NPDR2, NPDR3 and for the binary class classification the levels are normal and abnormal. The TPR and the TNR is 89.30 and 90.89% respectively [1]. Priya *et al.* found that the SVM has an accuracy score of 97.6% [4]. The logistic regression model gives an accuracy score of 88% where the SVM after training and using some pattern recognition tricks also known as kernel tricks gives an accuracy score of 88.3% [5].

b) Probabilistic Neural Network (PNN)

The PNN network modifies or controls a process by using its anticipated result and is used widely in classification and PR problems. The architecture of PNN consists of a layer of sequential layers of many interconnected processing neurons [4]. It simply populates the inputs to the neurons without performing any computation. It first came into picture by D.F Specht in 1966. Priya *et al.* found that the PNN has an accuracy score of 89.6% [4].

c) Bayesian Classification

In statistics Naïve Bayes Classifiers come under the family of simple probabilistic classifiers that uses Bayes' theorem with strong independent assumption between the features. It comes under the supervised machine learning technique that uses the Bayes theorem that assumes that the features don't depend upon another feature statically. Bayes hypothesis gives a strategy that ascertain the likelihood of a speculation from its earlier likelihood by watching the various information for the given theory and furthermore the watched information [4]. Priya *et al.* found that it gives an accuracy score of 94.4% [4].

d) CNN

Neural network is a computer system that replicates the human brain and the nervous system. Convolutional neural network deals with the study of DNN and is used to analyze the visual image. The system applies a scientific activity called convolution. It is an unusual kind of linear activity. CNN utilizes convolution rather than general network duplication in any event one of its processing layers. The hidden layers typically consist of a series of convolutional layer that convolve with a multiplication or other dot products. In identification of diabetic retinopathy, Laxmi *et al.* found that it gives an accuracy score of 96.97 and 98.46% at 20 and 30% of features and gives an AUC (area under curve) of 97.51 and 98.50 at 20 and 30% [3]. Jain *et al.* found that it gives an accuracy score of 96.52% on an average over 10 runs using data from the first data source and gives an accuracy score of 99.7% on same run from the second data source [8].

There are also many other techniques such as random forest classification (RF), k-NN, LDA, ANN, Adaboost, and many more. RF is a grouping of several decision trees which is used in ML. In this method the category which is selected has the most votes. Another technique is k-nearest neighbor is a basic technique of ML. Linear discrimination analysis is used to eliminate some of the spatial properties. By using a large dataset of image when we compare the LLDA algorithm with k-NN and SVM classification algorithm then it is found that the performance of LLDA is reduced to some extent [7]. SVM performs very well than LLDA and KNN. Adaboost is a technique that is also used for detection. It is used to design a mathematical model that act in an arranged way so that the dataset gets fit in tree structures. This is used for recognizing exudates [7].

24.2.3 Grading of DR

To grade or measure the severity of diabetic retinopathy we need a retina ophthalmoscopy and a skilled examiner. In general, to grade DR we need to visit to an eye hospital; there are different types of diabetic retinopathy [15]. They are categorized below in Table 24.1.

24.3 Dataset Used

Dataset is an important requirement for research in this field. Due to higher demand of datasets there are many datasets available in many websites like GitHub, Kaggle and many more. In this paper many datasets are used for research. Some of them are DIARET-DB, DIARET-DB0, DIARETDB1, STARE, IDRiD, MESSIDOR, e-ophtha, Kaggle, DRIVE, STARE, CHASE, DRiDB, ORIGA, SCES, AREDS, REVIEW, etc.

24.3.1 DIARETDB1

It is public database which is available online and contains digital images of retina for recognition of diabetic retinopathy. It has a total number of 89 images out of which 84 images have mild NPDR signs and the rest 5 images are normal which don't have any sign of the disease. The images of the eye were taken by a 50-degree field-of-view fundus camera with various picture setting. The images are given in Figures 24.3, 24.4, and 24.5 respectively.

Table 24.1 Grade features decision [11].

Grade	Features	Decision
R0: no DR	No abnormalities	Rescreen in 12 months
R1: Mild NPDR	Only MAs	Rescreen in 12 months
R2: Moderate NPDR	More than just MAs bt less than severe NPDR	Rescreen in 6 months
R3: Severe NPDR	- More than 20 HMs in each quadrant - Venous beading in two quadrants - Intraregional microvascular abnormalities	Refer
R4: PDR	- Any new vessels at OD or elsewhere - Vitreous/pre-retinal HM	Refer
M0: No ME	No EX or retinal thickening in posterior pole	12 month screening
M1: Mild ME	EXs or retinal thickening at posterior pole, >1 disc diameters from fovea	6 month screening
M2: Moderate ME	Same signs of mild ME but with 1 disc diameters or less from fovea, but not affecting fovea	Refer for laser treatment
M3: Severe ME	EXs or retinal thickening affecting center of fovea	Refer for laser treatment

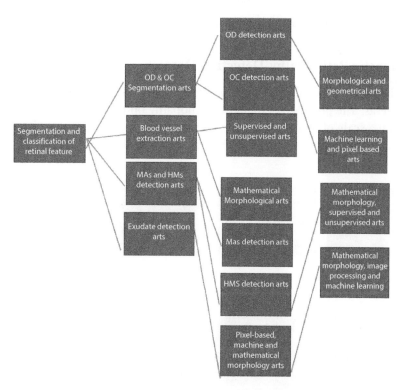

Figure 24.2 Computer aided diagnosis diagram for diabetic retinopathy detection using retinal fundus images [14].

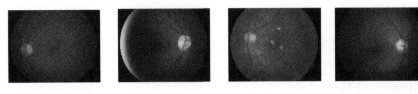

Figure 24.3 Some fundus images.

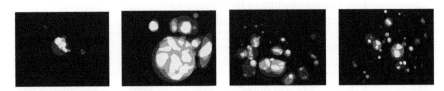

Figure 24.4 Some images of hard exudates and hemorrhages.

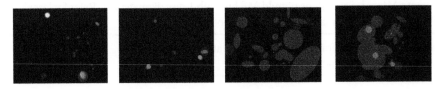

Figure 24.5 Some images of soft exudates and res small dots.

24.3.2 Diabetic Retinopathy-Detection Dataset

It is a publicly dataset available on Kaggle website. It contains an image of a retina taken by different cameras. The presence of diabetic retinopathy on the images has been rated by a psychiatrist on a scale of 0–4 in which 0 represents no DR and represents Proliferative D. Some images of that dataset are given in Figures 24.6 and 24.7 respectively.

Figure 24.6 Some images of the left eye.

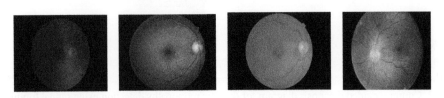

Figure 24.7 Some images of the right eye.

24.4   Methodology Used

Before using the dataset or collected images to train the model or test the model there are many operations that are performed on the image. Some of those methods are preprocessing of image, feature extraction, segmentation, classification, etc.

24.4.1   Pre-Processing

It is a technique in which the images are converted into fine images so that they can be used to train or test the machine. In this process many types of methods are used to complete this. Gray scale transformation, DWT transformation, green channel extraction, etc. are used. Image cropper is used to hide the patient information that is present on the image to maintain privacy. Image resizer is used to resize the image. Image augmentation is used to get healthy. Gray scale is used to convert the color image into gray scale image. Adaptive histogram equation is used to improve the contrast of the image. Other techniques are also used to preprocess the image.

24.4.2   Segmentation

It is used to decide visual representation into segments to simplify image analysis. FCM is a type of grouping used to separate data into separate clusters. The blood vessels present in the retina can be detected through segmentation [4].

Thresholding
One of the simplest exudates extraction method is gray level thresholding [14], the computer aided diagnosis diagram is shown in Figure 24.2, and the some fundus images are shown in Figure 24.3. There are five consecutive steps for segmentation of exudates. First histogram modeling of green channel is used to find an enhanced image which was further reshaped by mixture model statistical technique and then dynamic thresholding is applied to the image. Then automatic localization and masking of the optic disk is used. Lastly to obtain the sharp boundary of hard exudates edge strength of characterization and morphological operation is used [14].

Region Growing
It is an easy clustering technique that is based on area or region and is also referred to as a pixel-based image segmentation. It deals with the segmentation of initial seed points. In this procedure we inspect the adjacent pixels and determine whether to include the pixel in the region. Out of two criteria, image-based criteria have a greater accuracy score in terms of percentage. Hence we get a sufficient number exudate.

Clustering
Clustering means the assignment of a set into different subset so that the data in the subsets are similar in some sense. It is an unsupervised learning method used for statistical data analysis.

24.4.3 Feature Extraction

Feature extraction is used to derive measured data and values to support further learning and generalization process. To detect exudates, the green channel is pulled out from the RGB images because exudates looks most contrasted in this channel. Thresholding is used to produce an area of uniformity within an image based on some thresholding limit or minimum point. After these steps some of the feature values are extracted from the image. We also choose the features of the image efficiently. Feature selection is important as a data-set can have a number of features [5]. Feature importance is a built-in property that has a tree-based classifier. It sets a score for each attribute of data. The higher the score the more important is the feature. There are many other features like quality assessment, pre-screening, macula detection, etc. There are also many types of features like shape feature, color feature, statistics based feature and intensity based feature. We extract these feature using different techniques.

Apart from the color, statistical, and geometrical features, there are many other features that are used by the researchers for classification of leukemia, namely, Discrete Cosine Transformation (DCT), Gray Level Cooccurrence Matrix (GLCM), Gray level Run Length Matrix (GLRLM), Gray Level Difference Matrix (GLDM), Discrete Wavelet Transform (DWT), Stationary Wavelet Transform (SWT), Discrete Orthonormal STransform (DOST), etc. These features are global features and are calculated over the entire image.

24.4.4 Classification

Classification is a type of supervised learning which basically divides the data into classes. The common algorithm which is used for classification is K-nearest neighbor. The value of neighboring node which is used for prediction is termed ask. In unsupervised machine learning the technique seeks out the feature area using cluster approaches [7]. Many researchers use unsupervised classification algorithm. Logistic regression is another algorithm that is used for various classification. In LR algorithm, it is decided whether the example comes under category 0 or 1 by putting the features into the trained hypothesis [13].

There are many other types of classification algorithms. Some of them are listed below. Support vector machine (SVM) is a type of classification technique that is used for classification of normal and abnormal class for a particular disease. It comes under the category of supervised learning and consists of associated learning algorithm that analyzes the provided data for classification and regression analysis. The probabilistic neural network (PNN) is a type of neural network that modifies or controls a process by using its anticipated result and is used widely in classification and PR problems. The architecture of PNN consists of a layer of sequential layers of many interconnected processing neurons. It simply populates the inputs to the neurons without performing any computation. Naïve Bayes Classifiers come under the family of simple probabilistic classifiers that use Bayes' theorem with strong independent assumption between the features. RF is a grouping of several decision trees which is used in ML. In this method the category which is selected has the most votes. Convolutional neural network deals with the study of DNN and is used to analyze the visual image. The system applies a scientific activity called convolution. It is an unusual kind of linear activity. CNN utilizes convolution rather than general network duplication in any event one of its processing layers.

After all the preprocessing work the images are used to train the model. After successful training the model is used for testing.

24.5   Analysis of Results and Discussion

After all the training and testing we get the result. Support vector machine is the most used technique that is used for detection. Li *et al.* found the accuracy score for the five class classification task of diabetic retinopathy is 86.17% and for the binary class classification the accuracy score is 91.5%. The accuracy comparison of various classifiers by using different parameter optimization methods is listed in Table 24.2 and the result is shown in Figure 24.8. The names of the five class classification are normal, NPDR0, NPDR1, NPDR2, NPDR3 and for the binary class classification the levels are normal and abnormal. The performance measures of different classifiers in terms of TPR, TNR, and accuracy is listed in Table 24.3. The sensitivity and the specificity for the binary class classification is 0.8930 and 0.9089 respectively [1]. The logistic regression model gives an accuracy score of 88% where the SVM after training and using some pattern recognition tricks also known as kernel tricks gives an accuracy score of 88.3% [5]. Priya *et al.* found that SVM has an accuracy score of 97.6%,

Table 24.2 Accuracy comparison of various classifiers by using different parameter optimization methods.

	Classifier			
	SVM		TLBO	RF
Method	Without Optimization	With Optimization	-	-
Five-fold cross validation (using training data)	88.744%	96.5724%	-	-
Validation data	85.4%	79.6%		84.7%
Test data	86.1177%	81.0573%	86.17%	86.02%

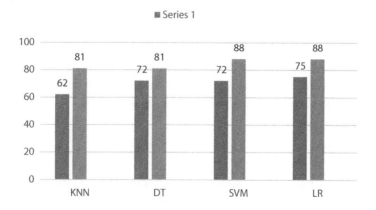

Figure 24.8 Comparison of accuracy among different classifiers.

Table 24.3 Performance measures of different classifiers in terms of TPR, TNR, and accuracy.

Models	TPR	TNR	Accuracy
PNN	90	88	89.6
Naïve Bayes	95	92	94.4
SVM	98	96	97.6

Table 24.4 Results of accuracy, precision, and recall from two different datasets.

Type	Metric	Retinal Institute of Karnataka	Friedrich Alexander University
COLOR1024 pixels	Precision, Recall	0.75, 0.77	0.66, 0.71
128 pixels red-free	Precision, Recall	1.0, 1.0	0.8, 0.8
1024 pixels- red-free	Precision, Recall	1.0, 1.0	0.8, 0.8
With augmentation	Precision, Recall	1.0, 1.0	0.8, 0.8
	Average accuracy	99.70%	96.52%

Table 24.5 Performance of the individual field-specific DCNNs in terms of AUC.

Month	F1	F2	F3	F4	F5	F6	F7
6	0.65 ± 0.12	0.65 ± 0.11	0.63 ± 0.09	0.59 ± 0.08	0.72 ± 0.11	0.66 ± 0.14	0.69 ± 0.12
12	0.68 ± 0.04	0.62 ± 0.07	0.67 ± 0.05	0.75 ± 0.06	0.70 ± 0.04	0.72 ± 0.05	0.74 ± 0.03
24	0.69 ± 0.07	0.61 ± 0.06	0.67 ± 0.04	0.68 ± 0.05	0.70 ± 0.03	0.65 ± 0.05	0.74 ± 0.04

Probabilistic Neural Network has an accuracy score of 89.6% and Bayesian Classification has an accuracy score of 94.4% [4]. The results of accuracy, precision, and recall from two different datasets is listed in Table 24.4. In identification of diabetic retinopathy, Laxmi *et al.* found an accuracy of 96.97% and 98.46% at 20 and 30% and found an AUC (Area under Curve) 97.51 and 98.50 at 20 and 30% [3]. Lorik Jain *et al.* found an average accuracy score of 96.52% on 10 runs using the first data source [8]. He also found an average score of 99.7% on 10 runs [8]. Filippo *et al.* found that their DL models were able to predict the disease with an area under the curve (AUC) of 0.68±0.13 0.79±0.05, and 0.77±0.04 respectively [12].

From the above result as shown in Table 24.5, we found that SVM and CNN is the most effective way to detect diabetic retinopathy. There are also many other techniques which is also efficient for disease detection can also be used for detection.

24.6 Conclusion

In this chapter, we have mainly focused to find an effective method for detection of diabetic retinopathy. From the above topic we found that using machine learning in disease detection can be very effective in detecting the disease. We can detect the disease at an earlier stage by using machine learning. If we can detect this disease at an early stage, then there is chance that we can cure it. If we can't detect this disease in the early stage, then it gets more and more dangerous day by day and there also exists a chance that the person can lost his vision permanently. We found that there many machine learning techniques like SVM, KNN, CNN, etc. that are efficient in detecting the disease. From the above survey we found that SVM is efficient in detecting the disease. There are many other work is left in this field for future so that the future researchers can do some innovative work in this field.

References

1. Li, Y.H., Yeh, N.N., Chen, S.J., Chung, Y.C., Computer-assisted diagnosis for diabetic retinopathy based on fundus images using deep convolutional neural network. *Mob. Inf. Syst.*, 1–14, 2019.
2. Chen, M., Hao, Y., Hwang, K., Wang, L., Wang, L., Disease prediction by machine learning over big data from healthcare communities. *IEEE Access*, 5, 8869–8879, 2017.
3. Kalia, A.A. and Uttarwar, V.U., Identification of Diabetic Retinopathy from fundus images using Machine Learning. *Natl. J. Comput. Appl. Sci.*, 2, 2, 1–4, 2019.
4. Priya, R. and Aruna, P., Diagnosis of diabetic retinopathy using machine learning techniques. *ICTACT J. Soft Comput.*, 3, 4, 563–575, 2013.
5. Huda, S.A., Ila, I.J., Sarder, S., Shamsujjoha, M., Ali, M.N.Y., An improved approach for detection of diabetic retinopathy using feature importance and machine learning algorithms, in: *2019 7th International Conference on Smart Computing & Communications (ICSCC)*, 2019, June, IEEE, pp. 1–5.
6. Bellemo, V., Lim, G., Rim, T.H., Tan, G.S., Cheung, C.Y., Sadda, S., Ting, D.S.W., Artificial intelligence screening for diabetic retinopathy: The real-world emerging application. *Curr. Diab. Rep.*, 19, 9, 72, 2019.
7. Satyananda, V., Anithalakshmi, K.C., Poornimanayaka, K., Sowmya, H., Diagnosis of Diabetic Retinopathy Using Machine Learning Techniques and Embedded Systems. *Perspect. Commun. Embedded-Syst. Signal-Process.-PiCES*, 2, 11, 346–348, 2019.
8. Jain, L., Murthy, H.S., Patel, C., Bansal, D., Retinal Eye Disease Detection Using Deep Learning, in: *2018 Fourteenth International Conference on Information Processing (ICINPRO)*, 2018, December, IEEE, pp. 1–6.
9. Ker, J., Wang, L., Rao, J., Lim, T., Deep learning applications in medical image analysis. *IEEE Access*, 6, 9375–9389, 2017.
10. Gadekallu, T.R., Khare, N., Bhattacharya, S., Singh, S., Reddy Maddikunta, P.K., Ra, I.H., Alazab, M., Early detection of diabetic retinopathy using PCA-firefly based deep learning model. *Electronics*, 9, 2, 274, 2020.
11. Asiri, N., Hussain, M., Al Adel, F., Alzaidi, N., Deep learning based computer-aided diagnosis systems for diabetic retinopathy: A survey. *Artif. Intell. Med.*, 99, 101701, 2019.
12. Arcadu, F., Benmansour, F., Maunz, A., Willis, J., Haskova, Z., Prunotto, M., Deep learning algorithm predicts diabetic retinopathy progression in individual patients. *NPJ Digital Med.*, 2, 1, 1–9, 2019.
13. Bhatia, K., Arora, S., Tomar, R., Diagnosis of diabetic retinopathy using machine learning classification algorithm, in: *2016 2nd International Conference on Next Generation Computing Technologies (NGCT)*, 2016, October, IEEE, pp. 347–351.
14. Joshi, S. and Karule, P.T., A review on exudates detection methods for diabetic retinopathy. *Biomed. Pharmacother.*, 97, 1454–1460, 2018.
15. Qureshi, I., Ma, J., Abbas, Q., Recent development on detection methods for the diagnosis of diabetic retinopathy. *Symmetry*, 11, 6, 749, 2019.

Index